Pushing back the boundar

The European Union
and Central and Eastern Europe

edited by
Mike Mannin

Manchester University Press
Manchester and New York

distributed exclusively in the USA by St. Martin's Press

Published by Manchester University Press
Oxford Road, Manchester M13 9NR, UK
and Room 400, 175 Fifth Avenue, New York, NY 10010, USA
http://www.man.ac.uk/mup

Distributed exclusively in the USA by
St. Martin's Press, Inc., 175 Fifth Avenue, New York,
NY 10010, USA

Distributed exclusively in Canada by
UBC Press, University of British Columbia, 6344 Memorial Road,
Vancouver, BC, Canada V6T 1Z2

British Library Cataloguing-in-Publication Data
A catalogue record for this book is available from the British Library

Library of Congress Cataloging-in-Publication Data applied for

ISBN 0 7190 5214 9 *hardback*
     0 7190 5215 7 *paperback*

First published 1999

06 05 04 03 02 01 00 99   10 9 8 7 6 5 4 3 2 1

Typeset in Sabon with Gill Sans display
by Action Publishing Technology Limited, Gloucester
Printed in Great Britain
by Biddles Ltd, Guildford and King's Lynn

Contents

Appendices

Tables

Contributors

Charlotte Bretherton is Senior Lecturer in European Studies and International Politics at Liverpool John Moores University. She is co-editor (with G. Ponton) of *Global Politics: An Introduction* (Blackwell), and has recently co-authored *The European Union as a Global Actor* (Routledge). She has also recently published several articles in the fields of gender issues in environmental change and women's networks in the European Union, and contributed to chapters on international relations in *An Introduction to Politics*, eds G. Ponton and P. Gill (Blackwell).

Terry Caslin is Principal Lecturer in Economics at Liverpool John Moores University, where he teaches public sector economics. He is co-author of *Theories of Welfare* (Routledge) with T. Forder *et al.*, and also with H. Vane of *Current Controversies in Economics* (Blackwell). He has taught at the Universities of Budapest and Salerno. He has researched and published in the economics of European integration, East European economic reform and regional aspects of economic policy.

Laszlo Czaban has taught at the Technical University of Budapest and the University of Economic Sciences and University of Natural Science, Budapest. He has worked for the European Commission as an economist 1992/3, and is currently Research Fellow at Leeds Business School. He has published widely in both Hungarian and English, contributing to *Industrial Transformations in Europe*, eds E. Dittrich *et al.* (Sage), *The Changing European Firm*, eds K. Kristensen and R. Whitley (Routledge), *Look East? Industrial Transformation in Eastern Europe*, eds J. Henderson *et al.* (Macmillan) and other books on Central and Eastern European economics.

Andrew Francis is Senior Lecturer in Geography and Urban Studies at Liverpool John Moores University, where he teaches in the fields of European environment policy and the geography of Central and Eastern Europe. He is co-author of *Environmental Planning in Britain and Germany* (University of Dortmund) and *Environmental Policy in the United Kingdom and Germany: Towards a Comparative Analysis* (Natural Built Environment Professions). His current research is on the spatial aspects of economic transformation in Poland and he has travelled and researched extensively in the region.

Mike Mannin is Principal Lecturer and Jean Monnet Chair in European Integration at Liverpool John Moores University. He is co-editor with D. Kermode of *The Redundant Counties: Participation and Electoral Choice* (Hesketh), and recently published 'Global Issues and the Challenge to Democratic Politics', in *An Introduction to Global Politics*, eds C. Bretherton and G. Ponton. He has also published in the fields of European Monetary Union, Structural Funding and French and Italian politics.

Linda Middleton is a History graduate currently pursuing postgraduate research into the social policies of Central and Eastern European states at Liverpool John Moores University.

Brian Newton is Senior Lecturer in Geography and Subject Leader in Urban Studies at Liverpool John Moores University, where he teaches in the field of European urban studies and the geography of Central and Eastern Europe. He is currently engaged in research examining the comparative analysis of privatisation strategies in Eastern Europe.

Linda Walsh is Senior Lecturer in Economics at Liverpool John Moores University. Her research interests include small and medium-sized enterprise cultural and economic transformation in Slovakia and the Czech Republic.

Preface

There has been little in European history since 1919 to rival the bewildering pace of change following the collapse of the post-Second World War Communist order in Eastern Europe. Thus the East–West, market–planned, liberal–Communist dichotomies, for long the coordinates of political action (and academic observation) of European state relations, have been replaced by a triumphal liberal democratic paradigm that seemed to be reflected in the successes of the European Union (EU) – itself part of the West's bulwark against an extension of Soviet hegemony.

In several senses, the EU has become a natural 'coordinate' for contemporary European state relations, and our assumption here is that the EU will remain for the foreseeable future the most important arbiter of 'East–West relations' in Europe. In consequence, it may be seen as the anchor point for a new continental stability. Nevertheless, unresolved issues within the EU, especially since the signing of the Treaty of Union in 1991, have challenged the very stability that Central and East European Countries (CEEC) so covet. The completion of the Single Market, Economic and Monetary Union (EMU), and the associated reform of EU policies, processes and institutions have made it difficult to predict what type of Union may exist in the first decade of the twenty-first century, and what advantages close EU–CEEC relationships might hold for both sides. In effect, the EU is a moving target for CEEC seeking access to its markets and political institutions in order to shore up their own futures.

This book discusses, critically, responses in both Eastern and Western Europe to these developments – culminating in *Agenda 2000*, the European Commission's proposed framework, published in June 1997, for managing these massive changes. Our focus is, thus, on the evolving relationship between the EU and CEEC, with particular emphasis upon the EU's proposed enlargement to the East. Hence a central concern is the extent to which the economic, political and cultural boundaries of the EU can be pushed. There is, however, a political symbiosis between these issues of enlargement and the internal challenges of policy deepening and institutional reform faced by the EU. The success of one would seem largely dependent upon the achievement of the others, in that, without an attempt to incorporate a 'nested' approach to EU futures, the *extent* of enlargement, or the *depth* of integration, or the *efficiency* of the Union as a deliverer of policies may be jeopardised. In *Agenda 2000* this integrated view is presented by the Commission as a logical outcome of the EU's responsibilities towards the wider Europe since the end of the Cold War, and in an analysis of the content, conclusions and the early reactions to *Agenda 2000*, this book attempts to unpick a Gordian knot.

The book's scope, therefore, reflects both the complexities of the subject matter and the research interests of the contributors. Part I covers the key 'dual transition' of state Socialist economic and political systems to liberal, market democracies. The success or failure of this transition will create conditions that are crucial to the stability of the region and thus its security – a third key dimension to EU–CEEC relations which we discuss. Analysis, in Part I, of two further issues allows us to observe societal reactions to transformation. Thus environmental policy and the position of women in post-Communist societies provide two tests: of the extent to which CEEC can, or indeed should, respond to external expectations of fundamental societal change; and of the ingenuousness of EU demands for such major transformations as 'imperative' conditions for deepened EU–CEEC relations. In examining these issues, several of the contradictions inherent in these relations become apparent, as do the distinctions and differences of treatment that the EU applies in its 'European policy'.

The first seven chapters of the book offer an EU-focused and, hence, primarily *West–East* view of Central and Eastern Europe (CEE) generally. As such they are broader in territorial coverage than Part II, which concentrates on the Visegrad Four (the Czech and Slovak Republics, Hungary and Poland) as key players in the enlargement debate. These countries were the first to pursue closer relations with the EU during the late 1980s, and their relatively longer experience of association with the EU provides greater opportunity for assessment of its impacts. In comparison, other CEEC, by virtue of their longer dependence on the USSR and/or particular economic and political difficulties, have only recently begun to deepen their involvement with the EU.

The focus of Part II is more evidently *East–West*, in that the case studies illustrate the perceived centrality of association with the EU to the economic and political transformation and domestic policies of the Visegrad countries. Despite the common aim of 'coming home' to the EU, the studies also illustrate the divergence of opinion, and indeed competition, that exists between the CEEC in anticipation of closer association with or accession to the EU. Our four case studies, in consequence, illustrate the *diversity* of the political, economic and social transformations that have occurred since 1989 and, therefore, of the challenges confronting the aim, set out in *Agenda 2000*, of applying equally an EU European policy. Thus, while Part I themes are reflected in the country portraits, each focuses upon those attributes or policy areas which, in each case, are of particular significance in shaping relations with the EU.

In Chapter 9, for example, the emphasis is upon Slovakia's current struggle to establish a consolidated liberal democracy acceptable to its domestic and external audiences. This may be contrasted with Hungary's relatively smooth and early economic transition, which successfully 'dealt with' its Communist elites. In consequence, a focus of the Hungarian chapter is on preconditions which helped shape that country's relatively successful contemporary political and economic transformation.

Hungary's relatively long-standing, gradualist transformation may be contrasted with that of the Czech Republic, characterised here as a country whose rigorous approach to economic change produced social pressure and distortions to market mechanisms that currently undermine the claim of its political elites to enjoy 'pole position' in a race to EU accession. Finally Poland, by far the largest of the aspirant member states, presents an opportunity to examine carefully the enormity of the tasks facing all CEEC in aligning themselves with the laws and procedures of the EU *acquis*.

In the compilation of this volume the editor, on behalf of his co-authors, gratefully acknowledges the contributions of the many officials of the European Commission, the EU delegations and ministries of Central and Eastern European states, and representatives of non-governmental organisations who gave their time, opinions and information during the research for this book. He also wishes to acknowledge the help of, and in several cases his total reliance upon the contributions of, long-suffering colleagues, friends and relations. These include Linda Pringle, Sue Meyer, Cathy Renton and Melissa Newton, whose patience in the production of readable typescripts was strained beyond most personal assistants' usual endurance. Thanks are also due to Phil Cubbin in the JMU Cartographic Unit, Paul du Feu, who proof-read several chapters, Geoff Ponton for assistance with the index, and Peter Gill, whose comments improved Chapter 4. Steve Mannin, offspring of the editor, proved conclusively that the vast amounts of public and family resources spent on his higher education had not been entirely wasted. Apologies must be offered to the spouses and partners of authors who suffered not just from their partners' preoccupation but also from the (occasional) terse enquiry from the editor as to the progress of the particular chapter(s) in their households. Finally I wish to thank my colleague, Charlotte Bretherton, for the intellectual and technical skills that she brought to the project, as well as her encouragement to the editor to complete the task. Despite my willingness to share the editorial spotlight with her, she declined, cleverly leaving the responsibility for all errors, omissions and misjudgements with me.

M. L. Mannin
New Brighton
October 1998

Abbreviations

AFD	Alliance of Free Democrats (Hungary)
AWS	Solidarity Election Action (Poland)
CAP	Common Agricultural Policy
CDU	Christian Democratic Union (GDR)
CEE	Central and Eastern Europe
CEEC	Central and Eastern European Countries
CEEC 5	Poland, Hungary, Estonia, Slovenia and the Czech Republic
CEEC 10	CEEC 5 and Slovakia, Romania, Bulgaria, Lithuania and Latvia
CEFTA	Central European Free Trade Area
CEI	Central European Initiative
CFSP	Common Foreign and Security Policy
CIS	Commonwealth of Independent States
CMEA	Council for Mutual Economic Assistance (Comecon)
Comecon	*See* CMEA
Cominform	Communist Information Bureau
CPSU	Communist Party of the Soviet Union
CSCE	Conference on Security and Cooperation in Europe (now OSCE)
CSFR	Czech and Slovak Federative Republic
CSSD	Social Democratic Party (Czech Republic)
DFES	Debt-For-Environment Swaps
DG	Directorate-General
DUS	Democratic Union of Slovakia
EA	Europe Agreement
EAEC	European Atomic Energy Authority (Euratom)
EAS	European Administrative Space
EBRD	European Bank for Reconstruction and Development
EC	European Community
ECSC	European Coal and Steel Community

ecu	European currency unit
EDC	European Defence Community
EEA	European Economic Area
EEC	European Economic Communities
EFTA	European Free Trade Association
EFTAN	European Free Trade Association Nations
EHRF	European Human Rights Foundation
EIB	European Investment Bank
EMS	European Monetary System
EMU	Economic and Monetary Union
EP	European Parliament
EU	European Union
FDI	Foreign Direct Investment
FIDESZ	Alliance of Young Democrats (Hungary)
FNP	Fund for National Property (Slovakia)
FRG	Federal Republic of Germany
G7	Group of 7
G24	Group of 24
GATT	General Agreement on Tariffs and Trade
GDI	Gender-related Development Index
GDP	Gross Domestic Product
GDR	German Democratic Republic
GEF	Global Environment Facility
GSP	Generalised System of Preferences
HDF	Hungarian Democratic Forum
HDI	Human Development Index
HSP	Hungarian Socialist Party
HSWP	Hungarian Socialist Workers' Party
HZDS	Movement for a Democratic Slovakia
IGC	Intergovernmental Conference
ILO	International Labour Organisation
IMF	International Monetary Fund
IRB	Investicna Banka Rozvojova (Slovakia)
JPC	Joint Parliamentary Committee
KDH	Christian Democratic Movement (Slovak Republic)
KDU–CSL	Christian Democratic Union (Czech Republic)
KOR	The Workers Defence Committee (Poland)
KSC	Czechoslovak Communist Party
LFA	Less Favoured Area
MDF	Hungarian Democratic Forum
MEP	Member of the European Parliament
MFN	Most Favoured Nation
MIS	Management Information System

NATO	North Atlantic Treaty Organisation
NEM	New Economic Mechanism (Hungary)
NGO	Non-Governmental Organisation
NIS	Newly Independent States
ODA	Civic Democratic Alliance (Czech Republic)
ODS	Civic Democratic Party (Czech Republic)
OECD	Organisation for Economic Cooperation and Development
OEEC	Organisation for European Economic Cooperation
OSCE	Organisation for Security and Cooperation in Europe (formerly CSCE)
PCA	Partnership and Cooperation Agreement
PfP	Partnership for Peace
Phare	Poland and Hungary: Assistance for Economic Reconstruction
PMU	Prime Minister's Unit (Hungary)
PTDP	Phare and Tacis Democracy Programme
PUWP	Polish United Workers' (Communist) Party
QMV	Qualified Majority Voting
SDL	Post-Communist Party of the Democratic Left (Slovakia)
SEA	Single European Act
SEM	Single European Market
SLD	Democratic Left Alliance (Poland)
SMEs	small and medium-sized enterprises
SNS	Slovak National Party
SPAR	Reinforced Pre-Accession Strategy
SZDSZ	Liberal Alliance (Hungary)
Tacis	Technical Assistance for the Commonwealth of Independent States
TCA	Trade Cooperation Agreement
TEN	Trans-European Network
TEU	Treaty of European Union (Maastricht)
UN	United Nations
USAID	US Agency for International Development
USSR	Union of Soviet Socialist Republics
UW	Freedom Union (Poland)
VLK	Forest Protection Movement (Slovakia)
VPN	Public Against Violence (Slovakia)
WEU	Western European Union
WTO	World Trade Organisation
WTO	Warsaw Treaty Organisation
ZRS	Workers' Association of Slovakia

The EU and CEE: the emerging union?

Europe Agreement (fast track)

Europe Agreement States

Phare/cooperation states

Tacis/Partnership states

European Union

Note: Relations with Belarus, Croatia and Yugoslavia (Former Republic of Yugoslavia) subject to 'conditionalities'.

Source: LJMU Cartographic Unit, 1998.

Part I

The EU and relations with CEE

1 Mike Mannin

EU–CEE relations: an overview

Either we export success to them or they export instability to us.
(Werner Hoyer, German Ministry for Foreign Affairs, *European*, 29 June–
5 July 1998)

The first Austrian presidency of the Union, commencing in July 1998, is
an appropriate institutional setting from which to consider the implications of Herr Hoyer's warning, and thus to introduce the *raison d'être* for
the following chapters. In a statement prior to the presidency succession,
the Austrian minister for foreign affairs, Wolfgang Schussel, reminded
member states of his country's unique geographical status: Austria, a
newly acceded EU state, shares around 50 per cent of its borders with four
of the candidates for accession; thus 'hardly any other country has as
great an interest in the success of enlargement' (*European Voice*, 2–8
July:14).

The Austrian presidency began one year after presentation of the
Amsterdam Treaty and *Agenda 2000* documents that, together, represent
a serious attempt by the Union and its member states to create a post-Cold
War institutional architecture for a wider Europe. Stage Three of EMU,
the creation of the Eurozone (May 1998) and the single currency (January
1999) place this strategic challenge alongside moves towards (and the
uncertainties surrounding) EU economic integration. The added complication of potential world recession and the real or perceived need to
respond to the pressures of 'globalisation' make for interesting times.

The following chapters aim to unravel and explain the convoluted
factors that have shaped contemporary EU–CEE relations and influenced
EU policy responses and potential institutional adaptations to incorporate
this 'new Europe'.

Part I outlines the main characteristics of EU relations with CEE, illus-
trating the ambivalent nature of policy initiatives by the EU as it struggles
to adapt to a new, post-Cold War environment. This part also examines
the extent and depth of CEE transformation as CEE governments struggle

to respond to complex internal and external pressures. Chapter 2 details
the progress of EU–CEE policy to its current reinforced pre-accession
status. The broader issues affecting the transformation of CEEC are
examined in separate chapters on economic change (Terry Caslin and
Laszlo Czaban) and democratic governance (Mike Mannin); the domestic
'dual transition' that entails so many uncomfortable policy choices for
CEE elites. The search for internal and external stability that follows in
part from these choices forms the subject of Charlotte Bretherton's
chapter on new security dilemmas for CEEC – in effect a third dimension
of transition. Two further Part I chapters reveal the extent of CEEC difficulties in making these transformations. In the case of environmental
policy, a legacy of Communist neglect cannot be overcome without
considerable commitment from cash-strapped CEE governments and
corresponding push–pull assistance by the EU and member states; and, as
Andrew Francis points out, new environmental problems are emerging
from the very success of transformation. From a quite different perspective, the gender issues associated with transformation expose the roots of
CEE social change and reveal the disproportionality of its negative effects
on women, as well as the relatively limited role that EU policies can have
in shaping life opportunities for half of CEE citizenry.

Both these last chapters reveal the deep-rooted structural and attitudinal
barriers that CEEC face in responding to the conditionalities imposed by
the EU and other external organisations. They also illustrate an 'expectation gap' that many commentators, as well as CEE decision makers, see as
impossible to bridge within timescales that are achievable in the context of
medium-term political choice and immediately available resources.

Part II of the book presents four portraits of transformation. As will be
evident in the brief historical overview that follows, it was with the
Visegrad Four (Poland, Hungary, Slovakia and the Czech Republic) and
East Germany that the EU commenced a rapidly implemented programme
of aid, trade, cooperation and, by March 1993, association through the
Europe Agreements (EAs). Their central role in twentieth-century history,
their 'advanced' political and economic status and their close relations
with Western Europe prior to the Second World War suggest that these
countries form a sub-region with 'a distinctive sense of its own identity'
(Hyde-Price 1996:1). Though our later discussion challenges this perspective, until quite recently EU policy towards the Visegrad countries was
based on an even-handed approach that tended to understate the differences that gradually emerged as political and economic transformation
unfolded. These differences – now apparent in the progress that these four
countries are making with regard to their association with the EU –
become evident in our analysis in Part II.

The broader CEE perspective is not neglected, however, as in Part I the
analysis of EU–CEE relations includes references wherever appropriate to

other players: the Baltic States, Slovenia, Bulgaria, Romania, the Balkans, the Newly Independent States (NIS) and inevitably Russia. We move, in effect, from a general analysis in Part I to the particular cases of EU relations with Hungary, Poland, the Czech Republic and Slovakia, and in doing so examine the complexities of the EU's most important and uncertain project for the millennium – Eastern enlargement.

The remainder of this introduction has three purposes. The first is to outline the contemporary history of EU–CEE relations in order to contextualise the important steps taken by the EU during 1997/8 within its *Agenda 2000* initiatives. The second is to examine the institutional parameters within which EU policy towards the CEEC is conducted. Third, and emanating from the historical and institutional analysis, comes a re-evaluation of theoretical perspectives pertaining to European integration.

EU–CEE relations: a historical context

Space permits only passing reference to periods prior to the end of the Cold War. However, a detailed chronology (Appendix I) outlines the main postwar events that have influenced EU–CEE relations. The Cold War that divided Europe into two dangerously armed camps also impacted on the domestic politics of European nation states as well as providing an impetus for sub-regional cooperation. Thus the Council of Europe, the Organisation for European Economic Cooperation (OEEC, later the Organisation for Economic Cooperation and Development – OECD), the Council for Mutual Economic Assistance (CMEA), the North Atlantic Treaty Organisation (NATO), the Warsaw Treaty Organisation (WTO), the Western European Union (WEU) and the European Economic Communities (EEC, later the European Community – EC) had by 1957 institutionalised the division of Europe into opposing militarised blocs, with clear boundaries and entry rules.

The relation between these sub-regional structures and their member states inevitably reflected the antagonisms between the main protagonists, the USSR and the USA. The bones of this crude dichotomy are as follows: an ideological, economic and military stand-off exemplified by limited and antagonistic multilateral dialogue between the several East–West international organisations, demonstrated by 'the debate between deaf mutes' that took place periodically between the EC and CMEA during the 1970s, continuing through the chillier climate of the second Cold War (Senior Nello 1991); and limited and piecemeal bilateral relations, driven by the economic self-interest of states, including the USSR, often in the face of the formal disapproval of the EC and CMEA. This dichotomy reflected divisions between respective member states towards emerging multilateral commercial policies as well as the particular interests of states whose bilateral relations were shaped by historic, cultural and political as well as economic interests that on occasions rode across the ideological line; a growing asymmetrical trade relationship in favour of the EC and characterised by protectionism, particularly by the Community, with regard to agricultural, steel and textile products (Pinder and Pinder 1975; Rollo and Smith 1993; Rollo 1990); an evident technology gap and shortage of consumer goods that by the mid-1980s placed state trading economies at a serious disadvantage within global markets; a gradual emergence of Commission responsibility for a Common Commercial Policy; and equally gradual recognition of this by the Soviet Union and CMEA. These and other factors form the background to the momentous economic and eventually political restructuring of Communist Europe, 1989/91, to which we now turn.[1]

Prelude to transition

The experience of recession in the West during the 1980s had resulted in a period of protectionism, slowing down European East–West trade just at a time of mounting Communist state indebtedness, a hard currency crisis, and a continuing and evident technology gap only surmountable by the import of Western knowledge and hardware. Since CMEA countries were not influential in the General Agreement on Tariffs and Trade (GATT) or any other international economic forum, the CMEA approached the Commission in summer 1984, with proposals for the establishment of a multilateral process.[2]

Gorbachev's accession as Secretary General of the Communist Party of the Soviet Union (CPSU) in March 1985 provided the shift in political climate necessary to remove those long-standing ideological blockages to EU–CMEA relations. By 1986, the EU had commenced direct and formal negotiations with individual CMEA states, and by the end of 1986 consultations between the CMEA Secretariat and the Commission had turned to negotiations. By the end of 1989 bilateral agreements on trade and economic cooperation had been concluded with Hungary, Poland and the Soviet Union itself.

EU Mediterranean enlargements (1981, 1986) and the development of a Single Market (1985–93) were part of the background and counterpoint to the initial acceptance of a reformist path by the Soviet politburo, leading to the restructuring programmes and political initiatives of Gorbachev's leadership. But both the EU *relance* and Soviet reforms need to be set in the global perspective of the 1980s. During the 1970s the rapid growth of the Pacific Rim economies, coupled with the relative decline of the USA, had led to a new climate of economic protectionism and increasing trade competition between the USA and the Pacific Rim countries which appeared to threaten economic growth in Europe. The collapse of the Bretton Woods system years earlier had already resulted in a new protectionism evident in fierce trade competition between the USA, the EU and Japan, and an attempt to establish a regional zone of economic stability in the shape of the European Monetary System (EMS). The weakening of the dollar and Wall Street as arbiters of the global market, together with unpalatable diplomatic and military rebuffs in Africa and South East Asia, produced an abrasive set of reactions from the USA.

The responses by the USSR and the EU were in some respects quite similar. Elites in both systems saw the need for economic transformation and regeneration. Initially, similar steps were taken towards integration and regional protection; in the case of the EU via the establishment of a Single Market, including Community-wide research programmes (for example, BRITE/ESPRIT/RACE) and the EMS; in the case of the USSR, through yet another relaunching of the CMEA, at the 1984 Moscow Summit (Bideleux 1996). A more 'liberal' attitude towards global trade was manifest in overtures to the EU for mutual recognition and in the more flexible attitude adopted by the Soviet Union to bilateral agreements between East and West European countries after 1985. By mid-1986 the USSR had applied for membership of the GATT.

The outcomes of these initiatives were, however, very different. The Single European Act (SEA) of 1987 proved a catalyst for a period of EU integration and economic growth leading to Maastricht and the Treaty of European Union (TEU). Attempts to resuscitate the CMEA by the Soviet Union, accompanied by the economic liberalism and political openness of *perestroika* and *glasnost*, sent conflicting messages to East European countries. Thus, while all CMEA economies were in serious difficulties, Poland's debt situation called for immediate attention, especially after the debt default of 1986. Western bank credit restructuring was agreed in 1987. A weakened Communist administration gave in to round-table talks in February 1989, which led to the first non-Communist government in September 1989. By contrast, the German Democratic Republic (GDR) and Czechoslovak elites took little advantage of Gorbachev's reforming example, remaining heavily critical of a non-socialist road to recovery. The varying responses emanated from a growing realisation that the USSR was directing its energies towards its own economic salvation, had little interest in managing and coordinating erstwhile satellite economies, and was also losing the political legitimacy to do so. Thus when Hungary, having signed the United Nations (UN) Convention on Refugees, began without hindrance the removal of fences along the Austrian border in May 1989, the Brezhnev Doctrine symbolically died.

Early EU responses to the new Europe: 1989–91

The withdrawal of Soviet control of CEE was to produce a mixture of political and economic changes at a bewildering pace. Polish elections in June 1989 showed a collapse in support for the Polish United Workers' (Communist) Party (PUWP); in the same month the Hungarian Communist Party central committee agreed to accelerate an already successful reform programme and commenced discussions with opposition parties for a peaceful democratic transition; the migratory haemorrhage of especially young and well-qualified East Germans to the Federal Republic continued via Hungary, with little hindrance from authorities; in July, in deliberately leaked discussions with Mitterand and more publicly in a speech made to the Council of Europe, Gorbachev made it evident that the new perspective on CEE self-determination was irreversible. While several issues remained unclarified, such as the Soviet position on German reunification, the inviolability of the Warsaw Pact, or indeed the extent of transformation from the socialist model that would be tolerated, there was little doubt that the commitment to *perestroika* and *glasnost* was formally and publicly extended to the CEEC. EU–CEE futures were to the fore of the Madrid Summit in June 1989, when EU trade cooperation and aid assistance were set against further CEEC commitments to political transformation.

One month later, at the Group of 7 (G7) Summit in Paris, the EU's pivotal status in reinforcing transformation received international recognition. Following groundwork laid by Jacques Delors in a White House meeting with President Bush in May, the G7 meeting delivered to the EU the role of international coordination of immediate aid to the CEEC. This was for the Commission 'an extraordinary and unsought acknowledgement of its status as an international actor in its own right' (Sedelmeier and Wallace 1996:335). For the US administration it was a tacit admission that the American government lacked the necessary economic strength and political will to provide an independent level of assistance commensurate with the enormity of the restructuring task. Other factors that contributed to the G7 decision were more positive. The EU had already set up machinery to facilitate coordination of policy towards Eastern Europe (Luxembourg, April 1989); since the EU had already opened the doors to EU–Soviet and CMEA rapprochement, the EU – compared with the USA – stood in a more favourable political light with the USSR and CEE as the ambassador of a new relationship. The USSR's absence from the International Monetary Fund (IMF), World Bank and OECD made them less appropriate as interventionist organisations than the EU; the uncertainties associated with the prospect of a united Germany would be minimised within the Union – a factor of interest to both the USSR and France. Finally, previous EU experience of aid programmes to the Third World underscored the importance of effective coordinating machinery; since immediate aid was to come from a variety of international sources and the EU had considerable experience with African, Caribbean and Pacific states, a coordination function was deemed an appropriate task for the Commission.

First steps

The donor group of OECD countries (the Group of 24 – G24) plus the IMF, World Bank, European Investment Bank (EIB), European Coal and Steel Community (ECSC), the Paris Club and later the European Bank for Reconstruction and Development (EBRD) (May 1990) were initially to provide aid to Poland and Hungary through the Phare programme (Poland and Hungary: Assistance for Economic Reconstruction) and through bilateral aid. The programme was later extended to Romania and East Germany (until unification) and to Czechoslovakia, Bulgaria and Yugoslavia.[3] Through a task force – the G24 Co-ordinating Unit – the Commission commenced the collation of information with respect to both donor input and recipient requirements.[4] Phare, however, did not provide funding for macro-economic stabilisation; its aim was to provide Community funding or cofunding directed towards sectoral transformation – in effect the well-established Community approach of directed redistribution towards micro-economic change.

The Phare programme was an important aspect of the broader G24 aid programme (Kramer 1993). By mid-1992 this G24 support, including assistance offered via the IMF, World Bank, EBRD and contributing states, amounted to ecus 47 billion, coordinated by the Community. The total Phare programme amounted to approximately ecu 1.47 billion (July 1992). Overall the Community and member states contributed approximately two-thirds of G24 funding, with Germany providing 50 per cent of EU member state funding 1989–93 (Kramer 1993:225).[5]

We have mentioned the rapid establishment of EU–CEEC bilateral trade cooperation agreements – the second economic response to the post-Wall scenario. By 1991 eight bilateral agreements, including one with the USSR, had been concluded. These, together with those with Slovenia, Albania and the Baltic States in 1992, had a common structure, varying in their detail with regard to specific needs of CEEC and the specific terms of EC member states. They were non-preferential agreements based on reciprocity associated with market liberalisation. In effect, this meant a staged lifting of quantitative import restrictions to the Community and the status of Most Favoured Nation (MFN). Their effect was limited, reflecting the cautious attitude of the EU actors, who understandably continued to view these new partners with some apprehension; what was offered therefore was no more than EC standard procedure for new foreign relations (Kramer 1993).

The earliest agreement, however (with Hungary, September 1988), and its subsequent amendment to more favourable terms in January 1990, were used as a springboard to stake Hungarian claims for early and full membership (Reisch 1993:33). Similar aspirations were echoed by the governments of Czechoslovakia and Poland (de Weydenthal 1992). While understandable in the climate of post-Wall euphoria and the uncertainties remaining with regard to the future of the Soviet Union, such aspirations were, from the Commission's perspective, unrealistic.

Post-Wall political manoeuvres

The autumn of 1989 saw a mostly enthusiastic and willing public commitment on behalf of the EU member states to assist in CEEC transformation. Moving from the generality of statements at the conclusion of the Hanover and Rhodes Summits (June and December 1988), where the potential of support was offered to CMEA states clearly deemed as 'reformist', the Strasbourg Summit (December 1989) presented the Community as a haven of political and economic stability; from such a cornerstone a new framework for EC/CEE relations could be constructed. From Strasbourg came Council support for rapid German reunification as well as agreement to inaugurate the EBRD as an inclusive policy instrument. East European and Russian representatives were to form part of its management structure; this contrasted with the deliberately divisive nature of EU–CEE relations during the Cold War.[6] For an illustration of the role of the EBRD in Poland see Chapter 11.

The imminent unification of Germany, achieved by October 1990, set several hares running. For West Germany unification delivered new political and economic opportunities, inside and outside the EU. It broadened the range of potential options available to the new Germany, both in terms of previous commitments to European integration and in shaping the direction of EU–CEE relations. France had always lent support to German unification, but based on an assumption that it could never actually happen (Le Gloannec 1989). The spectre of a 'new German question' with the potential of an unwelcome regional hegemony produced tremors in French foreign policy circles that temporarily reopened old debates over alignments.[7] At Strasbourg, however, President Mitterand opened a reinvigorated argument for enhanced integration as a means of both harnessing the new Germany and maintaining French influence over the European project. Thus, for different reasons, both Mitterand and Kohl presented unification as a catalyst for the further deepening of the Community and hence as a significant impetus to both political and economic reform of EU structures (Commission 1990).

Such arguments cut little ice with the (then) Thatcher UK government. For it, the development of extensive cooperation with CEEC was advocated both as an underpinning of fledgling market economies, and as a contribution to the dilution of the Delors–Mitterand European Project. A similar position was adopted by Portugal and Denmark.

For Mitterand, sustaining the 1992 Project would create the necessary political will and economic strength to support the economic and democratic transformation of CEEC. In reality, however, the prioritisation of EU integration implied an ante-chamber for CEE states, awaiting their turn for closer association and membership after economic and political hurdles were cleared. Economic and political union with concrete treaty agreements also implied tough entry conditions, so precluding CEEC from their goal of membership for years to come. The application of conditionalities to CEEC found favour with Spanish, Portuguese and Greek governments, who as new member states naturally perceived any major new claims on EU resources as a potential loss to their recently established position of 'deserving' recipient states.

The more generous stance of the West German government towards the CEEC in this period is evident in statements and actions during 1989–91. The unique relationship between the GDR and Federal Republic of Germany (FRG) prior to the unification, together with the FRG's position as the largest EU trading partner with the European CMEA countries, placed a high level of expectation by CEEC on Germany as an economic and political bridge to the EU (Lippert *et al.* 1993). In response, Bonn acknowledged its 'historic debt' as well as recognising the advantages of investment to Germany, particularly in Poland, Hungary and the Czechoslovak economies. New neighbours, however, produced new border problems, with the fear of 'migratory leakage' and a consequent domestic political backlash; there was therefore a need to assist economic transformation in adjoining CEE states to ameliorate any unwelcome invasion. The Federal Republic's *Ostpolitik* also contended with changed circumstances in the Soviet Union; thus emerged 'an unspoken political obligation to Moscow because of the largely unconditional Soviet unwillingness to accept German unification' (Lippert *et al.* 1993:108). Finally, the Commission initially had high expectations of a united Germany to provide the economic motor for, and political linkage between, the EC and CMEA states, and as such to play a key role in the coordination of trade policy and aid for restructuring (Commission 1990).[8]

During 1990 this commitment by the Kohl government was enhanced by the optimism of unification and its anticipated opportunities. The 'equalisation' of the East and West German economies was estimated to be achievable in ten years; a potentially huge consumer demand in East Germany, stoked by the Single European Market (SEM) and the parity given to the Ost mark, offered benefits to both West Germany and other

EU member states alike. Politically, it provided an incentive for further integration and would strengthen the Community's world role (Welfens 1993; Bulmer and Scott 1994). Thus Kohl and others in German government repeated unswerving commitment to EU integration 'which had always been seen as a *"precondition"*, and not a *substitute* for German unity' (Van Ham 1993:163).

Circumstances in Germany during 1991 challenged these assumptions: the costs to the Federal Republic were evidently greater than had been publicly stated a year before; 'equalisation' was now estimated at twenty years; taxation surcharges, public expenditure rises and East–West migration destabilised popular support in West Germany for both unification and moves towards European Monetary Union (Welfens 1993). The result was to be a growing gap between public and elite opinion regarding European integration and German involvement in CEE transition – costly ventures for a disturbed West German electorate. These factors, together with the growing crisis in Yugoslavia, and the loss of Gorbachev as an ally for *Ostpolitik*, led one commentator to conclude that 'the medium term effects of unification seem on balance to have made Germany more of an equal, weaker partner than a dominant member of the Community' (Lippert *et al.* 1993:131). At the Maastricht Summit of December 1991 there was less stridency in German demands for EU integration and a consciousness that transformation could only be effective within the context of other European organisations, including NATO. In effect the rapid extension of EU membership to CEEC looked, for the foreseeable future, unrealistic.

The emergence of a European policy

In the context of the internal debates concerning economic and institutional integration, and differing opinions on the role of the Union in assisting CEEC transformation, member states were poorly placed to agree on anything other than ameliatory and technical responses to the post-Wall scenario. There was no dominant voice with the political clout of a powerful state – no George Marshall or George Kennan and no interventionist US administration – to argue conclusively for a grand strategy and a major resource commitment of Marshall Plan proportions. In fact, 'just as the twelve were about to sit down to a rich diet of economic and monetary union, gatecrashers from the east start knocking on the door, threatening to gain admission to the club and to spoil the community feast!' (*Financial Times*, 24 January 1990). It was therefore the Commission, internationally tasked with the coordination of G24 aid, which was to respond with initiatives that for the most part did not 'go beyond the established instruments of Community foreign relations and the normal range of Western international activities in international restructuring' (Kramer 1993:234). This is not to say that the Commission did not have its own divisions regarding the signals to be given to CEE. The demise of the CMEA (by January 1991) was accompanied by several grand gestures, notably for an eastern European Free Trade Association (EFTA) as a precursor to closer affiliation, or a European Political Area by Frans Andriesen, the (then) external affairs commissioner.

Partly as a response to these ideas, and after several meetings during 1990, Poland, Hungary and Czechoslovakia signed the Declaration of Visegrad in February 1991, to develop regional cooperation between the three countries; the agreement also offered the Commission a target for negotiations calculated to enhance the chances of the (then) Visegrad Three for eventual EU membership. Overlapping these somewhat premature attempts at developing a new semi-detached European architecture were more traditional moves to reconsider the trade and cooperation agreements of 1989/90. The emergence of EAs as second-generation policy instruments represented a compromise between maximalist and minimalist positions evident in both the Council and Commission itself. A discussion of their effectiveness in assisting transformation is contained in subsequent chapters. Here we trace briefly their emergence during 1991.

Deteriorating economic circumstances in CEE were evident in several forms: in terms of debt crises – only Hungary and Czechoslovakia could borrow on the international markets during 1990, and Poland was saved from bankruptcy by a partial debt waiver via Paris Club Agreement in the spring of 1991; in terms of trade system collapse, especially of Soviet foreign trade with CEE – during 1991 CEE exports amounted to 30–40 per cent of 1990 levels; in terms of payments crisis – as the CEEC and the Soviet Union struggled with the change to hard currency payments; and in terms of deteriorating domestic economic circumstances – recession, increased unemployment, inflation and budget deficits (Koves 1992). In particular the escalating crisis in the Soviet Union, the single most important factor behind the collapse in trade, presented a dilemma to the EU that rendered the recently negotiated trade and cooperation agreements obsolete.

As early as April 1990 the Dublin Council meeting had called for a form of agreement to enhance new relationships with the CEEC (Commission 1990). Initial negotiations with Poland, Hungary and Czechoslovakia commenced in December 1990, revealing deep divisions of opinion and differing expectations between EU actors and CEE representatives (de Weydenthal 1992; Van Ham 1993; Reinicke 1992). The CEEC viewed any new Association Agreement as a transitional arrangement towards full membership. Their models were those of the Greek, Portuguese and Spanish Association Agreements, all of which contained cautious but clear statements of eventual membership and thus a clear-cut indication of where aspirant interests lay in the future (Preston 1997). It was not until April 1991 that a reluctant Council agreed to a preamble statement that referred to membership as an eventual but certainly not automatic outcome of association; subsequently, clauses associated with democratic and human rights and market principles were added to the preamble statements at the insistence of the European Parliament (EP). Similarly tough stances, influenced by sectoral interests, were taken with regard to market access. The resulting 'classical' association formula was, from the perspective of the CEEC, a disappointing outcome of the process.

It must also be remembered, however, that during this period EU priorities lay elsewhere, with the Maastricht negotiations and with the establishment of the European Economic Area for the EU and EFTA. It took the external shock of the Soviet coup in August 1991, and the fear of massive political regression in the USSR, to produce a flurry of statements from CEE and EU negotiators to speed up and conclude the agreements. By September, Central European governments had accepted what was probably the best deal they were likely to achieve in difficult circumstances, and the agreements were signed on 16 December, shortly after the conclusion of the Maastricht Summit and its framework treaty aimed at a significant deepening of relations between existing member states.

Near and far Europe: the parameters of EU *Ostpolitik*

The collapse of the Soviet Union in 1991, the breakdown of the Yugoslav Federation and the consequent redefinition of EU–Russian relations are significant for our analysis in several respects. Prior to 1991, the distinction between CEE, the Soviet Union and Yugoslavia was clearly marked; subsequently the status of the Baltic and Balkan States was radically altered and, inevitably, required EU policies commensurate with the maintenance of the Union's immediate security interests. Chapter 7 examines the politically charged notion of the 'return to Europe' and the factors that have contributed to identification with an EU 'cosmos'. Here we outline EU policy responses in the context of an emerging hierarchy of EU–East European relations.

From an early stage, policies adopted to assist the NIS of the former Soviet Union contrasted markedly in generosity, aims and implementation with policies towards CEEC. Like Phare, the EU's Technical Assistance for the Commonwealth of Independent States (Tacis) programme provides aid to fourteen countries of the ex-Soviet Union, and aims to foster partnership 'initiatives to develop societies based on political freedoms and prosperity' (Commission 1997a:1). However, Tacis received only half of Phare's commitment between 1991 and 1995 (2,268m ecu);

moreover, infrastructional aid (approximately one-third of each programme's commitment) shows a marked difference in agreed priorities, with banking/finance and transport/communications taking the bulk of Phare infrastructural funding, compared with around two-thirds of Tacis infrastructural support directed at the energy sector and with particular reference to nuclear safety. A similar distinction can be made in the application of the 'democracy' lines of Phare and Tacis (see Chapter 4). Over 80 per cent of Tacis funding was committed to two countries, the Russian Federation and the Ukraine; Phare aid was more evenly spread (Commission 1997b, 1997c).

Contrast may also be made between the emergence of the trade and cooperation agreements of the early 1990s and those that emerged later as Partnership and Cooperation Agreements (PCAs), concluded with NIS during 1996. The latter were 'to occupy a position between the trade and cooperation agreements and the European Agreements' that would allow for 'closer links and broader co-operation' (Commission 1993:784). What was significantly missing was any reference to a move towards Association similar to that on offer to the CEEC, though reference is made to the future establishment of a Free Trade Area in the PCA between Russia and the EU (Commission 1997d; Ardy 1997). While there are similarities in the political context of the EAs and PCAs, with reference to the maintenance of democratic values and human rights and an ongoing political dialogue through cooperation, councils and twice-yearly presidential meetings, the economic provisions do not greatly extend beyond the Trade Cooperation Agreements (TCAs) of 1990 and will be, in the case of Russia, superseded in some respects by WTO membership (Gower 1997).

Inclusion with the EA/Phare policy framework gives substantially different signals when compared with the PCA/Tacis nexus. Thus the decision to include the Baltic States in the Phare programme (1992), later reinforced by their EAs (1995), was a clear political message that they were, if not geographically, certainly politically part of CEE. Prior to the Essen Summit the European Parliament resolved as such, 'insisting in all consideration of the further enlargement of the EU' that the Baltic States 'must be regarded as part of Central and Eastern Europe' (European Parliament 1994).

Any slight doubt that Romania and Bulgaria would not enjoy near-Europe status, engendered by the lack of early invitation to negotiate an EA, was removed when, by the spring of 1993, the two countries signed similar agreements to the Visegrads (Phinnemore 1997). Since then, Slovenia, Albania and the remaining ex-Yugoslav Federation states (excluding Serbia-Montenegro and Croatia), through the extension of the Phare programme and separate trading agreements, have been included in the ambience of the 'near-European family'.

Thus three ex-NIS (the Baltics) and one ex-Yugoslavian state (Slovenia)

are included with the CEEC as association partners having evident accession potential. The Phare programme may be seen as delineating a further
group – Albania, Macedonia and Bosnia – as having the potential to
progress towards deeper association and, conceivably, to pre-accession
status in the (long-term) future (Commission 1998). No such formal
status is offered either to sixteen NIS, including Russia, Ukraine and
Moldova which now have both PCA agreements and Tacis aid, or those
which are in receipt of limited aid and trade agreements (see Table 1.1 and
also map, p. xviii).[9]

Table 1.1   Formal EU–CEE relations to 1998

Country	Application status	Form of agreement	Aid/technical assistance programme
Albania	–	TCA	Phare
Belarus	–	–	Suspended relations
Bosnia	–	TCA (pending)	Phare
Bulgaria	Pre-accession	EA	Phare
Croatia	–	Limited	Suspended
Czech Republic	Negotiating accession	EA	Phare
Estonia	Negotiating accession	EA	Phare
GDR	Incorporated	–	Structural funding
Hungary	Negotiating accession	EA	Phare
Latvia	Pre-accession	EA	Phare
Lithuania	Pre-accession	EA	Phare
Macedonia	–	TCA	Phare
Moldova	–	PCA	Tacis
Poland	Negotiating accession	EA	Phare
Romania	Pre-accession	EA	Phare
Russia	–	PCA	Tacis
Slovakia	Pre-accession	EA	Phare
Slovenia	Negotiating accession	EA	Phare
Ukraine	–	PCA	Tacis
Yugoslavia (Serbia/ Montenegro)	–	Suspended	OBANOVA (special assistance programme)

The list of factors that may explain this differentiation is inevitably
eclectic, reflecting the pragmatic and incremental nature of EU *Ostpolitik*
since 1989. Thus the different, less advanced, processes of economic and
political transition of the NIS; regional disputes; lack of clear socio-
cultural identity with Western Europe; and the broader perspectives and
influences on their future that emanated from the international community, including the USA, combine with other factors to result in the
PCA/Tacis distinction as evidently not just a separate path to accommodate different stages of transition, but leading 'to a different destination –
partnership – not membership' (Gower 1997:11).

One further and significant factor in observing the policy differential within EU *Ostpolitik* is, inevitably EU–Russian relations. Periodic domestic instability in Russia, the emergence of nationalism, the erratic nature of Yeltsin's leadership and the Chechnya problem served to encourage integrative policies associated with EU–CEEC (Phinnemore 1997), sensitise relations between the EU and other NIS, and complicate the smooth passage of stable EU–Russian relations that were perceived at an early stage as being vital to the progress of EU–CEE relations themselves (Van Ham 1993; Taylor 1996). The EP has expressed this dilemma rather more explicitly than appears in either official Council or Commission documentation.[10] But succinctly, prior to the Essen Summit (1994), the EP resolved that it was 'essential that enlargement of the Union towards the East be accompanied by a policy of closer co-operation with the European countries of the former Soviet Union' (European Parliament 1994).

The flurry of attention to EU–Russian relations surrounding the June 1997 launch of the *Agenda 2000* proposals indicated the continuing sensitivity shown by both parties to the EU's enlargement strategy. That relationship was not clarified by the assertion by Premier Chernomyrdin that Russia's aim was eventual membership of the Union (Gower 1997). While this may be dismissed as part of a periodically applied bargaining tactic to improve Russia's position *vis-à-vis* the EU, it may also illustrate the lack of clarity of objectives within the inclusive/exclusive EC–CEE policy frameworks that have emerged. The EP's Committee on External Relations lists a set of uncertainties resulting from what it calls 'the vagueness and uncertainty surrounding the final shape of the European project in the post *Agenda 2000* scenario and the broader consequences of the Union's significant policy shift towards Eurasia' (European Parliament 1997a:39).

The Community context of EU–CEEC relations

The EU association policy is founded upon the Treaties that have framed its common institutional structures and policy-making processes, and it is within this context that actors, especially the Commission, seek appropriate legal and institutional avenues for the development of EU–CEE relations. Thus the EAs have, as their genesis, Article 238; the extension of EIB activities beyond EU borders derives from Article 130; and the Treaty-based procedure for membership is described below. It is therefore worthwhile dwelling on some interpretations of the policy process at this point so as to be reminded of the formidable rules of engagement that surround EU–CEE relations.

The genesis of the policy process remains the systematic partnership of

Council of Ministers and Commission – the Monnet method (Wallace 1996:42). Moderated by emerging 'interventions' of the European Parliament, with the adjudicative role taken where appropriate by the European Court of Justice, the institutions are the gatekeepers through which European economic and political elites compete and develop common goals and values. The method relies on the Commission to deliver high-quality 'technocratic' policies based on prior agreement with non-governmental economic and political interests. The Council seeks to conciliate governmental interests; these may also include member states' expressed sectoral interests as well as particular national interests. Both Commission and Council may be advised by formal consultative bodies such as the EP, the Economic and Social Committee and, since Maastricht, the Committee of the Regions. Thus the Council–Commission tandem is surrounded by a plurality of other stakeholders in the Community policy area, both socio-economic interests and national policy makers. This model is closely associated with the theoretical and ideological features of neo-functionalism and therefore assumes the logic of integration and its socio-economic inevitability.

The countervailing model of the EU policy process shapes itself around the Gaullist method and its intergovernmentalist assumptions and expectations. The policy process in this model is focused on the Council and its various committees, including the Committee of Permanent Representatives, and is characterised by cautious negotiation around member states' interests – 'a guaranteed approach to policy extension and a sharp insistence on entrenching the interests of particular clients of policy in the policy rules of the institutions' (Wallace 1996:46). Further characteristics of this model include the distinction between high and low politics and the consequent divisions of responsibility for, and interest in, policies between the Council and the Commission; the focus of sectional interests not unnaturally at member state level and at early rather than later stages of the policy process; the spawning of Council and Commission consultative committees as a means of pre-negotiation; and the enhancement of tactical rather than technical negotiation for the Commission as it would need to progress policy through interstate bargaining – the stuff of 'comitology'.[11] While these models may have emerged from the experiences of specific periods of the history of the EU, they remain simplified frameworks within which we may observe the more complicated processes of the post-SEM/TEU Union and thus the context of more recent EU–CEE policies.

The Single Market and incremental decision taking

Earlier we suggested that the concept of the Single Market presented policy makers with an opportunity to respond positively to external economic challenges as well as to find common cause for EU enthusiasts in kick-starting a moribund Community. The impact on the policy process of the Community was similarly dynamic, in that it led to a series of process reforms, extended the reach of the Commission with regard to the range of its policies and the policy actors/clients necessary to sustain new initiatives. It also provided the political incentive for the Council to consider seriously the adequacy of its existing decision processes. In effect both neo-functional and intergovernmental methods needed overhaul if the SEA and its associated policies were to be delivered (Wallace and Young 1996). The subsequent fallout of new social, economic and environmental policies as a response to the anticipated negative aspects of the SEA only enhanced the need for consultation through networks that were to embrace new 'galvanised partnerships' (Scharpf 1994; Marks 1993; Mazey and Richardson 1992).

Correspondingly expanded EU budgetary demands to meet policy demands had two effects. They produced expectations of cooperation from both public and private organisations to facilitate take-up. They also produced the expectation of rapid and politically valid decisions in Council; that is, decisions that did not leave doubts that they were reached only through belligerent negotiation and reluctant acceptance. While the willingness to utilise Qualified Majority Voting (QMV) had already been noted prior to the SEA negotiations, it was subsequently accepted in its broader application rather more easily by member states than might have been anticipated (Wallace 1996:54).

The convoluted mix of deregulation and intervention which characterises the contemporary EU relies heavily on a sophisticated civil society, a systematic Commission/Council partnership, and the critical applause of European political elites, manufacturers and consumers (Middlemas 1995). It also includes a massive technical/legal effort on behalf of national and regional governments and private organisations to implement the associated *acquis* – a community method of 'co-option and regulation'.[12] While aspects of the EU policy arena remained outside this framework – and the Maastricht structure clearly indicates the strength of intergovernmentalism in Pillars II and III – the Single Market policy processes which parallel the first approaches of the CEEC towards closer association were dependent on an EU bureaucratic and political process more complex than ever, and relied upon incremental knowledge, sophisticated socio-economic structures and a post-industrial, market-led culture that seemed at times only just tolerated by existing member governments and citizens. It is in these circumstances that CEEC sought deeper association with, and accession to, this convoluted family of states.

The Treaty of Amsterdam

Unlike other Intergovernmental Conferences (IGCs), the one which culminated in the Amsterdam Treaty was *required* under Article N of the Treaty of Union of 1992. The official purpose of the 1996/7 IGC was to revise the European Treaties with the aim of ensuring the effectiveness of the mechanisms and institutions of the Community in the light of issues that remained unresolved from the Maastricht Treaty, the impact of EMU, and the necessity to prepare for the potential of enlargement to CEE. In the event other factors conspired to create a disappointing IGC outcome and the issue of institutional reform was ducked.[13]

Section Four of the Treaty – the Unions' Institutions – contained a Protocol on Enlargement that passed the responsibility for substantial Treaty amendment to a future 'accession' IGC. This is to be convened 'at least one year before the membership of the European Union shall exceed twenty'. At this future conference the postponed issues of Commission size, QMV extension, weighting of Council votes and, though not specifically mentioned, the further extension of EP powers would be resolved.[14] With regard to the Commission, Article One established that 'at the date of entry into force of the first enlargement of the Union ... the Commission shall comprise one national of each of the member states'. This was, however, to be linked to a prerequisite reform of the weighting of Council votes in a manner acceptable to all member states, especially those who would need compensation for the loss of a second member of the Commission.

The formal linkage of these three institutional reforms with enlargement looks likely to be no easier to resolve when it returns to an IGC agenda in a few years' time, when the larger member states are constitutionally legitimised in holding the enlargement talks hostage in exchange for institutional guarantees. Indeed, Spain enjoys a 'special case' protocol within the Treaty. One institutional issue was settled, however. The EP is to be restricted in size to a maximum of 700 (Article 137), a reform recommended by both the Commission and the EP itself. Subsequently, the Commission opinions in *Agenda 2000*, confirmed at the Luxembourg Council in December 1997, have confronted the institutional issue by recommending that accession negotiators should commence with six of the ten Association partners. More than this, the Commission sees the need to fix a date as early as possible in 2000 to effect further institutional reforms before the first enlargement. The EP and the Belgian and Italian governments have subsequently underlined the importance of achieving acceptable institutional arrangements well in advance of accession (European Parliament 1997b:3).

As a result of the failure of the Amsterdam Treaty, applicant states will begin the process of negotiation without the knowledge of how their countries will be represented in two of the major institutions of the club they wish to join. Neither is it clear how many seats in the EP will be made available, given that there is a reference in the Treaty to the establishment of fair representation for both large- and small-population states (Duff 1997:150). The next IGC will of necessity be seriously divided on this and other aspects of representational rights between large and small states.

The Commission mission

Since a major aspect of our analysis will focus upon the aspirations of CEE with regard to EU membership, it is worth examining the role of the Commission in accession negotiations. A Commission official guides us through the tasks (Avery 1995).

Accession negotiations are conducted bilaterally between member states and each of the applicant states. Thus the presidency presents a common position which has been agreed by the Council on a recommen-dation from the Commission. Since it is the primary role of the Commission to protect and enhance the Union, the Commission 'has to think not only what the member states will be prepared to agree amongst themselves, but also what the applicant country will be prepared to accept, and what will be equitable and workable in an enlarged union' (Avery 1995:2). In this context the Commission acts as both an internal and external mediator – playing the role of a trouble-shooter to assist in the solution of specific and difficult problems, in a less formal atmosphere than pertains at ministerial, ambassadorial or presidency level: 'the real discussions [take] place elsewhere, behind the scenes, often between the applicants, the Presidency and the Commission' (Avery 1995:3). In this more informal, often technical and 'realistic' atmosphere, the Commission's advice to candidate countries on what is possible in the political and often tendentious circumstances of the Council may be significant. We shall note later, however, that the Commission has prob-lems over its own internal coordination (see Chapter 2). Finally, the starting point for negotiation is based on an Opinion by the Commission, and the agenda for discussion is established around a set of compromises that reflect a Commission common position, the applicants' concerns and a 'realistic' assessment of the attitudes of member states.

The external and internal circumstances surrounding the CEE enlarge-ment place the Commission in a more complex position both technically and politically than in previous enlargements (Preston 1997). Instruments for pre-accession (the EAs, White Paper, 1995 and Phare), together with the several Council conclusions on the conditions within which accession should take place, established parameters within which the Commission must operate. Moreover the additional *acquis* particularly associated with

EMU and Pillars II and III of the TEU needed to be incorporated in a pre-accession strategy. Finally, policy reforms especially associated with the Common Agricultural Policy (CAP), competition policy and structural funding sprang not just from the imperatives of deepening/widening debate, but also from external factors including GATT/WTO negotiations and US pressures for market access (Burghardt and Cameron 1997).

Previous experience with accession presents useful comparisons for what emerged as a qualitatively and potentially quantitatively different experience for the EU. The first enlargement, with the exception of sectors within the Irish economy, was to countries whose economies and political systems were broadly compatible with the original Six. The second and third enlargements, to Greece (1981), Portugal and Spain (1986), were to countries whose political systems had emerged from authoritarianism comparatively recently and whose economies were considerably weaker than the existing member states'. However, each had an established market economy that, with an adapted structural policy supported by the EU, was expected to be able to compete in the emerging SEM. The fourth enlargement represents a shorter, smoother process, with accession negotiations lasting for little more than one year, representing the high level of preparedness of EFTA applicants, in part through their experiences of the European Economic Area (EEA) (Avery 1995; Preston 1997). (See also Table 1.2.)

Table 1.2   The accession timetable

Country	Application	Opinion of Commission	Opening of negotiations	End of negotiations	Accession
Turkey	14.04.87	14.12.89			
Austria	17.07.89	01.08.91	01.02.93	12.04.94	01.01.95
Sweden	01.07.91	31.07.92	01.02.93	12.04.94	01.01.95
Finland	18.03.92	04.11.92	01.02.93	12.04.94	01.01.95
Norway	25.11.92	24.03.93	05.04.93	12.04.94	
Switzerland	26.05.92				
Malta	16.07.90	30.06.93			
Cyprus	04.07.90	30.06.93	31.03.98		
Hungary	31.03.94	15.07.97	31.03.98		
Poland	05.04.94	15.07.97	31.03.98		
Romania	22.06.95	15.07.97			
Slovakia	27.06.95	15.07.97			
Estonia	24.11.95	15.07.97	31.03.98		
Latvia	13.10.95	15.07.97			
Lithuania	08.12.95	15.07.97			
Bulgaria	14.12.95	15.07.97			
Czech Republic	17.01.96	15.07.97	31.03.98		
Slovenia	10.06.96	15.07.97	31.03.98		

From this, we may deduce a number of factors relevant to the CEE pre-accession strategy as it is currently emerging. First, accession negotiations have been, with the exception of the second enlargement to Greece, conducted with groups of countries in separate, parallel negotiation. This for the most part has favoured the negotiation hand of the Union, which, assisted by the Commission, has presented a more coherent front than aspirant member states. These even in the EFTA accession did not produce a consistent group position in negotiation. This is hardly surprising, given the country-specific nature of accession problems and the inevitable rivalry for a successful outcome to accession proceedings that each country wishes to achieve. Second, the conclusion of 'grouped' negotiations has resulted in simultaneous accession dates. In this way the political, financial and administrative impact of enlargement is minimised and may be associated with the institutional and budgetary cycle of the Union. Third, formal acquiescence to the *acquis communautaire*, with only limited adjustment and derogation, has been an initial and vital aspect of Union negotiation; the use of agreed and often lengthy transitional periods has previously allowed new members the time necessary to adjust to Union rules, and allowed the Union time to make its own adjustments in the light of the post-accession situation.

Given the economic and administrative weaknesses of CEEC, and the exponential increase in the *acquis* since 1992, the practicality of transition periods and the application of derogation for CEE applicants presents huge problems for the fifth accession strategy. As will be seen, it has resulted in a pre-accession policy that depends upon adjustment of EU institutional and policy arrangements before enlargements can be implemented.

Some concluding threads: the Europeanisation of Europe?

For Lamberto Dini (1997:xxvii), 'in Amsterdam we saw a Europe that was all too often opaque, inclined to procrastination and ambiguity – a prisoner of interests sometimes more nationalistic than national'. The negotiations and the ensuing Treaty moved the 'European debate' only marginally from its historical parameters, that is, its imprisonment within a Cold War definition of (West) Europeanness, exclusivity and defensiveness against other, rival definitions of Europeanism in the shape of Fascism and communism. Events since the 1940s have seen the demise of those rival models and have, recently, radically altered the nature of the remaining model – a construct of the postwar Atlanticist pact that provided the *raison d'être* for the capitalist, interventionist character of the EU and the powerfully protective role of NATO. These changes have left remaining (EU) Europe with a moral and international obligation to provide a practising model, 'a new role for Europe in the world' (Hettne 1995:206).

While not discounting the potential for sub-regional disintegration and the perpetuation of the nation-state model that remains an unevenly influential force in both Western and Eastern Europe, Hettne argues that the potential for 'self-reliance', emerging from the interactive processes already achieved and responses to the external forces of global competition, is a likely outcome. Self-reliance, however, is not autarky, but 'is conceived of as a symmetric pattern of co-operation expressed on various [European] territorial levels and ultimately also in Europe's relations with the rest of the world' (Hettne 1995:213). The broad character of the (new) European model is within the liberal democratic hegemony that we describe below (see Chapter 4 and also Lalumiere 1992), but is also composed of a set of sometimes shared, sometimes competing values shaped by different cultural/historical experiences – Christian–secular; state–local, individualist–collective, etc. – with these and other factors apparent in the continual attempts by its members to redefine the character of the EU. Hence the problem of progress at Amsterdam and, for the CEEC, of joining a moving EU target, manifest in their struggle to operationalise increasing and complex sets of *acquis* (see Chapter 2). However, despite the nebulous features of the EU as a 'European model', it is to the EU as mainstream Europe to which the CEEC turned, rather than to the creation of a rival, post-Communist regional bloc, or to bilateral reintegration with the international community, as 'the start of a transition to the market economy, political pluralism and integration into the world' (Hettne 1995:247).

Perceptions of what Europe is are the preserve neither of the Commission nor of Danish Eurosceptics, Italian Federalists or Blairite pragmatists. The countries of Central, Eastern, Baltic and South Eastern Europe have different pre-Communist, Communist and post-Communist experiences that shape their contemporary identity, and thus their views of the European model and the EU as its embodiment (Hyde-Price 1996). Opting into a Western European family of capitalist democracies is likely to be selective in its progress; a function of the pragmatism of dominant EU actors and their perceptions of how far CEEC measure up to an emerging but still unclear vision of the European model.

The task of conceptualising 'New Europe' is therefore not easy. Integration theory, until recently, was contained within theoretical paradigms influenced by particular ideological and historical circumstances. Thus neo-functionalism and intergovernmentalism, the two major integration theories and their variants, spring from functionalist and neorealist political thought that sought, from different perspectives, to rationalise the international conditions of postwar Cold War Europe (Tranholm-Mikkelsen 1991; Webb 1983). Thus Mitrany (1944), Haas

(1957), Lindberg (1971) and Hoffmann (1966) reflected personal agendas – their vision for Europe – as well as the influence of the politico-economic environment in which they wrote. More recently, integration theory has moved from 'fields of vision' associated with postwar economic political and social 'realities' to the analysis of the EU 'beast' as a complex, multilevel system of governance (Risse-Kappen 1996). Academic recognition of the EU as an established, regional system of networks, structures, processes and interest coalitions (Peterson 1995) still owes its genesis to the concept of that same postwar/Cold War framework – in effect the *de facto* recognition of a now established but still *Western* European union of capital, liberalism and social regulation.

Theoretical perspectives on integration that are successfully to include the phenomenon of post-communism need to stretch further than the primarily middle-range (policy) analysis of recent years. One recent revision of neo-functionalism suggests an addition to the concept of spillover to include an international dimension, where anticipated EU expansion creates an enforced external spillover on the policies of aspirant members and member states (Miles, Redmond and Schwok 1998). The same authors suggest, paradoxically, that intergovernmentalism provides the most appropriate framework for explaining enlargement. We shall argue (in Chapter 2) that assumptions regarding the pre-eminence of national interests in agenda setting are curtailed by, first, the presentation by the Commission of 'integrated' policy packages – alike *Agenda 2000* – that became extremely difficult to unpick by member states; and, second, the tendency of national actors to discount 'long-term' consequences of major decisions, such as CEE enlargement, to overcome short-term veto problems (see also Smyrl 1998). In the context of CEE enlargement, therefore, broader idealist perspectives for a new Europe have emerged via Commission initiatives as part of the EU millennium agenda. Factors that have shaped that vision include: anticipation of an enhanced role for the EU as an international actor in the context of economic, technological and political globalisation; recognition of a historic, heterogeneous European identity and its geographic and cultural limits; and consciousness of the responsibility placed upon the EU to provide a model and leadership for the new Europe of the twenty-first century. At the same time, however, the EU's own vision remains uncertain and the EU model is inevitably challenged by the prospect of an Eastern enlargement. In these shifting and uncertain conditions the boundaries of EU–CEEC relations are being forged.

Notes

1 For a lucid examination of the history of the region see Hyde-Price (1996).

For a detailed neorealist account of postwar EU–CEE relations see Van Ham (1993). Lewis (1994) explores Central European postwar history and the rise and fall of communism in the region.

2 During the second half of 1983 the USSR brought a case through the European Court of Justice against the Commission, challenging anti-dumping measures considered to be unjustified – scarcely a positive initiative, but one that formally recognised the Community's policy role in international trade.

3 By October 1990 $15 million in grants and loans were pledged by G24 to Poland and Hungary; by 1991, with other recipients included, the figure needed revising to between £25 million and £30 million; approximately 500 million ecu were made available by the EU (Senior Nello 1991:194). Allocation of funds in the same period was approximately Hungary 26 per cent, Poland 34 per cent, Czechoslovakia 8 per cent, and Romania and Bulgaria 5 per cent each, with the remaining 22 per cent to other eligible countries.

4 The expectations of both donors and recipients were also canvassed via a relatively transparent information process available for all the actors concerned. The enormity of the coordination task involved was aptly portrayed in one commentator's matrix of policy choice/policy actor combinations – over 170 – with policy choices ranging from short-term balance of payments aid to building local political institutions, and actors ranging from the IMF to local government and individual firms (Rollo 1990). Initial stocktaking of available aid was followed by Phare programme recipients presenting detailed memoranda on their specific needs, assessed by EU missions sent to the countries involved. Immediate measures included food supplied to Poland (536 million ecus, 1989–90), rural development loans and agricultural assistance.

5 This support to 1993 included as follows (in ecus): Phare, 1 billion; single states' technical aid, 7.2 billion; emergency food aid, 1.5 billion; macro-economic stabilisation (Club of Paris), 11.4 billion; export credit, 10.2 billion; EIB, 1.7 billion.

6 The project was the brainchild of Jacques Attali, whose close attachment to President Mitterand allowed the plan a voice in the initial positioning of EU member states *vis-à-vis* the Eastern European 'problem'. Established in May 1990, the EBRD was designed as a joint activity owned by both the donors (EU and OECD member states and others) and the recipient countries, which would have a formal place in the Bank's policy-making mechanisms. Its dual mandate – to foster both economic and political transformation – together with the high-profile style proposed and later adopted by Attali as its first president, produced early controversy. The US administration was particularly concerned about the EU dominance of the Bank, as 51 per cent of its shares were controlled by EU member states: this together with the 'socialist dirigiste' leadership of Attali led to US insistence that at least 60 per cent of loans made should be to the private sector (Hughes 1993). This was to cause the Bank early problems in loan distribution, which was not helpful in countering later public criticism of its activities (Weber 1994).

7 For a brief period in 1989 a Franco-Russian stance on German unification emerged, mostly negative in tone and running along the lines of the destabilisation of European security that a change in borders would imply. The

straitjacket of the Strasbourg Summit, plus repeated assertions by Chancellor Kohl of commitment to EU integration as a vital aspect of a unified Germany, cut short this French flirtation with an old ally.

8　It is in the context of these factors that the Kohl government negotiated, during the winter of 1991, a series of 'Hermes' export guarantees with CMEA states, to sustain flagging trade with the East German *länder*, that flouted EC rules; agreed cojointly with the EC a zero-tariff transitional arrangement (from October 1990 to December 1992) from CMEA/East German *länder* trade; concluded initially, with Poland in 1991, a series of bilateral treaties with CEE that expressed support for its integration with the EU; and, with questionable effects, recognised Croatia and Slovenia, urging EU partners to follow suit (December 1991) (Bulmer and Paterson 1996; Thies 1994).

9　Currently (1998) Bosnia needs to fulfil the institutional arrangements of the Dayton/Paris agreement before negotiations for a Cooperation Agreement are possible; the former Yugoslav Republic of Macedonia and Albania are offered developing relationships with the EU as Phare/TCA agreements are effectively implemented. However, there is little hope for improved relations between the EU and the former Republic of Yugoslavia, though specific assistance is offered to Montenegro and Kosovo; a similar pessimistic perspective is offered for EU–Croatia relations, with the possibility that unless the position of Serb minorities improves trade preferences may be removed (Commission 1998) (*Uniting Europe*, 5–4/5/98).

10　Thus the Hansch Report (1992) saw the importance of cooperation with *non*-European states, 'in particular the United States and Canada, Russia and other republics on the territory of the former Soviet Union and with Turkey and the countries of the eastern and southern shores of the Mediterranean' (European Parliament 1992:519).

11　'Comitology' describes the system established shortly before the Hanover Summit (1988) to order competing institutional claims to policy responsibilities by defining what responsibilities may be ascribed to Commission, Council and Committee of Permanent Representatives.

12　For a lucid examination of EU governance in the light of internal and external challenges see Wallace (1996).

13　During 1996/7, issues surrounding EMU, European economic recession and the 'internal crisis' – mostly around the UK Conservative government's problems with the Union (and the UK electorate) – forced only limited progress in IGC negotiations. The election of two new governments, in Britain and France, prior to the final summit meeting added to the cautious climate that was emerging regarding the viability of major institutional reforms at this time. Member states' preoccupation with economic convergence and consequent domestic policy adjustments pushed the issue of rapid enlargement to CEE down the agenda of imperatives for action.

14　Until that time the Ioanniana Compromise (from 1994) would continue to apply to the exercise of QMV. The Compromise, forced on the Union by the UK, states that if Council members holding between twenty-three and twenty-five votes wish to oppose a measure otherwise to be decided by a Qualified Majority Vote of sixty-two, a reasonable period of time will be invoked to allow for an acceptable agreement to be achieved.

References

Ardy, B. (1997), Trade Relations between the European Union and the Russian Federation, Research Conference, *UACES*, Loughborough, 10–12 September.

Avery, G. (1995), *The Commission's Perspectives on the EFTA Accession Negotiations*, Sussex European Institute, Working Paper 12.

Bideleux, R. (1996), The Comecon Experiment, in R. Bideleux and R. Taylor (eds), *European Integration and Disintegration: East and West*, London, Routledge, 174–204.

Bulmer, S. and Paterson, W. E. (1996), Germany in the European Union: Gentle Giant or Emergent Leader?, *International Affairs*, 172:1, 9–32.

Burghardt, G. and Cameron, F. (1997), The Next Enlargement of the European Union, *European Foreign Affairs Review*, 2, 7–21.

Commission (1990), The European Community and German Unification, *Bulletin*, Supplement, April.

Commission (1993), *XXVth General Report on the Activities of the European Communities 1992*, Luxembourg, OOPEC.

Commission (1997a), *What is Tacis? Partnership and Cooperation with Newly Independent States*, Brussels, Tacis Information Unit, DG1A.

Commission (1997b), *New Policy Guidelines for the Phare Programme in the Framework of the Pre-accession Assistance*, 19 March, Brussels.

Commission (1997c), *The Tacis Programme Annual Report, 1996*, Directorate General for External Relations, COM(97) 400, Final.

Commission (1997d), *The European Union and the Russian Federation: Partnership and Cooperation Agreement*, Brussels, Tacis Information Unit, DG1A, 2500-11/EN.

Commission (1998), Bilateral Relations with the EU, *Uniting Europe*, 3, 7–8.

De Weydenthal, J. B. (1992), Czechoslovakia, Hungary and Poland Gain Associate Membership in the EC, *RFE–RL Research Report*, 6 February, 7.

Dini, L. (1997), The European Union after Amsterdam, in A. Duff (ed.), *The Treaty of Amsterdam: Text and Commentary*, London, Federal Trust and Sweet and Maxwell, xxv–xxviii.

Duff, A. (ed.) (1997), *The Treaty of Amsterdam: Text and Commentary*, London, Federal Trust and Sweet and Maxwell.

European Parliament (1992), *Report of the Committee on Institutional Affairs on the Structure and Strategy for the European Union with Regard to its Enlargement and the Creation of a Europe Wide Order*, 21 May, rapporteur K. Hansch, DOC.En/RR/298537.

European Parliament (1994), *Accession of Central and Eastern Countries*, Resolution A4081/94, OJEC No. C363/18.

European Parliament (1997a), *Report on Agenda 2000 (COM[97] 2000–C4–0371/97) Part A: Motion for a Resolution*, Committee on Foreign Affairs, Security and Defence Policy, rapporteurs A. Oostlander and E. Baron Crespo, Brussels, Doc.EN/RR/340/340343.

European Parliament (1997b), *Report on Agenda 2000 Part B: Explanatory Statements*, Brussels, Doc.EN/RR/340/340287.

European Voice (1997), 2–8 July.

Gower, J. (1997), The Partnership and Cooperation Agreement: Prospects for a

Constructive EU–Russia Relationship, Research Conference, *UACES*, Loughborough, 10–12 September.

Haas, E. (1957), *The Uniting of Europe*, Stanford, Stanford University Press.

Hettne, B. (1995), *Development Theory and the three Worlds: Towards an International Political Economy of Development*, Harlow, Longman.

Hoffmann, S. (1966), Obstinate or Obsolete: the Fate of the Nation State and the Case of Western Europe, *Daedalus*, 95, 862–915.

Hughes, M. (1993), Eastern Pain and Western Promise: The Reaction of Western Governments to the Economic Plight of the 'New Eastern Europe', *International Relations*, 10:6, 585–604.

Hyde-Price, A. (1996), *The International Politics of East Central Europe*, Manchester, Manchester University Press.

Koves, A. (1992), *Central and Eastern European Economies in Transition*, Oxford, Westview.

Kramer, H. (1993), The European Community's Response to the 'New Eastern Europe', *Journal of Common Market Studies*, 31:2, 213–44.

Lalumiere, C. (1992), The Council of Europe's Place in the New European Architecture, *NATO Review*, 40:5, 8–12.

Le Gloannec (1989), France's German Problem, in F.S. Larrabee (ed.), *The Two German States and European Security*, London, Macmillan.

Lewis, P. (1994), *Central Europe Since 1945*, Harlow, Longman.

Lindberg, L. N. (1971), *The Political Dynamics of European Integration*, Stanford, Stanford University Press.

Lippert, B. *et al.* (1993), *German Unification and EC Integration: German and British Perspectives*, London, Royal Institute of International Affairs.

Marks, G. (1993), Structural Policy and Multi-level Governance in the EC, in A. Cafruny and G. Rosenthal (eds), *The State of the European Community*, Harlow, Longman, 391–410.

Mazey, S. and Richardson, J. (1992), Environmental Groups and the EC: Challenges and Opportunities, *Environmental Politics*, 1:4, 109–28.

Middlemas, K. (1995), *Orchestrating Europe: The Informal Politics of the E.U. 1973–1995*, London, Fontana.

Miles, L., Redmond, J. and Schwok, R. (1998), Integration Theory and the Enlargement of the European Union, in J. Redmond and G. Rosenthal (eds), *The Expanding European Union: Past, Present and Future*, London, Lynne Rienner, 177–98.

Mitrany, D. (1944), *A Working Peace System*, London, Royal Institute of International Affairs and Broadwater Press.

Peterson, J. (1995), Policy Networks and European Policy Making: A Reply to Kassim, *West European Politics*, 18:2, 389–407.

Phinnemore, D. (1997), Six Years of the New EU Ostpolitik: The EU, Bulgaria and Romania, Research Conference, *UACES*, Loughborough, 10–12 September.

Pinder, J. and Pinder, P. (1975), *The European Community's Policy towards Central Europe*, London, Royal Institute for International Affairs.

Preston, C. (1997), *Enlargement and Integration in the European Union*, London, Routledge.

Reinicke, W. H. (1992), *Building a New Europe: The Challenge of System Transformation and Systemic Reform*, Washington, DC, Brookings Institution.

Reisch, A. (1993), Hungary Pursues Integration with the West, *RFE-RL Research Report*, 2:13, 32–8.

Risse-Kappen, T. (1996), Exploring the Nature of the Beast: International Relations Theory and Comparative Analysis Meet the European Union, *Journal of Common Market Studies*, 34:1, 53–80.

Rollo, J. and Smith, M. (1993), The Political Economy of Eastern European Trade With the European Community: Why So Sensitive?, *Economic Policy*, 16, 139–81.

Scharpf, F. W. (1994), Community and Autonomy: Multi-level Policy-Making in the European Union, *Journal of European Public Policy*, 1:2, 219–42.

Sedelmeier, U. and Wallace, H. (1996), Policies towards Central and Eastern Europe, in H. Wallace and W. Wallace (eds), *Policy-Making in the European Union*, Oxford, Oxford University Press, 353–88.

Senior Nello, S. (1991), *The New Europe: Changing Relations Between East and West*, New York, Harvester Wheatsheaf.

Smyrl, M. (1998), When (and How) do the Commission's Preferences Matter?, *Journal of Common Market Studies*, 36:1, 79–99.

Taylor, R. (1996), The Double Headed Eagle: Russia, East or West, in R. Bideleux and R. Taylor (eds), *European Integration and Disintegration: East and West*, London, Routledge, 225–51.

Thies, J. (1994), Germany and Eastern Europe: Between Past and Future, in A. Baring (ed.), *Germany's New Position in Europe – Problems and Perspectives*, London, Berg, 65–78.

Tranholm-Mikkelsen, J. (1991), New-functionalism: Obstinate or Obsolete? A Reappraisal in the Light of the New Dynamism of the EC, *Millennium*, 20:1, 1–22.

Van Ham, P. (1993), *The EC, Eastern Europe and European Unity: Discord, Collaboration and Integration since 1947*, London, Pinter.

Wallace, H. (1996), The Institutions of the EU: Experience and Experiments, in H. Wallace and W. Wallace (eds), *Policy-Making In the European Union*, Oxford, Oxford University Press, 37–70.

Wallace, H. and Young, A. R. (1996), The Single Market: A New Approach to Policy, in H. Wallace and W. Wallace (eds), *Policy-Making in the European Union*, Oxford, Oxford University Press, 125–55.

Webb, C. (1983), Theoretical Perspectives and Problems, in H. Wallace, W. Wallace and C. Webb (eds), *Policy-Making in the European Community*, Chichester, John Wiley, 1–42.

Weber, S. (1994), Origins of the European Bank for Reconstruction and Development, *International Organisation*, 48:1, 1–38.

Welfens, P. J. J. (1993), The New Germany in the EC, in A. Cafruny and G. Rosenthal (eds), *The State of the European Community: The Maastricht Debates and Beyond*, Harlow, Longman, 159–73.

Policies towards CEEC

The significance of the Cold War in shaping EU–CEE relations, and consequently the need for policy repositioning when it ended, is discussed in Chapter 1. Internally, the SEA engendered a vigorous debate regarding the future of European integration; externally the Union responded rapidly to the immediate needs of newly independent neighbours whose economic condition bordered on collapse. New policies were necessary, but they were required at a time of political and economic crisis in CEE and during a period of controversial internal adjustment to global pressures within the EU.

It would seem invidious to begin an investigation of EU–CEEC relations with the observation that a new chapter in those relations could not have begun at a worse time. Nonetheless, the pressures of a period of deepening of the Union, and its impact on EU and member state priorities, remains a determining factor in EU–CEEC relations.

The post-Maastricht debates and the Lisbon Summit

During 1991 the parlous economic situation of CEE, together with the collapse of the USSR and outbreak of civil war in Yugoslavia, combined to create an *annus horribilis* for the new democracies of Europe. Within the EU, during the same year, IGCs on Political and Economic and Monetary Union culminated in signature of the TEU in February 1992. At the same time, progress towards member state transposition of internal market directives into national law by the end of 1992, and the Delors II financial package, provided a platform from which further integration might be achieved. Optimism that the conclusions of the Maastricht Summit indicated progress towards resolution of several of the grand political and economic issues allowed attention to turn towards the widening question (Nugent 1993:2). Thus the Commission was requested, at Maastricht, to report to the Lisbon Council (June

1992) on the implications of enlargement.

A number of TEU provisions themselves have significance for enlarge-ment. Article N, for example, required a further IGC to consider the institutional consequences of enlargement beyond the anticipated European Free Trade Association Nations (EFTAN) accession, while Article O modified the accession procedures of the Rome Treaty to provide for the assent of the EP. Other conditions for accession – respect for human rights and democracy (Article F); and acceptance of the *acquis communautaire* – were formalised at Maastricht, as was the reinforce-ment of Article 3a(1) of the Treaty of Rome, which required that member states and the Community should adopt economic policies commensurate with the principles of a market economy.

In these and other provisions the TEU squared up to the 'new Europe', in the context of an emphatically *deepened* Union. In effect, after Maastricht, accession to the EU became considerably more complex, both procedurally and practically, than the original Article O requirement of being 'any European State'. So, while the Maastricht outcomes 'can be seen as a typical Community package making widening conditional on further deepening', the widening process became exponentially more complicated when compared with the Hague Summit of 1969, where deepening conditionalities were similarly set against British, Irish, Danish and Norwegian membership (Preston 1997a:97).

As in the case of CEEC, the end of the Cold War propelled other non-EU states into a reconsideration of the relationship with the EU – thus formal applications for membership were received from Austria, Finland, Norway and Sweden. There was 'a growing sense that the EC was "Europe" and non-membership of the former implied, in some sense, exclusion from the European mainstream' (Redmond 1993:213). More immediately, legal difficulties associated with the implementation of the EEA, and concern that the agreement would not prove a satisfactory substitute to full access to the internal market, escalated the pace of this fourth enlargement. The Commission's paper to the Lisbon Summit, 'The Challenge of Enlargement', examined the issues associated with these and other formal applications, together with the longer-term possibility of CEEC applications (Commission 1992a).

The Lisbon Summit is interesting not for its low-key presidency conclu-sions but for the Commission's recommendations, which outlined the issues arising from the potential membership of three groups of would-be members: the EFTAN, Cyprus/Malta/Turkey and, in the longer term, the CEEC. Full membership was deemed 'inappropriate' for those countries whose economic and political characteristics would not meet the progres-sively more difficult conditions set by the Community. Indeed, 'membership would be more likely to harm than to benefit the economy of such a country, and would disrupt the working of the Community' (para. 9). At best, CEEC and, for different reasons, Turkey, were perceived in the report as partners at arm's length; this contrasted with the conclusion that EFTAN, Cypriot and Maltese applications should not pose insuperable problems of an economic nature, with reservations attached to their ability to implement a Common Foreign and Security Policy (CFSP), the problems of micro-state institutional participation and the partition of Cyprus.

The report set out three basic conditions for membership – European identity, democratic status and respect for human rights. Though the latter might well have for its guide the Council of Europe's Declaration, neither democracy nor a European identity were defined. With regard to identity, the Commission recognised definitional characteristics – geography, historical and cultural elements, ideas, values, proximity and interaction – but left the boundaries of Europe 'subject to review by each succeeding generation . . . it is neither possible nor opportune to establish now the frontiers of the European Union, whose contours will be shaped over many years to come' (para. 7).

A more exclusive set of criteria related to the acceptance of the Community system and the capacity to implement it; this assumed a functioning and competitive market economy; an adequate legal/ administrative system in both the public and private sectors; and the capability to meet the political objectives of the CFSP and to take on the international agreements of the Community. Only temporary derogations and transitional periods could be negotiated. Here the Commission's prioritisation of internal cohesion and solidarity over enlargement were clearly apparent. Finally, in insisting that 'fundamental questions of decision making and the institutional framework cannot be evaded' (para. 25), the report emphasised the need to consider further institutional reform alongside enlargement beyond the EFTA countries.

As we shall see, subsequent Commission Opinions flesh out the details of an enlargement strategy. To a significant extent, however, its character is evident from the Lisbon Report. So, too, is a cautious policy tone indicating an evident preference for the maintenance of enhanced integration, with widening conditional on adequate internal and member state responses to reform of the EU's institutions.

While the Lisbon Summit accepted the Commission's conclusions regarding an early start to negotiations for EFTAN accession, a number of factors created a pessimistic backdrop for progress in EU–CEEC relations. These included difficulties with TEU ratification, the Exchange Rate Mechanism crisis and doubts over the viability of CFSP provisions following the failure of EU policy towards Yugoslavia. Thus the cautious approach to Eastern enlargement evident at Lisbon was reinforced by the difficult internal debates initiated by the TEU. Consequently the EAs with Czechoslovakia, Hungary and Poland were not ratified by the target date of

1 January 1993, though interim agreements were concluded early in 1992, and consideration of full membership was postponed until the Copenhagen Summit in June 1993. A subsequent Commission paper, *Towards a Closer Association* (Commission 1992b), set out a series of economic and political conditions, together with alternatives to membership, and was clearly negative in tone. There was also evidence of a growing reaction by interest groups to the freer market access for CEE products resulting from implementation of the EAs (Brewin 1993). This, coupled with the divergence of member state opinion over the goals of the new Union, further depressed expectations of the CEECs with regard to an early 'return to Europe'.

EU reservations regarding the future relationships with the CEEC were not only shaped by internal divisions, but also by conflicting messages from CEEC themselves with regard to economic and political transformation. While there was, in the early 1990s, clear evidence of diverse and fairly open trading patterns with Western Europe, currency convertibility, foreign investment, privatisation of public assets and economic restructuring, there remained serious levels of internal and external indebtedness, a weak financial services sector and desperately painful adjustments still to be made in public-sector spending and services (Dangerfield 1995; Ferreira 1995; Hughes 1993). Moreover, democratic transformation by the CEEC, though formally achieved by 1994, was not necessarily accompanied by citizen satisfaction with the achievements of democratic governance; and in some countries, such as Romania and Bulgaria, the change from authoritarianism to representative government was barely apparent. Initially there remained specific problems over minorities' rights, migration and border disputations, as well as the more general instability of the Balkans and uncertainties over Russian democratic progression that affected the security of the Baltic states. These issues of economic and political transformation and security are dealt with at length in the following chapters.

The EAs and EU internal politics

The EAs marked an important stage in EU–CEEC relations. Indeed, they were seen to 'constitute the basis of an orderly and long-term relationship between the EC and the states of Eastern Europe' (Kramer 1993:228). Here we examine the political circumstances within which they were negotiated and their implications for subsequent EU–CEE relations. The complex nature of EU policy making in the 1990s derives from the need to reconcile conflicting member state perspectives, both on EU integration and on enlargement. Since the EAs represent an attempt to accommodate the several preferences of member states on these matters, the evolving positions of member state governments during the negotiation process are worthy of consideration.

In the case of Germany, longer-term interests in the stability of CEEC competed with short-term economic sectoral pressures – especially from the German steel industry, whose 'federation claimed that even small additional quantities of low price allegedly subsidised CEE imports would seriously distort prices' (Sedelmeier 1994:13). The French government expressed concern over the potentially strengthened position of Germany within a more eastward-oriented Union, but also perceived advantage in reinforced strategic and trade links with CEEC. These were advanced through the promotion of a broader confederal framework to include the EU, CEEC and Soviet successor states. In the final negotiations, however, domestic pressure from farmers with regard to CEE beef imports turned the French government away from such a visionary future (Manners 1994; Sedelmeier 1994).

Britain's support for rapid progress with the EA negotiations, and indeed accession, was not disassociated from an underlying preference for an intergovernmental, trade-only character for the Union. However, Britain's supportive stance was belied by the government's reluctance to countenance immigration from CEEC, as well as an unwillingness to increase the relatively low level of British direct financial support. The geopolitical and economic interests of Italy also presented a less than clear position. Association with, indeed leadership of, an Alp Adriatica region was an Italian aim, as promotion of the Central European Initiative (CEI) showed. On the other hand, there were fears that economic and political union, to which Italy remained firmly commit-ted, would be undermined by any propensity towards a multi-speed Europe that might be encouraged by association/enlargement (Mannin 1997). Moreover, Italy's export-dependent economy was sensitive to the marginal impact of CEE imports.

In Spain, Portugal and Ireland concern focused upon preservation of existing levels of EU financial transfers. Conscious of the vulnerable nature of their own economic transformations, the cohesion states took a tough line on import safeguard clauses; it is noteworthy that the last import control included in the Final Agreement was to protect the Spanish steel industry against Visegrad imports (Manners 1994:11).

The EA outcomes

The EAs went beyond the previous TCAs in a number of ways. The aim was to establish a free-trade area between the EU and each country within a ten-year period, with the EU agreeing to abolish all tariffs within a five-year period, but subject to variations between individual countries, depending on the 'sensitivity' of products involved. 'Sensitivity' applies particularly to agricultural products, coal, steel and textiles. Here the Commission, negotiating bilaterally with each applicant, was constrained by a Council mandate which reflected various member state and sectoral interests. On two occasions, under pressure from CEEC demands for broader market access, the Commission sought bargaining room from the Council (Manners 1994:4–5).

In addition to conflict over trade issues, an acrimonious debate took place over the subject of future membership. The CEEC, in particular the Polish delegation, argued for a clear-cut statement on membership; the Commission had neither the mandate nor the political will to give more than a preamble commitment to membership as an ultimate and future objective.[1] Indeed, there was little support at this stage for any formal guarantee of eventual membership.

The trade element of the EAs was accompanied by agreements around financial, technical and economic cooperation – including supports for structural industrial change and research and development; energy; the environment and telecommunications. The commencement of approximation of laws, especially related to competition and state subsidy, indicated the importance accorded to Single Market compatibility; the CEEC were to introduce compatible legislation within three years. The gradual implementation of capital movement, together with movement of services and people, was an aim. However, movement of people was not acceptable to several EU member states desirous of keeping labour markets closed. CEEC were similarly concerned about the possible over-exposure of their emerging services sector (Preston 1997a:199). Application of the *acquis* was to be a major feature of later policy conditions but at this time was seen by CEEC as a further example of an emerging arm's-length approach by the EU towards membership (de Weydenthal 1994).

The provision in the EAs for political dialogue (referring to CFSP issues) and cultural dialogue was, however, perceived more positively. It was considered to provide formal recognition of the CEECs' special status in relation to the EU. In adding these elements to the essentially economic/trading nature of previous association agreements, the EU sought to relate political, legal, administrative and economic change in partner countries to future EU–CEE relations (Preston 1997b).

The formal institutions of association initially followed the traditional Community pattern, comprising bilateral Association Councils at ministerial level, supported by Association Committees at ambassadorial level and advisory Parliamentary Committees. The institutions were subsequently augmented and extended, first at the Copenhagen Summit (June 1993) and later at Essen in 1994, when the multilateral 'structured dialogue' was introduced. This centred upon CEE and EU ministerial meetings 'back to back' with corresponding Councils of Ministers, and annual meetings at head of state/government level in the margins of the European Council. These ministerial meetings were paralleled by approximately eighty Technical Committees comprising senior bureaucrats from the associated states and Commission officials.

In practice, even after the Essen Summit, there was considerable doubt from both sides regarding the efficacy, in particular, of multilateral dialogue. Complaints soon emerged that the structured dialogue was weak, lacked substantive content and resembled more an 'unstructured monologue' by a hectoring and dominant EU partner. On several occasions, association partners were denied access to Council agendas or the right of prior comment on papers (Philip Morris Institute for Public Policy Research 1994).[2]

The multidimensional nature of the EAs gave conflicting signals to CEEC. Presented by the Commission as a distinctive response to new times, on face value CEEC were given opportunities for participation in EU processes prior to the commencement of accession negotiations. In this sense the EAs were enhanced agreements compared with those struck with other associates, and, given the rapidity of their establishment, might be perceived as an initial 'reward' for progress in democratic transition. The enhanced dialogue was also to act as a catalyst for governmental re-organisation in the CEEC, to address directly the new demands of EU–CEEC association.[3]

Despite their innovative nature, the EAs remained primarily trade-led association agreements which reflected the asymmetrical nature of bargaining during the negotiation process. They were perceived by CEEC governments, and their supporters, as defensive in character. The reluctance to relax trade safeguard policies was particularly resented (Koves 1992; Rollo and Smith 1993; Baldwin *et al.* 1992). In consequence, the EAs were considered to be an unsatisfactory substitute for direct negotiation leading to accession.

Nevertheless, by 1995 ten CEE countries had entered into or were in the process of negotiating EAs. Since these Agreements provided a more intensive relationship with the EU than had been offered to other post-Communist states, they effectively contributed to the development of an outer and inner ring of EU–CEE–NIS relations, with distinct political advantage for those states on the inside track. Access to EU markets and aid programmes was clearly differentiated, providing a stronger framework for economic and political security for EA countries. In terms of their political and economic direction, this encouraged differentiation of the Baltic states from the other NIS. Similarly, the direction of Romanian and Bulgarian transformation was bolstered by the obligations of EA association, locking these countries into westward-oriented trade (Phinnemore 1997). However, the essentially bilateral character of EU–CEEC relations also had the effect of reinforcing the competitive character of intra-CEEC relations. Despite the attempts at collegiate responses through the Visegrad Memoranda (1992, 1993), the CEEC remained in a competitive situation as they vied for pole position in an accession race (Vachudova 1993).

Phare as an EU policy instrument

If the EAs can be viewed as reinforced examples of association arrangements that had some history, the Phare programme may be seen as a new instrument in its policy scope and aims. Phare, as already indicated, was the Union's immediate contribution to the G7 and later G24 response to the events of 1989. It evolved as the centrepiece of that programme and, latterly, as the main financial instrument of the pre-accession strategy.

The Commission, given the task of coordinating the entire G24 support framework, was also given full responsibility for the implementation of Phare; this was to be effected through a dedicated budget line and a special administration, set up within Directorate-General (DG) I (External Relations). Initially limited geographically to Poland and Hungary, and in time to 1992, the programme had expanded its application to ten countries by 1992, and was extended until 1997. By that date, thirteen CEEC had become eligible for Phare support, which had increased in commitments from under 500 million ecu (1990) to over 3,350 million ecu (1996) (see Table 2.1). The cumulative total commitment for the period 1989–96 was ecu 6,636 million in the form of non-reimbursable grants (Commission 1997a).

Table 2.1 Annual Phare commitments, contracts and payments

Year	Commitments	Contracts		Payments	
		Ecu (m)	%	Ecu (m)	%
1990	494.7	487.1	98	490.6	99
1991	773.6	773.4	100	738.8	96
1992	1,010.1	951.0	94	895.8	89
1993	1,007.2	814.9	81	710.0	70
1994	972.9	611.5	63	514.3	53
1995	1,154.7	411.5	36	282.2	24
1996	1,222.9	251.3	21	95.5	8
1990–93	3,288.6	3,026.4	92	2,835.2	86
1994–96	3,350.5	1,273.3	38	892.0	27

Source: Commission (1997d).

Phare's programme of technical assistance may be roughly divided into three periods: from 1989–91 when the emphasis was on technical assistance; from 1991–95 when support for public and private institutional reform was prioritised; and from 1995–98 when Phare was designated as the main financial instrument for the pre-accession strategy (see Table 2.2). A more specific role for Phare in pre-accession was outlined in

March 1997 (Commission 1997a) and later in *Agenda 2000* (Commission 1997c).

Table 2.2 Phare commitments by country by year

Country	1990–92	1993	1994	1995	1996	Total
Albania	120.0	75.0	49.0	88.0	53.0	385.0
Poland	577.8	225.0	206.8	174.0	203.0	1,388.5
Hungary	306.8	99.0	85.0	92.0	101.0	683.8
CSFR	232.7	0.0	0.0	0.0	0.0	232.7
Czech Republic	0.0	60.0	60.0	110.0	54.0	284.0
Slovakia	0.0	40.0	40.0	46.0	4.5	130.5
Lithuania	20.0	25.0	39.0	42.0	53.0	179.0
Estonia	10.0	12.0	22.5	24.0	61.8	130.3
Latvia	15.0	18.0	29.5	32.5	37.0	132.0
Romania	301.8	139.9	100.0	66.0	118.4	726.1
Bulgaria	223.3	85.2	85.0	83.0	62.5	539.0
Slovenia	9.0	11.0	24.0	25.0	22.0	91.0
Former Yugoslav Republic of Macedonia	10.0	25.0	25.0	25.0	25.0	110.0
Bosnia	37.3	0.0	0.0	0.0	140.0	177.3
Multicountry	276.7	86.0	86.0	104.0	125.5	704.2
Horizontal	143.8	119.1	119.1	243.2	162.2	742.6
Total	2,284.3	972.9	972.9	1,154.7	1,222.9	6,636.1

Source: Commission (1997d).

The continuing geographical expansion of the programme to states in different stages of transition has complicated what was originally a technical assistance programme to support the establishment of market economies in Poland and Hungary. However, the emergent difficulties in establishing social, civil, political and administrative structures and values to underpin the market led to a broadening of the definition of 'technical' and a greater range of programmes. In 1992, at the insistence of the EP, a modest 'democracy line' was created, tasked with the enhancement of democratic practice, establishing human rights, enforcing the rule of law and enhancing participation (see Chapter 4). By 1994–96, allocations in the related fields of civil society and democracy, administration, public institutions, education and social development amounted to approximately 29 per cent of overall Phare sectoral expenditure (see Table 2.3).

This increased range of activity has resulted in organisational complexity and a diversified set of delivery processes. Introduction of multiannual projects, cross-border cooperation, multicountry programmes and horizontal (Commission-initiated) programmes, as well as the coordination of support from other donors,[4] has greatly complicated the national demand-led programmes that constitute over three-quarters of Phare activities (Commission 1997d). Coordination of the programmes is

Table 2.3 Phare sectoral allocations by main sectors

Sector	1990–93		1994–96	
	Ecu (m)	%	Ecu (m)	%
Humanitarian, food and critical aid	337.7	10.3	180.0	5.4
Agricultural restructuring	392.8	12.3	85.5	2.6
Private sector (restructuring privatisation, SMEs,[a] financial sector, regional development)	876.4	26.7	611.2	18.2
Education, training and research (and Tempus)	431.0	13.1	443.4	13.2
Social development, employment, health	213.8	6.5	108.5	3.2
Environment (including nuclear safety)	325.9	9.9	215.0	6.4
Infrastructure	280.0	8.5	1,208.1	36.1
Administration, public institutions, legislation	164.5	5.0	275.2	8.2
Civil society and democratisation	34.0	1.0	66.4	2.0
Other	229.6	7.0	157.2	4.7
Total	3,285.7	100.0	3,350.5	100.0

Source: Commission (1997).

Note: [a]SMEs = Small and Medium-sized Enterprises.

undertaken by Directorate B of DG IA and, given the size of budget and range of responsibilities, the bureau has had a considerable profile in DG IA activities. The number of permanent central staff is relatively low, with the national programmes heavily reliant on 'on-site' delegations whose composition depends on temporary expert staffing. In effect, Phare, from an early stage, 'came to depend on an army of consultants from western Europe under contract to the Commission' (Sedelmeier and Wallace 1996:361).

Perhaps inevitably, the Phare decision processes have been criticised for their lack of direction, coordination and coherence. Thus, for example, while all CEE participants have established mechanisms through which their national priorities for use of Phare funding are established, this process rarely involved presentation of proposals 'according to pre-determined priorities and criteria' and resulted in bids being 'sometimes informally selected at the Phare national coordinators office' (Commission 1997d:20). Contracting-out procedures have produced criticisms ranging from lack of programme relevance to real needs to 'scamming', with the major benefit accruing to donor countries (Dangerfield 1995).

With regard to Commission management of the Phare programmes, criticisms have referred to inadequate and impermanent staffing; the high costs of tendering for contracts and discrimination against non-EU nationals in fund allocation (Allen and Smith 1997); delays in programme development and appointing consultants; lack of effective project evaluation mechanisms (Commission 1997d) and, until recently, the lack of a

Management Information System (MIS).[5] Internal competition between the bureaux of DG IA also undermined the external credibility of the programme (interview, January 1998; *European*, 20–26 April, 4–10 June 1998).

These problems must, however, be set in the context of Phare's operational field. The receiving countries may be perceived as problematic aid recipients, often providing limited, unreliable or misleading information that made project assessment difficult; nor did they provide sustained support for projects when completed, failing to continue, or even reversing, privatisation processes to the detriment of ongoing projects. Lack of resources within the Phare budget to provide comprehensive evaluation and monitoring also hindered effective project management and review (Commission 1997d).

Against these difficulties must be listed Phare's undoubtedly significant role in the transformation process. Since 1989 the programme of non-reimbursable grants has been extended in scope to cover a combined population of the thirteen partner countries of 105.3 million; single and co-financing activities extend to sixteen sectors, ranging from infrastructure and agricultural restructuring to consumer protection, equal opportunity for women and democratisation. Phare-committed funds amounted to 27 per cent of G24 aid from 1989–96 and, unlike loan- or interest-related financing, are not debt creating.

It could be argued that, without such large-scale technical assistance, other investors and donors would not have been so willing to contribute to the CEE transformation process, to the detriment of the domestic programmes for economic, administrative and societal reform. There has been a considerable change in programme emphasis since Phare's inception in 1989, and its role since mid-1997 has been recognised as accession-driven – that is, directly relating to the accession strategy in the fields of infrastructure investment and administrative reform. Ultimately, through its role in generating ideas and in providing technical assistance, Phare has made 'a major contribution to changes in attitudes and mentality' (Commission 1997d:55). As one Phare official opined, it was 'a case of from aid to brand name in seven years' (interview, 23 February 1998).

The Copenhagen and Essen Councils: towards a pre-accession agenda

At Copenhagen (June 1993) the European Council publicly conceded the possibility of membership for CEE countries with EAs. This commitment was reaffirmed at Essen (December 1994), when a pre-accession strategy within a structured EU–CEE relationship was launched. Thus the Copenhagen and Essen Council outcomes represent a formal commitment to the principle of CEE enlargement, and the framework within which the practical steps to accession could be achieved (Allen and Smith 1994). It was against this positive background that, by December 1995, eight CEEC, including the three ex-Soviet Baltic states, had made application for EU membership. Formal applications were subsequently received from the Czech Republic in January 1996 and Slovenia in June 1996.

The Copenhagen Council

In its communiqué the Council clearly stated that the Associated countries of CEE that desired membership would be admitted as soon as they were 'able to assume the obligations of membership by satisfying the economic and political conditions required' (Council of Ministers 1993a:12).

The Copenhagen criteria for membership
A candidate country must achieve:
- stability of institutions – guaranteeing democracy, the rule of law, human rights and respect for and protection of minorities;
- a functioning market economy;
- the capacity to cope with competitive pressures and market forces within the Union;
- capacity to take on membership obligations (the *acquis*), including adherence to *the aims* of EMU and political union.

In the general interest of both candidate countries and the EU the capacity of the Union to absorb new members while maintaining integration momentum is also an important consideration.

As we have seen, the achievement of those conditions was to be assisted by an upgraded dialogue between the EU and CEEC. This enhanced dialogue was accompanied by a more rapid and generous opening of EU markets, with a tariff reduction from 4 per cent to 2 per cent on sectors other than steel, textiles and agriculture by 1995. These concessions followed considerable criticism from Visegrad countries prior to the Summit, of the use of a comprehensive range of protective devices that impacted on over 40 per cent of all CEE exports.

A further dimension to EU–CEE relations was also announced at the Copenhagen Council. A Pact on Stability in Europe, proposed by the French Prime Minister Edward Balladur and eventually adopted in March 1995, aimed to provide a framework of preventative diplomacy to assist CEEC in resolving ethnic minority and border issues, and was to be one of the first actions emanating from the CFSP following entry into force of the TEU. The Stability Pact received a mixed reception from CEE governments, which saw it as a distraction from the membership issue (of both the EU and NATO).

The public acknowledgement that the EU would, rather than might, enlarge to the East, reflected a change in the internal climate of policy opinion within the Commission, and was underscored by external factors that encouraged a more positive reaction towards CEE from member states. After TEU ratification, the Commission's agenda was less crowded than during the previous four years and this, together with the changes to the Commission College (January 1993), allowed CEE relations a more important position on the policy agenda. The appointment of Hans van den Broek, the former Dutch Foreign Minister, as Commissioner responsible for DG IA (CFSP, relations with CEE and NIS), and Leon Brittan to DG I (external commercial relations) strengthened the external relations dimension of the Commission. Consequently, in the months before the Copenhagen Summit, support grew in the Commission for a more positive set of proposals, while opposition from the less positive member states and sectoral interests was eased (Sedelmeier 1994).

The Copenhagen outcome was also affected by consciousness of potential instability in the CEE region. The calamitous situation in Bosnia; the growing strength of Russian nationalism; economic and social unrest in Romania; political instability in Slovakia and Poland; and a recession that affected all CEEC – provided the background to the 1993 Danish and Belgian presidencies. Thus the interplay between these external events and a positive Commission/Council nexus pushed the subject of EU–CEEC relations to the top of the EU agenda.

The Essen Summit, the structured dialogue and the White Paper

The Danish presidency may be viewed as a watershed in EU–CEE relations for its consolidation of EU policies towards CEEC, their transparent statement and the establishment of a broad political consensus within the Council that CEEC accession was no longer a matter for dispute. What remained, crucially, was the *modus vivendi* for the application of the *acquis* and the financial framework and timetable within which association might be turned into accession.

Again the development of EU policy was influenced by external factors – including Vladimir Zhirinovsky's Russian electoral success in December 1993 and President Clinton's re-evaluation of the US 'Russia First' policy[6] – which gave additional weight to the arguments of Commission 'maximalists'. Their objective, to establish an effective framework for CEE accession, included awareness of the need for internal reform of the Community, coupled with recognition that, for CEEC, application of the *acquis* would be problematic. An alliance between Brittan and van den Broek on the need to establish this complex accession strategy provided the necessary leadership within the Commission. This was paralleled by continuing pressure from the Kohl government to sustain and deepen the association dialogue, and from the British and Italian governments, which sought to develop EU–CEE relations within Pillars II and III (the

Hurd/Andreatta initiative). Though less enthusiastic, France sustained a joint position with Germany during the German presidency; and, together with the Spanish government, saw advantage in adopting a flexible position on CEE accession in order to advance claims for a flanking EU policy response for the Mediterranean.

In Corfu (June 1994) the Council requested the Commission to prepare further proposals for an accession strategy, and in response the Commission produced two papers that were to form the backbone of the Essen Council outcomes (Commission 1994a, 1994b). At the same time the Commission gained a Council mandate to commence EA negotiations with the Baltic states and, when the Italians had resolved their dispute, with Slovenia. Later, following a Franco-German bilateral meeting (September 1994), the Council requested the Commission to prepare a White Paper that was to provide 'both a conceptual framework for the definition and delineation of the internal *acquis* and a detailed list of all the relevant legislation and policies in different sectors' (Preston 1997a:202).

The Essen Council decisions strengthened the framework of consultations established a year before at Copenhagen. Henceforth bilateral meetings would be more frequent and would be complemented by a more clearly structured multilateral framework 'to make co-operation a more normal part of the life of governments and Parliaments' (Commission 1995b:146). The first EU–CEE meeting at head-of-government level was held on the last day of the Essen Council – a symbolic beginning to the pre-accession strategy.

Of equal significance, though less publicly broadcast, were the intentions of the Council to move ahead with establishing conditions for the functioning of the Single Market as a prerequisite for accession. The conditions were to be more specifically detailed in the Commission's White Paper published five months later. Phare was proposed as the cornerstone of financial aid for adjustment, and a new bureau, the Technical Assistance Information Exchange Office, would provide a database of expertise and other information to assist CEE market adaptation. CEEC were expected to make progress towards adopting Single Market legislation as part of a planned accession process.

What did not emerge from Essen, as CEEC had requested, was any timetable for accession. Nor were there any concessions on what CEE governments regarded as the considerable remaining restrictions on EU market access.

The White Paper – the new testament?

The Commission White Paper (Commission 1995a) was discussed at the Cannes Summit in June 1995. Its purpose was to provide an authoritative guide – a 'bible' – to assist the associated countries in their attempts to approximate the daunting Single Market *acquis*. This was seen as a prior step to adoption of the entire *acquis* as a condition of membership. To this end the White Paper provides three 'commandments' (or as the Paper states, 'contributions') to facilitate the task of approximation:

- identify prescribed 'key' sectoral measures and their sequence of approximation;
- achieve structural reforms necessary to make legislation effective;
- focused use of Phare aid to achieve an intensive and coherent pre-accession programme.

The White Paper is said to mark 'the beginning of a process ... for the associated countries' (para. 6.3). However, 'the primary responsibility for the success of this process lies with the associated countries themselves' (para. 6.2).

While providing tangible aims for the CEECs, as well as prioritising steps towards market harmonisation, the daunting range of legal and economic transformation was made abundantly clear to CEEC; for some it represented yet another exercise in EU prevarication and deserved the title 'wait' rather than 'White' Paper. The EP's detailed opinion on the Paper (the Oostlander Report) reflected this concern (European Parliament 1996a). Notwithstanding criticisms of its conclusions in such areas as free movement, regional policy, the environment and women's rights (European Parliament 1996b), the White Paper is notable for EU–CEEC policy development in a number of ways.

First, it addresses Single Market issues across sectors that are monitored by the Commission DGs. Thus, in effect, the opportunity to depoliticise sectoral disputes and to reduce the impact of pressure groups is enhanced by a move towards a technical approach to implementation. This inevitably shifts the focus of policy initiation and implementation towards the Commission – effectively internalising EU–CEE relations rather than treating them as part of the external policy process. Second, prioritisation of Single Market transposition presents manageable targets for implementation by CEEC; thus giving traders and investors the necessary encouragement and security for ongoing and developing relations with the CEEC. However, it also had important implications for application of the full *acquis* in such fields as social and environmental policy – in effect, the separation of 'product' from 'process' that is implicit in such prioritisation – and has significant implications for both CEE societies and for the direction of the European project itself (Smith *et al.* 1995). Finally, coordination of the White Paper's implementation, including monitoring by the Commission, has put a heavy responsibility on the relevant DGs (DG XV, DG II, DG IV) and the coordinating capacity of DG IA.

These and other factors emerge as significant determinants in the processes surrounding the presentation of *Agenda 2000* and its implementation, to which we now turn.

The background to *Agenda 2000*

The prospect of enlargement has, on each of its occasions, generated internal debate among the member states – both in relation to issues of EU *raison d'être* and the particular and immediate perspectives of member states. As one Commission official has described it, 'Enlargement tends to be an occasion when existing members are forced – perhaps unwillingly – to face fundamental questions about what they want the Union to do and how they want to do it' (Avery 1995:2). This can give applicants the impression that their own negotiations with the EU are secondary to 'an ongoing negotiation within the Union itself' (Avery 1995:2).

The daunting tasks ahead were acknowledged in the Commission's submission to the Reflection Group which preceded the 1996–97 IGC. This was, nevertheless, a generally upbeat document in which enlargement and deepening were seen as compatible, and problems capable of solution (Commission 1995b:4). Evidently less sure of this, the Council produced conclusions that effectively postponed any further initiatives on enlargement until the conclusion of the IGC in June 1997. This followed friction between member states at the 1995 Madrid Summit, where Chancellor Kohl was unable to establish that Hungary, Poland and the Czech Republic would be guaranteed a similar start-date to accession negotiations as Cyprus and Malta. Kohl's resistance to commencement of further accession negotiations at that time conflicted with Finnish and Swedish support for the Baltic states and Austrian support for Slovenia.

In the event, it was agreed that the Commission should proceed with a detailed review of applicants' chances on a country basis, together with broader analyses of the impact of enlargement on existing EU budgetary and policy arrangements.

It was also agreed that differentiated application of criteria and separate accession timetables were not acceptable; and that negotiations would take place simultaneously, on the basis of common criteria, for all applicants (Council of Ministers 1995). A formal start to the IGC was agreed to coincide with the Turin Summit in March 1996; it was to conclude at the end of the Dutch presidency in June 1997.

The Commission Opinion was to include:

(i)   opinions on individual applications;
(ii) an examination of the impact of enlargement on EU policies;
(iii) a composite paper on enlargement (a pre-accession and accession strategy);

(iv) a detailed analysis of the current and future state of Union finances in the light of enlargement.

In effect, this amounted to a request for a thorough review of the Union's future policy commitments and resources, in the light of CEE accession within a foreseeable future. The task, it must be noted, was to take place as new EFTAN members embedded in the EU; during a period of extensive preparatory activity with regard to EMU Stage III; and in the run-up to the IGC itself. Member states were also preoccupied, if not by impending elections (Italy, UK, Greece and Spain), then by problems of recession and, in particular, unemployment and its political consequences (France and Germany). This, together with British intransigence over the BSE crisis and the ensuing paralysis of EU decision taking during 1996, presented an opportunity for reflection and preparation, from a positive perspective, or frustration and delay from the more impatient view of CEE applicants.

Composing the communication[7]

In producing *Agenda 2000* a main resource for the Commission was a country questionnaire, compiled by DG IA with the assistance of all other relevant DGs. Sent to each of the applicant countries during April 1996, it comprised 165 pages of detailed questions of relevance to the assessment of CEEC capacity to adopt the *acquis*. The questionnaires were with minor exceptions similar, essentially following the structure of the Commission, and the particular concerns of the Directorates, some of which were less reliant on the responses than others.[8] The responses by CEE governments were analysed by the relevant DG upon their return before July, and DG assessments formed the basis of a final compilation within DG IA. As well as providing detailed technical information, the questionnaires also demonstrated the administrative capabilities of the applicants in providing the type of information routinely required by the Commission from member states.

The replies amounted to 1,000–5,000 pages from each country and varied in quality of response. There was consequently a period of verification after July when the Commission checked with the CEE embassies of member states, Commission delegations or the CEE governments themselves on the accuracy and comprehensiveness of the replies. The difficult task of condensing this and other evidence of the readiness of the applicant states was the responsibility of the Enlargement Team in DG IA.[9] The Team was (and remains) relatively small. Consequently it sought cooperation for the completion of its tasks from DG IA country desks, the larger DG IA bureaucracy associated with implementation of the Phare programme, and 'consultants and various experts' (interview, February 1998). Other sources of information and verification included reports and opinions from international organisations such as the OECD, the Council of Europe and the World Bank, as well as from member states and the EP. In preparing the *Agenda 2000* country reports, Enlargement Team responsibilities were allocated horizontally by subject.

While questionnaire responses were a significant factor in the country assessments, they were less relevant in areas requiring qualitative assessment, where intelligence gathering was more salient – for example, the evaluation of administrative and judicial capacities and some aspects of macro-economic change. The Impact Study and composite paper on enlargement strategy drew on a plethora of Commission papers published during 1995–97 in response both to enlargement matters and to ongoing debates surrounding EMU and institutional and policy reform. In particular, the necessary reforms to the CAP and structural funding had already been flagged in Commission reports to the Madrid Council. Finally, completion of *Agenda 2000* documentation was predicated on the outcome of the IGC and, in particular, the institutional reforms which, it was hoped, would be agreed in time for the June 1997 Amsterdam Summit.

Agenda 2000

As requested, the Commission presented, in *Agenda 2000*, both its Opinions on the applications of the Association countries, and a two-volume Communication that constitutes a comprehensive reply to the Madrid Council's requests. Thus *Agenda 2000* 'outlines in a single framework the broad perspectives for the development of the Union and its policies beyond the turn of the century, the horizontal issues relating to enlargement, and the future financial framework beyond 2000 taking account of the prospects of an enlarged Union' (Commission 1997b:3). Its aims are, consequently, both cautious and ambitious. Not only does it promote the strategic inevitability of EU enlargement to the East, it also sets out a programme for internal institutional and policy reform as prerequisites for enlargement.[10] There is, in addition, a financial framework that is calculated to be politically acceptable to member states and viable within existing economic conditions. Finally, the pre-accession/accession strategy seeks to recognise the different status of applicants, yet attempts to keep all aboard in allowing entrance to a 'regatta', with the prize of full membership for all who cross the finishing line.

The contents of *Agenda 2000* are summarised in Appendix 2. Volume I, *For a Stronger and Wider Union*, examines the current state of the Union, the criteria for accession and its potential impact on the EU, together with the necessary changes to Union policies associated with enlargement. It also proposes a financial framework within which the pre-accession and enlargement recommendations could take place. Volume II, *The Challenge of Enlargement*, details the Commission's Reinforced Pre-Accession Strategy (SPAR), outlining priorities and measures for financial assistance. An impact study examines the potential effects of accession on applicant countries and concludes with an overall assessment of the bene-fits, strains and adjustments relating both to the EU and CEEC. Opinions on the merits of each application, of roughly equal length and structure, were presented separately to the Council.

In its final recommendations, the Commission emphasised the inclusive nature of the enlargement process – in that all CEE applicants would be involved in SPAR. Moreover, bilateral discussions were to start simulta-neously with all applicants (commencement was agreed at the December Luxembourg Council for 30 March 1998). Only five CEEC, however – Hungary, Poland, Estonia, the Czech Republic and Slovenia – were to open formal accession negotiations. These countries were considered to be suitable for membership in the medium term 'if they maintain and strongly sustain their efforts of preparation' (Commission 1997b:69). There was, however, no guarantee of accession negotiations *concluding* simultaneously.

For all applicants, preparation for accession is to be reinforced through individual Accession Partnerships, and progress will be reviewed annually by the Commission. The existing multilateral structured dialogue is to be replaced by a Presidency/Commission bilateral discussion format, comple-mented by an annual European Conference, at head-of-government level, to discuss primarily Pillar II and III issues.

Enlargement of the Union to a possible twenty-six member states (the CEEC 10 plus Cyprus) remains conditional on pre-achieved institutional reforms and a reassessment of EU policies, in particular structural funding and the CAP.[11] The accompanying financial framework sought, in the context of EMU convergence criteria, 'to provide coherent coverage within reasonable budget limits for the development of Community poli-cies and the impact of the Union taking in new members' (Commission 1997b).[12]

The strategy for accession

The key feature of SPAR is a new instrument – the Accession Partnership – which will 'mobilize all forms of assistance to the applicant countries within a single framework' (Council of Ministers 1997:3). The Partnerships jointly agreed by the applicants and the EU establish the prioritisation of, especially, the White Paper *acquis* and access to

Community resources. Implementation of the Partnerships is to be reviewed annually and, in the absence of positive reports from the Commission, financial assistance could be blocked (*Guardian*, 28 March 1998). Pre-accession aid is substantially increased: 'For the first time in its history, the EU has put in place a pre-accession strategy whose *financial package* is the Union's way of compensating the adaptation efforts required of the applicant countries' (European Parliament 1997a:35).[13] Moreover, the Commission recommended, and the Council agreed, the principle of 'catch-up' support for the countries in greatest need (the 'pre-ins'), financed in part from non-takeup of previous Phare funding (interview, February 1998). Phare itself is to be accession- rather than demand-driven, with about 30 per cent of funding directed towards institution building, particularly associated with the reinforcement of administrative and judicial capacity, and 70 per cent to support the adoption and application of the *acquis*. The Partnerships will involve a continuous bilateral dialogue within principles and priorities determined by the Council, and in which the Commission will play a close 'tutorial' role.[14]

The Commission's annual monitoring of the Partnership process will involve mini-reviews, particularly focused on areas where further or rapid progress is required. The lack of opportunity for opt-outs or even a long transition period was made clear from the outset, as was the asymmetrical and uncompromising character of the dialogue. As one senior official from DG IA stated, 'Opt-outs are for us. Not for them!' (François Lamoureaux, quoted in the *Guardian*, 4 March 1998).

The 'ins' and 'pre-ins' – pecking towards accession

In applying the criteria, and in presenting its Opinions, the Commission stresses its role as interpreter of the conclusions of the Copenhagen Council. Thus each application, it is claimed, is analysed 'on its merits but according to the same criteria as the other applications ... to ensure [treatment] on an equal basis' (Commission 1997c). There is an examination of the ability of each country to meet conditions for membership in both current and future situations as appropriate, with 'future' defined as a five-year medium term. Hence the implication is that first-wave accessions might be achieved by 2002/03.

Table 2.4 summarises the Commission Opinion on each of the Copenhagen criteria including, under economic criteria, the additional assessments of the applicants' fitness for EMU entry; it also subdivides Opinions on administrative capacity between bureaucratic and judicial capabilities. While the use of terminology by the Commission is not entirely consistent, there is an evident taxonomy based on absolute and relative evaluation, on which Opinions and recommendations rest.[15]

Final recommendations, and thus the choice between 'ins' and 'pre-ins', were left to the Commission College, which received documentation without country recommendations. While there was 'fierce debate', no changes were made to the analysis – the Commissioners simply added their recommendations. In the final analysis Hungary, the Czech Republic and Poland were established as clear contenders for fast-track treatment. At this point the line might have been drawn; however, the Commission went on to include Slovenia and also Estonia, whose performance in overall economic performance was seen as superior to that of Latvia (interview, Commission 1998). Here Commissioner Hans van den Broek has argued:

> Sometimes in politics it is necessary to take hard decisions, however tempting it may be to gloss over them. The Member States recognised this when they asked the Commission to prepare opinions on the applications ... We left no stone unturned in ensuring that our analysis was as objective and as complete as possible. The essential accuracy of the Commission's assessment has been acknowledged by the Member States and the applicants themselves. (van den Broek 1997)

Before commenting on the factors that may have influenced this analysis, the Copenhagen criteria are examined as they were applied to the candidate countries.

For the Commission the effective functioning of democracy was 'primordial' in the assessment of readiness for membership. This necessitated the Commission going beyond the mere acceptance of idealist democratic statements by applicants, to a careful examination of procedural democracy *currently* practised, and the efficacy of institutions and processes in support of that practice. Here opinion was sought from the EP, the Council of Europe, the Organisation for Security and Cooperation in Europe (OSCE) and Non-Governmental Organisations (NGOs). The assessment relates to the situation in June 1997, taking into account any scheduled changes. As Table 2.4 indicates, the Commission found that, while operational democratic constitutions and judiciaries were evident in most countries, all applicants 'have flaws in the rule of law that they need to put right' (Commission 1997c:43). A lack of suitably qualified judges, poorly paid and ill-trained police and lack of an autonomous local government system were seen as shared problems needing attention. In particular, Romania and Bulgaria, until changes evident during 1997, had not moved sufficiently far from Communist practices for them to enjoy the soubriquet of having 'the characteristics of democracy'. However, the most damning criticism was left for Slovakia, where there remained 'a gap between the letter of constitutional texts and political practice' with the rule of law and democracy 'not yet sufficiently deeply rooted' (Commission 1997c:43).

Table 2.4 *Agenda 2000*: Country Opinions, a summary

	Political criteria		Economic criteria			
	Democracy, rule of law (current)	Human rights, minorities (current)	Market economy (current)	Competitive pressures (future)	EMU entry (future)	EMU Stage III (future)
Romania	On its way to political criteria	A number of shortcomings: court/police procedures; integration of Roma; child protection	Considerable progress towards	Serious difficulties to cope	Premature to judge	Still poses problems
Bulgaria	On its way to political criteria	Considerable efforts to improve judicial and police processes	Progress limited by absence of commitment	Not be able to cope	Premature to judge	Could pose serious problems
Estonia	Presents characteristics of a democracy	Needs to accelerate naturalisation of Russian-speaking non-citizens	Functioning market economy	Should be able to progress to cope	Premature to judge	Should pose few problems
Lithuania	Presents characteristics of a democracy	Guarantees and respects	Considerable progress towards	Serious difficulties to cope	Premature to judge	Still poses problems
Latvia	Presents characteristics of a democracy	Needs to accelerate naturalisation of Russian minority	Considerable progress towards	Serious difficulties to cope	Premature to judge	Poses no problems
Czech Republic	Presents characteristics of a democracy	Guarantees rights and respects	Functioning market economy	Able to cope	Premature to judge	Poses no problems
Poland	Presents characteristics of a democracy	Guarantees rights and respects	Functioning market economy	Able to cope	Premature to judge	Poses no problems
Hungary	Presents characteristics of a democracy	Guarantees rights and respects	Functioning market economy	Able to cope	Premature to judge	Poses no problems
Slovakia	Unstable institutions; lack of rootedness; shortcomings	Independence of judiciary and police questioned; also rights of Hungarians and Roma	Most reforms introduced	Able to cope	Premature to judge	Should pose no difficulties[a]
Slovenia	Presents characteristics of a democracy	Guarantees rights and respects	Functioning market economy	Able to cope	Premature to judge	Could present some difficulties

Notes: [a]There is an inconsistency in the Opinion para. 3.3 with the final conclusion, which indicates that Slovakia participation could present 'some difficulties'.

Table 2.4 (continued)

	Membership obligations			Administrative capacity	
	Single Market participant (future)	Other acquis (future)	Caveats (future)	Bureaucracy (future)	Judiciary (future)
Romania	Has not taken on essential elements; participation uncertain	Has not taken on essential elements; considerable efforts required	Considerable efforts in environment; transport; employment; social affairs; justice; home affairs; agriculture	Major sustained effort	Not yet possible to judge
Bulgaria	Not possible to envisage full participation	Uncertain whether obligations can be achieved	Considerable efforts in environment; transport; energy; justice; home affairs; agriculture	Substantial admin. reform indispensable	Difficult to judge prospects
Estonia	Full participation with further effort	Particular efforts needed	Particular efforts in environment	Needs major effort of reform	Not yet possible to judge
Lithuania	Full participation with considerable further effort	Particular efforts needed	Particular efforts in agriculture; energy; environment	Needs major reinforced effort of reform	Definite evaluation difficult at this stage
Latvia	Full participation with considerable further effort	Particular efforts needed	Particular efforts in agriculture; environment	Needs major reinforced effort of reform	Definite evaluation difficult at this stage
Czech Republic	Should be capable of applying fully	Should be capable of applying in many areas	Particular efforts in agriculture; environment; energy	Significant and sustained reform needed	Not yet possible to judge
Poland	Should become available to participate fully	Should be able to apply in several areas	Particular efforts in agriculture; environment; transport	Needs further admin. reform, but could be in place	Further admin. reform, but could be in place
Hungary	Should be capable of applying fully	Should be capable of applying	Particular efforts in environment; customs control; energy	Structures should be in place with reform	Should be in place
Slovakia	Can be expected to have implemented/ adopted most of the acquis	Should not have particular difficulty in (several) fields	Substantial efforts in industry; environment; transport; customs borders	Structures could be in place with reform	Difficult to judge progress
Slovenia	Has to make considerable efforts	Has to make considerable efforts	Important progress in environment; employment; social affairs; energy	Structures could be in place with reform	Difficult to judge progress[b]

[b]There is an inconsistency with the Opinion in para. 4.3 which suggests that the judicial system could be in a position to apply the law in the medium term, if necessary means are taken.
Source: Commission (1997c).

With regard to respect for human rights and minorities, while all countries have acceded to the Council of Europe's Convention on Human
Rights and Fundamental Freedoms, concern was expressed in a number of
cases regarding the independence of the media. Moreover, the particular
problems of 'non-citizens' in Estonia and Latvia were considered to be
potentially destabilising. A concern over discrimination against the Roma
minority in several countries was also expressed. Ultimately, however, it
was concluded that 'only one applicant State – Slovakia does not satisfy
the political conditions laid down by the European Council in
Copenhagen' (Commission 1997c:45).[16]

With regard to economic criteria, the Commission was mindful of the
fact that all states will participate fully in EMU if not within the Euro area,
and that the convergence criteria 'are key points of reference for stability
oriented macro-economic policies' (Commission 1997f:51). The country
conclusions on economic criteria contrast markedly with those on political
criteria. None of the applicants 'fully meets the two economic conditions
(market economy/competitive pressures) of Copenhagen today although
some should be able to do so in a few years from now' (Commission
1997b:46). However, five have functioning market economies, with a
sixth, Slovakia, coming close in terms of legislation and systemic features,
but lacking 'transparency in implementation' (Commission 1997b:47).
None of the applicants is currently able to withstand the hurly-burly of the
internal market with two, Hungary and Poland, able to meet market pressures in the medium term. Three others – the Czech Republic, Slovenia and
Slovakia – should achieve this, with strengthened efforts. Estonia's external
imbalances caused 'concern'. By contrast, Bulgaria was given up to ten
years' fairly hard labour to meet this criterion.

With regard to EMU, the Commission's Opinion was less nuanced: it
was considered unlikely that any of the new members would be full
participants in the Euro area at point of entry. Thus the major challenge
will be adoption of the EMU *acquis* as non-participating countries. If this
is measured in terms of the ability to meet the criteria for future Stage III
entry, then only the Czech Republic, Hungary, Poland and Latvia will
have 'no problems' in achieving this. Estonia should have few problems;
Slovenia, however, may face some difficulties in meeting Stage III criteria.

Detailed examination of the current and future capabilities of the applicants in meeting their full obligations under the *acquis* comprises the major
part of each Opinion. Here there is considerable emphasis upon the applicants' ability to implement Single Market measures. The Czech Republic,
Hungary and Poland were deemed capable of fully applying the SEM in the
medium term; Estonia needed further, and Slovenia considerable, effort to
meet SEM obligations. Slovakia, whose Opinion was presented slightly
differently to others in several fields, was expected to have adopted or
implemented most SEM *acquis* in the medium term. Latvia and Lithuania

both needed considerable further effort. With regard to the other *acquis*, only Hungary gains fairly confident comprehensive approval for its ability to meet obligations – to a lesser (Poland) or greater (Bulgaria) degree, each country is found wanting, and each receives specific commentary on those fields that are considered to warrant most attention.

Finally, the Copenhagen criteria associated with the administrative capacity of each applicant are worth attention. With regard to bureaucratic capacity, once again Hungary is judged able to reach a satisfactory level with less effort than Poland, Slovakia and Slovenia. Czech bureaucracy would need a significant and sustained, and Estonian a major, effort of reform. Perhaps more problematic is the reluctance of the Commission to state positively, save in the case of Hungary and Slovenia, that judicial systems of sufficient calibre would be in place within the medium term. This finding was noted with great concern by the EP (European Parliament 1997c:42). Commission concern about institutional capacity is also evident from the redirection of the Phare programme – indeed, institutional reform has become a key issue in the enlargement debate (Fornier 1997; Sigma 1997; see also Chapter 3).[17]

Agenda 2000: reactions

> Nobody can really contest the assessments made. (Senior Commission Official, pre-Luxembourg Seminar, December 1997)

The Commission's confident presentation of its conclusions received endorsement at the Luxembourg Council when, for the most part, the *Agenda 2000* strategy for enlargement was accepted (Council 1997:2). Similarly, the EP, in its lengthy resolution on *Agenda 2000*, while noting 'some factual inaccuracies', supported the Commission's evaluations of applicant countries and the proposed strategy towards enlargement (European Parliament 1997a).

Member state perspectives on enlargement remain less uniform than the Luxembourg Council's endorsement of the Commission strategy would suggest. While Germany, Austria and the UK indicated their support for the Commission's proposals, Italy, Denmark and Sweden argued for full accession negotiations to commence simultaneously with all ten CEE applicants. Greece and France proposed full negotiations with Bulgaria and Romania (*European Voice* 1997, July; Avery and Cameron 1998). More particularly, Germany's consistent preference for fast-tracking only for Poland, Hungary and the Czech Republic; Sweden and Finland's support for the Baltic states;[18] and Spain and Portugal's lukewarm support for the whole project remain as potential influences over EU–CEEC relations. Ultimately, the political flexibility offered by the Commission accession strategy gives both 'maximilists' and 'minimalists' further opportunities to influence the pace of negotiations. This, coupled with the propensity for member states to discount proposals having medium- and long-term implications (Smyrl 1998), appears to have influenced the Luxembourg presidency conclusions. What emerges, nevertheless, is a lack of shared vision on the part of member states; and the potential for serious divisions over enlargement issues in the relatively short period left to the next IGC.[19]

Selection of candidates for early accession

In assessing the validity of Commission proposals and Council decisions on enlargement, some consideration of the political influences on the ranking of 'ins' and 'pre-ins' is invited, especially with regard to the inclusion of Slovenia and Estonia in the fast-track process. An attempt to assign numerical weighting to the various conclusions reached in the Commission country Opinions (see Tables 2.5 and 2.6) suggests a rank order that largely matches the Commission's perspective on individual applicants' fitness for purpose. This gives Hungary, Poland and the Czech Republic a clear lead; Slovenia, Estonia and Slovakia follow; Lithuania and Latvia form a third group; and Romania and Bulgaria clearly fall outside consideration for the medium term.

With regard to Romania and Bulgaria, it is evident that these countries have consistently lagged behind the Visegrad Four in various respects, including their contractual relations with the EU (Phinnemore 1997:16). For very different reasons Slovakia, despite recognised achievements in economic transformation and, interestingly, a good administrative capability, fails to meet the vital criterion of democratic respectability. Slovakia's awkward relationship with the EU forms part of Chapter 11 and will be dealt with there. Here, attention focuses on the 'front-row status' of Estonia and Slovenia – countries which, until 1991, did not exist as independent states.

The case of Slovenia

A justification for Slovenia's inclusion alongside the Visegrad 'ins' appears to present less difficulty than the case for Estonia. Slovenia, it is argued, had 'begun to be strongly integrated with the EU much earlier than any other former socialist country' (Stanovnik and Svetlicic 1996:3). When part of the Yugoslav Federation, Slovenia played a vital role in the country's external trading pattern, accounting for more than one-third of its convertible exports to the EU (Milner 1994); Foreign Direct Investment (FDI) in Slovenia began in 1967 and, by 1994, 60 per cent of inward investment originated from Austria, Germany, Italy and France. With a per capita Gross Domestic Product (GDP) of ecu 7,240 (1995), it has by

Table 2.5 EU criteria for membership: numerical score

Country	Political		Economic			Membership obligations			Administrative capacity	
	Democracy	Human rights	Market economy	Competitive pressures	EMU Stage III	Single Market	Other acquis	Caveats	Bureaucracy	Judiciary
Poland	3	3	3	3	3	4	4	3	4	2
Hungary	3	3	3	3	3	4	3	3	4	3
Slovakia	1	2	3	3	2	3	4	–	4	–
Slovenia	3	3	3	3	2	2	2	2	4	–
Romania	2	–	2	–	–	–	2	–	–	–
Bulgaria	2	–	–	0	–	–	–	–	–	–
Estonia	3	2	3	2	2	3	2	3	3	–
Lithuania	3	3	2	–	–	2	2	3	–	–
Latvia	3	2	2	–	–	2	2	3	2	–
Czech Republic	3	3	3	3	3	4	4	3	2	–
Possible scores	1–3	1–3	1–3	0–3	1–3	1–4	1–4	1–3	1–4	1–3

Source: Commission (1997c).

Table 2.6   Rank order of applicants based on
Agenda 2000 analysis

Hungary	33
Poland	32
Czech Republic	29
Slovenia	25
Estonia	24
Slovakia	23
Lithuania	19
Latvia	18
Romania	13
Bulgaria	10

far the highest GDP of the CEEC 10 (the nearest is the Czech Republic, at ecu 3,490).[20] Moreover, with an average growth rate over the past three years of 5 per cent, unemployment at around 7.5 per cent, an agricultural workforce of 7 per cent, a well-developed service sector, good progress in industrial restructuring and a skilled workforce, the prognosis for Slovenia's ability to compete within the EU is positive.

Unlike Estonia, Slovenia has no substantial minority population and receives a quite positive assessment of its viability as a democratic state (Vanhanen 1997). A long-running dispute with Italy bequeathed after independence from Yugoslavia was settled, in 1996, within the terms of the Slovenian Europe Agreement. Despite Commission reservations over the pace of privatisation, agricultural developments and application of several *acquis* (see Table 2.4), the Commission Opinion shows little reluctance in inviting Slovenia to participate in the first tranche of accession negotiations.

On the other hand, why bother with a newly created state with a population of only two million that neatly buffered part of the EU's borders from more problematic and dangerously unstable neighbours? Part of the explanation, it may be argued, lies in the relatively unproblematic relationship between Slovenia and the EU. Having largely satisfied the Copenhagen criteria, there can be no strong objection to rapid accession to the EU. Moreover, for other Balkan states, EU/Slovenia relations present a model that might be envied and hopefully emulated. Slovenia, therefore, may be seen to have political and strategic significance beyond its contribution to the south-eastern extension of Trans-European Networks (TENs) (European Parliament 1997b:38).

The Estonian case

Estonia, despite its similar league position, presents a more complex picture for fast-track inclusion. Estonia's economic turnaround since

1991 has been dramatic. There has been an explosive growth of the trade and services sectors, against a background of decreasing volumes of agricultural and industrial output. Trade patterns altered rapidly from the exclusive Soviet/Confederation of Independent States (CIS) orientation to the EU, especially to Finland, Germany and Sweden (Finland accounting for around 30 per cent of Estonian exports and 19 per cent of imports). Investment from these three countries – especially in modernising the ice-free port of Tallinn – places Estonia as an intermediate link in the servicing of goods and passenger traffic, and similarly in servicing transport flows, both to Russia and to Scandinavia.

From the outset Estonia's access to the Western institutions was strongly supported by the Nordic countries. Estonia's Free Trade Agreements with the EU entered into force on the same day (1 January 1995) as Swedish and Finnish entry to the Union, and these countries strongly supported the upgrading of EU–Estonian relations. While similar support was offered to the other Baltic states, Estonia has emerged as rather more than first among equals in terms of political and economic investments from Scandinavia. This can be explained to some large degree by the rapid steps taken to establish in Estonia what is 'today one of the most liberal trade regimes in the world' (Commission 1997f:19). This includes a relatively small unsubsidised agricultural sector, whose only threat to EU interests is its example as an effective market-based system! (Terk 1995:114).

Other favourable opinions were reached – on Estonia's low DM-linked exchange rate; low unit labour costs; the competitiveness of the banking sector; the healthy state of FDI and the significant steps taken in implementing the Single Market *acquis*. This, together with a highly educated workforce and rapidly developing telecommunications and information technology sector (Estonia has more personal computers per head than France) adds to the possibility of Estonia as an important link between 'the wealthy markets and the technical and management skills of the Nordic countries' and 'Eastern regions rich in raw materials ... an economic challenge of an all European nature' (Terk 1995:116).

In several senses, however, the strengths of Estonia's economic transformation are balanced by political weaknesses which, it could be argued, the Commission has chosen to underplay in its recommendations. The policies of the newly established Estonian government after 1990 reflected bitter experiences of cultural and economic imperialism. This was evident from the immediate de-Russification of the political administrative process.[21] Thus, from its inception as an independent state, Estonia's nationalism has taken the form of a fiercely inclusive model, where the 'other' is clearly manifest in attitudes towards Russians and all factors associated with the authoritarianism of Soviet/Communist structures and values.

This has been expressed via the restoration of an Estonian-dominated state structure, the return of private ownership and the recognition of individual (Estonian) rights. Here the early and very strict application of regulations dating from 1938 on rights to citizenship, automatically excluded all but a small percentage of non-Estonians from citizenship of the new state (Kirch and Kirch 1995). It was not until the intervention of 'European experts' a year later that changes to the law gave Russian non-citizens protection as a recognised minority (Jarve 1995). Nevertheless, citizenship remains subject to a test of knowledge of the Estonian language. Despite the application of rather easier rules regarding pass rates, from 1997, and support from Phare for language programmes, the Commission recognises that at current rates 'a large percentage of the Estonian population will continue to remain stateless for a long time' (Commission 1997f:14). Part of the problem lies with sectors of the Russian minority who, for reasons associated with their own cultural protection, do not wish to become part of a Western, market-oriented Estonia.[22] While this applies less to Russians living in the western part of Estonia and Tallinn, where there is evidence of a high rate of Russian involvement in SMEs and high rates of citizenship take-up, the emergence of a regional socio-economic division based on ethnic origins remains a strong possibility (Serenov 1995).

One further issue is worthy of consideration, given the problem that 'fast-track' status itself presents to Estonian transformation. The de-Russification of the administrative and particularly the judicial systems has led to a shortage of able and adequately trained public servants of a high degree of integrity.[23] Similarly, the effectiveness of the police in combating organised crime and corruption is also questioned by the Commission (Commission 1997f:103).

There are, thus, a number of problems attending early Estonian accession – in the context of rapid marketisation, privatisation and deregulation, but problematic re-regulation of the new economic and social order. In addition, various commentators point to the implications of the EU's departure from its practice of according similar treatment to the Baltic states – in particular, the divisions that are likely to occur as the 'in'/'pre-in' categorisation accentuates the differences between countries that share similar and testing interests (Girnius 1998).

Why five?

Are we to conclude, therefore, that choice of the five 'ins' by the Commission reflected overall economic performance and progress? Certainly, one senior Commission official closely involved with preparation of *Agenda 2000* denied any covert political weighting of the criteria, while stressing that minority rights issues were taken very seriously;

another reiterated the Commission position that the 'pre-ins' will have every opportunity within the pre-accession strategy to 'catch up' currently more favoured applicants, so that countries like Latvia 'may join the negotiations later but could join sooner' (interview, 12 December 1997). Despite these assurances, our examination of the Slovenian and Estonian cases invites consideration of other decisional influences associated both with internal institutional matters and with the broader political and strategic landscape.

First, the Commission's recommendation to include five CEEC plus Cyprus triggers Article II of the Amsterdam Protocol on Institutional Reform, which requires that 'at least one year before EU membership exceeds twenty', a comprehensive review of the Union's institutions and procedures must be undertaken. Subsequently the EP and the Belgian, Italian and French governments have called for institutional reforms to be firmly in place prior to any further enlargement (European Parliament 1997c:91). In recommending a potential Union of twenty-one in the medium term, the Commission, arguably, is attempting not only to sustain the dwindling enthusiasm for institutional reform demonstrated by the Council at Amsterdam, but also to increase the momentum for vital policy reforms, especially in the fields of structural funding and the CAP. Here, while reforms are necessary for the progress of enlargement, they are also required if the EU is fully to meet commitments made during the Uruguay Round of international trade negotiations.

If we add to these interrelated political priorities a strategic dimension, then the inclusion of the five may perhaps be more comprehensively understood. *Agenda 2000* was published shortly after the NATO Madrid Summit (July 1997), when the Czech Republic, Hungary and Poland were invited to open negotiations for NATO membership. Despite lobbying by various existing NATO members, on behalf of Romania and Slovenia in particular, the US government refused to countenance NATO enlargement beyond the Visegrad Three. While there is no evidence of formal coordination between EU and NATO policy towards CEEC, there clearly exists a case for consideration of their complementarity. Membership of both organisations is sought by the CEEC but the decision to offer early NATO membership only to the three least insecure applicants may be seen as excessively influenced by residual fears of Russia as a military threat and the vagaries of US domestic politics (see Chapter 7). In this context the EU inclusion of Estonia and Slovenia reflects concern for regional stability, with Estonia and Slovenia as flagships for EU good practice and influence in the Baltic and Balkan regions, should their progress lead to early membership. Thus, for instance, the treatment of the Russian minority in Estonia can only be enhanced by the tutelage of the Union, as progress towards membership depends, in part, upon the application of minority rights. Latvian treatment of its Russian minority might be anticipated to follow such good practice.

Ultimately, then, *Agenda 2000* poses big questions. It imposes upon member states the need to consider the interconnections between enlargement, the internal coherence of the Union, and external pressures and policy commitments in the post-Cold War policy environment of the wider Europe.

Conclusion

In this chapter we have traced the incremental development of the EU's 'European' policy, which culminated in *Agenda 2000*, 'a strategy for strengthening growth, competitiveness and employment, for modernising key policies and for extending the Union's borders through enlargement as far eastwards as the Ukraine, Belarus and Moldova' (Commission 1997g:l).

Practical steps have now been taken towards securing that vision, including the convening of the first European Conference in London (March 1998) and the commencement of bilateral entry negotiations with the five CEEC 'ins' plus Cyprus. Each Association country has produced its Accession Partnership – on which the progress of negotiations towards accession will be based – and papers on the proposed reforms of the CAP and structural funding have been published by the Commission (Commission 1998). Thus, while no timetable for the conclusion of accession negotiations has been set, there has been movement along the road towards enlargement.

Debates during and since the Amsterdam Summit have necessitated consideration not just of the piecemeal enlargement of the Union, but have brought into focus a broader vision of a 'new European order' – a suitable subject for the political and moral analysis that is inevitably taking place as the millennium approaches. The Commission itself, anxious to be part of that analysis, has attempted to seize the initiative. As Sedelmeier and Wallace point out (1996:383), it is the Commission that has periodically been able to inject critical redefinitions of approach; and 'only *with active engagement by the Commission* have policy ideas become policy instruments'.

In recent years, Commission intervention has been assisted by the emergence of 'integrated' approaches to policy – exemplified by the 1985 Integrated Mediterranean Policy and the 1988 structural fund reforms. This integrated approach is the Commission's response to the complex policy impacts of the SEA in the areas of environment, social policy, health and safety; and the need to coordinate the disparate problem-solving approaches of the DGs in the light of their new regulatory responsibilities (Smyrl 1998). An integrated approach, in contrast with a sectoral approach to problem solving, concentrates techniques and resources on objectives by facilitating coordination of Community instruments over time. As Smyrl suggests, by redefining Mediterranean or regional problems in this manner, 'the Commission went well beyond the role of informal agenda setting ascribed to it by principal–agent models of EC policy-making' (Smyrl 1998:89–90).

While the Council/presidency retains overall responsibility for the enlargement process, the integrated nature of many aspects of the *Agenda 2000* programme presents a scenario far more difficult to unpick by the member states; nor will it be easy for the Council/presidency to delay presentation of favourable reviews on individual country accession progress. The political balancing act that the Commission undertook in presenting potential resolutions to internal institutional and other problems, together with the theoretical win–win solution it offers to the disparate problems faced by the Association countries, brings an ingenuity to *Agenda 2000* that, at least initially, member states have stepped back to admire. The fear of CEEC, however, is of potential disingenuousness – there is a sense that they enter the EU accession game as pawns, not players, in a member state/institutional struggle for the future of the Union.

Notes

1 As one alternative, in a climate of divergent and mostly conservative preferences from member states, Commissioner Andriessen put forward the concept of a European Political Area with affiliate membership as a half-way house to full integration. This was not welcomed by the CEEC, which perceived it as a stalling tactic.

2 Hans van den Broek, not unsympathetic to the demands of CEEC, revealed the dilemmas of the Commission in progressing and deepening Association dialogue: 'there is a fear – and this is not a new one – that we risk becoming overstretched if we offer too much substance in the engagements we take on regarding third countries'. He also articulated Commission concerns regarding the 'legal implications of bringing East Europeans into more Councils'. He concluded that 'when talking to these countries we still tend to think in terms of our dealings with all third countries, which are conducted through our external relations departments ... we have to get used to the notion that we are talking to genuine partners' (quoted in Philip Morris Institute for Public Policy Research 1994:43).

3 The Polish response to the anticipated demands of the EA had, by January 1997, evolved into a National Strategy for Integration, with associated ministerial machinery and committed administrative resources (Preston 1997b).

4 One example is the Bangkok facility, a joint Phare–EBRD activity through which Phare provides assistance to support EBRD investment strategy.

5 The lack of an MIS, together with the high turnover of staff and reliance on temporary consultants, had resulted in loss of information and heavy reliance on individual knowledge (interview, January 1998).

6 Domestic and international considerations led President Clinton to accept the need for closer US–CEE and thus NATO–EU–CEE relationships, and in a visit to Berlin (summer 1994), a working group was established to coordinate EU–US policies towards the East.

7 Information for this section is based on interviews with Commission officials and advisers conducted during and after the presentation of *Agenda 2000*. The conclusions reached, however, are those of the author.

8 DG II (Economic and Financial Affairs), with its considerable involvement in economic developments in CEE, was less reliant on questionnaire information than DG XV (Financial Institutions and Company Law), which had little prior knowledge yet was deeply involved in assessing progress towards implementing aspects of the *acquis*.

9 Officially established in September 1996, the Enlargement Team had a pre-existence from early 1996 in the shape of two special advisers at Director level – one with responsibility for the assessment of CEEC' membership capabilities, the other for the Impact Study – on the potential consequences for the EU of enlargement.

10 The Commission notes, with some irritation, the inadequacy of the institutional reforms agreed at the recent (June 1997) Amsterdam Summit (Commission 1997b, 1997g; *European Voice*, June 1997, p. 7). Consequently the introduction to *Agenda 2000* emphasises the need for urgent reforms 'well before 2000' and for a new IGC, after 2000, to negotiate the thorough reform of institutions which was evidently beyond the political capabilities of leaders at Amsterdam.

11 Concern with internal cohesion during and after the accession of countries whose GDP is only one-third the EU average necessitates a reformulation of structural funding so as to simplify its objectives and concentrate its impact. Stuctural funding objectives are to be reduced to three, with a concentration of funding upon 35–40 per cent of the Union's population (down from 51 per cent). Strict enforcement of the 75 per cent qualifying criterion for Objective One funding and the 90 per cent criterion for cohesion funding will alter the existing pattern of eligibility. Over the period 2000–06, ecu 275 billion are to be devoted to structural cohesion funds, an increase of ecu 75 billion over the previous five years. However, ecu 45 billion were proposed for CEEC, including ecu 7 billion for pre-accession. Similarly, absorption of the CEE farming sector, that could entail a 50 per cent increase in agricultural production and a 100 per cent increase in farm labour, would necessitate a further shift in the CAP towards a market-based policy to enable CEEC entry to a reformed CAP. Cuts in price supports for beef, cereal and dairy products are to be cushioned by direct payments – income support for farmers – and transition periods. The net result would be a temporary increase in CAP expenditure over the period (2000–06) from ecu 98 billion (1999) to ecu 114 billion (2006).

12 The financial framework is contained within the EU's own resources expenditure limit of 1.27 per cent GDP. On the assumption of 2.5 per cent average annual growth within the EU, and 4 per cent within the CEEC, additional

resources of around ecu 20 billion would accrue. Since projected total spending would rise to around 17 per cent and the anticipated own resources availability could be approximately 24 per cent, there should be a cushion of reserves to allow for 'eventualities'. The figures are predicated on the assumption of an increase of six members – any more would need a re-evaluation of the 1.27 per cent own resources ceiling. Overall, taking into account reforms to structural funding and the CAP, there will be 'a deterioration in the budgetary condition of the current Member States, but this cannot give rise to compensation' (Commission 1997b).

13 Pre-accession aid worth ecu 21 million over the period 2000–06 will be supplemented by ecu 54 billion to support first-stage applicant adjustment and integration within Community policies from a mid-way point in the financial cycle.

14 Early evidence of the strict application of pre-accession criteria was seen in an ecu 34 million cut in 1998 Phare allocation to Poland (from ecu 212 million) as some projects were not considered to be directly associated with membership preparation. The Polish Prime Minister subsequently sacked the Minister considered responsible for the loss (Central Europe Online, 26 May 1998).

15 One Commission official stressed the care taken in using phrases consistently, but indicated the possibility of differences according to subject area. Thus expressions of caution on future capabilities may in some cases indicate no more than a lack of information on a subject area, rather than an adverse judgement. This was particularly so in the evaluation of judicial capabilities (interview, February 1998).

16 In its opinions on *Agenda 2000* the EP, itself a source of information from which the Commission made its evaluation, largely accepted the political criteria conclusions. In its resolution it stressed that special attention should be paid to the Phare democracy programme but also argued for cooperation with the Council of Europe and the OSCE to keep the human rights situation under review (Resolution 37). More particularly, it called for the abolition of the death penalty as a prerequisite for membership.

17 One established consultant, however, suggested that the political timescale for establishing an acceptable level of administrative and judicial capacity was 'totally at odds with the reality of implementing the *acquis*' (interview, January 1998). A less pessimistic note was sounded by a Commission official, who while agreeing that all candidates were in 'tricky situations', suggested that the reluctance to give definitive statements on judicial capacity was more a reflection of the lack of information on which the Commissioners were able to base their opinion; and that the position of applicants should not be seen as 'apocalyptic' (interview, March 1998).

18 In a statement prior to Amsterdam, the three Presidents of the Baltic states publicly thanked Nordic members for their interventions on behalf of Baltic accession. In the event, Sweden's, and especially Finland's, strong championing of the Estonian cause resulted in a less than optimal outcome for Latvia and Lithuania.

19 The German government's admittedly pre-election rhetoric over its paymaster role, at the Cardiff Summit (June 1998), is illustrative of the political sensitivities to which the assession process is subject.

20 Nevertheless it compares, at 59 per cent of the EU average, only with the poorest of EU states (Portugal, ecu 7,770 and Greece ecu 8,360).
21 Estonia, again, is a small new state (population 1.5 million), though between 1920 and 1940 it enjoyed independent democratic constitutional status until its annexation by the USSR in 1940 and, later, its occupation by Germany. The subsequent return of Soviet rule brought with it a period of Russification, including mass migration and deportation so that, by 1989, 40 per cent of the population was of non-Estonian, mostly Slav, origin (Kirch and Kirch 1995).
22 This is especially true of the north-eastern region, where not only is Russian nationalism still a powerful force, but the nostalgia for a state-based economy and the values so attached is also powerful. Ex-Soviet migrants, especially in the north-eastern enclave, 'know practically nothing about the history, culture of the land and nation in which they are living' and have only recently realised 'that they live in the territory of another foreign state' (Kirch and Kirch 1995:45).
23 One ex-Minister of Justice pointed to the inadequacy of post-Communist judges, particularly at Court of First Instance level, remarking somewhat ruefully that 'at least their predecessors had a grasp of legal procedure, even if they were Communists' (interview, December 1997).

References

Allen, D. and Smith, M. (1994), External Policy Developments, *Journal of Common Market Studies*, Annual Review of Activities 1993, 33, 69–86.
Allen, D. and Smith, M. (1997), External Policy Developments, *Journal of Common Market Studies*, Annual Review of Activities, 1996, 35, 73–94.
Avery, G. (1995), *The Commission's Perspectives on the EFTA Accession Negotiations*, Sussex European Institute, Working Paper 12.
Avery, G. and Cameron, F. (1998), *The Enlargement of the European Union*, Sheffield, Sheffield Academic Press.
Baldwin, R. *et al.* (1992), *Monitoring European Integration: Is Bigger Better? The Economics of EC Enlargement*, London, Centre for Economic Policy Research.
Brewin, C. (1993), External Policy Developments, *Journal of Common Market Studies*, Annual Review of Activities 1992, 31, 71–86.
Central Europe Online (1998), *Polish PM Says He Will Make Tough Choices on the EU*, http://www.ceo/news/98030907.
Commission (1992a), Europe: The Challenge of Enlargement, *Bulletin*, Supplement, Luxembourg, March.
Commission (1992b), *Towards a Closer Association with the Countries of Central and Eastern Europe*. Report by the Commission to the European Council, 11–12 December, Sec/92/2/Jol.
Commission (1994a), *The Europe Agreements and Beyond: A Strategy to Prepare the Countries of Central and Eastern Europe for Accession*, COM(94) 320, Final, 13 July.
Commission (1994b), *Follow up to Commission Communication on the 'Europe Agreements and Beyond': A Strategy to Prepare for Accession*, COM(94) 361, Final, 27 July.

Commission (1995a), White Paper: *Preparation of the Associated Countries of Central and Eastern Europe for the Integration into the Internal Market of the Union*, COM(95) 163, Final, 3 May.

Commission (1995b), *Commission Report for the Reflection Group*, Directorate-General for Information, Luxembourg.

Commission (1997a), *New Policy Guidelines for the Phare Programme in the Framework of the Pre-accession Assistance*, Brussels, 19 March.

Commission (1997b), *Agenda 2000 – for a Stronger and Wider Union*, Vol. 1, COM(97) 2000, Final, Brussels, 15 July.

Commission (1997c), *Agenda 2000 – The Challenge of Enlargement*, Vol. 2, Doc/97/6, Brussels, 16 July.

Commission (1997d), *Phare – an Interim Report*, Directorate-General for External Relations, Evaluation Unit (DG IAF/5), Brussels, June.

Commission (1997e), *The European Union and the Russian Federation – Partnership and Cooperation Agreement*, DG 1A Information Unit, Brussels, November.

Commission (1997f), *Agenda 2000 – Commission Opinion on Estonia's Application for Membership of the European Union*, Doc/97/12, Brussels.

Commission (1997g), Agenda 2000 for a Stronger and Wider Union, DG X, *Information for the European Citizen*, Brussels.

Commission (1998), *Agenda 2000 – the Legislative Proposals*, DN: 1P/98/258, Brussels, March.

Council of Ministers (1993a), *Conclusions of the Presidency, Copenhagen, 21–22 June*, Brussels, General Secretariat of the Council.

Council of Ministers (1995), *Presidency Conclusions, Madrid*, Brussels, General Secretariat of the Council, 15–16 December.

Council of Ministers (1997), *Presidency Conclusions, Luxembourg*, Brussels, General Secretariat of the Council, 12–13 December.

Dangerfield, M. V. (1995), The Economic Opening of Central and Eastern Europe: Continuity and Change in Foreign Economic Relations, *Journal of European Integration*, 19:1, 5–43.

De Weydenthal, J. B. (1994), East Central Europe and the EU: Forging Political Ties, *RFE-RL Research Report*, 3:29, 16–18.

European Parliament (1996a), *Report on the Preparation of the Countries of Central and Eastern Europe for Accession to the Union, on the Basis of the White Paper on the Subject (Com (95) 0163 – C4 – 0166/95)*, Rapporteur Mr A. A. Oostlander, Doc.EN/RR/296/296750, 28 March.

European Parliament (1996b), *Annex (Oostlander Report): Opinions of the Other Committees*, Doc.EN/RR/296/2967, 28 March.

European Parliament (1997a), *Report on Agenda 2000 (Com[97] 2000 – C4 – 0371/97) Part A: Motion for a Resolution*, Committee on Foreign Affairs, Security and Defence Policy, Rapporteurs Mr A. A. Oostlander, Mr E. Baron Crespo, Doc.EN/RR/340/340343.

European Parliament (1997b), *Report on Agenda 2000, Part B: Explanatory Statements*, Doc.EN/RR/340/340287.

European Parliament (1997c), *Report on Agenda 2000, Part C: Opinions of the EP's Committees*, Doc.EN/RR/340/340348.

European Voice (1997), 14 and 17 July.

Ferreira, M. P. (1995), The Impact of Liberalisation of East West Trade, *Europe–Asia Studies*, 47:7, 1205–24.

Fornier, J. (1997), Administrative Reform in the Commission's Opinions Concerning the Accession of Central and Eastern European Countries to the European Union, *Multi Country Seminar on European Integration and Public Administration Reform, Athens*, 8–10 October, Paris, Sigma and OECD.

Girnius, K. (1998), The Race Is On, *Transitions*, 5:4, 48–51.

Guardian (1998), EU Gets Tough with Entrants, 28 March.

Hughes, M. (1993), Eastern Pain and Western Promise: The Reaction of Western Governments to the Economic Plight of the 'New Eastern Europe', *International Relations*, 10:16, 585–604.

Jarve, P. (1995), Transition to Democracy, *Nationalities Papers*, 23:1, 19–27.

Kirch, M. and Kirch, A. (1995), Ethnic Relations: Estonians and Non-Estonians, *Nationalities Papers*, 23:1, 43–59.

Koves, A. (1992), *Central and Eastern European Economies in Transition*, Oxford, Westview.

Kramer, H. (1993), The European Community's Response to the 'New Eastern Europe', *Journal of Common Market Studies*, 31:2, 213–44.

Manners, I. (1994), *The Negotiation of the EC Association Agreements with the Visegrad Countries*, British International Studies Association Annual Conference, Warwick, December.

Mannin, M. (1997), Italy, European Monetary Union and the Intergovernmental Conference: Squaring the Circle, *Contemporary Politics*, 3:2, 137–50.

Milner, M. (1994), Tiny Slovenia Eyes the Big League, *Guardian*, 30 October.

Nugent, N. (1993), The Treaty On European Union – Looking Rather Different Twelve Months On, *Journal of Common Market Studies*, Annual Review of Activities 1992, 31, 2–9.

Philip Morris Institute for Public Policy Research (1994), *Is The West Doing Enough For Eastern Europe?*, Brussels, Philip Morris Institute.

Phinnemore, D. (1997), Six Years of the New EU Ostpolitik: The EU, Bulgaria and Romania, Research Conference, UACES, Loughborough, 10–12 September.

Preston, C. (1997a), *Enlargement and Integration in the European Union*, London, Routledge and UACES.

Preston, C. (1997b), Poland and EU Membership – Current Issues and Future Prospects, UACES conference, *Enlarging the European Union – the Way Forward*, Birmingham, July.

Redmond, J. (1993), The Wider Europe: Extending the Membership of the EC, in A. W. Cafruny and G. G. Rosenthal (eds), *The State of the European Community – the Maastricht Debates and Beyond*, Harlow, Longman, 209–25.

Rollo, J. and Smith, M. (1993), The Political Economy of Eastern European Trade with the European Community – Why So Sensitive?, *Economic Policy*, 16, 139–81.

Sedelmeier, U. (1994), *The European Union's Association Policy Towards Central and Eastern Europe: Political and Economic Rationales in Conflict*, Sussex European Institute, Working Paper No. 7.

Sedelmeier, U. and Wallace, H. (1996), Policies towards Central and Eastern

Europe, in H. Wallace and W. Wallace (eds), *Policy Making in the European Union*, Oxford, Oxford University Press, 353–88.

Serenov, A. (1995), Russian Assembly: The Formation of a Legal State and Russophone Community in the Estonian Republic, *Nationalities Papers*, 23:1, 235–41.

Sigma (1997), *Reliable Public Administration*, Conference, Governance and Integration, Rotterdam, 29–30 May, Paris, Sigma and OECD.

Smith, A. *et al.* (1995), *The EU & CEE: Pre-accession Strategies*, Working Papers in Contemporary European Studies, Sussex European Institute, Working Paper No. 15.

Smyrl, M. E. (1998), When (and How) Do Commission Preferences Matter? *Journal of Common Market Studies*, 36, 79–100.

Stanovnik, P. and Svetlicic, M. (1996), Slovenia and the European Union, paper delivered at Experts' Meeting, *The Economic Aspects of Slovenia's Integration into the European Union*, TEPSA and University of Ljubljana, Bled.

Terk, E. (1995), A Changing Economy in a Changing Society, *Nationalities Papers*, 23:1, 103–17.

Vachudova, M. A. (1993), The Visegrad Four: No Alternative to Cooperation, *RFE-RL Research Report*, 2:34, 38–47.

Van den Broek, H. (1997), *The Prospect of EU Enlargement*, speech to International Press Institute, the Future of Europe Brussels Centre, Commission Dn.Speech 97/264, 27 November.

Vanhanen, T. (1997), *Prospects for Democracy – A Study of 172 Countries*, London, Routledge.

3 Terry Caslin and Laszlo Czaban

Economic transformation in CEE

This chapter examines the common economic legacies and challenges that face the post-Communist states of the former 'Soviet bloc'. The end of the Cold War had created a more liberal environment within Eastern Europe and the revolutions of 1989 saw the widespread rejection of state social-ism as a model for economic development. The CEEC are now endeavouring to establish robust market-type economic systems alongside democratic political institutions. The focus of the chapter is thus on the economic transition, that is the process which leads to the establishment of the market economy. This process has implications for, and is inter-woven with, profound political and social changes. These changes will not be the primary focus of this chapter but they are emphasised in other chapters of this book.

The transition from a command to a market economy is the movement towards a new system for the production and allocation of resources. It involves changes in the institutional system, including enterprises and legal structures, liberalisation of prices and wages, and liberalisation of trade. Transition must be accompanied by stabilisation policy, which aims to achieve a low and predictable level of inflation and to prevent large fluctuations in output and in the level of employment. Monetary and fiscal policy are the relevant instruments here. Transition and stabilisation must be distinguished from the concept of economic development, which refers to improvements in the standard of living and economic and politi-cal rights. However, the concepts are closely interrelated. Transition and stabilisation policies aim, ultimately, to promote growth and develop-ment.

The transformation of the economic system in the CEEC will be seen to involve two major issues: transformation of the institutional system of macro- and micro-economic management, and the creation of the precon-ditions for sustainable economic development in the new environment.

Many scholars of the early 1990s predicted a relatively swift transition of the state socialist countries (for a review see, for example, Jackson

1992). Their arguments focused on the rapid changes of the institutional systems, which were supposed to alter enterprise behaviour (effective management, closure of non-viable companies and the growth of profitable ones) and help the integration of these economies into the world market. This in turn would result in sustainable economic growth and the underpinning of the legitimacy of liberal democracy in the region. Contrary to these assumptions, the transition has proven to be a rather incremental and past-dependent process with a high level of market and institutional uncertainties (Tatur 1995), in spite of the rapid introduction of new institutions and the stability of the new political regimes in these countries.

The chapter is divided into six sections. The first section examines the common heritage of the CEEC, the legacies of state socialism. The second section considers the changes in the institutional system, including an assessment of the alleged dichotomy between 'shock therapy' and 'gradual transformation'. Privatisation is the focus of the third section, an issue which continues to be at the very centre of the reform process in most countries. Enterprise restructuring and corporate governance are here seen as integral parts of the privatisation programmes. FDI has been a key issue in the transformation process, and this is examined in the fourth section. The fifth section reviews the consolidation of the transformation process to date, and the final section poses the question as to how far transition is relevant in the context of the enlargement of the EU, and considers a number of transition indicators.

Legacies of state socialism

In this section we summarise those common features of state socialist macro- and micro-economic management, while pointing out important differences between countries, which can be expected to have a significant effect on the transition in the medium term.

The central feature of the state socialist economic system was bureaucratic planning (although in Hungary and the former Yugoslavia the central planning authorities had only informal means to keep the companies in line in the second half of the 1980s). In the planning process every actor – companies, ministries, central planning authorities, unions and party organisations – engaged in a bargaining process to gain additional resources for fulfilling the plans imposed on them. As the main objective was to fulfil the plan targets, defined either in monetary terms or in kind, companies tended to accumulate and hide production resources from the central authorities. The attempts of central authorities, through foreign trade, price, subsidy and other policies, to correct these 'imperfections' of the planning system were always *ex post facto* and limited, as, in general, there is a limited capability of regulators to obtain sufficient information on the regulated economic units.

The management of the companies was interested in their growth to increase their bargaining power (Grancelli 1995; Szalai 1991). The resources for this growth were allocated mainly by the state (either directly or through the banking system), in accordance with the objectives of the central plan (Revesz 1990) rather than with profitability considerations, despite the attempts to introduce such criteria in all the state socialist countries from time to time. There was thus no effective economic limit to the growth of the companies. This is referred to as 'the soft-budget constraint' in the literature (Kornai 1986).

These two factors, the prime growth objective and the hoarding of resources by companies, resulted in the 'shortage economy'. This phrase expresses not so much a general shortage as inefficient allocation of resources and a constant tendency of the economy to overheat. It also means that the shortage was not primarily concerned with the consumer goods markets.

The shortage as an expression of unreliable timing and quality of supply by suppliers (in most state socialist countries the commodity channels – who supplies to whom – were also directed by the state) led companies to integrate component manufacturing into the organisation of the company. They were often encouraged by the central authorities, for example GDR *Kombinats*. As a result, state socialist companies tended to be not only large, but also a combination of often sub-optimal units. Plants were often built in particular locations simply to provide employment in rural areas.

The growing size of companies and the close cooperation between company management, company party and trade union organisations made the central authorities extremely vulnerable to capture by particular pressure groups or lobbies. Thus their capability to define macro-economic development priorities declined, especially after the 1960s (Szalai 1991). This declining efficiency of central planning was expressed not only in worsening economic indicators and the reduced ability to meet the technological challenges of the world economy from the 1970s, but also in the fragmentation of the state organisation, as witnessed by warring factions of the bureaucracy and politicians. The state socialist organisation was responsible for macro-economic management and the transmission of the economic policy to the companies through regulations, plan targets, commodity channels, funding, and so on, and was also involved in the strategic and operational management (either formally or informally) of companies. The disorganisation of central planning thus spread rapidly to the enterprise sphere (Whitley and Czaban 1998).

Turning to company structure, we find that these large and vertically integrated companies had a steep hierarchic structure with a chief executive officer at the top, usually appointed by the state (though in Hungary and Yugoslavia they were appointed by the company councils, dominated by the management, from 1985 and 1974 respectively). Correspondingly, the organisational structure was functional, with a large number of managerial levels. Because of this functional structure the company centre often retained decision making on basic operational issues, while production units lacked functional personnel.

Within the work organisation, because of the shortages and obsolescent machinery, skilled workers had a strong position, as they were able to cope with unforeseen situations. Consequently, first-line supervisors, who were likely to be promoted from the shop floor, were responsible for ensuring production rather than managing the workforce; thus the distance between operators and foremen or forewomen was small.

Wages were regulated nationally and there was a labour shortage in most periods. State legislation discouraged labour mobility, so once the major waves of industrialisation had passed, people often spent their entire career in one company, sometimes in one unit. This encouraged internal promotion (often linked to vocational training), and thus most managers at all levels of the state socialist firm had no experience of working in various companies or sectors. As the state encouraged vocational and general education for those to be promoted, the educational level of state socialist management did, however, increase significantly in the 1970s–1980s.

The combination of these factors – pressure to fulfil plan objectives, the growth prerogative, the need to utilise economies of scale, and the company-related expertise of the workforce and management – encouraged narrow product lines with very little customisation (mass production of standardised products), little product innovation (or incremental at the most) and single-purpose machinery. This tendency became especially strong as CMEA trade developed, because this trade was based on large-batch sales in a large, stable and guaranteed market (Hitchens *et al.* 1995). In CMEA trade, customer–supplier relations were exclusively mediated by intergovernmental agreements. Companies cooperated only to a limited extent with their suppliers and customers, thus cross-industry associations were weak. On the other hand they cooperated closely, and often informally, with companies in the same branch to increase the bargaining power of the sector.

In most state socialist countries companies engaged in trade with Western companies had no direct contact with them, as foreign trade was mediated by specialised, state-run foreign trade companies (Clague 1992). While in CMEA trade the smaller state socialist countries exported finished goods to the Soviet Union in exchange for energy, raw materials and specialised machinery, in OECD trade they mainly supplied components, basic products or highly customised finished goods in small quantities. OECD exports were subsidised by the state, or companies cross-subsidised the prices of these goods, as the large-batch exports to the CMEA countries covered the fixed costs.

The changes in the institutional system

Although reforms of the above system were initiated in a number of countries from the 1960s (Berend 1990) and its deterioration became evident in the 1980s (see Chapter 1), it was the political change of 1989–91 that abolished the ground on which this system could operate. The economic literature usually discusses these changes in terms of the dichotomy between shock therapy and a gradual approach; that is, while governments of some of the CEEC applied a shock to transform the institutional system (and thus the behaviour of economic actors), other countries applied a gradual transformation.[1] Neither empirical nor logical evidence supports this dichotomy. All CEEC applied shock therapy to start with, and under various pressures they shifted to more gradual alteration of the existing system, although there were differences in the degree of 'shock', ranging from Poland through Hungary to Czechoslovakia and Slovenia. In terms of logical reconstruction of the transition, the abolition of certain crucial institutions of central planning and the introduction of certain crucial institutions of a market economy made the continuation of old behaviours and the maintenance of the existing economic structure impossible; thus by definition these were shock therapies. Kaser and Allsopp (1993) point out that countries that followed shock therapy and those that pursued a more gradual approach applied similar macro-economic measures. On the other hand, shock therapies create high market and institutional uncertainties that actually inhibit deep and sustainable changes and eventually give way to more gradual approaches. Thus, instead of seeing shock therapies and gradual approaches in terms of dichotomy, we can consider them as historic sequences in the transition from state socialism to a kind of capitalist economy.

The origins of shock therapies can be traced back to Friedman's adaptive expectations hypothesis (Friedman 1977) and its application in Chile in the middle of the 1970s, although Friedman criticised some of the policy measures applied in the transformation of the CEEC. The essence of this approach is the assumption that the existing income distribution encourages behaviours that maintain and reinforce the existing institutional system and the role of agents. According to the assumptions of this model, to change these behaviours a shock is needed which is large enough to force the economic agents to give up their behaviours. This type of policy had been applied mainly in Latin America in the 1980s to combat spiralling inflation. However, in 1990 Jeffrey Sachs worked out an econometric model of transplanting the Latin American experiences to the transformation of Eastern Europe (Sachs 1992, 1994).

According to this concept, on a particular day (D-day) all direct production subsidies and price subsidies are abolished, prices deregulated, foreign trade, market entries and exits liberalised, housing marketised and an external labour market created, with liberalisation of wages and redundancies. At the same time the state initiates a large-scale privatisation. The expected behaviour of economic agents as a response to the above changes can be summarised as follows: cuts in subsidies reduce domestic demand, but the liberalisation allows companies to adjust their capacity and workforce to the new level of demand. It might be expected then that some of the companies would have to cut significantly both their output and employment. The cuts in subsidy and the falling output result in contracting domestic markets, which in turn force companies to find export markets. The growing exports pay for the growing imports (both capital and consumer goods) deriving from the import liberalisation, as exporters of the advanced countries seek to exploit the domestic markets of the region hungry for sophisticated Western goods after the shortage economy. Those companies then which are unable to find new markets are deselected (wound up), while companies successfully switching markets are rewarded; that is, incomes are redistributed from the 'bad' companies to the 'good' ones. If the shock is large enough, economic actors are unable to adjust their existing behaviour and strategy to the new situation, but have to abandon these completely and adopt new ones.

This approach then seemingly aimed at solving the two major issues of the transformation of the countries concerned: social transformation (liberalisation and privatisation) and sustainable economic growth (efficient companies being rewarded). This in turn would underpin the developing political democracy. There were, however, two major concerns with this approach (Taylor 1991): (1) nobody really knew how big the shock had to be; and (2) retaining the metaphor from medical science, it was possible that the shock would kill the patient; that is, the reward for the sufferance of the shock was in the womb of the future and it was by no means certain that it could be delivered.

The most extensive introduction of shock therapy took place in Poland. Apart from the persistent high inflation, industrial output fell by 36 per cent in 1991, and official, previously unknown, unemployment reached 13 per cent. The economic recession on this scale, unknown since the Great Depression of 1929–33, rapidly undermined the legitimacy of the new regimes, which led to first the abandonment of some of the measures of shock therapy and then to a shift to an incremental modification of the macro-economic institutional system. The failure of the shock therapy derived from the negligence, inherent in this economic thinking, of the existing economic system (Rybczynski 1991), the 'real' behaviour of economic agents (Aslund 1994), the world economic context (Gowen 1995), and the time lag between the introduction of the institutional changes and changes in the behaviour of economic agents (Whitley and Czaban 1998).

As a result of the collapsing domestic market, companies followed an 'each for itself' strategy, which undermined the long-term, established, intercompany relationships (e.g. instead of selling products, companies sold their raw and basic materials, switched suppliers without notice, etc.). The now contracting CEEC domestic economies, flooded with cheap, 'dumped' Western imports, forced local companies to flee to export markets. As the CMEA trade collapsed in 1991, export markets meant the markets of the OECD countries. For example, Poland's hard currency exports in the chemical industry increased by more than 50 per cent, and metallurgy and agriculture by more than 40 per cent, in 1990 (*The Economist*, 19 January 1991). Table 3.1 shows selected East European countries' share of the OECD market over the period.

Table 3.1 East European countries' share of the OECD market (% change of market share, 1979–92)

Period	Bulgaria	Czechoslovakia	Hungary	Poland	Romania
1979–86	−18.5	−44.0	−7.8	−32.3	−46.3
1986–89	−19.9	0.9	1.5	−23.5	−27.8
1989–92	59.1	82.4	36.4	49.2	−55.1

Note: The inward concentration of CMEA member countries' trade had been accompanied by loss of market shares outside the CMEA. From 1989 the reforms led to a strong reversal of these trends (except for Romania).
Source: OECD (various years).

The competition, however, became heightened as all CEEC tried to switch their CMEA exports to OECD markets, and companies of the regions tried to sell their goods in these markets instead of the domestic economy. All this took place in 1990–91, when the recession in the European economies was about to start. The reaction of the EU was market protection measures, anti-dumping procedures (in the steel and chemical industries) and quota restrictions.

As the switch between markets became restricted in this way, one of the crucial elements of shock therapy collapsed: the deselecting of inefficient companies became not so much that of particular companies as of entire industrial branches, irrespective of their profitability. This is demonstrated by the falling output (and from 1992 exports) in the sectors which Matropasqua and Roli (1994) described as competitive export branches: food processing in Poland and Hungary; the chemical industry in Hungary; coal in Poland; energy in Czechoslovakia; and textiles, garments and metallurgy in all the three countries.

Because of the existing interbranch relations, cemented in the previous forty years, the secondary effect of the collapse of the CMEA markets, contracting domestic markets and restrictive OECD markets emerged just before the economy of the region could have recovered from the shock of liberalisation. This second shock pushed the hoped-for fast recovery into the infinite future, as all industrial branches now slipped into free-fall recession.

Behaviour at company level was also different from that expected. Although companies indeed shed their workforce (especially non-production workers) and closed production units, the latter closures were seriously hindered by the sunk costs, especially in capital-intensive sectors. Instead of full-scale closures, companies attempted to sell their products at the price of variable cost plus profits, thereby eating into their capital (Scott 1992). This allowed those companies having large enough capital, or capital that was already written off, to survive the 'hard times', but at the cost of the future, as not only were they unable to generate internal funds for future investment, but depreciation funds were also used to cover running costs.

The crisis in the enterprise sphere started to spread into the banking system after a short period of one or one-and-a-half years. The traditionally undercapitalised East European companies (Kornai 1986) were characterised by an equity/debt ratio unusually low by West European standards, though not unusual in the economies of the Far East.[2] Financing a low equity/debt ratio is possible under two conditions: if the company's cash flow is continuous and plentiful, and if the margin (including depreciation) is high enough to cover the principal and interest payments. As shown above, the first condition was undermined by the waves of market shocks, and the latter not only by the low margins squeezed by the sharp competition, but also by high inflation that required high nominal interest rates. The banks' deteriorating balance sheets, which required a growing interest rate spread to cover the mounting losses, meant the adjustment of lending strategy, especially in the context of the sharp competition for savings.

The deteriorating conditions in the banking sector affected the shock therapy in two ways. On the one hand, banks had to accumulate large risk provisions to cover the potential loss from non-performing debts, which resulted in low or non-tax payments. On the other hand, banks refrained from providing fresh loans to the enterprise sector either openly or requiring such high collateral as could not have been satisfied under normal circumstances. As statistics show, bank loans for investment became virtually unknown in CEE and loans for working capital fell rapidly (Bonin and Szekely 1994). The falling banking activity, when other financial institutions, such as stock exchanges, were absent in the region, meant that reallocation of resources from the 'bad' companies to the 'good' ones

– that is, modernisation of the capital base, upgrading or introducing new products, spending on entering new markets, and so on – became impossible from financial sources.

The crisis in the banking sector in the region threatened widespread insolvency of banks, which in turn would have deepened the economic recession and would have undermined the legitimacy of the transition to a kind of capitalist economy (Gomulka 1994). This threat, alongside the falling level of production and growing social problems, was sufficient to prompt governments to leave the path of shock therapy and try to introduce the institutions of a market economy more gradually, allowing the economic actors to adjust their behaviour to the new situation and if necessary provide state resources at the crucial points, such as bank consolidation programmes and the 'bailing out' of some large companies.

Privatisation

Privatisation was the central question of the transition programmes, as the ideological assumption was coincidental with the need to create a social base to the transition (Batt 1991). The ideological assumption derived directly from neo-classical economics. It was that private entrepreneurs are the actors, who, to maximise their profit, are able to operate companies efficiently and in this way engender general social well-being. The state, on the contrary, is unable to ensure the efficient operation of state firms and wastes economic resources. On the pragmatic side, governments of the region were convinced that in the new social system a broad ownership structure was required. Some of these governments were genuinely convinced that they had to compensate the population for the suffering under communism, and all of them competed to show to Western governments and international organisations, especially the EU, that they were ahead of the others in implementing the principles of the capitalist economy (Gowen 1995).

Privatisation was a phenomenon also being experienced in advanced economies. A liberalisation in economic ideas was a common thread in the EU Single Market and in market reform in the East. There was an increasingly wide belief in the merits of competition, deregulation and private ownership as the dominant mode of production. Privatisation was no longer a British eccentricity but a major fact of life throughout the EU. However, the sheer size of state property to be transferred to private owners, the lack of institutions of privatisation (such as a stock exchange), the lack of an operating market system, and the lack of savings available for investment suggested that privatisation in the CEEC context was going to be a substantially different process from selling nationalised industries in the advanced countries.

Privatisation in CEE faced a gap that could not be bridged: the lack of savings available for investment. In the most developed CEEC the ratio between the value of state property (without land) to aggregated household savings was about ten to one (EBRD 1997). Additionally, there were no ready means to establish the value of the state property in the new market environment, as the book value represented the historic cost; and even if some approximations (such as business valuation based on profits and cash flow) were available, these valuations became increasingly doubtful as the business environment changed at a swift pace.[3] These conditions offered three solutions to the new governments of the region: a long process of privatisation, leaving the government responsible for managing the state property for a relatively long period; the introduction of a form of subsidy to potential buyers of state property, which can hardly be considered a market-conforming measure; or the sale of state property to those with purchasing power, namely foreign investors.

The third option failed at the beginning of the 1990s, as foreign investors did not queue up to buy a large number of state enterprises in the region. This is witnessed by the Hungarian First Privatisation Programme, where the government listed the fifty most marketable companies for sale to foreign investors and managed to sell only a handful in two years. From this 'failure', two 'ideal typical' privatisation methods emerged: voucher privatisation and trade sale.

Although all countries used both methods, the former was the dominant method in the Czech Republic (and prior to this in Czechoslovakia), while the latter was dominant in Hungary. In principle, the extent to which trade sale was applied by the governments of the region depended on the indebtedness of the state. Thus, while in a formal sense it was a method of privatisation, in substance it was a debt/equity swap.

Voucher privatisation in its Czech form meant that all citizens were entitled to buy, for a nominal price, vouchers that entitled them to bid for shares in state-owned companies put on sale. Some specially selected companies were not available for voucher privatisation, most notably Skoda, which was acquired by Volkswagen; these were sold to foreign investors. As companies were gradually introduced to sale, the Czech government established investment funds, partly or fully owned by banks, which pooled people's vouchers. These investment funds were closed-end investment funds, so people could not move out of them once they entered. Applying this method, the Czech government could claim a rapid privatisation of the bulk of the state-owned enterprises (see also Chapter 10). Nevertheless, as most companies offered over 50 per cent of their share issue as vouchers, investment funds have often become the most important shareholders (Lastovicka and Mejstrik 1995). For this reason Dangerfield (1997) refers to this type of privatisation as 'pseudo-privatisation'.

Trade sale is a widely used method of privatisation in Western countries. In this, the state owner announces either an open or a closed tender and ranks the bidders according to set criteria. The bidder coming out at the top of the list has the right to purchase the company. The success of the privatisation in this case would depend on the interest of the potential bidders and the criteria set by the government. The first condition in the CEEC context meant attracting the interest of foreign investors. The second condition proved to lack transparency and was open to struggle within the ministries and power groups, as the governments lacked clear priorities to set criteria as to whether, beyond the offer price, such conditions as future investment, employment and market access should also be considered, and if so, how these could be enforced. As the Skoda case illustrates, even if such criteria are considered and set, the governments are often not in the position to force large multinationals, the most desirable buyers, to fulfil promises. Thus, in 1993, the Czech government had to accept Volkswagen's significantly downward revised investment and output plans, in spite of the fact that these plans were an integral part of the acquisition contract between the government and Volkswagen (Havas 1997; Myant 1997).

Governments of the CEEC and many Western advisers expected privatisation to be the remedy to most of the problems of transformation (Csaba 1995). However, the transfer of state assets to the private sector in the privatisation process is a legal action; thus ownership *per se* has only a legal meaning and says nothing about the operation, the management and the strategy of the company. As research on the Far East, continental Europe and other regions of the world has demonstrated, the Anglo-Saxon model of corporate governance, which describes the relationship between shareholders and senior managers, has a significantly different meaning in other business systems (Whitley 1991, 1992). Experiences in CEE also show that ownership is not sufficient for analysing the firm: the analysis has to go beyond the type of ownership to control.

An important initial distinction in terms of type of control can be made between 'insider' and 'outsider' control. Companies whose new owners have been unable and/or unwilling to take over control of strategic decisions and of the way strategies are implemented can be considered to be under 'insider control'. This also applies in cases where the managers have become the new owners (Brom and Orenstein 1994). In these firms, though exceptions exist, the controllers are more embedded in existing organisational, strategic and employment patterns than in firms under 'outsider' control; thus the pattern of changes can be expected to be different and triggered by factors other than the change of control or ownership. Additionally, we need to distinguish between types of outsider control. Most privately owned and controlled firms, especially those under foreign ownership and control, can be expected to pursue growth and profit goals. State-controlled firms, on the other hand, are likely to pursue more varied and contradictory objectives, as political pressures and connections fluctuate. Thus it can be expected that private controllers are more able to alter company development patterns systematically than state agencies. Finally, distinctions should be made between domestic privately controlled firms and foreign-controlled firms, since it is the latter that have more ready access to the financial means to implement changes in company development. A large body of research demonstrates that foreign owners, even if taking a minority or small majority stake in state-owned companies, acquire an effective managerial control (Havas 1997). It should also be noted that in an environment of high market and institutional uncertainties, the financial position of the company can be as important in determining and implementing strategy as ownership, and may also influence control, as it may be expected that owners of companies in financial trouble would exercise closer control.

Of the two major privatisation methods, voucher privatisation clearly favoured insider control. People exchanging vouchers for company shares were much too remote and fragmented to exercise any influence on the way the company was run. Moreover, under the privatisation law, managers were responsible for developing privatisation strategies, and until 1992 they were not even compelled to give information about their firms to other parties who might be interested in developing a competing privatisation plan (Kotrba 1995). Investment funds pooling vouchers and bidding for company shares acted as portfolio investors, and thus did not take control on strategic issues. However, as the dominant actors in these investment funds were the banks, the role of the portfolio investor was also compromised. Banks were not only owners of the companies through the investment funds, but also creditors of these companies; not to mention that until recently banks were state owned. Although this inter-locking situation is not unknown in other economies (e.g. East Germany, Germany), the Czech case was substantially different for two reasons. First, companies already carried large debts (and often had difficulties in servicing them), while they needed new funding for restructuring. Second, banks did not have the expertise and interest to take over managerial control, or at least close control of the management, of the company. It created a situation in which the management of the companies were the *de facto* controllers, with no means to implement the necessary restructuring, obstructed in carrying out restructuring both by their embeddedness in the existing coalitions of the companies and by their contradictory roles as managers and controllers (Whitley 1992).

As is mentioned above, the trade sale method favours foreign invest-ment, mainly strategic investment, although portfolio investment also started to grow around the middle of the 1990s. However, the expectations of a quick restructuring of acquired companies were not realised in this case either. Foreign companies entering the region in the early 1990s did so mainly to get access to the CMEA markets and exploit the advantages of the protected domestic markets in these countries. A second motive was tariff jumping. These motives, however, did not require large-scale company restructuring, only cutting waste and excess cost from the production organisation. With the collapse of the CMEA and trade between the former CMEA countries, and with the liberalisation of foreign trade, this strategy became obsolete. The foreign-owned companies were confined to domestic markets, often facing competition from imports; thus they were faced with the same options as other, non-foreign-owned, companies: that is, switching markets or capturing the domestic market. In order to be successful in this situation, the subsidiaries needed resources for upgrading their products, introducing new products and renewing their obsolete capital base. These, in turn, required an extensive shake-up of the management of the company: training for both management and the workforce, restructuring the production control and decision-making structures, and implementing quality assurance. Carrying out all these elements of corporate restructuring, finally, required reform of the organisational structure.

Foreign investors, therefore, had to commit further funding to the acquired companies. This funding, on the one hand, was subject to the investor's global corporate strategy and, on the other hand, required the ensuring of the efficient use of the additional resources. The latter requirement, because of the high market and institutional uncertainty and unfamiliarity with the environment, involved placing controllers from the foreign investor in the company and implementing regulations which would ensure the efficiency of control. Moreover, these regulations had to become part of corporate behaviour, which often meant conflicts between the culture of the country of origin of the investor and that of the host country, as well as conflicts between the corporate culture of the investor and the acquired company. As a result, except for green-field investment and for a number of investors who had a well-established integration strategy and had committed sufficient resources for implementing this strategy, the restructuring process, even in foreign-owned firms, proved to be long relative to the expectations of the host governments.[4]

FDI in CEE

Foreign ownership became dominant only in the Hungarian economy in CEE (EBRD 1997), as a result of the realisation of trade sale privatisation by the socialist–liberal coalition government. Foreign owners came to control a large proportion of industrial output and exports as well as utilities. In some countries anti-foreign investment sentiments increased significantly in the 1990s, most notably in the Czech Republic. This derived from the fact that there was no mechanism that would ensure the compatibility of the motives of foreign investors and those of the host governments, which eventually led to disappointment and misplaced hopes in the role of FDI in the region.

With foreign trade liberalisation, the attraction to foreign investors of exploiting the protected markets of the CEEC faded away, especially from around 1993, when the more coherently applied competition policy of governments stopped the questionable practice of selling private monopolies to foreign investors. Additionally, the collapse of the CMEA and the insolvency of companies in the former Soviet Union made it unfeasible for foreign investors to use their acquisitions in the CEEC as a springboard for investment towards the East. As these period-specific motives for investment in the region may be described as efficiency-seeking and strategic-asset-seeking investment strategies, the CEEC offered a number of opportunities to efficiency-seeking investors: a large supply of relatively cheap and skilled labour; cheaper sources of inputs from the former Soviet Union; its closeness to the EU's huge markets; and, for non-EU investors, the EAs between these countries and the EU. The most notable aspect of these EAs was the 'country of origin' rule, which allowed for combining the value of production in these countries so that goods could be exported to the EU market under the quota of one of these countries.

These objectives of the investors did not necessarily correspond to the expectations of the governments. Governments in the CEEC expected the upgrading of production facilities, increasing output and employment, and the transfer of knowledge and technique. These expectations were only partially realised. At the beginning of the 1990s many Western investors reduced output projections from their CEE subsidiaries (E.C. in the automotive industry: see Havas 1997), and as the domestic markets in these countries recovered at a relatively slow pace the upward projections remained modest. While foreign investment often resulted in an increased output in the acquired company, it also caused falling overall output, because existing suppliers were abandoned in favour of the first-tier suppliers of the investors (Czaban and Henderson 1998).

As these investments often aimed only at exploiting the cheap labour in the region, labour-intensive technologies and assembly factories have been developed, which do not contribute to an increase in the technological level of these countries. In extreme cases (Myant 1998), foreign investment actually reduced the engineering capacity of firms, through closure of up-stream production and research and development units and through digression into basic component manufacturing or assembly of supplied parts of components. Nevertheless, there are counter-examples (e.g. Audi's and General Electric's investment in Hungary), when, partly as a result of the change in the corporate strategy of the foreign investor, partly because of the changes in market conditions, foreign investors invested heavily in these units in the acquired firms.

These particular investment strategies are characteristic only of EU investors, as they do not have to meet local content regulations.[5] As opposed to this strategy, non-EU investors, once having committed funding to investment in the region, have to follow a different development path, including regional cooperation between subsidiaries (Daewoo) and technology transfer and close cooperation with domestic suppliers (Suzuki). However, the strategic (and high value-added) segments of production are rarely moved to the region even in these cases, in spite of the fact that in such a way the local content requirement could easily be met and in many countries the manufacturing capabilities are now present.

The obvious danger of the prevalence of these types of foreign investment in the region derives from the fact that real wages have increased in the region and wage differences, when accounting for productivity differences, are narrowing between the CEEC and the EU. Considering that the transfer of these production operations between locations is fast and easy, and that foreign companies have so far been the main driving force of the integration of the CEEC economies into the world economy, the risk exposure of these countries to short-term changes in competitive advantages and the business cycle of the world economy has become extremely high.

Strategic-asset-seeking strategies are not unknown in CEE, though they are confined mainly to primary industries, particularly in the former Soviet Union, formerly defence-related industries (laser technology), or highly specialised, niche market producers. In these cases the aim of the investment is acquiring these assets. While empirical evidence shows that in many cases the survival of these industries depended on foreign investment, the accusation that the CEE governments were 'selling off the family silver' was almost inevitable. This laid them open to accusations that the sale of these 'jewels' was not necessary for survival or further development, or that the price received for them was too low.[6]

It is only since 1990 that the authorities of the CEEC have started to accumulate experience with respect to the regulation of these strategic asset investments. Regulation is focused on preventing the transfer of the strategic asset (e.g. research and development) from the country; the acquisition of a monopoly position on the basis of the strategic asset; and the winding up of the operation in order to abolish competition in the domestic and third markets.

The consolidation of the transformation process

By 1994–95, the decline of GDP ceased in the CEEC and some economic growth had been registered. Although the growth rates in the second half of the 1990s are higher than in the advanced countries, they are lower than in the newly industrialised countries, even if the crisis of 1997 is accounted for, and still need to make up the decline of the first half of the 1990s.

Parallel with these changes, the institutions established in the earlier phase of the transition have been consolidated, and their operation has become more routine and predictable. With this the trust in formal procedures and authorities has increased. Although the CEEC are undeniably at different stages of these developments, the tendency in all of these countries, partly because of the technical assistance and expectations of the international organisations, is to point to larger autonomy of the bureaucracy from politics and, as the privatisation process approaches its end, the autonomy of the economy from bureaucracy. The country studies of *Agenda 2000* clearly illustrate these differences (see also Chapter 2 and Part II case studies).

The calmer and more predictable business environment appears to be a greater attraction to foreign investment, as statistics on FDI flows demonstrate. In this environment corporate restructuring appears to take a shorter time, especially in foreign-owned companies. Table 3.2 shows FDI inflows for the period 1994–97.

Table 3.2 FDI (net inflows recorded in the balance of payments, $m)

Country	1994	1995	1996	1997 (projection)	Cumulative FDI inflows, 1989–97	FDI inflows as % of GDP, 1997
Czech Republic	105	82	100	575	1000	5.6
Estonia	212	199	111	131	809	2.8
Hungary	1097	4453	1986	2100	15403	4.7
Latvia	155	244	379	415	1287	7.6
Lithuania	31	72	152	327	612	3.6
Poland	542	1134	2741	3044	8442	2.3
Romania	347	404	415	998	2389	2.9
Slovakia	203	183	177	150	912	0.8
Slovenia	128	176	186	321	1074	1.8

Source: EBRD (1998).

Nevertheless the CEEC are faced with further tasks and objectives. Apart from the larger exposure to risks discussed in the previous section, their preparation for joining the EU and restructuring in the micro-sphere require further policy measures and resources. All of these countries face objections by various EU member states, either because of some of their competitive sectors (e.g. agriculture and food processing), or because they would constitute the poorest economies of the Union and thus would be entitled to a larger slice of the structural funds under the current rules. Some of the regulations (e.g. taxation in Poland, banking in the Czech Republic) do not satisfy some of the criteria expected by international organisations.

Agenda 2000 embodies a very large number of extremely detailed and demanding obligations (see Appendix 2). Some of these require the strengthening and adjustment of public institutions; for instance, regarding the regulation of product standards of competition. Others will have strong implications particularly for infrastructure enterprises and financial institutions. For example, in infrastructure there will be emphasis on integrating transport and communication systems to ensure the smooth functioning of the internal market. For enterprises, EU rules for health and safety in the workplace and environmental standards will be of particular significance, with major implications for restructuring and investment. Financial institutions will be expected to perform to higher standards of financial strength and transparency than at present.

How far is transition relevant?

A key stage in the development of a framework for relations between the EU and Eastern Europe was the declaration of accession criteria by the European Council at the Copenhagen Summit in June 1993 (see Chapter 2). A crucial criterion was that of the existence of a functioning market economy and the capacity to cope with competitive pressure within the Union. Since the very basis of the EU is the internal market, it is incumbent on member states to make the existence of this market possible. This is inextricably connected both economically and politically with the existence of a market economy and a national economy strong enough to meet Community-wide competition. The issue of enlargement of the EU is a fundamental part of the process of economic transition for the region and is of vital historical significance both for those countries seeking accession and for those who are already members. Unfortunately, the various dimensions of economic transition discussed above do not translate into a ready set of indicators to assess progress. Indicators such as inflation, unemployment and the size of the state deficit provide some idea of the progress of stabilisation, but it is extremely difficult to quantify the structural changes under way. Following the introduction of radical economic programmes during 1990 and 1991, the economies of Central Europe experienced a deep 'transformational recession', a recession that turned out to be much deeper than expected. The cumulative contraction of the Central European economies between 1989 and 1992 has been estimated at about 30 per cent. However, the next few years saw a number of positive developments, in particular the re-emergence of economic growth in the region as a whole. The turnaround in GDP in the region is an important signal and a reflection of the progress made with structural reforms. Table 3.3 shows aggregate growth in the CEEC 10.

Table 3.3 Growth in real GDP in the CEEC 10

Country	Percentage change							Estimated level of real GDP, 1997	Projected level of real GDP, 1998
	1992	1993	1994	1995	1996	1997	1998		
Bulgaria	−7.3	−1.5	1.8	2.1	−10.9	−7.4	2.5	63	64
Czech Republic	−3.3	0.6	3.2	6.4	3.9	1.0	2.0	98	100
Estonia	−14.2	−8.5	−1.8	4.3	4.0	10.0	5.5	78	82
Hungary	−3.1	−0.6	2.9	1.5	1.3	4.3	4.5	90	94
Latvia	−34.9	−14.9	0.6	−0.8	2.8	6.0	6.0	56	59
Lithuania	−37.7	−12.1	−11.3	2.3	5.1	5.7	5.5	43	45
Poland	2.6	3.8	5.2	7.0	6.1	6.9	5.5	112	118
Romania	−8.7	1.5	3.9	7.1	4.1	−6.6	−2.0	82	81
Slovakia	−6.5	−3.7	4.9	6.8	6.9	6.5	3.5	96	99
Slovenia	−5.5	2.8	5.3	4.1	3.1	3.3	3.8	98	102

Note: 1989 = 100.
Source: EBRD (1997).

Table 3.4 shows that inflation performance in the region has continued to improve. However, as in the case of GDP growth, there have been some reversals in individual countries and all have some way to go before achieving levels of inflation comparable with the EU average of 1.8 per cent.

Table 3.4 Inflation in the CEEC 10 (% change in year-end retail/consumer price level)

Country	1992	1993	1994	1995	1996	1997 (estimate)	1998 (projection)
Bulgaria	79.4	63.8	121.9	32.9	310.8	578.6	17.0
Czech Republic	12.7	18.2	9.7	7.9	8.6	10.0	11.5
Estonia	953.5	35.6	42.0	29.0	15.0	12.0	11.0
Hungary	21.6	21.1	21.2	28.3	19.8	18.4	14.0
Latvia	959.0	35.0	26.0	23.0	13.1	2.0	5.0
Lithuania	1161.1	188.8	45.0	35.5	13.1	8.5	6.8
Poland	44.3	37.6	29.4	21.6	18.5	13.2	10.0
Romania	199.2	295.5	61.7	27.8	56.9	151.6	47.0
Slovakia	9.1	25.1	11.7	7.2	5.4	6.4	7.0
Slovenia	92.9	22.9	18.3	8.6	8.8	9.4	8.0

Source: EBRD (1997).

With the exception of Estonia and Latvia, all countries in the region are running fiscal deficits (government expenditure in excess of revenue). In fact transitory fiscal deficits seem to have become a characteristic of the transition process. Fiscal reforms, including the reorganisation of public expenditure, the reform of pensions and the creation of an efficient and market-oriented civil service, are widely seen as crucial if investor confidence is to be retained. Any delays in such reforms will continue to be an important source of instability and are likely to cause very high real interest rates in a number of countries. The incompleteness of fiscal reform will continue to place a heavy reliance on monetary policy for the purposes of macro-economic stabilisation.

Having said that, it is probably fair to say that monetary policies have led the way in restoring macro-economic stability, albeit with, at times, extraordinarily high real rates of interest. *Agenda 2000* stipulates that to secure macro-economic performance, fiscal positions must be put on a sound long-term basis. In many countries there are still difficult adjustments to be made on both the revenue and expenditure sides. As a broad generalisation it can be said that in the western part of the region the challenges will be particularly severe in controlling expenditure, and in the rest in raising revenue. These macro-economic issues cannot be separated from the general process of reforms. As elsewhere in the transition, improving policy on the fiscal front requires attention not only to building institutions, but also to promoting and enforcing responsible behaviour both inside and outside government. Indeed, *Agenda 2000* argues that applicant countries' administrative and judicial capacity is of crucial importance for the adoption, implementation and enforcement of the *acquis* and for the efficient use of financial support.

Turning to the progress in market-oriented transition, Table 3.5 shows that the private sector is now in excess of half of the economy in all of the CEEC 10. It should be noted that even in countries where the private sector is of the order of two-thirds or more, the figures need to be interpreted with caution. For example, in Poland the private sector was always dominant in agriculture and that might give an inflated view of the progress of privatisation. The figure of 75 per cent for the Czech Republic includes many enterprises in which the state, through the National Property Fund, continues to hold a minority share. However, it is certainly true that many countries joined the EU with levels of public sector involvement in the economy close to those in the most advanced transition countries now (Rollo 1997).

Another consideration, though not strictly related to market-oriented transition, is the level of income per head. Table 3.5 also shows GDP per head at purchasing power parities in 1996. The figures suggest that Slovenia and the Czech Republic were at 86 per cent of the 1996 Greek level, Slovakia was approaching three-quarters of that level, Hungary and

Table 3.5 The market and income per head in CEE

Country	Private sector value added as % of GDP, 1996	GDP per capita at PPP,[b] 1996
Bulgaria	46(50)[a]	4230
Czech Republic	75	9770
Estonia	67	4431
Hungary	73(78)[a]	6410
Latvia	55	3484
Lithuania	68	4766
Poland	65	5400
Romania	55	4591
Slovakia	71(77)[a]	7970
Slovenia	55	10594

Notes: [a] Official estimates for 1997.
[b] PPP = purchasing power parity. The country's nominal GDP per capita in local currency is divided by the PPP, defined as the number of units of the country's currency required to buy the same amount of goods and services in the domestic market as $1 would buy in the USA.
Source: EBRD (1997).

Poland around a half and the rest more than a third. Undoubtedly, these numbers will change. However, it is estimated that countries such as Poland, currently growing at around 6 or 7 per cent a year, could catch up in twenty years and be enjoying an income per head comparable with that of the UK today (see Rollo and Stern 1992). It can of course be argued that relative income is not by itself a criterion for membership of the EU. After all, none of Spain, Portugal, Greece or Ireland would have qualified for membership in the 1970s and 1980s if that had been the case. In fact, modern work points to trade integration and the compatibility of economic systems as more relevant criteria. This brings us back to the transition issue.

On trade integration the picture is promising. The EU is far and away the main trading partner of the countries of CEE. In the aftermath of the demise of the CMEA, all of the CEEC quickly reoriented their trade flows towards the EU. In a very short space of time, the EU became the CEEC' main trading partner, replacing trade with their former partners in CMEA. From 1989 to 1995, the EU's share in the external trade of the Visegrad Four, Bulgaria and Romania nearly doubled and in 1998 accounted for 63 per cent of exports and 60 per cent of imports, making the EU by far their main trading partner. In the early years of transition it was possible to argue that the trade shares simply reflected the collapse of sales in the East. However, these high trade shares have been sustained, particularly in the Visegrad Four, and it looks as if the process of trade integration with the EU is firmly in place. Table 3.6, which relates to 1995, indicates the role of different partners in the external trade of the CEEC 10 from 1989 to 1995.

Table 3.6 The role of different partners in the external trade of the CEEC 10, 1989–95 (%)

Country	Exports		Imports	
	1989	1995	1989	1995
EU	35	63	36	60
USA	2	2	2	3
Japan	1	1	1	1
Ex-CMEA	47	23	48	24
Rest of world	15	11	13	12

Source: IMF (1997).

It is worth noting that there have been several examples of regional cooperation among the CEEC, one of which is the Central European Free Trade Area (CEFTA). After the dissolution of the CMEA in the summer of 1991 and the collapse of regional trade at the beginning of the 1990s, 1994 was the first year in which trade between the CEEC recovered at all strongly. This trend has continued since, especially among the CEFTA countries. However, the weight of intra-group trade in total CEE trade remains relatively small. For example, in 1997 exports by CEFTA countries to other CEFTA countries varied between 5 per cent of total exports for Poland and Slovenia to 8 per cent for the Czech Republic and Slovakia. In addition, institutional cooperation within CEFTA is weak. Each country appears to believe that it can obtain EU membership faster on an individual rather than collective basis. Indeed, it would appear that a more significant level of regional economic and trade cooperation among CEEC will be the result of successful integration into the global economy, and primarily of joining the EU, and not vice versa (Kawecka-Wyrzkowska 1996).

We move finally to the criterion of the compatibility of economic systems, in particular to the question of regulatory integration. The European Commission's White Paper of May 1995 (European Commission 1995) aimed at preparing the associated countries of CEE for integration into the internal market through the implementation of a detailed programme of law approximation. The underlying intentions of the White Paper are clear. In aligning their internal legislation with the EU rules in such a crucial field as the internal market, the associated countries will reinforce the competitiveness of their economies and allow the expansion of business. They will also be better able to meet the Copenhagen criteria regarding accession, particularly the requirement of the existence of a functioning market economy and the capacity to cope with competitive pressures. The CEEC 10 are to a greater or lesser extent putting into their legislation the list of EU directives. The question of implementation is difficult to monitor. Effective competition policy is clearly important in reassuring the existing members of the EU that the transition states are resolutely committed to reform (see Fingleton *et al.* 1996 for a discussion of implementation).

Progress in competition policy in the CEEC 10 has been driven primarily by the incentives of harmonisation with EU policies. Legislation has been enacted and new institutions created such that the legislative framework is now compatible with EU standards in most of these countries, with the exception of Bulgaria. There have been clear indications of active enforcement of competition legislation in the Czech Republic, Hungary, Poland, Slovenia and the Baltic States. These range over case reviews, recommendations and fines, although significant actions to reduce the abuse of significant market power have still been limited. This is particularly true in the case of the natural monopolies. It should be noted that for smaller countries such as the Baltic States, external trade acts as a major competitive force in the economy. In all countries liberal regimes towards foreign trade and foreign investment assure some competitive pressure on most domestic companies. The Estonian trade regime, for example, is very liberal – all tariff and non-tariff barriers to imports and exports, including those on imported agricultural and food products, were abolished in the early reform years.

Another consideration, particularly in the light of high-profile banking crises in several transition economies in the period 1995–98, is the need for improvements in the regulatory structure. After an initial period of rapid and virtually unregulated expansion, a widespread recognition has emerged among countries at all stages of transition of the need to consolidate and strengthen the banking sector. Most countries have initiated a programme of bank restructuring. In addition, progress has been made in enhancing the supervisory capacities of central banks, tightening prudential regulations, and increasing capital requirements to prevent the re-emergence of systemic problems in the banking sector. Notwithstanding the recent progress, the banking system in most of the transition economies remains fundamentally underdeveloped. However, there are also some more positive indicators. Poland, Hungary and the Czech Republic are OECD members. The Visegrad Four together with Romania and Slovenia are members of the World Trade Organisation (WTO). These provide some guarantees about rules and practices which should apply in trade relations, and remedies where they are not applied. Table 3.7 summarises progress to date in transition in the CEEC.

Conclusion

Many of the legacies of state socialism still survive in the CEEC, in the form of industrial structure, managerial and employee behaviour, and the

Table 3.7 Progress in transition in the CEEC 10

Countries' private sector share in GDP (%) mid-1997		Enterprises			Markets and Trade			Financial Institutions	
		Large-scale privatisation	Small-scale privatisation	Enterprise restructuring	Price liberalisation	Trade and foreign exchange	Competition policy	Banking reforms	Security markets
Bulgaria	50	3[a]	3	2	3	4	2	3	2
Czech Republic	75	4	4*[b]	3	3	4*	3	3	2
Estonia	70	4	4*	3	3	4	3	3	3
Hungary	75	4	4*	3	3	4*	3	4	3
Latvia	60	3	4	3	3	4	3	3	2
Lithuania	70	3	4	3	3	4	2	3	2
Poland	65	3	4*	3	3	4*	3	3	3
Romania	60	3	3	2	3	4	2	3	2
Slovakia	75	4	4*	3	3	4*	3	3	2
Slovenia	50	3	4*	3	3	4*	2	3	3

Notes:
[a] The scoring runs from 1 for least advanced or little progress, through 4 for comprehensive or advanced reform, to 4* for the standard of advanced industrial economies.
[b] Most advanced industrial economies would qualify for the 4* rating for about all of the transition indicators.
Source: EBRD (1997).

strategic behaviour of firms (such as narrow product lines, little attention to customisation and little diversification). Market pressures have eliminated companies rather than forcing them to move to new product lines or diversify, partly as a result of companies' lacking the resources to do so. In the case of companies acquired by foreign firms, the fact that most of these were acquired because of the products they produced, and for their markets, encouraged the maintenance of the existing product lines even though upgrades or new products within the product lines have been introduced.

Although changes at the level of firms are much less than at macrolevel, and these are evolutionary rather than revolutionary, in some countries the accumulation of changes – institutional changes, the operation of new institutions, the more competitive business environment, the spread of Western management techniques and foreign investment – has started to challenge the deep structural legacies of state socialism. Nevertheless, many of these factors also contribute to maintaining the legacies of the past. The relatively small size of domestic markets in CEE is favourable to monopolies. The lack of resources to introduce high-quality products and the relatively low production cost are favourable for producing standardised products in large batches. The capital-intensive nature of these production systems and the relatively large size of the dominant companies result in incremental changes over a relatively long period. Business success in these conditions largely depends on the volume of output, which, in turn, encourages the competition for market share in mass product markets. As a result, these companies must compete in prices and thus have to cut cost. However, the cuts in cost in the early 1990s were a one-off exercise, and with increasing labour costs throughout the region, companies are being forced to abandon this strategy, while the means of developing or implementing new strategies are often scarce.

Manager-controlled companies, lacking the access to additional capital on acceptable terms, seek niche market products, although this is partly a consequence of their size. The long-term success of this strategy will depend on the value-added on these products as well as the flexibility of the companies (moving in and out of the markets). An alternative to this strategy has emerged in those countries where large multinationals invested in production facilities and where the large-company sector is non-integrated vertically. The strategy is to become suppliers to large multinational or domestic companies. The survival of these smaller companies will then depend on the performance of the large companies and the strategies of the multinationals.

Eastern European countries still lack a domestic agent for the current industrial transformation. Neither of the classic historical agents – indigenous industrial capitalists and/or an able state organisation – has as yet emerged in the region. Consequently the crucial factor in the redesigning of the economy may well have to be foreign investment (Czaban 1998; Henderson 1998).

Thus various controllers are likely to develop different paths for restructuring company organisation and product lines and will manage the restructured companies in different ways, depending on their power to develop such strategies, the level of their control, their size, technology (capital intensity), available resources and market position. Within these various development paths and management methods certain dominant forms will undoubtedly develop, namely the forms characteristic to those companies that dominate the market – those effectively owned by foreign firms.

We have noted that growth is returning in the region as the transition enters a new phase. There is, however, great diversity. While some of the more advanced CEEC such as the Czech Republic and Hungary are already in the second phase, a few are still enmeshed in the problems of the first. Most countries of the region are already market economies to a greater or lesser degree. New institutions are being built, the legitimacy of the new regimes has been reinforced and, partly as a consequence, foreign investment has reached a 'critical mass'; the most important elements of the capitalist economy have become rooted in CEE. In this context it is worth reflecting that 'joining Europe' is simply a synonym for establishing a market economy that is an organic part of the global and of the European economy. The typical EU reminder that enlargement will be a protracted affair is at odds with its emphasis on the CEEC' need for swift transition to market economies. Joining Europe, as seen from the CEEC, is not just a question of joining a dynamic form of regional integration – the EU – instead of the defunct CMEA, but one of integration into the international economy after forty years of involuntary seclusion. For these countries, Europe is not so much a geographical area distinct from America or Asia as one of the key centres of a global economic system previously closed to them by the CMEA structure. Their aim is to join the world economy, and for clear geographical reasons they must become part of the EU regional integration to do so.

Notes

1 For a review of 'shock therapy' versus 'gradual change' in the CEEC, see Koves (1992).
2 The equity/debt ratio is the ratio between the risk-bearing ordinary shares of limited companies and the fixed interest-bearing securities, such as debentures, which are normally secured on the firms' fixed assets.
3 In order to sell, a value needs to be assigned to the firm. Improved accounting methods are a necessary, but far from sufficient, condition for this, as the value of a firm is the discounted value of its expected future profit stream. The valu-

ation of firms in transition economies is considerably more complex than in mature market economies, as their future viability and performance are hard to assess in a highly unsettled environment.

4 'Industrial restructuring' refers to the difficult and prolonged tasks of structural reform that are needed to improve enterprise efficiency. Improvements rest on being able to improve hard budget constraints on enterprises: reducing subsidies, limiting the extent of tax arrears and tax evasion, bringing about rational credit allocation by banks, and controlling inter-enterprise credit and inter-enterprise arrears. Clearly industrial restructuring is a much more complex task than liberalisation.

5 EU investors can simply develop assembly factories utilising components produced in the home country rather than locally supplied products. Non-EU investors must meet regulations concerning the percentage of locally supplied content.

6 Selling prices are not only difficult to establish but also the cause of domestic political warfare. It is policies with regard to the pace of privatisation that inspire protests against the 'selling out' of state property. A significant portion of the national wealth cannot be sold in a very short period of time at reasonable prices. FDI is in the initial stages of rapid development, but the absolute numbers of Western investors willing to bid for large state-owned enterprises remain small. According to data published by the United Nations, 88 per cent of the 10,700 joint ventures existing in the CEEC 5 in December 1990 were established in the single year of 1990 (see Koves (1992)).

References

Aslund, A. (1994), Lessons of the first four years of systemic change in Eastern Europe, *Journal of Comparative Economics*, 19:1, 17–31.

Batt, J. (1991), *East Central Europe from Reform to Transformation*, Pinter, Royal Institute of International Affairs.

Berend, I. (1990), *The Hungarian Economic Reforms 1953–1988*, Cambridge, Cambridge University Press.

Bonin, J. and Szekely, I. (1994), *The Development and Reform of Financial Systems in Central and Eastern Europe*, Aldershot, Edward Elgar.

Brom, K. and Orenstein, M. (1994), The privatised sector in the Czech Republic: government and bank control in a transitional economy, *Europe–Asia Studies*, 46:6, 893–928.

Clague, C. (1992), The journey to a market economy, in C. Clague and G. Rausser (eds), *The Emergence of Market Economies in Eastern Europe*, Cambridge MA, Blackwell, 2–15.

Csaba, L. (ed.) (1995), *The Capitalist Revolution in Eastern Europe – A Contribution to the Economic Theory of Systemic Change*, Aldershot, Edward Elgar.

Czaban, L. (1998), Ideologies, economic policies and social change: the cyclical nature of Hungary's transformation, in J. Henderson (ed.), *Industrial Transformation in Eastern Europe in the Light of the East Asian Experience*, London, Macmillan, 224–44.

Czaban, L. and Henderson, J. (1998), Global commodity chains and economic transformation in Eastern Europe: problematic issues from the Hungarian experience, paper presented at the International Institute of Labour Studies – ILO Workshop on Global Production and Local Jobs, Geneva, March.

Dangerfield, M. (1997), The business culture in the Czech Republic, in M. Bateman (ed.), *Business Cultures in Central and Eastern Europe*, Oxford, Butterworth-Heinemann, 1–34.

EBRD (1997), *Transition Report Update*, London, European Bank for Reconstruction and Development.

EBRD (1998), *Transition Report Update*, London, European Bank for Reconstruction and Development.

European Commission (1995), White Paper, 163 final, Brussels, European Commission.

Fingleton, J., Fox, E., Nevin, D. and Seabright, P. (1996), *Competition Policy and the Transformation of Central Europe*, London, CEPR.

Friedman, M. (1977), Nobel lecture: inflation and unemployment, *Journal of Political Economy*, 3, 451–72.

Gomulka, S. (1994), Economic and political constraints during transition, *Journal of Comparative Economics*, 19:2, 84–106.

Gowen, P. (1995), Neo-liberal theory and practice for Eastern Europe, *New Left Review*, 213, 3–60.

Grancelli, B. (1995), Organizational change: towards a new east–west comparison, *Organization Studies*, 16, 1–26.

Havas, A. (1997), Foreign direct investment and intra-industry trade: the case of the automotive industry in Central Europe, in D. A. Dyker (ed.), *The Technology of Transition: Science and Technology Policies for Transition Countries*, Budapest, Central European University Press, 211–40.

Henderson, J. (1998), On appropriate models for transformation in Eastern Europe, in J. Henderson (ed.), *Industrial Transformation in Eastern Europe in the Light of the East Asian Experience*, London, Macmillan, 3–25.

Hitchens, D. W. M. N., Birnie, J. E., Hamar, J., Wagner, K. and Zemplinerova, A. (1995), *Competitiveness of Industry in the Czech Republic and Hungary*, Aldershot, Avebury.

IMF (1997), *International Financial Statistics Yearbook*, Washington, DC, IMF.

Jackson, M. (1992), Constraints on systemic transition and their policy implications, *Oxford Review of Economic Policy*, 7:4, 16–26.

Kaser, M. and Allsopp, A. (1993), The assessment: macroeconomic transition in Eastern Europe 1989–91, *Oxford Review of Economic Policy*, 8:1, 1–14.

Kawecka-Wyrzykowska, E. (1996), On the benefits of the accession for Western and Eastern Europe, in L. Ambrus-Lakatos and M. E. Schaffer (eds), *Coming to Terms with Accession*, Warsaw, Institute for East–West Studies.

Kornai, J. (1986), The soft budget constraint, *Kyklos*, 39, 3–30.

Kotrba, J. (1995), Privatisation process in the Czech Republic: players and winners, in J. Svejnar (ed.), *The Czech Republic and Economic Transformation in Eastern Europe*, San Diego, Academic Press, 112–46.

Koves, A. (1992), *Central and East European Economies in Transition*, Boulder, Westview.

Lastovicka, A. and Mejstrik, M. (1995), Corporate governance and share prices in voucher privatised companies, in J. Svenjar (ed.), *The Czech Republic and Economic Transition in Eastern Europe*, London, Academic Press, 199–209.

Matropasqua, C. and Roli, V. (1994), Industrial countries protectionism with respect to Eastern Europe: the impact of the Association Agreements concluded with the EC on the exports of Poland, Czechoslovakia and Hungary, *World Economy*, 17:2, 151–71.

Myant, M. (1997), Foreign direct investment and industrial restructuring in the Czech Republic, paper presented at the Workshop on Central and Eastern Europe: Institutional change and industrial development, Tannishus, Denmark, November.

Revesz, G. (1990), *Perestroika in Eastern Europe: Hungary's Economic Transformation 1945–1988*, Boulder, Westview.

Rollo, J. (1997), Economic aspects of EU enlargement to the East, in M. Marescau (ed.), *Enlarging the European Union*, London, Longman, 252–75.

Rollo, J. and Stern, J. (1992), Growth and trade prospects for Central and Eastern Europe, *World Economy*, September, 645–69.

Rybczynski, T. (1991), The sequencing of reform, *Oxford Review of Economic Policy*, 7:4, 26–34.

Sachs, J. (1992), The economic transformation of Eastern Europe: the case of Poland, *Economics of Planning*, 25:1, 5–19.

Sachs, J. (1994), Life in the emergency room, in J. Williamson (ed.), *The Political Economy of Policy Reform*, Washington, DC, Institute for International Economics, 203–23.

Scott, N. (1992), The implications of the transition for foreign trade and investment, *Oxford Review of Economic Policy*, 8:1, 44–57.

Szalai, E. (1991), Integration of special interests in the Hungarian economy: the struggle between large companies and the party and state bureaucracy, *Journal of Comparative Economics*, 15, 284–303.

Tatur, M. (1995), Towards corporatism? The transformation of interest policy and interest regulation in Eastern Europe, in E. Dittrich, G. Schmidt and R. Whitley (eds), *Industrial Transformation in Europe*, London, Sage, 163–84.

Taylor, P. (1991), The market meets its match: lessons for the future from the transition's initial years, *Journal of Comparative Economics*, 19:1.

Vojnic, D. (1993), Some issues on macro-economic stabilisation policy in the economies in transition, in L. Somogyi (ed.), *The Political Economy of the Transition Process in Eastern Europe*, Aldershot, Edward Elgar, 227–39.

Whitley, R. (1991), *Business Systems in East Asia*, London, Sage.

Whitley, R. (1992), Societies, firms and markets: the social structuring of business systems, in R. Whitley (ed.), *European Business Systems*, London, Sage.

Whitley, R. and Czaban, L. (1998), Institutional change and enterprise transformation in an emergent capitalist economy: the case of Hungary, *Organisation Studies*, 18, 259–80.

4 Mike Mannin

Democratic governance in CEE: the conditions for change

> Please accept my resignation. I do not want to belong to any club that will accept me as a member. (Groucho Marx, 1932)

While the EU is not the only club in town, in practice its rules of membership make it the most exclusive and, once admitted, the costs of membership, like those of Lloyd's, are high, with no guarantee of a satisfactory return on initial investment. Modifications to the Treaty of Rome through to Amsterdam in 1997 have produced a complex 'European model' (Hettne 1995) that has led to a re-evaluation of what role democratic government should play in relation to the overlapping and competing local, regional and national values, structures and processes within the EU. So what signals are necessary to ensure internal adherence to EU club rules, and what barriers are necessary to maintain the high standards of club membership?

Membership of the EU confers, in a permanent manner, political choices and economic and social opportunities that are interdependent, given the conceptual connectivity assumed within the ideals and application of liberal democracy (Held 1995). Thus we shall argue that democratic conditions for EU membership go far beyond a simple formal definition, and are connected to specific aims of economic and social well-being to sustain the cohesion of the Union – in effect, European 'good governance'. More recently, the Copenhagen criteria as applied in *Agenda 2000* ensure that the range of *acquis* now considered appropriate to EU–CEEC membership concern issues of governance far deeper in their implications than those of the late 1970s. Democratic practice, it seems, now extends not just to public processes, but includes socio-economic activity in its broader reaches.

This chapter seeks to outline the involvement of the EU in the democratisation of CEE, the significance that such transformation has for the enlargement prospects of the Association countries, and the wider implications that democratisation brings for societal progress and security in

Europe. The first section places the events of 1989 in the broader context of globalisation and liberalisation, and introduces briefly some of the conceptual conundrums associated with the term 'democracy' itself.

The global environment of democratisation

'The surge of democratic governments starting in 1974 and continuing through the early 1990's is probably *the* political sign of our time' (Munck 1994). In the period 1974–94, according to one evaluation, the number of political systems designated as 'democratic' increased from 44 to 107 (Shin 1994); the fall of the Berlin Wall exacerbated this trend. As we suggest in Chapter 1, a major agent for change was the impact of global forces on markets and capital movements, resulting in pressures to liberalise trading relations and reduce the role of government in domestic market activity. By 1989 this had already affected Western markets, but also CEE economies encouraged by Gorbachev's reformist Soviet admin- istration. The reduction of Soviet involvement in the economic and political affairs of many Second and Third World states and the corre- sponding reactions of the USA and its allies resulted in a marked challenge to political and economic orthodoxies of Cold War stand-off between communism and capitalism (Fukuyama 1989). This, together with the questioning of Keynesian-style economic management in established Western political systems, also in part a result of global pressures, led to a re-evaluation of the role of government, as the notion of the state and the concepts of democracy and liberalism were examined in the light of this post-Cold War environment. Correspondingly, there emerged a search for valid theoretical perspectives on the process of democratisation (Held 1993; Shin 1994; Remmer 1995; Munck and Leff 1997; Pridham 1997). These new, or in several cases revisited, perspectives included a series of premises about this 'third wave' of democratisation (Huntington 1991).

First, and significantly for our evaluation of CEEC democratisation, there was a recognition of the interrelationship between the democratisa- tion process and international involvement. As Huntington and others point out, the study of democracy has in previous periods concentrated on state-centric explanations of its emergence and survival, often associated with the concept of modernisation and assumptions regarding societal development. While the latter still has a significant part to play in analy- sis, the current wave of democratisation has been propelled by a confluence of domestic and international factors, 'with international factors playing the more influential role in Eastern Europe' (Shin 1994:153). Such exogenous forces as sanctions, aid based on conditional- ity, achievement of internationally stipulated political and economic standards, and direct intervention either of a civil or military character, have helped shape the nature and the pace of democratisation in such new democracies as South Africa, Sierra Leone, Slovenia, Benin and Bulgaria. We can also point to the 'demonstration effect' of transition, reinforced by the greater opportunity for global communication that has emerged in recent years (Schmitter and Karl 1992). It is in the context of the globalisation of ideas that we may explore a second parameter of 'third-wave' democracy – the dominant global model – liberal democracy.

Globalisation, liberalism and democratisation

The potential for the dissemination of ideas on a global stage has been intensified in recent years by enhanced global communications networks. This is not to deny that ideas were not previously exportable, but merely to point to technology that has allowed, in very recent times, not only a significant intensification of a global connectedness but also a *consciousness of that connectedness* not previously apparent in international discourse (Bretherton 1996:11). The gradual withering of one set of global values – communism – and the upsurge of ideas associated with global capitalism served only to heighten the ubiquity of values such as the market, choice, liberalism, individualism and freedom, and the democratic paradigm within which such values can flourish. We have already mentioned the problems of Western state economic management and the recourse during the 1980s to neoliberal solutions. In effect this global 'big idea' was, prior to 1989, already part of Western intellectual and political discourse on the nature of democratisation and governance in the late twentieth century. Thus Fukuyama's 'end of history' thesis contained assumptions about political and economic adaptation that were already being applied in several Western states; these were to emerge as prescriptions for governance in the new political economies of both the Third and Second World during the 1990s (Gills and Rocamora 1992; Leftwich 1993).

The consequences for the character of democracy in this third wave, and thus the conceptual parameters within which transforming governments operated, are significant. We may initially observe that in any debate about democracy, while the term may have universal currency, the problem emerges when establishing a common value for its particular characteristics. We will therefore distinguish between *idealist* conceptions of democracy expressed in terms of goals – equality, freedom, justice, happiness; *procedural* definitions usually associated with process – individual control and access to decision making; citizen rights and responsibilities; and institutional procedures and powers. The former may be evaluated in terms of universal ideals or relative moral judgements –

the latter through the prism of law, agreed regulations and working rules. However, while we may accept they are sides to the same coin (Beetham 1993), there is inevitably a tension between the application of democratic ideals and democratic procedures which reflects in the prioritisation of their characteristics by governments. Thus the struggle between the achievements of individual liberties and social equality, or plural intervention and 'effective' leadership, remains an old and enduring debate around which 'models' of democracy are defined and argued (Held 1995).

Without wishing to enter more of that debate than is necessary, the factors mentioned above which have led to the pre-eminence of neoliberal values and their global dissemination lead inevitably to the emergence of a dominant model of democracy within which both idealist and procedural characteristics are judged – liberal democracy – 'with its stress on individual freedoms, on limited state activity especially in the economy and the representation of interests via elected public forums and group participation – a democracy founded on individualism' as a predominant value (Mannin 1996: 223). Thus more recent empirical research on democracy, following global trends, has stressed 'a procedural or minimalist conception of democracy over a substantive or maximalist conception embracing economic equality or social justice; that procedural conception has gained more acceptance even amongst mass publics' (Shin 1994:142).[1]

At this point there is a need to distinguish our terms: here, *democratisation* is used to describe a general political process; the term *democratic transition* may be perceived as the period from the demise of an authoritarian regime and the establishment of new political processes and elite leadership, within formal constitutionally established institutions. *Democratic transformation* involves the routinisation of elite behaviour within those rules and practices and the inevitable destruction of previous processes and machinery not compatible with democratic values (Przeworski 1991). *Democratic consolidation* involves the permeation of democratic practices and its internalisation by the populace through the emergence of a civil society. Each of these stages involves both symbolic and substantive demonstrations of support by both domestic *and* international actors.

If the 'third wave' has brought with it a reprioritisation of the characteristics *of liberal democracy*, and recognition of international involvement in that prioritisation, a third premise struggles uncomfortably from these factors – that the transformation of, in our case Communist regimes, to stable liberal democracies must be achieved through a *dual transformation* – of both political and economic systems – in parallel and potentially in conflict (Encarnación 1996). The problem is particularly acute in post-Communist transformations, given the previously high level of state intervention experienced by generations of CEE citizens; the

legacy of industrial but unmodern economic systems; the inefficient agricultural sectors within a traditional rural society; the rigid, channelled
character of formal participation within stifling authoritarian governmental regimes and therefore the uncertain character of an emerging civil
society – these and other shadows of communism are the background to
the hopes of the market, democratic freedoms and representative and
responsible politics thrust across this entrenched and unhappy environment.[2]

The academic debate relating to dual transformation includes, therefore, not just the examination of stages of democratic and economic
development, definition and measurement (Vanhanen 1997; O'Donnell
and Schmitter 1986; Freedom House 1996; Shin 1994), but also the relationships between the two processes. It has produced a plethora of
prescriptive advice and causal explanation,[3] particularly regarding the
sequencing of reforms. This is not merely a question of economic versus
political liberalisation – what comes first – but the recognition that prior
factors associated with pre-Communist, Communist and transition
experiences shape the transformation experience and thus affect the mix
of political and economic liberalism best suited for 'optimal' transformation (Haggard and Kaufman 1995). The prescriptions that have emerged
present conflicting views (Munck 1994; Huber *et al.* 1991); but without
substantive economic policy outcomes, compliance and participation will
not be attainable and democratic transition is weakened.

One other conceptualisation of democratisation stresses the salience of
the agency of constitutional choices by actors earlier in the transition
process. Thus the 'rise of epoch-making leaders such as Mandela, De
Klerk, Walesa, Gorbachev, Yeltsin and Havel mark these periods and
indeed fully justify emphasis on choice and crafting' (Munck 1994:370).
These choices lead to the creation of institutional structures and elite
consensus that either support or undermine democratic transformation,
especially during periods of economic downturn and citizen disappointment (O'Donnell and Schmitter 1986; Higley and Gunther 1992). As will
be seen in the next sections, the political and economic legacies of CEEC
and the international penetration of their futures by Western liberal
predilections have further complicated an already complex arena for
democratisation.

Liberalism and a civil society

We have argued that external preferences for democratic values in CEE
have been primarily of the liberal variant. Liberalism in this context
relates to individualism and hence the political, economic, social and
moral rights of the individual; the role of governments is thus to maximise

those individual liberties by assuring the rule of law, economic regulation and encouraging social mores that enhance separateness and its respect – an emphasis on individual rights over the concept of state supported community – in effect classical liberalism. Hirst (1997) gives three reasons why this is not just a political fad: that nation states can no longer achieve/maintain a monopoly of governing functions; that public services have become diverse and complex, needing delivery systems appropriate to this complexity; that economies are diversifying such that central regulation is inappropriate for market needs and impossible to apply effectively. Thus government is applied to support the private sector's power to manage in a 'market economy' (Hirst 1997:122).

Democracy in this sophisticated neoclassical form rests on clear distinction between public and private activity, both of which are protected by representative government and a responsible administration; public activity is supported by a broad arena of 'secondary associations' capable of encouraging and representing private activity within established cultural and legal limits. These represent a barrier to the 'creeping interventionism' of the state, or more particularly, elite control of the state. The idea of 'civil society' refines classical liberalism to provide liberal democratic processes a place within a free market environment; it became a vital aspect of the social organisation that underpins 'the effective democratic order and involves trade unions, professional associations, the independent media and other social and economic groupings which help to integrate different sections of the community' (Wiseman 1993:436). The existence of a civil society also blunts the detrimental impact of competitive freedoms and unbridled capitalism; assists the emergence of clear-cut minority rights and tolerance; develops equal, fair application of policy regulations and process by state implementers and adjudicators; and results in a responsible, responsive concept of citizenship. These and other characteristics must be assisted by an informed and free flow of public information and, inevitably, political elites who, by example, reinforce these values in their exercise of open, limited and responsible governance. Such values must also permeate commercial practice in order for it to operate in a *liberal* market – a factor of particular significance for an effective Single Market and clearly evident in Commission Opinions in *Agenda 2000*.

However, the tensions that have emerged in Western liberal states, as they apply market-based solutions to their problems, is testimony to the difficulties in sustaining liberal democratic governance and civil society within the most established political ground. Startling electoral swings in Canada (1993), Italy (1994), Britain and France (1997), and short-lived regimes (in Sweden, New Zealand, Denmark and Italy) during the early 1990s are testimony of the reactions of electorates to the pain of neoliberal solutions. The occasional, though so far limited, successes of

nationalist and extreme right parties, and the resulting impact on the
stability of 'moderate' parties and party systems, is not helped by the
aggressively competitive and more politically promiscuous role of the
international media. The battle for market share by a global, deregulated
and technologically pervasive communications network has encouraged a
corresponding change in political style and has enhanced the role of the
strong leader; this may be redefining the relationship between citizens and
political elites towards a democratic process of less sophistication than is
needed for the effective application of a liberal democratic model as
outlined above, and as prescribed for transforming CEEC. Thus the threat
of CEE demagogic populism springs not just from the pains of economic
transformation but also from the interpretation of Western democratic
experiences and opportunities for political communication that lend
themselves to 'inspired' leadership and simple solutions to complex problems (Greskovits 1996). It is against a somewhat disturbing set of
democratic practices, manifest not least by several of the member states of
the EU, that we may observe the concept and application of international
conditionalities as applied to CEE states.

Conditionality and the role of international organisations

Conditions attached to international support for economic and political
change are not new. During the Cold War support was ideologically
driven, such that there was little commitment to follow through to logical
conclusions the implications of Western aid and loans to Third World
states: that is, to oversee the major economic restructuring or establishing
liberal 'good' governance for poor authoritarian states (Leftwich 1993;
Gills and Rocamora 1992). 'Until quite recently, western governments,
the World Bank and the International Monetary Fund ... have displayed
no serious or consistent interest in promoting good governance or democracy. Such concerns were regularly eclipsed by foreign policy
considerations or overseas economic interests' (Leftwich 1993:608).[4]

The experiences of structural adjustment, tied to loan and aid
programmes of the 1980s, with stages of 'stabilisation' and 'adjustment',
revealed the need to establish appropriate levels of political commitment
and bureaucratic competence in recipient countries as integral parts of
successful structural change (Leftwich 1993). This experience, together
with the theoretical justification of neoliberalism, propelled what
amounted to an integrated Western perspective on the role of economic
aid and loans, involving a simultaneous and symbiotic transformation of
economic systems through structural adjustments and political change, to
incorporate individual freedom. Thus evidence of good governance went
beyond sound financial management to include legitimate, institution-

alised and democratic modes of political decision taking. By 1991 support for these aims was evident in public pronouncements from all major Western governments and such widely divergent international organisations as the OECD, the Organisation of African Unity, the Commonwealth, the EBRD, NATO and, of course, the EU (Leftwich 1993:611; Pridham 1997).

The benefits of international recognition are broad and reciprocal in their impact – on internal and external security; on investments and creditworthiness; on the success or failure of particular leadership elites to secure power; on the fate of minorities; on the direction of cultural and social patterns. The emergence of a democratising CEE, however, represents a special case and has attracted the particular attention of one such international actor, the EU.

CEE and the democratisation process

In Chapter 2 we discussed the significance of EAs and the *Agenda 2000* Opinions that assume the achievement by the CEEC of certain economic and political qualities. Similarly, the distinction between Phare and Tacis status made by the EU holds symbolic as well as substantive value for the countries involved. We may therefore observe democratic (and economic) development, from transition to transformation, paralleling EU–CEE policy changes through progress from cooperation and trade agreements to Phare aid and association through EAs. In the same way the ranking order of countries within *Agenda 2000* evaluation may also be seen to represent the EU's opinion on individual country progression to democratic consolidation; only when sufficient evidence of 'good governance' is available will full entry be permitted. What emerges is a progression of EU–CEE relations that is shaped initially by the timing and extent of democratic transition and the particular circumstances of transition/transformation in each country concerned.

Thus our description below of the successes and problems of CEE democratisation is divided into two periods that parallel emerging EU–CEE policies of the 1990s: a period of democratic *transition to transformation* lasting from 1989 to 1994, coinciding with the entry of most of the CEEC 10 into EAs; and the period of *transformation to consolidation* that, we may argue, began in 1994/5 and remains as yet incomplete. This is influenced by CEEC responses to EU demands for evidence of good governance in such policy instruments as the EAs, the White Paper and, more recently, *Agenda 2000* and the strengthened pre-accession process.

CEE: from transition to transformation

As with economic transformation to a basic market economy, by 1994 the rapid transition from authoritarian to democratic structures seemed complete for CEE as well as for the Baltic ex-Soviet successor states. In the case of the former, competitive elections (1989–91) had established a majority will, and allowed for the re-emergence of social groups such as the private peasantry, Church, trade unions, and ethnic and cultural groups – in effect, the bones of civil society. International recognition of successful transition was evident in the membership offered to CEEC and successor states by organisations such as the Council of Europe, as well as their willingness to subscribe to human rights and minorities treaties. Together with political and legal aspects of conditionalities attached to support from the IMF, International Bank of Reconstruction, EBRD and EU, this provided concrete incentives to sustain transition, and with the establishment of a market economy, provided barriers to the return of communism. Political freedoms in the shape of multiparty systems and electoral choice were reinforced by the rapid establishment of a free and competitive press and public access to new sources of television from both within CEEC and, more importantly, from Western Europe. Voter turnout, with the exception of Hungary and Poland, was high, falling slightly in second-round parliamentary elections where they had occurred (Brown 1994:30–3).

However, as Gordon Smith observes, transition contains the characteristic of uncertainty and the possibility of reversibility, and 'has to be treated as open-ended with regard to its final outcomes' (Smith 1994: 116). The destinations of several countries were unclear: for newly independent Slovakia under Merciar; Albania, whose weak parliamentary system veered towards a powerful presidential model after 1992 under Berisha; Ilescu's Romania, its government peppered with prominent figures from the Communist era; and Bulgaria, whose first major privatisation did not begin until May 1993. These examples evinced little confidence in a necessarily liberal democratic future. There were also the particular difficulties of the newly established Baltic states, whose relations with Russia were complicated by substantial Russian minorities of uncertain status and loyalties, as well as unresolved issues of the continuing Russian military presence; and a destabilised and warring Balkans that precluded the consideration of even the relatively trouble-free states of Slovenia and Macedonia as permanent additions to a European democratic family. Both these states had the added complication of border disputes with EU member states, Italy and Greece. Finally, there were the question marks hanging over Russian democracy and its potentially destabilising effects on its western neighbours.

Even the more optimistic perspectives of successful political transition observed in the cases of Hungary, Poland and the newly formed Czech Republic were not without qualification. Thus, by 1992, the early successes of Hungary's gradualist transition were challenged by a period of economic downturn (Reisch 1993) and the rise of nationalist, populist opinion, including criticism of ex-Communists in the privatisation process, hostility towards Jews and Roma and 'foreign' intervention in Hungarian transformation, as well as irredentist protestations (East and Ponton 1997). In the case of Poland, whose Solidarity movement had challenged Communist regimes since 1980, the first free elections in 1991 resulted in a fragmented parliament of twenty-nine parties with a turnout of only 43 per cent. International indebtedness and 'shock therapy' under-mined regime popularity, producing five cabinets in the period 1989–93. Centre-right policies, while pleasing international investors, eventually rallied left and ex-Communist opposition to form a post-Communist government (October 1993). This 'nostalgia for communist comfort' (Denton and Mortimer 1994) was also evident in Slovak politics, together with a powerful nationalist dimension. These were factors contributing to the Czech/Slovak 'velvet divorce' (January 1993) and the formation of the clearly less liberal Meciar government (Rehak and Kirillov 1995). Deteriorating economic performance, together with less than amicable post-divorce relations with the Czech Republic, produced considerable doubt over Slovakia's continued 'first-order' status regarding future membership of the EU (Pehe 1993).

In contrast, the fortunes of the Czech Republic developed in almost inverse proportion to Slovakia, with exceptional economic progress and political stability under the 'technocratic', market-friendly coalition of Vaclav Klaus and the internationally respected President Vaclav Havel (Musil 1994). After independence Klaus and others evinced total confi-dence that the new Republic was by far the best candidate for membership of Western Europe's security and economic organisations (Okalicsanyi 1993). By arguing so stridently, however, Klaus revealed the lack of common purpose among even the most advanced CEEC (Pithart 1994). Even relative economic and political stability, it seemed, brought its own difficulties in the delineation of EU–CEE relations.

The factors that shaped the period of democratic transition in CEEC are significant for two reasons. First, since these factors are inherently political, they affect the nature of subsequent transformation and consoli-dation. Thus, while there are other elements shaping the democratisation process, the mode of transition left its own legacy. In particular, the re-lationships between old and new elites during transition would seem to carry considerable significance for the way in which institutional struc-tures and political configurations are transformed. Also, the positioning of Communist parties and opposition groupings and the mode of power transferral during the transition period differed in several CEEC

(Ishiyama 1995; Welsh 1994; Munck and Leff 1997), leaving substantially different patterns of political stratification, party systems, policy choices, institutional change, and thus opportunities for democratic transformation and consolidation.[5] Second, and consequentially, evident differences in the democratisation process between CEEC gave opportunities for what emerged as a sometimes aggressive competitive external promotion of political maturity against the political and economic difficulties of rivals in the race to 'rejoin Europe'.

CEE: from democratic transformation to consolidation?

Democratic transformation chiefly involves the routinisation of elite behaviour within already established formal rules and practices, and the eradication of previous processes/practices not compatible with democracy. Democratic consolidation involves the permeation of practice and its internalisation by citizens, assisted by the emergence of a confident civil society, that contributes to, and, where necessary, will challenge, elites working within the formal democratic process. We have argued that, far from being perceived as a purely academic construct, the requirements of the *acquis* and their implementation require evidence from CEEC of such consolidation through evident 'good governance' as a necessary symbol of their progress towards accession. By 1995 each of the CEEC 10 claimed full restoration of democratic processes and the marginalisation of anti-democratic forces, such that 'it seems whatever their mutual differences, all CEECs have gone beyond the point of a return to the ancien régime' (Kaldor and Vejvoda 1997:60). Can we justify this claim of successful democratic transformation, or are there still nagging doubts over the quality of democratic practice, that may be a 'mirage of democracy' (Kaldor and Vejvoda 1997:61)?

Agenda 2000 is only one of several recent evaluations of democratisation in the region. Such organisations as Freedom House (1997), the US State Department (1996), the EBRD (1995), the European Human Rights Foundation (EHRF), the Council of Europe, the OECD and others have joined with academic studies in what amounts to a perpetual health check of the CEEC' transformation process. What emerges are fairly consistent conclusions regarding CEE democratisation, with the general consensus of opinion suggesting clear evidence of transformation in the case of all the CEEC 10. Where opinions are nuanced is on the progression to what in one report is termed 'consolidated democracy' (Karatnychy *et al.* 1997). As we have seen, the acceptance of all but Slovakia by the EU as having satisfied the (formal) political conditions laid down at Copenhagen was accompanied by the recognition that progress in the actual practice of (substantive) democracy, and protecting minorities, was still necessary in several countries. According to Agenda 2000, only Hungary, Slovenia, the Czech Republic, Poland and Lithuania emerge as having relatively few substantive problems. A report prepared for the US Agency for International Development (USAID) by Freedom House (1997), which surveyed twenty-five CEE and NIS states, concludes that, of these, there are eighteen electoral democracies in operation, of which seven may be classified as 'consolidated democratic states with market economies' (Karatnychy *et al.* 1997:6). These are the Visegrads less Slovakia, and each of the three Baltic states, that have established a 'significant' degree of political and economic freedom, together with 'the basis for a vibrant civil society'. Slovakia, Bulgaria and Romania are ranked with Russia, Moldova, the Ukraine, Croatia, Georgia and others as *transitional governments*, whose common feature is instability.[6]

In an examination of selected CEEC, as part of an evaluation of Phare/Tacis democracy programmes, progress towards formal democracy was considered more or less established, except for Estonia, which failed to provide an inclusive citizenship. Formal democracy was weakest in Slovakia and Romania, but nevertheless was considered to exist (ISA Consult 1997).[7] A more critical commentary was evident when substantive democracy was considered, with all countries varying in degrees of weakness, especially in the application of the rule of law and tendency to centralisation. However, 'the aspect of substantive democracy that is slowest and hardest to achieve is a democratic political culture' (ISA Consult 1997: 19) which is handicapped, in all countries examined, by an authoritarian legacy that manifests itself in low levels of trust in political processes and actors, belief in individualism and political participation.

Other evaluations also present different conclusions for CEEC democratisation since 1989. There is general agreement on only three of the CEEC 10 confirming characteristics of democratic consolidation (Hungary, Poland and Slovenia), with the Kaldor and Vejvoda analysis expressing some doubts over the Czech Republic's progress in the substantive application of democracy. Significantly, the democratic progression in Slovakia is considered pessimistically by both ISA Consult and Freedom House, with the former particularly concerned, also, over problems of Estonian–Russian minority/citizenship.[8] More recently, similar problems over the smaller but still significant Russian minority in Latvia have resulted in Russian, US and EU criticisms (*Guardian*, 5 April 1998). Moreover, Romania's first effective change of government (November 1996) is uncertain evidence that basic human rights issues, protection of minorities and substantial political and administrative reforms will be achieved (Mihas 1997). In effect, the evidence of progress towards democratic consolidation by the CEEC is varied, and solid evidence of putting 'the principles of democracy and the rule of law ... into practice in daily life' (Commission 1997:43) is confined to a limited and still criticised group of candidate countries.

The plethora of comparative studies on political transformation in CEE since 1989 examine the prospects for democracy from several perspectives.[9] What follows is a brief examination of the particularities of CEE democratisation and their implications for the direction of EU–CEE policies.

A third way?

While the period 1989–92 saw the eradication of Communist authoritarian rule in Eastern Europe, it did not necessarily entail either the complete demise of Communist values nor authoritarian government. The centralising nature of a dominant ideology and its machinery was unlikely to disappear within the medium term, even within the best of contemporary circumstances. As J. F. Brown suggests, country transformations are affected by pre-Communist and post-Communist factors that combine to create an environment within which democratisation is shaped. Pre-Second World War geopolitical factors: old alliances and enmities towards Russia, Germany and the countries bordering on to them; socio-cultural connectivities; ethnic and religious and historical association with the three empires prior to 1918; these are all a necessary part of 'understanding the changing pattern of international politics in East–Central Europe that have coloured the nature of politics in individual states in the region' (Hyde-Price 1996:69). The re-emergence of political Catholicism and Eastern Orthodoxy, the problem of disaffected ethnic minorities and diasporas (Hungarian, Roma, Russian, German), and from these the unfinished business of national identity and disputed borders, manifest themselves within a now 'open society'. The danger of new 'little imperialisms' is evident, and may be a significant part of Eastern European political rediscovery (Brown 1994:13).

Layered across quite varied pre-Cold War CEE histories was the common Communist experience itself, but even this had its ideological variants in the Yugoslav, Albanian and Romanian 'models' that challenged the dominant Soviet Leninist orthodoxy. Even within the 'dominant' model, Hungarian New Economic Policy and its social and political implications contrast with 'the fated orthodoxy of Czechoslovakia and the GDR' (Henderson and Robinson 1997: 20), while the oppositional forces in Poland after martial law (1981) maintained a critical political presence not evident in the post-1968 Czech politics that remained 'normalised' to 1989. What was common, however, was one essential feature; each country was ruled by a single party whose 'power dominated and corrupted all these variations in political structure *in some way or another* so that all post communist states shared a common legacy and problem: overcoming the destruction of independent social economic and political life wrought by their ruling communist power' (Henderson and Robinson 1997:8). Thus democratic transition and transformation involved the eradication of democratic centralism and its organisational structures. This leaves a clutch of 'remaindered' problems for governance that cling on after the (re)establishment of formal democratic processes and gave rise to consideration of a Third Way for economic and political transformation unique to the experiences of post-Communist states (Hettne 1995; Lewis 1994; Batt 1994).

Evidence for the current state of public uncertainty over the progress achieved in democratising the CEEC may be seen in the results of several surveys, not least Central and Eastern Eurobarometer analysis of citizen expectations of democratic progress and their perspectives on human rights. In 1997, of the CEEC 10 citizens, 51 per cent were largely dissatisfied with the way democracy was developing, with only the Poles (57:33) showing more satisfaction than dissatisfaction. This contrasted with the negative outlook in Bulgaria (21:33), Slovakia (25:74) and Hungary (30:64). Attitudes towards the working of democracy showed marginally more dissatisfaction (overall 41:53 per cent CEEC 10), with only Poland and Romania having over 40 per cent of citizens satisfied with their country's democratic practice. Respect for human rights also received critical appraisal; in the CEEC 10, 51 per cent thought there was not much respect/no respect for individual human rights; 45 per cent thought there was some or a great deal of respect; 'first-wave' entrants' citizens' views on respect for human rights were evenly split (45:46), though this varied between 61 per cent of Hungarian citizens reasonably content with their individual rights to 50 per cent of Poles who were not (Commission 1998). In this context, the role of the EU and other international organisations as guarantors of both democracy and human rights may well be seen as a significant factor explaining why particular groups of CEE citizens have high expectations of future EU–CEE relations, though overall support for EU membership seems motivated by primarily economic factors (Commission 1998:34; Rose and Haenpfer 1994).[10]

From the discussion above we argue that communism has left its mark on post-Communist political culture, if not uniformly across Eastern Europe, at least with sufficient visibility for several aspects of its legacy to remain clearly problematic for a smooth pathway to democratic consolidation. The problem for the CEEC is that in order to become fully Westernised (in effect, to gain the desired status of EU membership), they must become democratically consolidated; but in order to become democratically consolidated they need the recognition and support of the EU that in turn demands evidence of democratic consolidation. In this context democratic consolidation takes on a particular and EU-driven character to which CEEC attempt to respond, handicapped by their own particular post-Communist democratic cultures and economic difficulties.

Thus the success of democratisation in post-Communist countries depends 'to a significant extent upon the activities of ex-Communists for their numbers are too large and their political prominence too great to be ignored' (Rose 1996:15). Their prominence is manifest in their continuing roles within public administration and political processes in many countries and/or their transference into the private sector.[11] Whether purged from the public sector and re-emerging in Estonian urban markets, or adapting their political organisation and ideological messages to form part of a governing elite, as in Hungary, post-Communists form part of the emerging political deal. Their adaptation, suggests Rose, is assisted by the fact that few were doctrinaire believers; rather, that they fit the image of 'opportunistic adherents', so shifting their behaviour to fit new political rules.[12] In this sense, democracy, for the older generations especially, represents only *one* form of (European) solution to people's problems and thus stands against not just communism but also fascist authoritarianism as other tried and not entirely rejected alternatives (Rose 1996). However, Havel's maxim that 'the Third Way leads to the Third World' seems an apposite summary of the feelings of many CEE citizens, who perceive they have few alternatives for their future well-being than the painful path to democratic consolidation (Batt 1994).

Substantive issues for democratic consolidation

Four areas serve as examples of consolidating democratic political institutions and processes in the light of prior Communist experience, and are significant for their importance as dependable evidence of 'good governance'. These are a reformed (central) bureaucracy; legal processes that guarantee the rule of law; the establishment of decentralised systems of government; and the emergence of a deep layer of NGOs; all of which are significant (though not the only) ingredients of a civil society and thus a consolidated democracy. They also form important aspects of the political, administrative and economic requirements that applicant countries must meet if they are to become suitably equipped EU club members, and therefore in the context of EU–CEE relations, commend themselves for our attention.

Central bureaucracy

At the 1997 Rotterdam Conference on Governance and European Integration, the link between democracy, government and governance is clearly stated. Thus:

Government is about stabilising order and stability by making power predictable. *Democracy* is the expression of the will to bring governmental power under control of the people. *Governance* stresses that government is inseparably tied to civil society without which justice and effective policy is impossible; *Substantive democracy,* is democracy that works in practice; it is also important to create and promote civil society traditions, (to include) a profound political administrative culture.

(Netherlands Presidency of the EU 1997)

Reform of the state apparatus to achieve this 'profundity' is not without its difficulties.

No country except for East Germany and the Czech Republic, has 'decommunised' its central administration in a systematic and pervasive manner. Where it has been attempted, the use of lustration laws has been piecemeal, often with the real aim of discrediting political opponents, for example in Poland and Slovakia; and when past Communist governments were returned to power – Hungary, Lithuania and Bulgaria – lustration laws were rapidly shelved, so making the whole activity a political rather than an administrative initiative (Brown 1997).

Against decommunisation remains the strong argument of operational necessity: continuity, administrative expertise, and linkages between political and economic processes needed to be sustained to oversee the changes demanded by 'democratic' forces. However, CEE civil services are still perceived by their citizens as clientelistic and politically dependent rather than Weberian, neutral, public institutions (Kaldor and Vejvoda 1997). Moreover, the transference from the role of public technocrat to private entrepreneur via privatisation programmes has resulted in a significant number of the previous nomenclature becoming part of the new entrepreneurial class. Corruption and/or a self-seeking use of the market has been the unfortunate consequence, assisted by inefficiencies of tax and business regulation of the 'new' public administration. Clientelism with the associated potential for bribery and corruption 'become the normal way for doing even the most menial administrative business' (Kaldor and Vejvoda 1997:75).

The country-specific studies of *Agenda 2000* catalogue horizontal, vertical and sectoral administrative problems that currently beset all the CEEC 10.[13] An analysis of the Commission's findings (Fournier 1997) indicates that criticism far outweighs praise in the sectoral review, with particular and universal criticisms of the administration of indirect taxation and consumer protection, transport safety (except Slovenia), and health and safety at work (except Hungary and Poland). Significantly, the Commission found widespread civil service corruption, seen as a major problem for public credibility (Fournier 1997:7), with only Slovenia showing no evidence of significant civil service corruption. Few civil services have comprehensive legislation governing their activities, with the Czech Republic, Romania and Bulgaria with no Civil Service Act of any kind. The last two countries and Slovakia have the most serious problems of political interference. Overstaffing in routine administration – especially in Poland and Bulgaria – runs alongside shortages of skilled staff in specific sectors, especially those associated with the *acquis* (Czech Republic, Estonia, Latvia, Poland and Slovenia), and in part related to the low wages of public-sector posts compared with the emerging private sector. Here the irony of international conditionality that demands reductions in public spending levels is evident enough. Civil service reform is observed as piecemeal in most countries; the implementation of Accession Partnerships will certainly address this as a matter of urgency.[14] For the most part, countries have established coordinating structures for EU affairs, though the coordination between ministries for other purposes is often inadequate (Preston 1997).

A Rotterdam Conference paper (Sigma 1997) considers EU–CEE policy in this area. While acknowledging that there is no basis in EU rules regarding public management, it finds that there does emerge an *obligation de résultat*, as well as the demand to sustain consistency between domestic and EU policy over time. This, together with the emphasis by the Commission on the requirements of economic administration to achieve integration and thus market efficiency, has led to the emergence of what is termed 'European Administrative Space' (EAS), developing from the frequent meetings of member state bureaucrats with and through Commission officials. EAS is emerging 'with its own traditions which build on but surpass the distinctive administrative traditions of the Union' (Sigma 1997:3). It is this space that CEEC administration must attempt to fill as a prerequisite for the acceptable working of democratic processes, markets and the political objectives of integrating economies and societies with the EU.[15]

Legal systems and processes

As Istvan Pogany suggests, it is 'extraordinarily naive to imagine that human or social conduct has changed simply *because* the laws and political institutions have' (Pogany 1996:159). Thus there is inevitably a noticeable time lag between the adoption of constitutions that rest on the rule of law and the emergence of protective and proactive legal rules and their effective implementation. Once again the different legacies of CEEC affect the working of structures and processes that, on face value, seem similar.

Post-Communist countries have, within their legal systems and processes, elements of pre-Communist, Communist and post-Communist experiences. In cases where a pre-Communist liberal system existed, an embryo rule of law may be found; in the body of Communist law, the experiences of regulation are predominant; in the post-Communist legal reforms, civil and economic laws may have developed significantly.[16] Without judicial systems of a suitable international standard, question marks remain over the democratisation process; and 'without a legal system capable of achieving EU ends the possibility of accession is remote' (interview, Commission official, December 1998).

In establishing a constitutional framework within which the rule of law is applied, 'constitution makers in the CEECs demonstrated their concern for both (individual) right and social justice', but in general favour communitarian constitutionalism over a rights-led framework, thus 'emphasising the "nation" as opposed to the citizen' (Kaldor and Vejvoda 1997:67). This is not unusual, given the protective and interventionist role of post-Communist transforming governments and their immediate Communist pasts. What it has led to, however, are concerns over the individual and collective rights of minorities; a tension between the 'remaindered' Marxist values of social and economic rights and the often externally generated neoliberal criticisms of CEEC government policies (Holmes 1997); a somewhat overbearing attitude and on occasion a direct intervention by governments in media and judicial freedoms; law enforcement agencies that struggle to implement new economic and criminal regulations in under-resourced circumstances – a recipe for corruption; and administrative law that is struggling to overcome the reluctance of its implementers to accept 'the idea that government can be brought to account in the courts' (Galligan 1997:132).

As we have already indicated, concern over the application and administration of justice is shown in a number of recent international reports. The 1996 Freedom House survey of democratic transition addresses a broad range of legal applications in CEE and NIS states, finding Hungarian courts and the constitutional court independent of political interference but expressing concern over *de facto* discrimination against the Roma community in Hungary (and the Czech Republic) that is not adequately dealt with by the police or in the courts; neither are media freedoms clearly established and legally protected. There was also a dearth of adequately trained lawyers, a problem common in most CEEC 10. In Poland and Slovakia, the judiciary were not seen as wholly free from political interference, with most Polish judges identified as 'holdovers' from the previous regime. Estonia's relatively independent judicial system works within the framework of tightly controlled citizens' rights, and has considerable recruitment and training problems associated with its de-communisation process. Other critical problems include the connivance of black marketeers with police and state officials in Romania and the lack of effective criminal law enforcement in Latvia and Estonia (Kaldor and Vejvoda 1997); the general reluctance to open up administration to judicial and quasi-judicial review (Galligan 1997); and a concern with the incidence of criminality associated with social and ethnic divisions, economic expectations and opportunities that slows the development of a civic culture that must replace imposed Communist values (Kaldor and Vejvoda 1997).

When addressing legal and judicial issues, *Agenda 2000* is also specifically critical of the CEEC' administration and implementation of judicial and quasi-judicial processes, observing for the most part virtually the same shortcomings – of court overload, inexperienced judicial personnel, lengthy court proceedings, and the amount and range of new law that renders enforcement extraordinarily difficult. While there is specific praise for some judicial aspects (the constitutional courts of Bulgaria, Poland, Slovakia and Slovenia) and criticism (of penal procedures in Bulgaria and the role of the Prosecutor-General in Lithuania) the Commission's general evaluation 'remains highly circumspect' (Fournier 1997). That circumspection can be explained by a number of factors: that expressions of caution regarding progress were a reflection of the lack of information in this area (interview, Commission, February 1998); that the quality of some member states' judicial processes was less than satisfactory, thus blunting critical appraisal of evidently transforming systems; that judicial and law enforcement processes were capable of a fast learning curve, given the right internal policies and external encouragement; that in the light of the formal stress placed upon human rights criteria and the capabilities of applicants to administer the *acquis* in total, objective critical appraisal in this area was capable of destroying the whole accession process for all but a couple of aspirants (Slovenia and Hungary). In the event, conclusions in this area were finalised at a late stage in the report process and at the 'highest' Commission level (interview, Commission, March 1998). In this sense these innocuous conclusions have an element of Damoclean judgement about them; for the time being, the jury of the EU court remains out on the subject of legal transformation.

Decentralisation in CEE and democratic consolidation

Consideration of the role of decentralisation in democratisation and governance is important for two main reasons. First, if consolidation involves the permeation of political practice and its internalisation by citizens it must then include the experience of decentralised modes of government as a vital part of that practice. Historically, sub-state politics has been a vital component of European political development, and, as such, is part of the compact that allows civil society to exist. Second, the EU concepts of social partnership and subsidiarity are now part of the 'process culture' of the EU. So, given the stultifying nature of forty years of democratic centralism, the establishment of decentralised modes of governance is a tough but appropriate test of CEE democratic consolidation (Coulson

1995). Furthermore, if, as Emil Kirchner suggests, market reform has outpaced the establishment of democratic values, civil society and local *and* regional government, decentralisation remains as a vital component of democratic consolidation and *economic* transformation (Kirchner 1997). While such ideas are not new, having their origins in development theories of the 1950s and 1960s, they have been revitalised by the CEEC overriding medium-term interest in 'joining Europe', and the salience of the decentralised partnership of central and meso-governments expected by the EU as part of Community policy implementation.

So, regional and local governance could have a threefold position in the scheme of accession. It could help to compensate for the sometimes poor or erratic performance of central government in social and economic outcomes as part of a new democratic accountability; it could provide a complementary arena for the delivering of the type of services necessary to sustain the SEM *acquis* (in such fields as consumer and environmental protection, and health and safety at work) and third, it '[could] reinforce the activities of NGOs, including specialised interest organisations', so reinforcing the process of democratic consolidation (Kirchner 1997:3). Two factors mitigate against a speedy move to decentralisation; in several senses a new democratic centralism remains in CEE, as countries have prioritised the rebuilding of national central institutions and directed limited resources accordingly; old democratic centralism, as we suggest above, dies hard, both with regard to bureaucratic processes and in the continuing belief in technocracy and centrally directed governance. This has meant a serious shortage of resources when local and regional economic initiatives and political direction have been attempted.[17] In consequence, an ill-funded local government system resulting in low salaries and standing for local officials only exacerbates levels of corruption and deficiencies in local service (ISA Consult 1997).

Agenda 2000 pays little attention to local government save to describe the different systems and to point to its excessive financial dependence on central government (in Poland, the Czech Republic, Romania and Bulgaria). A much more upbeat assessment of its potential role is contained in the Rotterdam Conference final document, where local government is elevated to 'a foundation stone of the democratic state; a source of learning for governments'; as a means of brokering state and civil society; encouraging partnership and co-government; and 'playing a role in political integration and cohesion in Europe through its contribution to and implementation of EU policies in building relations across national borders' (Netherlands Presidency of the EU 1997:4). The latter point is argued further by Kirchner, who points to the growing and potentially powerful impact of cross-border initiatives at local and regional levels between CEEC and neighbouring EU states and within 'Euro-Regions' (Kirchner 1997).[18] Thus it is argued that the potential for inter-

and intra-regional cooperation is one that is worth developing, especially in the context of those perspectives on integration that stress the salience of networks, regional policies, partnerships and multilevel EU governance (Marks 1993).

The emergence of NGOs

It is not surprising that the growth and penetration of NGOs in CEE has been nominated as 'one of the most remarkable features of post communist transition' (ISA Consult 1997:20). Within populations still suspicious of the state and critical of the role of political parties, it would seem self-evident that the development of a civil society, and thus the consolidation of CEE democracy, is served well by the opportunities that NGOs offer. These may be seen as a training ground for public participation; an institutional setting that encourages an ethical context to social and political conduct; and an antidote or opposition to the power of the state and the market. Thus it could well be that in contemporary Eastern European conditions it is this sector where democrats are trained and established (ISA Consult 1997:22).

Of course the emergence of NGOs as part of the establishment of a 'civil society' was itself an important aspect of the initial opposition to communism and part of the period of democratic transition during, and prior to, the late 1980s (Welsh 1994). To some considerable extent, the development of such contemporary perspectives on late twentieth-century democracy as 'communitarianism', 'associationalism', 'stakeholding' or 'cosmopolitanism' (Etzioni 1995; Hirst 1997; Held 1995) owes much to the ideas of dissident thinkers such as Havel and Michnik.[19] In effect, civil society in CEE in the form of officially accepted or unofficially established NGOs was a vital precursor to the revolutionary change of 1989; the need for 'active citizenship' to combat state power, remoralise society and provide organisational focus and political impetus to the mobilisation of society has since formed much of the intellectual debate on democracy in Eastern and Western fora (Hirst 1997).

As with other democratic processes in CEE, there are major differences in the numbers and nature of emergent NGOs, reflecting the region's varied historic and contemporary experiences. Hungary presents a success story, with more than 50,000 NGOs officially registered such that 'civil society must be perceived as a third societal sector beside the economic and state sectors' (ISA Consult 1997:52). Of significance is the emergence of NGOs organised by the Roma, whose interests do not seem effectively represented by a still prejudiced Hungarian society. A more pessimistic view is taken of the emergence of Romanian NGOs. Officially registered organisations have increased in recent years to 12,000, but volunteer involvement is low, with many having 'only a fractional existence, having been created to hide economic activities under a non-profit cover' (ISA Consult 1997:109). Though, since the 1996 election, the government has promised a more favourable climate, the NGO sector has suffered several years of hostility from the post-Communist Illescu regime that, together with poor and declining living standards, has created a scenario for an uncertain democratic future. Slovakia's similarly uncertain political destination has, however, not precluded an abundant growth in NGOs: indeed, one argument for what amounts to the brightest element of Slovak democratisation is that citizens, unsure of their formal freedoms and disillusioned by the representational qualities of political parties, have turned to 'own resources' to achieve political objectives. This phenomenon is also assisted by the more cooperative and local traditions in Slovak society when compared with the Czech Republic (Kaldor and Vejvoda 1997).[20]

Despite the favourable signs of civil activity in some CEEC, and with all the advantages that this brings to democratic consolidation, the geographical spread and functional range of NGOs are uneven. In some CEEC, such as the Baltic states and Bulgaria, numbers are low and those involved tend to be from the intellectual middle class – already participative and democratic in outlook. The attraction of voluntary support is also uneven; the highest proportion of workers in the sector are women (ISA Consult 1997), and NGOs in CEE remain greatly dependent on Western finance. It is, of course, inevitable that the greatest numbers, range and recorded activity of NGOs are in those CEEC with the most extensive evidence of other democratic consolidation – for example, Poland, the Czech Republic and Hungary, which have good media access and supportive laws of assembly and interest articulation. Given the range of activities of NGOs as providers of services, as advocacy groups, as protectors of social, ethnic and religious minorities or as promoters of women's issues, their role is potentially dramatic; in consequence, relationships with the state or specific governments have, in several countries, been fraught with mutual hostility. This is most noticeable in Slovakia, Romania to 1996 and the Czech Republic, where President Havel has argued that the centralist neoliberal policies of the Klaus government have undermined the participatory aspects of democratic transformation (East and Pontin 1997).[21] There remain doubts, however, over the clientelistic character of NGOs, given the degree of financial support made available by international organisations and the genuineness of local demand, and thus their contribution to a growing sense of civic values (Kaldor and Vejvoda 1997). The EU's formal contribution to these and other democratic impulses is examined below.

The democracy line to the EU

There is considerable evidence of official EU support for democratisation, including the increasing attention being given to the task of 'institution building' that has emerged as sufficiently important an aim to capture 30 per cent of Phare funding within *Agenda 2000*'s reinforced accession strategy. 'Institution building', in this context, represents a somewhat nebulous set of interrelated arenas that in turn reflect the complexity of establishing a civil society and thus a consolidated democracy. As we pointed out in Chapter 2, by 1996 the related fields of civil and society democracy, public administration and institutions, and education and social development had already reached the 30 per cent share of sectoral developments, and in *Agenda 2000* progress towards substantive democracy ('the degree that individuals can influence the conditions in which they live', *European Dialogue* 1998) became an official mantra of Commission opinion.

The broader EU context on democracy is outlined in the document *The External Dimension of Human Rights*, which clearly indicates the international framework of those policies (Commission 1996a).[22] Furthermore, Copenhagen criteria established a conditional framework that included specific reference to democracy, human rights and effective governance. Finally, the Treaty of Amsterdam (1997) afforded Union respect for the European Convention (Article F) and its enforcement via the threat of sanction on member states which breach it (Article F1). Importantly for our analysis, the Union recognises 'the interdependence between human rights, democracy and development' (Commission 1996a: 1). It is in this broader context that the EU has developed its policies to assist the process of democratisation.

International aid for democratisation in CEE is neither the preserve of the EU nor a new phenomenon. Bilateral aid from member states, of which the British Know-How Fund is but one example; from the USA and other states, through government-funded and quasi-independent organisations such as USAID; NGOs, of which the Soros Foundation is the most well known (and generous); and from the Council of Europe, the OECD, NATO and the UN, has been forthcoming from an early stage. There has always been a plethora of grant/aid programmes in support of democracy and good governance. While some coordination between international organisations and NGOs has been attempted, as we shall see below, it remains relatively limited. In consequence it is difficult to assess the amounts offered, especially by NGOs and foundations, though one estimate put the figure at $500 million in the period 1990–95. Indeed, one estimate of total Soros Foundation expenditure on democracy, civil society and educational activities between 1990 and 1996 was $1277.6 million (Randel and German 1997).

The EU's democracy programme developed out of an EP initiative in 1992, following the criticism of Romanian progress on human rights and the resultant block of Phare funding. Parliament's partial control over the Phare budget has allowed it a degree of influence over scheme guidelines and thus the nature of 'institutional' aid (Hartwig 1997). Demand for funding under the scheme's guidelines led to its expansion by 1993 to include Tacis countries (the Phare and Tacis Democracy Programme, PTDP), with its management by an external Brussels-based NGO, the EHRF.[23]

The general objectives of the scheme are to increase knowledge of democratic practices at national/local levels; and to support the work of NGOs to transfer technical skills and expertise in the fields of democratic and legal practice to expert and professional groups in CEE. Financing involves partnerships between NGOs in both the member states and CEE. In the period 1993–96, approximately ecu 76 million were allocated to the programme, of which 56 per cent was spent in Phare countries and 44 per cent in Tacis countries. Projects are of three types: *macro-projects*, that should have a 'European' dimension and are directed towards sustained activities supported by member state and CEE partnerships – for example, Strengthening Parliamentary Practice in Estonia (Institute of European Affairs, Ireland and the Chancellery of the Estonian Riigikogu), and Democratic Control of Armed Forces (the Atlantic Club Bulgaria and the UK Democracy Partnership Consortium); *micro-projects* – mainly local projects managed by EU country delegations, in response to citizen initiatives – for example, pupils' self-government at schools in the Lomza Viovodship (Poland); cooperation between Roma/non Roma groups in Romanian localities; and seminars designed to strengthen the position of women in Slovenian business (Commission 1996b); plus a small number of *ad hoc projects* that are selected and managed by the Commission.

The ISA Consult evaluation of the democracy programme (1997) presents, for the most part, a positive view of the scheme, finding that the most significant effect of the programme has been in 'the contribution of the growth of a lively NGO sector in all countries' (ISA Consult 1997: 11), but particularly in Phare rather than Tacis countries, whose experience of totalitarian political culture was longer and deeper. What distinguished EU programme activity from others was the EU label, which seemed to represent a badge of legitimacy 'that especially in the case of Slovakia, offered some protection from the arbitrary action of governments'. Also the concept of partnership and, importantly, the bottom-up approach for application and lack of need for CEEC government approval for the project, contrasted with other Phare and Tacis activities. These projects also represented a 'political' signal about the character of the EU – with cross-border partnership and transparency evidently part of the programme activity. Micro-projects were seen as a significant contribution to 'second-generation' NGOs. However, the scale of democracy line assistance is comparatively minor when considering the magnitude of the tasks and the timescales associated with accession, especially in the fields of public administration and the application of the law. Several ISA Consult recommendations seem to be incorporated in recent amendments to the programme that, in the light of *Agenda 2000*'s accession-driven model, entail a strategic (government-led) rather than demand-driven approach.[24]

The Democratic Initiatives of the EP are broader than their particular interest in Phare/Tacis aid programmes. Parliament itself provides a learning process for CEEC parliamentarians through its formal and informal association with colleagues and political groupings from CEE Joint Parliamentary Committees (JPCs); the administration of the JPCs is served by a common secretariat in Brussels, but meetings take place in both the Association country and Brussels; thus, 'on a regular basis representatives from the associated country's government, the Commission and the Council Presidency attend meetings and answer questions from parliamentarians' from the CEEC and EU (Hartwig 1997:7). Also, meetings between the President of the EP and the Presidents of CEE Parliaments have supplemented JPCs and mirror the EP and member state parliamentary process. These strengthened contacts between the EP and CEEC political elites are, it can be argued, of greater significance since the EP has the Treaty power to reject the accession of new states. In this context, CEEC parliamentarians must respond to the European parliamentary process positively for fear of losing the status of 'democratic partnership' and thus the support of a (mostly benevolent) teacher and critic. Also of significance has been the role of EU party federations in vetting the democratic credentials of CEE political parties that seek membership of EU political groupings and international federations (Pridham 1997).

Other EU initiatives in support of democratisation have involved co-operation with international organisations, in particular the Council of Europe and the OSCE. Council of Europe/EU Joint Country Programmes have been applied in the Baltic states and Albania, with thematic programmes for CEEC in the fields of fighting corruption and organised crime and assisting minorities. These initiatives work in cooperation with the Phare and Tacis programmes. The EU also works with the OSCE within its 'human dimension' programme and has increasingly cooperated with the OSCE in election monitoring and addressing the problems of national minorities (Hyde-Price 1997). The Commission thus works in close association with the OSCE Bureau of Democratic Institutions and Human Rights, the OSCE High Commissioner for National Minorities, and the UN Human Rights Centre. Evident from the preceding discussion, however, is that the EU's interest in CEE democratisation involves the integration of several other policy areas in order to create the best climate for good governance, the 'advanced conditionalities' for democratisation prescribed in *Agenda 2000*.

Conclusion

> So far as democratisation is concerned, the EU is the most important actor in Europe. (Geoffrey Pridham 1997).

Despite not being the only club in town, as we suggested in our introduction, we have argued that the circumstances of the post-Cold War era, the position that the EU now holds as a regional actor, and the wishes of the CEEC to join the EU, are significant features in any analysis of CEE political and economic transformation. The democratisation process, for many states during the last twenty years of the twentieth century, has taken place within the context of globalisation – of economies, technologies, ideas and politics; furthermore, the increasingly dominant 'global vision' of democracy – the liberal democratic paradigm – has shaped, indeed constrained, the choices of those countries seeking to reinvent their political processes. These factors, together with pre- and post-Communist experiences for the particular countries, provide a complex backdrop to the CEE democratisation process. It is the common experiences of over forty years of communism, however, nuanced within individual political systems, that is the heaviest baggage to be carried, adapted or dispensed with. Post-communism, therefore, is a phenomenon within which pre-Communist history and post-Cold War liberalism collide with the remains of socialist authoritarianism, with varying consequences for the consolidation of liberal democracy in CEEC.

A dual transformation – a triple process, if one includes the adjustments to a new set of security issues (Chapter 7) – is thus contextualised within the vicissitudes of global markets in general, and the conditionalities of the EU in particular – to which CEEC must adjust. The need to establish free markets necessitates the establishment of appropriate political formations; the need to gain access to external economic support to assist in transformation results in the close attention of international actors. For CEEC this means proof of 'good governance' – conditionality within a liberal market paradigm – the liberal triumphalist dictum. The EU, however, presents to CEE is own conditions – reinforced by the need to ensure compliance with club rules designed to sustain the existing Union in a global market. Consequently, the Copenhagen political criteria and their subsequent elaboration in the *Agenda 2000* process involve the application of both 'idealist' and 'substantive' characteristics of democracy; thus the EU–CEEC 10 discourse regarding democratisation involves not only profound changes to political institutions, but also to governmental and administrative processes, such that there emerge civil society traditions commensurate with consolidated democracy (Netherlands Presidency of the EU 1997).

Democracy working in practice (effective democratic governance) cuts across a broad range of transformation issues – from the civic rights of Russian minorities in Estonia to corrupt policing in Romania; from flawed constitutional practice in Slovakia, to fears for media freedoms in Hungary. These, and many more, issues must be addressed before full external recognition for democratic maturity – EU membership – is achievable. *Agenda 2000* and other evaluations present mixed evidence in support of the CEEC' ability to meet these criteria in the medium term. This is especially problematic when observing the hurdles that seem to impede achievement of the necessary standards in administrative and legal capacity. The Commission has also clearly stated its intention of rigorously applying criteria associated with establishing individual rights. But the extent to which cultural change to accompany legal frameworks can be exogenously induced is debatable, especially in the light of the example of some existing member states in such areas as gender and minority rights. Can the emergence of 'civil society' be anticipated in regions, if not whole countries, where the main concern is day-to-day existence? The pressures of dual transition must inevitably continue to test the opinion of CEEC citizens that 'democracy' can deliver the good life, and expectations of elites that EU membership is an affordable political goal. In these circumstances it could be that the rigid application of EU political criteria may take a back seat to economic criteria; and that the calculation of both EU and CEEC decision makers may be that what matters most is the marketisation, not the democratisation, of CEE.

Notes

1 For a presentation of definitions of democracy in several forms see William R. Reisinger in Gray (1997). For an erudite discussion of theoretical interpretations of democracy, see Vanhanen (1997).

2 Thus for J. F. Brown (1994:1), 'Eastern Europe is engaged with a revolution as it copes with a legacy. Both are intimidating ... The legacy is bequeathed not only by communism but by elements in the pre-communist history of the region, influencing and hampering it, directly and indirectly. Indeed the most constraining part of the legacy is *pre*-communist; the national re-assertiveness that was repressed by communism but never submerged by it.'

3 For a lucid review of academic perspectives on democratic and economic transformation see Remmer (1995), who argues that global economic changes and democratisation cannot be addressed in total isolation from each other. Global economic changes have provoked and deepened economic difficulties

in societies undergoing democratisation, economic constraints have strengthened the impact of international forces upon regime change and sustainability, and the internationalisation of processes of domestic political choice has augmented the diversity of societies experiencing democratic transition (p. 118).

4 The resignation of Indonesia's dictator Suharto, in part hastened by critical commentary from the USA after thirty years of unswerving support, is one example of the more 'principled' stance taken by the USA, now able to regard democracy as a value rather than as a political football.

5 Munch and Leff contrast the negotiated process of transition (extrication) in Hungary; the 'rupture' experience of Czechoslovakia and Estonia; transaction where incumbent elites acquiesce to transition and subsequently acquire a stake in the new regime (Poland); and transition from above (Bulgaria) where old elites sustained a powerful influence over the transition process.

6 In its Comparative Survey of Freedom (Freedom House 1996) the survey takes a broadly neoliberal view of political rights and civil liberties and suggests that a free society may be defined in essentially democratic procedural terms, the extent of democracy governed by the choice offered to people to determine *the system* and their leaders. They point to a close correlation between the establishment of political freedoms and market choice in the speed of progress from transition to consolidation.

7 In all, the ISA group examined five CEEC (Slovakia, Hungary, Estonia, Romania and Poland) and four Tacis countries (Russia, Georgia, Belarus and Kazakhstan).

8 Events in Slovakia during and after the rows over a successor to President Kovac (March 1998) have only exacerbated international uncertainty over the effectiveness of the Slovak constitution and thus its desirability. This has not been enhanced by a long period of political instability likely at least until legislative elections in September 1998.

9 Thus J. F. Brown's historical/cultural analysis (1994); the Project on Democratisation and Political Participation in Post Communist Societies series edited by Karen Dawisha and Bruce Parrott (see Dawisha and Parrott 1997); Arend Lijhart and Carlos Waisman's *Institutional Design in New Democracies* (Boulder, Westview Press, 1999); Geoffrey Pridham and Paul Lewis's explanation of the salience of party systems, *Stabilizing Fragile Democracies* (London, Routledge, 1996); Pridham and Vanhanen's focus on the importance of international factors for CEE democratisation, *Democratisation in Eastern Europe: Domestic and International Perspectives* (London, Routledge, 1994) and Vanhanen's broad-based empirical observations in *Prospects for Democracy* (London, Routledge, 1997) represent some of the comparativist approaches recently undertaken.

10 A 1994 analysis comparing Eastern European attitudes towards past, present and future regimes found for the most part, on a scale ranking of worst to best, that citizens ranked Communist regimes as least well respected (43 per cent), with current regimes at 53 per cent (Rose and Haenpfer 1994). The study is interesting in that there is an attempt to analyse, from the individual's perspective, the dynamics of transformation. Citizens were divided into four groupings – *democrats* (37 per cent), who mostly support/applaud the

existing pluralist system; (32 per cent) *reactionaries*, who mostly support the previous authoritarian regime; *sceptics* (25 per cent), who disapprove of old and current regimes; and *compliants*, who see positive benefits in old and new (20 per cent). Their projections for the future, however, are less polarised than might be anticipated, with democrats, compliants and sceptics showing mostly positive expectations towards the medium-term prospects for democracy in their countries.

11   In one survey of Hungary, Poland and Russia the numbers of former party members still contemporary in elites were as follows: Russia 83.4 per cent political elite; 77.7 per cent cultural elite; 84 per cent state sector economic elite; 52.7 per cent private sector elite. Poland 56.9 per cent economic elite; 30 per cent political elite; 30 per cent cultural elite. Hungary 66 per cent economic elite; 31.7 per cent political elite; 55.6 per cent cultural elite. ((1995), I. Szeleyi, D. Truman and E. Wnuk-Lopinski (eds), *Elites in Poland, Russia and Hungary: Change or Reproduction?*, Warsaw Polish Academy of Sciences, Institute of Political Studies).

12   Rose describes the possession of a party card as the equivalent of an MBA in the market economy; 'a credential of an individual who could behave dishonestly or honestly, whichever way suited his or her convenience' (Rose 1996: 16).

13   Critical commentary is contained in horizontal analyses of: political criteria where, for instance, a Romanian change of government is said to have improved the Communist inherited administrative processes; in Slovakia where the functioning of central government is too closely controlled by Meciar's ruling political elite; in Latvia where access to the professions including the bureaucracy is closed to certain minorities; administrative criteria where the transformation and implementation of *acquis* can only be achieved in the major part and in the medium term by three countries – Hungary, Poland and the Czech Republic; Slovakia, Estonia, Lithuania and Slovenia will be able to do so only with 'a considerable and sustained increase in their efforts' (Commission 1997); and economic criteria: where the ability of applicants to effectively transpose and implement economic *acquis*, especially those associated with the SEM, is evaluated in depth. Sectoral evaluation of administrative capacity is also undertaken in fields such as agriculture, the environment, transport, nuclear safety, the implementation of justice and home affairs – in law enforcement, frontier protection and in particular the applicants' fight against organised crime, drugs, human trafficking and terrorism, 'where the lack of trained and experienced manpower [*sic*] is a common feature' (Commission 1997:59).

14   What the Commission did not do is recommend any particular bureaucratic model, process or mode of operation. Thus there is no debate around the concepts of a Weberian model versus new public management, nor is any model of central–decentralised relations recommended. What may be deduced from the *avis* is that CEEC should at the least: produce a civil service act; support a career rather than political civil service; ensure the independence of public administration from political authority; and provide adequate training and relevant pay levels for its public servants (Fournier 1997).

15 Administrative reform represents a fundamental task of political leadership and resource application that, for one established adviser on the subject, had only recently been recognised by the EU as a major problem of political and economic transformation (interview, January 1998). It was further suggested that the need to establish effective legal systems, resource management and control systems (horizontal reforms) is more pressing than the reforms of ministries (vertical reforms). Indeed, horizontal control mechanisms did not exist before 1989, and though the 1995 White Paper recognised this as a serious problem, it was not until *Agenda 2000* that it was included as a significant aspect of the Commission *avis* (interview, January 1998).

16 It is only in Czechoslovakian inter-war experiences that the rule of law has been embedded for any lengthy period; the Polish experience of democratic constitutionalism lasted for only five years (1921–26); Hungary's rule of law was circumscribed by several authoritarian populist regimes; and the Baltic states, Yugoslavia, Bulgaria and Romania experienced periods of democratic nominalism and authoritarianism that left little evidence of a judicial culture based on the rule of democratically legitimised laws.

17 Thus, Estonia has 46 town and 209 rural municipalities that are democratically elected. Since 1993 more responsibilities than inexperienced councillors or ill-trained local officials can handle have been accompanied by inadequate local and national resource allocation. Serious regional and cultural problems in the Russian-dominated north-eastern area have resulted in considerable mistrust between local and national politicians (Hanson 1993; Henderson and Robinson 1997). Where regional tiers of central governments exist, as in Hungary, Slovakia and Slovenia, a struggle for power between local and regional priorities has emerged (Kaldor and Vejvoda 1997). Romanian local government remains a victim of the centralist tendencies within the constitution, in part driven by the fear of Hungarian separatism.

18 Kirchner lists nine Euro regions involving Germany, Austria and the Visegrad states involved in eight programme areas of cooperation. This, in some cases, has extended to *inter*regional cooperation, e.g. the Hungarian Balaton Region with the French Pays de la Loire in the fields of culture and tourism (Kirchner 1997:7–8).

19 For example, see Havel's essay 'The Power and the Powerless', in *Living in Truth* (London, Faber and Faber, 1987) or Michnik's *Letters from Prison* (Berkeley, University of California Press, 1987). For an analysis of civil society and Communist collapse, see Hirst (1997).

20 In an attempt to avoid government interference in their activities, at least to 1996, the Slovak 'independent' NGO sector is organised into national and regional forms of association. The more political organisations (civic advocacy groups) have developed cooperative networks such that 'it is certainly arguable that the most effective (Slovak) opposition as well as independent action comes from this sector' (ISA Consult 1997:147).

21 More cooperative relationships between governments and NGOs are evident in Hungary, contemporary Romania and Estonia, where through cooperation with such organisations as the President's Round Table, the Ethnic Rights Information Centre and the Estonian Institute for Human Rights, active support for democratic processes is offered (ISA Consult 1997).

22 The principles that guide the EU's action in the field of human rights and
    democracy spring from the UN Charter (1948) and other sources such as the
    European Convention (1949), the Charter of Paris 1991, the Vienna
    Conference on Human Rights (1993) and the Beijing Conference on Women
    (1993).
23 The EHRF was established in 1980 by the Commission to promote world-
    wide human rights and since 1994 has provided, on a contract basis, technical
    assistance for the PTDP.
24 The danger in this for the bottom-up 'success' of the programme was recog-
    nised in the Commission, where one official admitted the differences in
    opinion within the Commission, some of whom feared loss of the spon-
    taneous nature of NGO 'development encouraged by the Democracy
    Programme to date' (European Dialogue 1996). From the perspectives of
    CEEC applicants the generally slow process from application to receipt of
    funding and rapid turnover of Brussels staffing has led to the demise of
    several smaller projects, again a valuable learning experience for would-be
    members.

References

Batt, J. (1994), The Political Transformation of East-Central Europe, in H. Maill
    (ed.), *Redefining Europe*, London, Pinter and Royal Institute for International
    Affairs.
Beetham, D. (1993), Liberal Democracy and the Limits of Democratisation, in D.
    Held (ed.), *Prospects for Democracy*, Oxford, Blackwell, 55–74.
Bretherton, C. (1996), Introduction: Global Politics in the 1990s, in C.A.
    Bretherton and G. Ponton (eds), *Global Politics – an Introduction*, Oxford,
    Blackwell, 1–19.
Brown, J. F. (1994), *Hopes and Shadows – Eastern Europe after Communism*,
    Harlow, Longman.
Brown, J. F. (1997), Goodbye (and Good Riddance) to De-communisation,
    Transitions, 4:2, 28–34.
Commission (1996a), *The External Dimension of Human Rights Policy*, Brussels,
    DGIA.
Commission (1996b), *The EU's Phare and Tacis Democracy Programme: Micro
    Projects in Operation*, Brussels, DGIA/EHRF.
Commission (1997), *Agenda 2000 – for a Stronger and Wider Union*, Vol. 1,
    COM(97)2000, Final, Brussels, 15 July.
Commission (1998), *Central and Eastern Eurobarometer*, 8, Brussels, March.
Coulson, A. (ed.) (1995), *Local Government in Eastern Europe: Establishing
    Democracy at the Grassroots*, London, Edward Elgar.
Dawisha, K. A. and Parrott, B. (1997), *Politics, Power and the Struggle for
    Democracy in South-East Europe*, Cambridge, Cambridge University Press.
Denton, N. and Mortimer, L. (1994), Nostalgia for Communist Comfort,
    Financial Times, 5 May.
East, R. and Pontin, J. (1997), *Revolution and Change in Central Europe*,
    London, Pinter.

EBRD (1995), *Transition Report*, London, European Bank for Reconstruction and Development, November.

Encarnación, O. G. (1996), The Politics of Dual Transition, *Comparative Politics*, 28:4, 477–92.

Etzioni, A. (1995), *The Spirit of Community*, London, Fontana.

European Dialogue (1996), *Democracy goes Hand in Hand with European Union Membership*, http://europa.euint/en/comm/dg10/intocom/eur-dial/96ila4so.html, January–February.

European Dialogue (1998), *Democracy*, http://europa.euint/en/comm/dg10/intocom/eur-dial/98i2a0so.html, March–April.

Fournier, J. (1997), Administrative Reform in the Commission's Opinions Concerning the Accession of Central and Eastern European Countries to the European Union, *Multi-Country Seminar on European Integration and Public Administration Reform, Athens*, 8–10 October, Paris, Sigma and OECD.

Freedom House (1997), *Freedom in the World: The Annual Survey of Political Rights and Civil Liberties 1995–6*, www.freedomhouse.org/library/freedom96

Fukuyama, F. (1989), The End of History, *The National Interest*, Summer, 3–18.

Galligan, D. (1997), Administrative Procedures and the Supervision of Administration, in Hungary, Poland, Bulgaria, Estonia and Albania, *Sigma Papers*, 17, Paris, Sigma and OECD.

Gills, B. and Rocamora, J. (1992), Low Intensity Democracy, *Third World Quarterly*, 13:3, 501–24.

Gray, R. D. (ed.) (1997), *Democratic Theory and Post Communist Change*, Englewood Cliffs, Prentice Hall.

Greskovits, B. (1996), Demagogic Populism in Eastern Europe?, *Telos*, February, 91–106.

Haggard, S. and Kaufman, R. (1995), *The Political Economy of Democratic Transitions*, Princeton, Princeton University Press.

Hanson, P. (1993), Estonia's Narva Problem, Narva's Estonia Problem, *RFE/RL Research Report*, 2:18, 17–23.

Hartwig, I. (1997), The Role of the European Parliament in Shaping the EU's Strategy on Central and Eastern Europe, Research Conference, *UACES*, Loughborough, 10–12 September.

Held, D. (ed.) (1993), *Prospects for Democracy – North, South, East, West*, Cambridge, Polity Press.

Held, D. (1995), *Democracy and Global Order*, Oxford, Polity Press.

Henderson, K. and Robinson, N. (1997), *Post Communist Politics – an Introduction*, London, Prentice Hall.

Hettne, B. (1995), *Development Theory and the Third World: Towards an International Political Economy of Development*, Harlow, Longman.

Higley, J. and Gunther, R. (eds) (1992), *Elites and Democratic Consolidation in Latin America and Southern Europe*, Cambridge, Cambridge University Press.

Hirst, P. (1997), *From Statism to Pluralism*, London, UCL Press.

Holmes, L. (1997), *Post-Communism – an Introduction*, Cambridge, Polity Press.

Huber, E., Rueschmeyer, D. and Stephens, J. D. (1991), The Impact of Economic Development on Democracy, *Journal of Economic Perspectives*, 7, Summer.

Huntington, S. (1991), *The Third Wave: Democratisation in the Late Twentieth Century*, Norman, University of Oklahoma Press.

Hyde-Price, A. (1996), *The International Politics of East-Central Europe*, Manchester, Manchester University Press.

Hyde-Price, A. (1997), The OSCE and European Security, in B. Park and W. Rees (eds), *Reconceptualising European Security*, London, Longman.

ISA Consult (1997), *Final Report – Evaluation of the Phare and Tacis Democracy Programme 1992–1997*, European Institute, Brighton/Hamburg, Sussex University and GJW Europe.

Ishiyama, J. T. (1995), Communist Parties in Transition, *Comparative Politics*, 27:2, 147–66.

Kaldor, M. and Vejvoda, I. (1997), Democratisation in CEE Countries, *International Affairs*, 73:1, 59–82.

Karatnychy, A. (1997), *Political and Economic Reform in East Central Europe and the New Independent States: A Progress Report*, Freedom House, http://www:/freedomhouse.org/NIT/intro-karatnychy.html

Karatnychy, A., Motyl, A. and Shor, B. (eds) (1997), *Nations in Transition*, New Brunswick, NJ, Freedom House, Transaction Publishers.

Kirchner, E. (1997), Decentralisation and Interregional Cooperation in Central Europe, Research Conference, *UACES*, Loughborough, 10–12 September.

Leftwich, A. (1993), Governance, Democracy and Development in the Third World, *Third World Quarterly*, 14:3, 605–24.

Lewis, P. (1994), *Central Europe since 1994*, Harlow, Longman.

Mannin, M. (1996), Global Issues and the Challenge to Democratic Politics, in C. A. Bretherton and G. Ponton (eds), *Global Politics – an Introduction*, Oxford, Blackwell, 220–46.

Marks, G. (1993), Structural Policy and Multilevel Governance in the EC, in A. W. Cafruny and G. G. Rosenthal (eds), *The State of the European Community (Vol. 2) – The Maastricht Debates and Beyond*, Harlow, Longman, 391–410.

Mihas, D. E. M. (1997), Romania between Balkan Nationalism and Democratic Transition, *Politics*, 17:3, 175–81.

Munck, G. L. (1994), Democratic Transitions in a Comparative Perspective, *Comparative Politics*, 26:3, 355–75.

Munck, G. L. and Leff, C. S. (1997), Modes of Transition and Democratisation, *Comparative Politics*, 29:3, 343–62.

Musil, J. (1994), Europe between Integration and Disintegration, *Czech Sociological Review*, 2:1, 5–19.

Netherlands Presidency of the EU (1997), Governance and European Integration: Final Document, *Conference: Netherlands Presidency of the EU*, Rotterdam, 29–30 May.

O'Donnell, G. and Schmitter, P. (1986), *Transitions from Authoritarian Rule: Tentative Conclusions about Uncertain Democracies*, Baltimore, Johns Hopkins University Press.

Okolicsanyi, A. (1993), Visegrad Triangle's Free Trade Zone, *RFE-RL Research Report*, 2:3, 33–7.

Pehe, J. (1993), Czech–Slovak Relations Deteriorate, *RFE-RL Research Report*, 2:18, 1–5.

Pithart, P. (1994), Only One Year Old and Deeper In Debt, *Guardian*, 4 January, 16.

Pogany, I. (1996), Constitution Making or Constitutional Transformation in Post-Communist Societies, in R. Bellamy and D. Castiglione (eds), *Constitutionalism in Transformation: European and Theoretical Perspective*, Oxford, Blackwell.

Preston, C. (1997), Poland and EU Membership – Current Issues and Future Prospects, Conference: Enlarging the European Union – the Way Forward; Birmingham, *UACES*, July.

Pridham, G. (1997), Regime Change, Democratic Conditionality and Transnational Party Linkages: The Case of Eastern Europe, paper for Workshop on Democratisation and the Changing Global Order, *ECPR*, University of Bern, 27 February–4 March.

Przeworski, J. (1991), *Democracy and the Market: Political and Economic Reforms in Eastern Europe and Latin America*, New York, Cambridge University Press.

Randel, J. and German, T. (eds) (1997), *The Reality of Aid – an Independent Review of Development Cooperation*, London, Earthscan.

Rehak, L. and Kirillov, V. (1995), Slovakia as a New Factor in European Politics, *International Relations*, 71:1, 47–64.

Reisch, A. A. (1993), Hungary Pursues Integration with the West, *RFE-RL Research Report*, 2:13, 32–8.

Remmer, K. L. (1995), New Theoretical Perspectives on Democratisation, *Comparative Politics*, 28:1, 103–22.

Rose, R. (1996), Ex-Communists in Post-Communist Societies, *Political Quarterly*, 67:1, 14–25.

Rose, R. and Haenpfer, C. (1994), Mass Response to Transformation, *Europe–Asia Studies*, 46:1, 3–28.

Schmitter, P. and Karl, T. (1992), The Types of Democracy Emerging in Southern and Eastern Europe, and South and Central America, in P. Volten (ed.), *Bound to Change: Consolidating Democracy in East-Central Europe*, New York, Westview, 28–68.

Shin, D. C. (1994), On the Third Wave of Democratisation, *World Politics*, 47:3, 135–70.

Sigma (1997), Reliable Public Administration, conference paper, Rotterdam, 29–30 May, *Support for Improvement in Governance and Management*, Paris, Sigma.

Smith, G. (1994), Can Liberal Democracy Span the European Divide?, in H. Maill (ed.), *Redefining Europe*, London, Pinter and Royal Institute for International Affairs, 113–28.

US State Department (1996), *Country Reports on Human Rights Practices*, Washington, DC, State Department, Bureau of Democracy, Human Rights and Labour, http//www.usis.usemb.se/human.

Vanhanen, T. (1997), *Prospects for Democracy – a Study of 172 Countries*, London, Routledge.

Welsh, H. (1994), Political Transition Processes in Central and Eastern Europe, *Comparative Politics*, 26:4, 379–94.

Wiseman, J. (1993), Democracy and the New Pluralism in Africa, *Third World Quarterly*, 14:3, 439–49.

5 Charlotte Bretherton

Women and transformation in CEEC: challenging the EU women's policy?

The impacts on CEE societies of the multidimensional transformation process have inevitably been differentiated by gender. Since the status of women is an indicator of the health of society, gender relations can be viewed, in the context of CEEC transformation, as 'a microcosm of the process and impact of social change itself' (Einhorn 1993:17). Moreover, as we shall see, the gender dimensions of transformation raise difficult issues for EU–CEEC relations in general; and challenge the EU women's policy in particular.

The women's policy is the most fully developed aspect of social policy provision at EU level (Hoskyns 1996). It has evolved considerably since the late 1970s, and now comprises two distinct elements. The central core of the women's policy has been, and remains, a series of legislative measures which seek to promote equality of treatment in the context of paid work. This important but relatively narrowly focused aspect of the women's policy is referred to, below, as the 'equal opportunity policy'. The second element of the women's policy comprises a range of broadly based initiatives and programmes which aim generally to enhance the social status and political influence of women. In the context of EU–CEEC relations, both aspects of the women's policy have significance – equal opportunity policy relates to economic transformation; the more broadly based measures have significance for the processes of democratisation.

EU policy on equal opportunity for women and men is an expanding element of the *acquis* which should, in principle, be adopted in full by candidate countries. However, its relevance in the context of CEEC is the subject of controversy. It is challenged, first, by the argument that, in order to facilitate CEEC accession, much of the social policy *acquis* should be set aside. Indeed, some commentators are prepared to consider permanent derogations from social policy provisions; not only for CEEC but also for existing member states – on the grounds that 'Some groups of European citizens could choose to create competitive advantages for themselves by accepting lower environmental quality or poorer social protection' (Smith *et al.* 1996:5). These arguments demonstrate the importance of equal opportunity policy for the enlargement debate. Equality issues epitomise the tensions – and possibly the difficult choices – between deepening and widening. It is in precisely such areas that fears concerning the potential impact of enlargement on existing policy achievements seem best founded.

The second challenge to the equal opportunity *acquis* emanates not from Western supporters of enlargement, but from CEE women themselves. This challenge is fundamental, in that it questions the premises which underlie EU policy and thus raises difficult issues concerning the relevance to CEE societies of externally generated principles and practices which fail to build upon, accommodate or even acknowledge the historical and contemporary experiences of CEE women.

Similar difficulties arise when considering the relevance of policies which aim to enhance women's social and political status more broadly. The contemporary situation of women in CEEC raises concerns about the balanced and healthy development of civil society, and hence the democratisation process. Since possession of a stable democracy is the first criterion for EU membership, women's participation in formal political processes, and in civil society more broadly, has significance for EU–CEEC relations as accession approaches.

Before exploring these issues in greater depth, it should be noted that they are extremely sensitive. East–West dialogue between women on these matters has frequently been characterised by tension and mutual misunderstanding – hence a Hungarian commentator's observation that she has 'found more gaps between Western and Eastern views on women than exist on most other issues' (Bollobás 1993:202).[1] There is a danger, moreover, that a focus upon East–West divisions will obscure the differences in women's experiences, and the many issues which divide them, *within* both the East and the West. Thus divergences of experience between Greek and Finnish women, for example, are as great as those between Slovenian and Polish women. A focus on 'national' differences also brings the risk of homogenising women's experience. Disparities based on socio-economic status and rural–urban divisions are important influences on women's priorities; and the issues of concern to ethnic minority or migrant women may differ markedly from those of the majority.

Failure properly to consider the variety of women's experience has important implications. Not only does it impede understanding of the complexity of gender relations within and between societies – it also impacts upon policy. Thus, in the context of the EU, 'until very recently, what "women" actually meant in terms of EU policy was "white women in paid employment"' (Hoskyns 1996:9). Clearly the capacity of the EU women's policy to accommodate difference must be a measure of its relevance, not least in the context of enlargement. Inevitably, we cannot properly explore these questions in a short chapter, although they are reflected in our assessment of the implications of enlargement for the EU women's policy. First, however, the relevance of EU policy is considered in relation to economic transformation and democratisation.

Economic transformation and the equal opportunity *acquis*

Neither the impacts of transformation nor the contemporary attitudes of CEE women can be understood without reference to the experiences of state socialism. Consequently we begin this section with a brief overview of women's situation prior to 1989. Since the EU equal opportunities *acquis* comprises a series of legislative measures relating to the workplace, and to the reconciliation of work and family life, it is upon these aspects of women's experience that we will focus.[2]

Women and work under state socialism

From the 1950s, following the consolidation of state socialist regimes across CEEC, women's participation in paid work increased considerably. By 1980 women comprised almost half the labour force of the region – a significantly higher proportion than in EU member states at that time – and by 1989 the majority of women of working age were in full-time paid employment. In (then) Czechoslovakia, for example, almost 94 per cent of women worked outside the home (Šiklová 1993:75). This level of labour force participation by women reflected both economic and political factors.

The strong emphasis on women's entry into paid work by state social-ist governments reflected a high demand for labour in the economy, and was supported by ideological commitment to women's 'emancipation' – for which involvement in paid work was seen as an essential precondition. From this perspective, moreover, achievement of emancipation was not equated with attainment of managerial status but with women's partici-pation in non-traditional areas of work; that is, 'whether a woman was capable to drive [*sic*] a tractor or operate a crane' (Subhan 1996:18). As a consequence, 'Some women were willing to become equal to men at any price' (Kiczková and Farkašová 1993:85). Nevertheless, for most CEE women, paid work was both an economic necessity and a source of social identity and status independent from men.

Across CEEC, women's labour force participation was supported by a range of policies and provisions intended to facilitate the reconciliation of work and family life. Thus paid maternity leave for a period of four to six months was the norm throughout the region, and in several countries, including Czechoslovakia, Poland and Hungary, there was provision for extended leave of up to three years. In addition, there were various levels of entitlement to annual paid leave to care for sick children.[3] Heavily subsidised kindergarten provision, for children from the age of three, was almost universal and was, for the most part, highly valued by parents. Crèche provision for infants under three, however, was less widely available but also less popular – women preferred to make other arrangements or to take extended leave. A range of other subsidised supports for family life, such as after-school childcare, children's summer camps or laundry facilities, were frequently provided by the state or at the level of the enterprise. Finally, in most CEEC, the right to abortion was available to women from the mid-1950s, although in some countries qualifications to this right were introduced or increased in the early 1970s. This matter is discussed further below.

In principle, the rights and provisions which supported women's participation in paid work under state socialism were socially progressive and favourable to women. Indeed, despite the expansion of the EU equal opportunities *acquis*, they have yet to be achieved in the West. Thus, from a Czech perspective, 'Rights that Western women are still fighting for are taken for granted here' (Šiklová 1998:33). Since these issues are important for the development and application of EU equality policy, it is instructive to examine the impacts of the state socialist model in practice.

Despite legislation providing for equal pay, the strong rhetoric of women's equality in the workplace and women's generally high level of educational attainment in CEEC, in practice the 'gender gap' in income resembled that in the EU. Thus women in CEEC earned, on average, between 66 and 75 per cent of male wages across all sectors of the economy (Einhorn 1993:122). This income differential reflects a vertical and horizontal segmentation of the labour force which, again, is not dissimilar to the pattern which prevails in the West. Thus, in CEEC, women were poorly represented in the heavy industrial and mining sectors which were prioritised, and remunerated accordingly, under state socialism. Indeed, in several CEEC women were (and in some cases remain) legally barred from employment in occupations regarded as particularly arduous. In Poland, for example, women have been excluded, since 1979, from ninety occupations in eighteen employment sectors (Subhan 1996:30). In consequence, despite the rhetoric of the 'heroine worker-mother' undertaking the heaviest of tasks, women were clustered in light industry and in administrative and service sectors – in occupations which were accorded low status and attracted low pay. In other areas, such as medicine, women were well represented, but earned considerably less than men in the same profession (30 per cent on average) – reflecting the fact that in the East, as in the West, senior positions were dominated by men. Thus in Hungary, for example, only 12.5 per cent of managerial positions were occupied by women in 1980; the figure for Czechoslovakia in 1989 was comparable at 14 per cent (Einhorn 1993:273; Heitlinger 1993:97).

This failure to achieve equality in the workplace reflects fundamental flaws and contradictions in the state socialist model of emancipation. Prioritisation of women's role in the public sphere, in particular paid work, reflected an approach to equality based upon 'sameness'. Thus, women were obliged to compete with men in a work environment dominated by men and by male norms and expectations of behaviour. At the same time, since childcare provision was based upon an exclusively maternal definition of parenting, women were accorded special treatment in relation to their reproductive role. The results of this combination of equal treatment in relation to production and special treatment in relation to reproduction were twofold. First, women suffered a particularly heavy, and frequently debilitating, double burden of domestic and paid work. Second, women's career progression was impeded by their special treatment in terms of extended leave for parental responsibilities and earlier retirement than men. A second impediment to women's career progression was the closed and inaccessible nomenclatura system, through which senior positions were filled and other privileges granted. While women comprised almost half the workforce, they were 'by no means half of the nomenclatura' (Makkai 1994:193). In the political and ideological climate of state socialism, little space was provided for discussion of these gender disparities.

An important, and telling, consequence of women's experiences under state socialism was the significant fall in the birthrate across CEEC. Indeed, by the late 1960s, the one-child family had become increasingly prevalent. Thus it is in the context of anxiety about falling birth rates that CEE governments introduced substantially increased material supports for maternity from the 1970s. A related concern has been the high rate of abortion across the region, which reflected poor availability of reliable contraception as well as unwillingness to reproduce. In Hungary in the late 1960s, for example, there were 134 abortions for every 100 live births (United Nations Children's Fund 1994:60). As a consequence, in Hungary, Bulgaria, and most particularly in Romania, restrictions to the availability of abortion were introduced from the 1970s. The abortion issue remained a subject of concern and debate in several CEEC during the 1980s; it provided a powerful symbol of the failure of the state socialist model of emancipation.

Economic transformation and women's work

From the outset it was clear that the processes of marketisation and privatisation would create unemployment in CEEC. For social-psychological as well as economic reasons, it was also anticipated that

unemployment would, and indeed should, affect women disproportionately.

Psychologically, in societies with little recent experience of unemployment, there were fears among men that failure to compete with women in
the new labour market 'might prove men's weakness' (Malinowska
1995:42). There was also a complementary belief that women would be
better able to adjust to unemployment, since they could devote themselves
to home and family, whereas unemployed men 'drank, stole or went
fishing' (Reszke 1995:16). Economically, as we have seen, the extensive
maternity leave and other benefits accruing to women made them expensive and 'unreliable' employees. Moreover, the costs of supporting
maternity, including subsidised childcare, appeared to be unsustainable in
circumstances where the state sector was contracting rapidly and market
disciplines were beginning to affect all sectors.

For all these reasons, and in the context of women's heavy burden of
work and the still declining birth rate, it seemed appropriate that women
in the East should leave the workforce in order to support men and
produce families, as women in the West had done after the Second World
War.[4] Women's reactions to this 'new' social model were ambivalent; they
have remained so.

For the new CEE governments after 1989, women's position in society
was an early matter of concern – and an important aspect of the broader
repudiation of the previous system. Thus, in the rhetoric of CEE politicians, the 'heroine worker-mother' of state socialism was replaced by
highly traditional images of women. 'The woman-mother for whom pregnancy is a blessing, must be an idol' announced Marcin Libicki, Poland's
(then) representative at the Council of Europe (quoted in Malinowska
1995:41). Women who questioned the new model of womanhood
attracted particular derision; earning the label 'feminist' – a term of abuse
in several CEEC.[5] Thus feminism, according to Czech President Vaclav
Havel, is a refuge for 'bored housewives and dissatisfied mistresses'
(quoted in Watson 1993:73). The intensity of this rhetoric, and of the
broader societal debate about women's role which it accompanied, varied
between CEEC. Throughout the region, however, it crystallised around
the issue of abortion.

In Poland, where the Catholic Church is particularly influential, there
was an emotional debate which resulted in an almost complete ban on
abortion in 1993 (Heinen and Matuchniak-Krasuska 1995). Although
Poland's legislation on abortion was relaxed in 1996, the issue remains
highly charged. In Hungary, also, a draft law banning abortion generated
'one of the first big discussions of the newly elected parliament' (Kiss
1991:53). While this law was not adopted, the Hungarian Constitutional
Court subsequently ruled that 'performing abortions without proper justification is against the spirit of the Constitution' (quoted in Subhan

1996:34). Similar debates took place in the Czech Republic and Slovakia. However, the intention to introduce a more restrictive policy in Slovakia than was proposed by the Czech government generated fears of 'abortion tourism', and no action was taken (Subhan 1996). Even in Slovenia, where an autonomous women's movement has existed since the early 1980s and anti-feminism has been less intense than elsewhere in the region, there was resistance to reinsertion of reproductive rights clauses into the constitution of the new state (Jalusic 1997). Only in Romania, where abortion was previously almost unobtainable, has access to abortion increased.

Following this high-profile debate, there was a significant decrease in the number of legal abortions performed in Poland, Hungary and the Czech Republic by 1992.[6] Despite this, the gradual decline in the birth rate continued across the region (Subhan 1996:68). This is a very clear demonstration of women's feelings of uncertainty and insecurity; and their ambivalence about the 'woman-mother' role they have been called upon to play. As Jalusic (1997:216) has argued, in Slovenia, as elsewhere, the abortion debate was ultimately about women's place in society.

Despite the expectation that women would, more or less willingly, embrace the housewife role offered to them, in practice the impact of economic change on women's employment has been mixed. Since 1989 there has been a significant increase in unemployment generally across the region, and in all countries (except Hungary) women figure disproportionately among the unemployed. In 1994 the percentage unemployment rates for selected countries were as follows:

	Bulgaria	Hungary	Poland	Romania	Czech Republic
Women	19.0	12.5	15.5	10.5	5.4
Men	18.7	14.6	11.9	6.3	4.8

(International Labour Organisation (ILO), in Subhan 1996:38)

The differences between countries reflect policy preferences and cultural factors; inevitably, also, they reflect different methods of measuring unemployment. While these tend, in all cases, to underestimate women's unemployment, this is particularly so in the case of Hungary, where women have been discouraged from registering as unemployed. Consequently the figures above conceal the fact that a relatively large number of Hungarian women have left the labour force (Wyzan 1998:14).[7]

While there are clear disparities between male and female unemployment, there has not been the exodus of women from the labour force that the 'woman-mother' model might predict. There are a number of explanations for this, which reflect both supply and demand factors. In terms of labour supply, there is considerable evidence that women both need to work, for financial reasons, and want to work, for status and other social reasons (Watson 1993; Millard 1995; Dodds 1998).[8] Here the greatly reduced availability, and increased cost, of childcare provision has been an impediment to women across CEE (United Nations Children's Fund 1994). This impacts particularly upon the lowest income groups, so that women who are single parents or from ethnic minorities suffer disproportionately (Watson 1993; Ferge 1997).

Consideration of demand for labour in contemporary CEEC reveals a complex picture. As a consequence of the contraction of the male-dominated heavy industrial and mining sectors, men have increasingly sought employment in the lower paid service sectors previously dominated by women. This reveals the most significant problem facing women in the labour market; women, once unemployed, are significantly less likely than men to be re-employed. Indeed in several CEEC, including Hungary, Poland and Slovakia, discriminatory practices in recruitment are 'rife and quite open' (Watson 1993:80). In addition to the open (and legal) practice of advertising job vacancies by gender, a number of informal practices are reported, including demanding assurances from potential employees that they do not plan to have children (Subhan 1996:41). There is also evidence that women's 'urgent need to obtain work' makes them vulnerable to sexual harassment in the workplace (United Nations Children's Fund 1994:70).

While women have yet to organise themselves politically to fight against this discrimination and mistreatment, they have demonstrated their unwillingness to give up employment – through, for example, taking advantage of the new opportunities for entrepreneurship. Thus in Hungary there were, by 1993, 'many successful women entrepreneurs', while a number of women were 'prominent and successful' in new areas of work, including the president of the Budapest Stock Exchange (Bollobás 1993:203). In the Czech Republic the proportion of women entrepreneurs in 1994 was also 'quite high' – at 21 per cent (United Nations Children's Fund 1994:54). Nevertheless, women in CEEC, as elsewhere, are over-represented among smaller, less capital-intensive types of business – reflecting women's relatively poor access to credit (Watson 1993:78).

The labour market impacts of economic transformation have not been gender neutral. In 1989 the majority of women, across CEEC, were in paid employment, albeit concentrated in poorly paid, low-status jobs. Today, even these jobs are increasingly unavailable to women. As unemployment has risen, men have been systematically favoured by employers, both in laying off and recruiting workers. In these circumstances it might appear that the EU equal opportunity *acquis* has a great deal to offer CEE women. In practice, however, the situation is rather more complex.

A place for the EU equal opportunity policy?

In assessing the relevance of EU policy, four factors demand consideration: the pan-European context of the debate; the content and evolution of EU policy; the attitudes of CEE women towards equality issues; and CEEC equal opportunity provision and the EU *acquis*.

The pan-European context

Despite the difficulties faced by CEE women, it would be mistaken to assume that their position is, in general, less favourable than that of EU women. Comparison is difficult, perhaps untenable, due to the very different experiences of women between and within the East and West. Even when considered at the most superficial level, the situation is complex.

Examination of the UN Development Programme (1997) 'Gender-related Development Index' (GDI) reveals that, in all CEEC, the position of women is relatively favourable when compared with the overall level of human development. This is not the case for several EU member states; indeed the GDI ranking of three (Ireland, Luxembourg and Portugal) falls below that of Slovenia, the Czech Republic and Slovakia (see Table 5.1).[9] It is noteworthy that a strongly positive relationship between GDI and overall human development is almost entirely confined to the former state socialist countries and, to a lesser extent, the Nordic countries, evidently reflecting egalitarian principles and high levels of social welfare provision.[10]

Within the EU, a variety of social welfare models coexist. Their outcomes are gendered, as the significant divergence in GDI ranking within the EU indicates.[11] Consequently, the social policy model adopted during the transition to capitalism will have great importance for CEE women. As will be evident from other chapters in this book, these models are likely to vary considerably between CEEC. For example, the present Estonian government is strongly oriented towards liberal, market-based solutions; while, in Slovenia, the evolving social model more closely resembles the Nordic pattern. A consequence of these policy differences is likely to be further widening of the GDI gap between the two countries, both of which have opened formal negotiations for accession to the EU. Thus, enlargement to the East, and the increased heterogeneity which this will entail, provides the background against which EU policy must be assessed.

Evolution of EU equal opportunity policy

EU policy originated from Article 119 of the Treaty of Rome, which provided for equal pay for equal work and was inserted, at the insistence

Table 5.1   Gender-related Human Development Index

Country	HDI rank[a]	GDI rank[b]	HDI rank minus GDI rank[c]
France	2	6	−4
Netherlands	6	11	−5
Finland	8	7	+1
Sweden	10	3	+7
Spain	11	19	−8
Austria	12	15	−3
Belgium	13	14	−1
UK	15	13	+2
Ireland	17	29	−12
Denmark	18	10	+8
Germany	19	16	+3
Greece	20	21	−1
Italy	21	23	−2
Luxembourg	27	38	−11
Portugal	31	30	0
Slovenia	35	24	+10
Czech Republic	39	25	+12
Slovakia	42	26	+13
Hungary	48	34	+11
Poland	58	37	+13
Bulgaria	69	49	+10
Estonia	71	52	+8
Lithuania	76	55	+8
Romania	79	59	+8
Latvia	92	67	+11

Notes:

[a] The HDI (Human Development Index) is a composite figure based on life expectancy at birth, the adult literacy rate, the combined enrolment ratio in primary, secondary and tertiary education, and real and adjusted GDP per capita. Figures are based on data for 1994. Rank indicates position out of 175 countries.

[b] In the GDI the criteria on which the HDI is based are expressed separately for men and women. GDP figures are replaced by earned income share. Rank indicates position out of 146 countries due to the absence of data by gender for 29 countries.

[c] A positive figure indicates that the GDI rank is better than the HDI rank, a negative figure the opposite. Calculations have been adjusted to allow for the countries with entries only in the HDI.

Source: Adapted from UN Development Programme (1997), 149–51.

of the French government, in order to avoid unfair competition in the Common Market. Despite this fragile basis, the policy developed incrementally during the 1970s and 1980s, largely as a result of women's political activism (Hoskyns 1996). A series of Directives was passed, which were intended to combat discrimination against women in the workplace.[12] Essentially, these Directives reflected liberal notions of equal treatment; that is, women were to compete on 'equal' terms with men, without special provision or positive action. In principle, these measures mirrored the equal treatment measures of state socialism.

During the 1990s the emphasis of EU policy has changed in two respects. First, an element of special treatment has been introduced. This is reflected in two Directives – one on the treatment of pregnant workers and women returning to work after childbirth, a second on parental leave. In addition, there has been a series of Resolutions and Recommendations on matters such as childcare and sexual harassment in the workplace.[13] Notions of positive action have also recently been introduced, amid great controversy – indeed, the legality of positive action has twice been tested in the European Court of Justice (Commission 1997–98). The present, rather complicated situation should be clarified on entry into force of the Amsterdam Treaty, which permits 'specific advantages . . . for the under-represented sex' (Article 141, ex Article 119).[14]

In consequence the equal opportunity *acquis* will in future reflect three principles – equal treatment, special treatment and positive action – although the first remains predominant. Moreover, the Amsterdam Treaty introduces a further important principle, that of mainstreaming, which is intended to apply across all policy areas and is discussed below. The evolution of these principles reflects the thinking of women who have been actively involved in influencing EU policy; that is, elite women – lawyers, politicians and officials of national organisations – who enjoy access to the resources necessary to operate at the EU level. Nevertheless, a range of women's networks do provide links, however tenuous, between elite women and women's groups at the grassroots level. This allows the needs and interests of women from a range of backgrounds to be articulated and discussed in various fora, including at the EU level (Bretherton and Sperling 1996).

CEE women's perspectives on equality issues

Policy towards women in Eastern Europe during the state socialist period did not reflect women's expressed needs or demands. Its principles, whether in terms of equal treatment or special treatment, were imposed upon women. In addition, there was little opportunity to challenge, or even seriously discuss, the content or effectiveness of policy in this area. Even today public debate on these matters remains limited. In the words of a Hungarian commentator, 'a description of how women see their own situation is completely lacking. Their voices – their critical considered voices – are rarely heard in public' (Acsady 1998:77).

In consequence, for CEE women, EU equality policy represents a further imposition of extraneous principles which take no account of their experience. Thus, among (primarily academic) Eastern European commentators there is a fundamental questioning of the perceived agenda of Western feminists and, by implication, much of the EU *acquis* – for two principal reasons. First, for CEE women, the issues pursued by Western women are redolent of

> the various benefits women enjoyed in the Communist societies, such as full employment, free health care, maternity leave, and cheap abortion (which) only sound appealing to foreign observers, to whom these words have different and much more positive meanings. In Hungarian – as well as Czech, Slovak, Polish and Russian – these words sound pitiful, cheap, poor and gloomy, because that is the reality they evoke. (Bollobás 1993:203)

Not only has the gap between rhetoric and reality under state socialism ensured that the principles of Western equality policies are questioned, it has also made CEE women extremely sceptical of attempts to address their needs through legislation. In the West, also, there is an implementation gap, and a justifiable scepticism about the effectiveness of legal remedies. Nevertheless, in the context of the EU, women have proved adept at exploiting the possibilities of legislation (Hoskyns 1996; Mazey 1998).

An explanation for CEE women's relative lack of involvement with equality issues can be found in the second element of their critique of Western feminism – which again reflects the legacy of state socialism. CEE women do not, for the most part, see their problems in terms of inequality with men. In the Czech Republic, for example, 'women have felt themselves to be struggling alongside their men against other oppressors' (Šiklová 1998:30). Similar sentiments are expressed by Polish women who were active in Solidarity in the early years (Hauser *et al.* 1993:261). Consequently, despite the fact that they are suffering disproportionately from the negative impacts of transformation processes, many women remain optimistic that a positive outcome to these processes will benefit society in general – 'Once again we want to believe that the change of economic base will solve all other problems, including relations between men and women' (Šiklová 1998:35).

In the context of major, rapid and unpredictable change, it is understandable that CEE women require time to adjust and to reflect; and that they are not prepared to accept uncritically policies and prescriptions put forward by Western women who have not shared their experiences. Nevertheless, in the context of the enhanced pre-accession strategies put in place following publication of *Agenda 2000* in June 1997, all CEE governments are under great pressure to ensure that their policies accord with the EU *acquis*. If CEE women are to influence the pre-accession and accession processes, there is no time for reflection.

CEEC equal opportunity provision and the EU *acquis*

The expansion of the EU equal opportunity *acquis* presents CEE governments seeking accession with a moving target in this area, as in others. Given the overall scope of EU policy, however, it is inevitable that priority has been given to areas which impinge most directly upon the EU's accession criteria, in particular the Single Market *acquis*.[15] Nevertheless, the Commission's Opinions on CEEC readiness for accession (attached to *Agenda 2000*) surveyed all policy areas, including equal opportunity.

It was concluded that, in all applicant countries, the basic provisions of EU anti-discrimination law were covered by national legislation (Commission 1997a). However, in respect of the Czech Republic, Hungary and Slovakia, the entire policy area is dealt with in a single (similar) sentence. Rather more space is devoted to the failure of CEE governments to insist on the EU's preferred labelling for cigarette packets. In the case of Slovenia, an additional sentence refers to parental leave. The remaining Opinions, which stretch to three sentences, make specific reference to failure to respect non-discrimination principles in relation to equal pay. In none of the Opinions, however, is there reference to systematic discrimination against women in recruitment.[16]

Concern at the superficial treatment of equality issues in *Agenda 2000* has been expressed by Members of the EP (MEPs), among others (European Parliament 1997a). There is particular anxiety about policy implementation, which is 'severely hampered by the unequal way in which present difficulties affect women and men' (Birgitta Ahlqvist, MEP, quoted in Commission 1997b). Implementation is undoubtedly an important issue, and a number of serious impediments to implementation can be identified – most of which are evident in all CEEC. These include absence of case law; lack of specialist legal training in equal opportunities; failure to provide guidance to employers and employees; lack of an independent national body to monitor equal opportunity matters; and low levels of public awareness concerning the meaning and practice of discrimination (Scheppele 1995; interview with Commission official, October 1997).

Some of these deficiencies will be remedied following accession to the EU; or in anticipation, as has been the case for existing member states.[17] Indeed, CEE governments have already shown awareness of EU requirements in this policy area. In Slovenia, for example, establishment of a parliamentary commission and a government office for women has been part of a 'well planned effort to do anything that will enhance the country's chance of being admitted into the European Union' (Renne 1997:6). And in the case of Hungary:

> Problems of gender were pushed to the side until Hungarian politicians bumped into European expectations about gender discrimination. Soon, government offices, boards and departments were established to institu-

tionalise the defense of women's interests. The only people missing from the picture were women. (Acsady 1998:78)

This lack of input from women is, perhaps, the single most significant factor affecting policy implementation. Even more importantly, it also inhibits the development of policies which respond to the needs of women. While reflecting, in part, the ambivalence of CEE women concerning equality issues, it is also indicative of the generally low level of women's participation in lobbying and policy-making activities in CEEC. It is to these matters that we now turn.

Political participation and the development of civil society

In the post-Cold War ideological climate, the EU has accorded increasing significance to the liberal democratic credentials of Associated countries. Indeed, for CEE candidate members, the development of stable democratic institutions is an essential prerequisite. In order fully to satisfy the political criteria for membership, 'achievement' of democracy must involve more than the establishment of formal institutions and procedures. There must also be widespread understanding of, and support for, the norms and practices which uphold liberal democratic systems. As will be evident from Chapter 4, democratic consolidation is a problematic and long-term process. It places considerable demands, not only upon elites, but also upon the general public, who are required to demonstrate the level and forms of participation deemed appropriate to citizens of a pluralistic, liberal democracy.

The political behaviour of women in CEEC thus becomes an important issue, which should inform the accession debate – both because women comprise more than half the population and because 'the principle of equality between the sexes is one of the basic principles of the European model of democracy' (Commission 1996:23). This model encompasses both elite participation and the broader involvement of women in the creation of a viable civil society. Below we examine each of these areas before considering the role of the EU in supporting the political involvement of CEE women.

Women in CEE political elites

In relation to elite participation, achievement of a gender balance in decision making is a central aim of the EU women's policy.[18] This reflects the view that 'The unbalanced representation of women in representative, administrative and advisory bodies, in the media, finance, justice and public administration, manifests a democratic deficit and deprives these

institutions of their full legitimacy' (Commission 1996:23). During the
state socialist period women's representation in the formal political
system, particularly in national parliaments, was relatively high when
compared with EU levels.[19] However, the gap between the rhetoric and
reality of women's political participation was very great. Representation
in national parliaments was predetermined by quota, and women's
participation was regarded as a duty.[20] In consequence, this was achieved
at great cost – not only did it place additional burdens on women, it also
generated perceptions, among women and men, that women's participation in public affairs was a ritual imposed from above to symbolise the
'achievement' of equality.[21] This perception reflects the fact that parliaments themselves played a largely symbolic role. Power lay with the
Communist Party apparatus and in the Politburo. Here, women were
frequently *un*represented; nowhere, throughout the state socialist period,
did women's representation on the Politburo exceed 5 per cent (Janova
and Sineau 1992:121).

An immediate effect of the demise of state socialism was a spectacular
fall, of almost 75 per cent on average (from 26 per cent to 7 per cent), in
the proportion of women in the national parliaments of CEEC (Lokau
1998). These figures are indicative of a broader tendency in societies
undergoing democratisation – as parliaments become more meaningful,
and the role of politicians more prestigious, there is a tendency to oust
women (Randall 1987; Einhorn 1993). In CEEC, where women are as
highly educated as men, and the new democratic procedures are unfamil-
iar to men and women alike, this 'cannot be readily justified in terms of
the superior experience, skills or qualifications of men' (Watson
1993:72). Rather, the 'rise of masculinism' reflects the highly traditional
political cultures of CEEC (Heinen 1992; Watson 1993, Waylen 1994).
As one Hungarian politician has put it: 'These are half-feudalistic, agrarian societies which have then had forty years of socialist dictatorship. You
cannot see women leaders in either form of society' (Anna Petrasovits,
quoted in Einhorn 1993:152).

Despite the social conservatism still evident in CEEC, there has been,
since 1994, an increase in women's representation, to an average of
approximately 10 per cent (Subhan 1996; Druker 1998). However, the
legacy of the previous system is such that there is great reluctance to introduce mechanisms, such as quotas, to promote women's candidacy –
although the Hungarian Socialist Party has recently done so (Lokau
1998). Clearly this has implications for strategies, associated with the EU
women's policy, to promote gender balance.

It is important to note that similar problems are evident in a number of
current EU member states. Indeed, the UN Development Programme, in
attempting to measure gender empowerment (as distinct from the socio-
economic GDI referred to above), places Hungary above France (United

Nations Development Programme 1997:152–4). It is very noticeable, however, that gender empowerment data – that is, the proportion of parliamentarians, administrators, managers and professional and technical workers who are women – are available only for Hungary and Poland. There are no entries for the remaining CEEC (and NIS). The generally poor availability of data by gender reflects the low importance given to this matter by CEE governments.[22] This is a particular problem in areas such as public administration, where information is not readily available. It has significance not only for domestic policy making but also for the conduct of accession negotiations. Here it is telling that representatives of two EU-funded organisations involved in supporting public-sector developments in CEEC were unable (in June 1998) to provide a gender breakdown of senior officials in CEEC; indeed, in one case, there was surprise that this information should be requested. This has implications for EU policy on 'mainstreaming', as we shall see below.

Despite improvements since 1994, women are under-represented at the elite level in CEEC, as in the EU. Moreover, elite women, if they are to represent the varied interests of women in their societies, depend for information and support upon an organised constituency at the grassroots level – and thus upon women's involvement in civil society.

Civil society and women's grassroots participation

In assessing CEEC democratic transition, great significance has been attached to the development of 'civil society' – that is, 'self-organized groups or institutions capable of preserving an autonomous public sphere which would guarantee individual liberty and check abuses of the state' (Kaldor and Vejvoda 1997:76). It is through participation in NGOs that the norms and practices characteristic of Western 'civil society' are to be learned by CEEC citizens (ISA Consult 1997:22). This would suggest an important role for women's organisations in the evolution of civil society.

In practice, the development of women's organisations in the new democracies has been hesitant (Renne 1997; Acsady 1998; Penn 1998; Šiklová 1998). This reflects, in part, the heavy responsibilities borne by women in CEEC. But, again, it is also a legacy of the past. For forty years, the only women's organisations officially permitted were those sponsored by the Communist Party; and in Hungary, as elsewhere, 'The Communists banned all thinking and action that challenged the role of the single official women's organization, the Soviet-type National Alliance of Hungarian Women' (Bollobás 1993:202). Consequently, since dissident organisations such as Charter 77 and Solidarity were mixed (albeit male-dominated), there was neither a tradition of non-official women's groups nor an opportunity to develop a critical analysis of women's position in society. Thus the ambivalence of CEE women concerning equality issues in the workplace, noted above, applies equally to involvement with women's organisations. In the Czech Republic, as elsewhere in the region, women's 'recently acquired freedom is understood as the freedom not to have to organize ourselves into politicized groups' (Šiklová 1998:34).

Despite an understandable lack of enthusiasm for participating in formal organisations, women across CEE have become involved in numerous, primarily small and local, groups organised around issues such as domestic violence – a previously unacknowledged problem in CEEC (Renne 1997). Indeed in Poland, where the abortion issue provided a focus for cooperative action by a range of disparate women's groups, there has recently been a national campaign against violence against women, which gained considerable media support (Regulska and Roseman 1998:28). Conversely, in Hungary, where women's groups are seen as lacking 'authentic Hungarianness', complaints about sexual harassment in the workplace were dismissed, in a recent media debate, on the grounds that 'men's reactions are natural and should be accepted as compliments rather than assaults' (Acsady 1998:77). The situation in Slovenia provides a further contrast, in that women's successful and high-profile mobilisation in defence of the constitutional right to abortion was greeted by the press as 'the first civil demonstration' to take place in the new state (Jalusic 1997:215).

The particular character of women's groups inevitably reflects cultural and other differences between CEEC, and will continue to do so. Across the region, however, a principal focus has been upon issues of immediate concern to women – reproductive rights and violence against women. Less attention has been devoted to broader economic issues and their impact on women's lives (Penn 1998:50); and even less to promoting women's political participation and involvement in government, which 'seem more and more like long-term projects' (Renne 1997:7). We now consider what support the EU can offer to these 'projects'.

Women's participation and the role of the EU

The women's policy, as indicated above, has a central aim of promoting women's participation in decision making. There are three areas where there is a potential for EU involvement – making space for women at the EU level, encouraging development of grassroots organisations and policy mainstreaming.

Women's involvement with the EU system

Compared with national policy systems, both East and West, the EU policy environment is relatively welcoming to women. The EP, for example, has a proactive Committee on Women's Rights; and most member states send a more balanced representation to the EP than exists in national parliaments. The Commission, despite the almost exclusively male composition of the College until recently, has a tradition of encouraging input from women's organisations and has been proactive in supporting the establishment of transnational women's networks at EU level. Thus in Brussels there has developed a 'more favourable policy-making venue for women than is evident in most national capitals' (Mazey 1998:138).

CEE women will bring to the EU valuable experience and insights; for example, Western women have much to learn about the costs of competing on 'equal' terms with men. Thus the accession of CEEC will provide new opportunities for pan-European networking between women, which should prove mutually beneficial. Full realisation of these benefits, however, depends upon development, at grassroots level, of a stronger ethos of critical engagement with the political system.

Support for grassroots women's organisations in CEEC

Since 1992 the EU has supported the development of NGOs in CEEC through the Phare and Tacis Democracy Programme. This Programme has relevance for women for three reasons. First, NGOs in CEEC are primarily staffed by women, who thus gain knowledge and experience (ISA Consult 1997:23). Second, NGOs are, in general, more likely than political parties to raise 'relatively unpopular issues such as feminism' (ISA Consult 1997:27). And, third, equal opportunities and non-discrimination (grouped with minority rights) form one of the Programme's eight designated areas of activity. Here a number of projects have been supported, many of which are judged to have been effective.[23] Several have sought to promote women's political participation; others have targeted or sought to include marginalised or minority women (European Dialogue 1998). While mainly small in scale, these programmes are valued by NGOs for the moral support and recognition which the EU logo and funding bring. On occasion this has also provided protection from the effects of government disapproval (ISA Consult 1997:31).

This activity area has, nevertheless, been a relatively minor focus of the overall Programme; and in some countries (notably Hungary) it has been insufficiently prioritised (ISA Consult 1997). In principle, there will be a need to remedy this when the mainstreaming provisions of the Amsterdam Treaty enter into force.

Mainstreaming equality – a new policy challenge

The Amsterdam Treaty places among the overarching Principles of the European Community the provision that, in *all* its activities, 'the

Community shall aim to eliminate inequalities, and to promote equality, between men and women' (TEC Article 3.2). The significance for the accession process of this cross-policy 'mainstreaming' provision has already been emphasised by the EP – in a formal reminder to the Commission that 'mainstreaming should be an important element in the enlargement negotiations' (European Parliament 1997b:34). As noted above, this should have implications for all EU-funded programmes. And for CEE governments preparing for accession, it potentially adds a further dimension to policy approximation in all areas.

As the Commission's somewhat ponderous definition indicates, mainstreaming will, in principle, have considerable significance for the EU and member states. Mainstreaming involves

> the systematic integration of the respective situations, priorities and needs of women and men in all policies and with a view to promoting equality between women and men and mobilising all general policies and measures specifically for the purpose of achieving equality by actively and openly taking into account, at the planning stage, their effects on the respective situations of women and men in implementation, monitoring and evaluation. (Commission 1998:2)

Mainstreaming will not be easy to implement, however. To be effective it needs the active support of key staff in all policy areas and the allocation of resources – to fund, *inter alia*, gender-awareness training for personnel, collection of gender-disaggregated statistics and appropriate monitoring procedures. Ideally, there would also be sanctions for non-compliance (Rees 1998:192).[24]

In practice, this level of commitment is unlikely to be forthcoming from existing member states; while, for CEE candidate members, introduction of mainstreaming would be a considerable burden. In consequence, this expansion of the equality *acquis* will reinforce arguments that the more challenging and/or costly elements of EU social policy should be set aside to facilitate CEEC accession. Hence, while mainstreaming may be important as a consciousness-raising exercise, vigilance will be needed to ensure that it does not become a low-cost, lip-service substitute for the special programmes currently associated with the women's policy. This makes the critical engagement of CEE women with policy systems at all levels, including the EU level, even more necessary.

Conclusion

As a result of the transformation processes in CEEC, women are today less visible politically and less secure economically than during the state socialist period. For the most part, however, there is little nostalgia among women for the old regimes. As we have seen, the cost to women of high levels of participation in paid work, and in the formal political system, was reflected in falling birth rates across CEEC. Nevertheless, rejection of the former model has not been accompanied by unquestioning acceptance of a traditional, maternal role. Thus the importance of the abortion issue, and the level of women's mobilisation around it, has not simply been a diversion from the major economic and political issues confronting CEE women; rather, it symbolises real conflict over women's role in society and the desire of many women to exercise choice in determining that role. Beyond this most fundamental aspect of choice, however, there has been relatively little debate among women about their roles and political priorities in the new democracies. In consequence, despite the advanced stage of pre-accession processes, CEE women are not well prepared to consider the implications of EU membership; nor for influencing policy processes during the pre-accession period.

The situation of women raises general questions about the readiness of CEEC for accession, particularly in relation to democratic criteria such as the balanced development of civil society. However, it raises very particular issues, and challenges, for the EU women's policy. First, the increased heterogeneity of the EU will fuel concerns about the responsiveness of EU policy to the very different needs and interests of Europe's women. And, second, enlargement will impose upon CEE women policies which do not reflect their experiences and to which they are indifferent or even opposed.

These challenges are not necessarily insuperable. At present the women's policy reflects a number of potentially competing principles – equal treatment, special treatment, positive action and mainstreaming. While these principles have been incorporated in response to pressure from Western women, there is no settled consensus on the most appropriate balance between them. There is thus room for manoeuvre as the policy evolves; and space for CEE women to influence debates on its future direction. Indeed, there is a very real need for inputs from CEE women, both because their ideas, advice and experience will be valuable; and because lack of involvement by, or opposition from, CEE women will reinforce the arguments of the policy's opponents within the EU and in CEEC. Policy implementation in this area is not without cost – and it contravenes the liberal principles of market enthusiasts in Estonia as in the UK.

The EU women's policy is by no means ideal, but it provides a continually evolving framework which, with the help of CEE women, can be adapted to meet a wider range of needs and interests. In consequence, there is an urgent need for engagement by CEE women in debates which would facilitate the articulation of their needs and demands – at the grassroots, national and EU levels. It is unfortunate that the exigencies of the accession process provide little opportunity for these debates to proceed at a pace determined by CEE women themselves.

Notes

1   The difficulties, challenges and rewards of dialogue between Eastern and Western women are charted by a number of commentators, including Cockburn (1992), Funk (1993), Busheikin (1997), Penn (1998) and Drakulic (1998).
2   Other aspects of market reform undoubtedly impinge, both significantly and disproportionately, upon women's lives – for example, increased food prices and reductions in public-sector services such as health care.
3   These provisions varied between countries. They were particularly generous in the former GDR, while in Czechoslovakia, by the late 1970s, direct and indirect supports for maternity comprised approximately 11 per cent of the annual budget (Heitlinger 1993:98). In some countries, for example Poland, extended maternity leave was unpaid although, following reforms in 1981, an 'educational benefit' was frequently available in practice (Millard 1995:65). In Hungary, however, women were paid up to 75 per cent of their previous wage during extended maternity leave in the 1980s. Entitlement to paid leave to care for sick children was also generous – sixty days annually for children under three, and thirty days annually for children between three and six years of age (Subhan 1996). These provisions reflected, in part, a particular need for women's labour in Hungary (United Nations Children's Fund 1994:19).
4   In Germany, for example, it was expected that female employment levels in the East would quickly approximate those in the West. According to the Federal Minister for Women (in 1991), 'This is natural because the opportunity to be a housewife did not really exist in the GDR' (quoted in Dodds 1998:178–9). Subsequent experience has shown that women in the former GDR have not accepted this situation. 'They find it unbearable to stay at home. It makes them feel useless and redundant' (Dodds 1998:179).
5   There is much evidence of this phenomenon in the Czech Republic, Poland and Hungary. In Romania and Bulgaria, where the articulation of women's views is very weak, such matters are not much debated. In Slovenia, however, anti-feminism has been less prevalent.
6   In Slovakia and Bulgaria there was a relatively small decline in the abortion rate, while there was a marked increase in Romania following legalisation of abortion.
7   In charting the changing status of Hungarian women since 1989, Acsady (1995, 1998) estimates that almost half the women of employment age are now 'confined to the four walls of their homes' (1998:78).
8   In the case of Hungary, where women have made little protest about their 'housewification', Acsady's research found 'an ambiguity: the glorified housewife does not feel happy in her current role but she does not admit it openly. She admits her unhappiness to the interviewer, who guarantees anonymity, but she would never revolt against public representations of the housewife as a happy and content being' (Acsady 1998:78).

9   It is interesting to contrast the UN Development Programme rankings with those derived from the Commission Opinions in *Agenda 2000* (see Chapter 2). However, the Programme's indices of human development are based solely upon socio-economic criteria, whereas the EU Opinions include political criteria, in particular measures of democratisation.

10 This applies also to the NIS not included in Table 5.1. The 'missing' high-ranking countries in terms of GDI are Canada – ranked first in the HDI and GDI – Norway (2), Iceland (4), the USA (5) and New Zealand (8).

11 For a comparative analysis of the gender implications of different social policy models operating within the EU, see Sainsbury (1994).

12 A useful summary of EU policy development in this field is provided in Commission (1996); and a full treatment, together with critical analysis, in Hoskyns (1996).

13 Unlike Directives, Recommendations and Resolutions are not legally binding upon member states but are intended to influence both policy and practice. During the 1990s they have reflected the increasingly broad basis of the EU's medium-term Action Programmes on equal opportunities. In addition, these Programmes have generated a number of initiatives, including the promotion of transnational research networks to study various aspects of women's lives – in the economy; in reconciling work and family life; in decision making and in the exercise of rights (Commission 1996).

14 The provision at Article 141.4 reads as follows: 'With a view to ensuring full equality in practice between men and women in working life, the principle of equal treatment shall not prevent any Member State from maintaining or adopting measures providing for specific advantages in order to make it easier for the under-represented sex to pursue a vocational activity or to prevent or compensate for disadvantages in professional careers.'

15 This has been increasingly the case since publication of the Commission's (1995) White Paper. See Chapter 2 for a fuller discussion of this matter.

16 The Opinion on Poland typifies this 'extended' version: 'On equal opportunity, the basic provisions of EC non-discrimination law between women and men are covered by Polish legislation, but the non-discrimination principle is not always respected in areas such as equal pay for equal work. The difference in pay between women and men is considerable. Legal adaptation is also necessary for parental leave' (Commission 1997a:14). Interestingly, the Opinion does not refer to the continued (legal) practice in Poland of reserving certain jobs for men (Subhan 1996:30).

17 The UK government, for example, introduced legislation prior to accession, in anticipation of Article 119 provisions (Meehan and Collins 1996).

18 These aims are furthered by various means, including dissemination of information, promotion of transnational NGO networks, funding of research, the European Woman of the Year project and annual prizes for women film-makers.

19 For an East–West comparative study of women's political participation prior to 1989, see Janova and Sineau (1992).

20 Recruiting women to fill the quotas was sometimes difficult. For example, in Romania, under the Ceauşescu regime, the women's quota was regularly increased to demonstrate 'progress'.

21 Anna Petrasovits, Hungarian Social Democrat leader in 1990, referred to
    women politicians under the previous regime as 'token women ... silly,
    stupid little women who sit there' (quoted in Einhorn 1993:152). In several
    CEEC, women MPs were known as 'milkmaid politicians' (Waylen
    1994:345).
22 In a report for the Soros Foundation, A. Posadskaya-Vanderbeck (1998:7)
    notes impediments to her research through 'lack of commitment of govern-
    ments in the region to collecting and disseminating sex-disaggregated data'.
    The US State Department, in its 1996 Human Rights Report, merely notes
    'low levels' of participation by women in public-sector managerial positions.
    Only in the case of Slovenia are women said to be 'frequently encountered in
    government executive departments' (US Department of State 1997:9).
23 In 1996, thirty-five projects were in operation, eleven of them in Romania,
    where there has been a dearth of women's activity (European Human Rights
    Foundation 1996). An evaluation of the Programme highlighted as particu-
    larly successful the 'Women in Modern Society' project in Romania (ISA
    Consult 1997:59).
24 Rees (1998) provides an excellent discussion of the concept of mainstreaming
    and its application in the EU and elsewhere.

References

Acsady, J. (1995), Shifting attitudes and expectations in Hungary, *Transitions*,
    1:16, 22–3.
Acsady, J. (1998), Still willing to grin and bear it, *Transitions*, 5:1, 76–9.
Bollobás, E. (1993), 'Totalitarian lib': the legacy of communism for Hungarian
    Women, in N. Funk and M. Mueller (eds), *Gender Politics and Post-
    Communism*, London, Routledge, 201–6.
Bretherton, C. and Sperling, L. (1996), Women's networks and the European
    Union: towards an inclusive approach, *Journal of Common Market Studies*,
    34:4, 487–508.
Busheikin, L. (1997), Is sisterhood really global? Western feminism in Eastern
    Europe, in T. Renne (ed.), *Ana's Land: Sisterhood in Eastern Europe*, Boulder,
    Westview, 12–22.
Cockburn, C. (1992), The European forum of socialist feminists: talking on the
    volcano, *Women's Studies International Forum*, 15:1, 53–6.
Commission (1995), *Preparation of the Associated Countries of Central and
    Eastern Europe for Integration into the Internal Market of the Union*,
    COM(95)163, Final.
Commission (1996), *Fourth Medium-Term Community Action Programme on
    Equal Opportunities for Women and Men (1996–2000)*, Brussels, Equal
    Opportunities Unit, V/231b/96.
Commission (1997a), *Paragraphs of the Commission's Opinions on the CEECs
    Applications for Membership of the European Union, which Identify a
    Number of Shortcomings and which are Regrouped per Direction of DGV*,
    V/E/4, October.
Commission (1997b), *Women of Europe Newsletter*, 74, October.

Commission (1997–98), *Women of Europe Newsletter*, 76, December–January.

Commission (1998), *Women of Europe Newsletter*, 78, April.

Dodds, D. (1998), Five years after unification: East German women in transition, *Women's Studies International Forum*, 21:2, 175–82.

Drakulic, S. (1998), What we learned from Western feminists, *Transitions*, 5:1, 42–7.

Druker, J. (1998), The underrepresented sex, *Transitions*, 5:1, 62–3.

Einhorn, B. (1993), *Cinderella Goes to Market: Citizenship, Gender and Women's Movements in East Central Europe*, London, Verso.

European Dialogue (1998), *Baltics Promote women*, March–April, http://europa.eu.int/en/comm/dg10/infcom/eur.

European Human Rights Foundation (1996), *The European Union's Phare and Tacis Democracy Programme: Micro-projects in Operation 1996*, Brussels, EHRF.

European Parliament (1997a), *Opinion on the Commission Communication 'Agenda 2000 – For a Stronger and Wider Europe'*, PE 224.339/PartC/Fin.

European Parliament (1997b), *Resolution on the Annual Report from the Commission: Equal Opportunities for Women and Men in the European Union 1996*, PE 261.933, 16 September.

Ferge, Z. (1997), Combating gender bias: round two, *Transitions*, 7:5, 72–3.

Funk, N. (1993), Feminism East and West, in N. Funk and M. Mueller (eds), *Gender Politics and Post-Communism*, London, Routledge, 331–6.

Hauser, E., Heyns, B. and Mansbridge, J. (1993), Feminism in the interstices of politics and culture: Poland in transition, in N. Funk and M. Mueller (eds), *Gender Politics and Post-Communism*, London, Routledge, 257–73.

Heinen, J. (1992), Polish democracy is a masculine democracy, *Women's Studies International Forum*, 15:1, 129–38.

Heinen, J. and Matuchniak-Krasuska, A. (1995), Abortion in Poland: a vicious circle or a good use of rhetoric?, *Women's Studies International Forum*, 18:1, 27–33.

Heitlinger, A. (1993), The impact of the transition from communism on the status of women in the Czech and Slovak Republics, in N. Funk and M. Mueller (eds), *Gender Politics and Post-Communism*, London, Routledge, 95–108.

Hoskyns, C. (1996), *Integrating Gender: Women, Law and Politics in the European Union*, London, Verso.

ISA Consult (1997), *Final Report: Evaluation of the Phare and Tacis Democracy Programme 1992–1997*, European Commission, DG-1A-53-98.

Jalusic, V. (1993), It's a shame! The campaign for constitutional reproductive rights in Slovenia, in T. Renne (ed.), *Ana's Land: Sisterhood in Eastern Europe*, Boulder, Westview, 212–17.

Janova, M. and Sineau, M. (1992), Women's participation in political power in Europe: an essay in East–West comparison, *Women's Studies International Forum*, 15:1, 115–28.

Kaldor, M. and Vejvoda, I. (1997), Democratization in central and east European countries, *International Affairs*, 73:1, 59–82.

Kiczková, Z. and Farkasová, E. (1993), The emancipation of women: a concept that failed, in N. Funk and M. Mueller (eds), *Gender Politics and Post-Communism*, London, Routledge, 84–94.

Kiss, Y. (1991), The second 'no': women in Hungary, *Feminist Review*, 39, 49–57.

Lokau, S. (1998), Number of female politicians plummets in Eastern Europe, *Central Europe Online*, http//www.centraleruope.com/eco/news, 3 February.

Makkai, T. (1994), Social policy and gender in Eastern Europe, in D. Sainsbury (ed.), *Gendering Welfare States*, London, Sage, 188–205.

Malinowska, E. (1995), Socio-political changes in Poland and the problem of sex discrimination, *Women's Studies International Forum*, 18:1, 35–43.

Mazey, S. (1998), The European Union and women's rights: from the Europeanization of national agendas to the nationalization of a European agenda?, *Journal of European Public Policy*, 5:1, 131–52.

Meehan, E. and Collins, E. (1996), Women, the European Union and Britain, *Parliamentary Affairs*, 49:1, 221–34.

Millard, F. (1995), Women in Poland: the impact of post-communist transformation 1989–94, *Journal of Area Studies*, 6, 62–73.

Penn, S. (1998), Looking East, looking West, *Transitions*, 5:1, 48–51.

Posadskaya-Vanderbeck, A. (1998), Redefining democratization: the gender challenge, *Women's Program*, Soros Foundation, http://www.soros.org/wp/concept.htm.

Randall, V. (1987), *Women and Politics: An International Perspective*, Basingstoke, Macmillan.

Rees, T. (1998), *Mainstreaming Equality in the European Union*, London, Routledge.

Regulska, J. and Roseman, M. J. (1998), What is gender? *Transitions*, 5:1, 24–9.

Renne, T. (1997), Disparaging digressions: sisterhood in East-Central Europe, in T. Renne (ed.), *Ana's Land: Sisterhood in Eastern Europe*, Boulder, Westview, 1–11.

Reszke, I. (1995), How a positive image can have a negative impact: stereotypes of unemployed women and men in liberated Poland, *Women's Studies International Forum*, 18:1, 13–17.

Sainsbury, D. (ed.) (1994), *Gendering Welfare States*, London, Sage.

Scheppele, K. L. (1995), Women's rights in Eastern Europe, *East European Constitutional Review*, Winter, 66–9.

Šiklová, J. (1993), Are women in Central and Eastern Europe conservative?, in N. Funk and M. Mueller (eds), *Gender Politics and Post-Communism*, London, Routledge, 74–83.

Šiklová, J. (1998), Why we resist Western-style feminism, *Transitions*, 5:1, 30–5.

Smith, A., Holmes, P., Sedelmeier, U., Smith, E., Wallace, H. and Young, A. (1996), *The European Union and Central and Eastern Europe: Pre-Accession Strategies*, University of Sussex, Sussex European Institute, Working Paper 15.

Subhan, A. (1996), Central and Eastern European women: a portrait, *Women's Rights Series*, W8, Brussels, European Parliament, Directorate-General for Research.

UN Children's Fund (1994), *Women and Gender in Countries in Transition: A UNICEF Perspective*, New York, UNICEF.

UN Development Programme (1997), *Human Development Report 1997*, Oxford, Oxford University Press.

US Department of State (1997), *1996 Human Rights Report*, Washington, DC, Bureau of Democracy, Human Rights and Labor.

Watson, P. (1993), The rise of masculinism in Eastern Europe, *New Left Review*, 198, 71–82.

Waylen, G. (1994), Women and democratization: conceptualizing gender relations in transition politics, *World Politics*, 46:3, 327–54.

Wyzan, M. (1998), Unemployed unequally? Nearly equally empty pocketbooks in the wake of reforms, *Transitions*, 5:1, 14–15.

6 Andrew Francis

Environmental issues in CEEC transformation: environment as a challenge to enlargement

Since the 1980s the environment has moved to centre stage as a problem requiring urgent attention. The Rio de Janeiro Earth Summit of 1992 and the progress review, Rio + Five, held in New York in 1997,[1] carried forward global action on issues such as climate change and biodiversity. The formulation at Rio of Agenda 21, and its constituent Local Agenda 21, gave practical expression to earlier concepts of sustainable development proposed by the Brundtland Commission in 1987. The EU member states and CEEC played an active role in these gatherings and the follow-up work. Now CEEC are candidates to join the EU and it is clear that environmental issues are a major challenge in the enlargement process.

The chapter commences by briefly discussing the importance of the environment as an aspect of EU policy making. There follows an outline of the current challenges which will, in part, inform ongoing negotiations. The emergence of the environment, both as a catalyst to transformation and as a major burden to CEEC, sets the context for two reviews. First, since environmental aid has been vital in preparing the way towards enlargement, some aspects of external assistance are discussed. Second, the main focus of the chapter is to analyse events in the period 1996–98. The views expressed by the European Commission in *Agenda 2000* provide the central issues for resolution, especially the necessity for candidates to comply fully with EU environmental legislation in the near future.

The context and problems

Environmental policy has been one of the fastest growing areas of EU activity. From the early 1970s, and the introduction of the first Community Action Programme on the Environment, the number of items of EU environmental legislation rose from about five per annum to more than twenty per annum in the 1980s. By the time of the EU Council Resolution on a Community programme of policy and action in relation to the environment and sustainable development in 1993, four Community Action Programmes on the Environment had given rise to approximately 200 pieces of legislation covering pollution of the atmosphere, water and soil, water management, safeguards in relation to chemicals and biotechnology, product standards, environmental impact assessments and nature protection.

State of the environment reporting indicated, however, a slow but relentless deterioration within the member states, notwithstanding the measures taken via the Action Programmes. Rising concerns at the global level have added to the EU's responsibilities in the international field. Since the Rio Summit, the EU has been engaged in 'two sets of challenging interactions with other parts of the world in dialogues about sustainability' (Osborn 1997:259). Apart from the many serious problems that the developing countries face, there are the environmental implications of the political and economic progress in CEEC – indeed, these were emphasised in the 1993 Resolution.

A major element in the history of environmental policy which operates at EU level, and one which is at the root of current difficulties for CEEC, has been the creation of a comprehensive set of rules to govern national efforts. Mainly through the means of Directives, one should appreciate that 'Since the 1970s the European Community has thus moved from providing little more than a loose framework for the development of common environmental policies, to being a firm institutional platform for the formulation of such policies' (Liefferink *et al.* 1993:4).

Chapter 1 briefly examines the complex and evolving character of EU policy making and the actors involved. Particularly since the mid-1980s, environmental policy has been addressed at Community level – supported by rulings of the European Court of Justice and legitimated by the SEA and, especially, the TEU. For existing members of the Union, much national progress in environmental protection over the past decades can be ascribed to the transposition of EU legislation. For the candidate members of CEE, then, meeting the requirements of the environmental *acquis* can be viewed both as an obligation and a severe challenge. Not only is there a considerable amount of legislation to transpose, but there are major problems in designing structures to carry out effective implementation. These problems are made even more daunting by factors arising both from the legacy with which the CEEC are burdened and from current debates over changing societal priorities and the real costs of accession.

One positive outcome since the 1980s has been that both existing and candidate members of the EU recognise the advantages of dealing with certain environmental issues at the international level, for example, trans-boundary air and water pollution. But it is important to understand the reality of environmental policy making. In practice, it is argued, member states are 'pursuing quite separate national interests in pressing for or opposing common environmental action – and these interests may vary across issues' (Liefferink *et al.* 1993:6). In consequence, CEE candidates may interpret the motives of some existing members for pursuing very strict environmental standards, and lobbying for these to be raised at the EU level, as simply a ploy to limit their ability to enter potential markets. Similarly, the high environmental costs incurred may have a seriously detrimental effect on economic performance.

It should also be noted that, even for well-established and generally well-intentioned member states, the ability to comply, or the temptation not to comply, has been an ongoing problem. Thus implementation of a range of Directives, for example on environmental impact assessment, has resulted in some disappointment, and, in some cases, necessitated the commencement of legal action. Moreover, experience in the existing member states suggests that environmental policy is an area that is very susceptible to changes in public perception and concern. Thus the over-zealous pursuit of high environmental standards is difficult to accept at times of economic downturn. Ultimately, the message from the existing member states is that the operation of an effective EU environmental policy relies on the commitment and willingness, not only of national governments, but of businesses and citizens, to give meaning to the legis-lation. An example here is the 'big idea' of sustainability, which underlies the Fifth Community Action Programme on the Environment. One can already note tensions at national level, and beyond, between two mean-ings of sustainability – as an environmental goal or as an economic goal (in terms of sustainable economic growth).

With these experiences in mind, it is possible to identify additional problems that are emerging for CEEC in the environmental field. First, there is no doubt that all the candidate countries find themselves in a greatly disadvantaged position when it comes to solving their environ-mental problems. As we shall see, there is a huge backlog of tasks resulting from decades of neglect. Sustainability, therefore, takes on a third meaning, because acceptable environmental standards can only be achieved through a sustained commitment of resources of all kinds – financial, human and technical – over the long term. A further question arises over the share of this effort that can be derived from CEE national budgets and the proportion to be expected via interstate transfers and international aid. What has been achieved via these mechanisms will be discussed later. The financing of environmental improvement then raises another difficult question, for in the process of meeting accession require-ments in other economic and social areas, there will inevitably be competition for scarce resources. Finally, one can see new environmental problems emerging as a consequence of the very successes of transforma-tion, for example air pollution from rapid increases in the use of private cars. Public attitudes will be especially important here, because consumerism in all its forms could not be seen to be thwarted by environmental controls, especially in the light of past decades of privation.

Recent work by Caddy (1997) suggests additional problems that have emerged from the relationship between CEEC and the EU. In a dynamic policy area such as environment, there is the problem of the 'moving target' of the EU *acquis*. CEEC, having adopted, at great expense, all the necessary components of current policy, may find themselves with new elements to implement. The asymmetric nature of policy relationships so far, skewed heavily in favour of the EU, has left little room for consideration of the policy experience in the candidate countries. CEE policy makers may feel that their accumulated experience, and good practice in fields such as nature conservation, is undervalued or even ignored. The possible reshaping of EU policy in areas such as agriculture, discussed within the context of *Agenda 2000*, might be just the sort of area where CEE experience of low-intensity, eco-friendly practices could be useful. There is scope for the EU to be much more of an environmental learning institution during this process. Here Lofstedt and Sjostedt's (1996) appraisal of environmental aid programmes to Eastern Europe offers many suggestions to policy makers which would help to overcome this skewed relationship.

The emergence of environment as an issue on the transformation and enlargement agendas

When the CEEC began their transformation from highly centralised, state-controlled economies to free-market systems, the environment was, from the very beginning, a major issue on the agenda. In the former Czechoslovakia, for example, one of the catalysts for the 'Velvet Revolution' was a demonstration at Teplice in November 1989, when approximately 1,000 demonstrators cried 'We want clean air!', 'Oxygen!' and 'We want healthy children!' (Moldan 1996). This demonstration on environmental issues was overtaken by the wider political events of November and December of that year. However, the location of this environmental protest was significant, for it took place in arguably the most environmentally devastated region of Europe, the so-called 'Sulphur (or Black) Triangle'. The generally parlous state of the wider Eastern–Central European environment had been noted by Western researchers (Rugg 1985; Carter 1985); and warnings had been issued, both officially and unofficially, by environmental experts working in the region over several decades. Moreover, the link between environmental quality and public health had been pointed out by medical experts in the many 'hot spots' created by polluting heavy industry, such as Upper Silesia (Alcamo 1992).

Indeed, the legacy of environmental destruction under communism led Rugg (1985) to conclude that socialist decision makers regarded the environment in terms of potential productivity rather than potential habitability. Thus Carter and Turnock (1996) argued that Communist parties throughout the region made public declarations concerning the priority given to sound environmental management, but in practice the opposite was the case.

A general problem, hardly unique to the CEE region, was that for several decades natural resources were regarded as 'free goods'; thus a (short-sighted) judgement was made that it was not worth devoting sizeable budgets to environmental protection. In consequence, two particular areas that it has been found necessary to support in CEEC have been pollution research and monitoring – for in the past, it was as if Communist governments were insulating themselves from the reality of environmental degradation by avoiding gathering the harsh facts (Carter and Turnock 1996).

During 1990 the European Commission funded a major study (Bachtler 1992a) to review the socio-economic conditions and trends at national and regional level in six CEEC – Bulgaria, the former Czechoslovakia, Hungary, Poland, Romania and the former Yugoslavia. The study recorded the nature and vast scale of environmental problems in these countries, while various particular problems were highlighted in a later article (Bachtler 1992b). First, rapid industrialisation and massive exploitation of natural resources were combined with inadequate environmental controls or consideration of environmental impacts. A particular culprit, with regard to air pollution, was the use of low-grade brown coal as an energy source. Moreover, industrial and transport technologies were inefficient, and older locations, particularly in Poland and the former Czechoslovakia, were said to be facing the most serious problems. Added to the visible despoilation of forests and the countryside were less visible, but related, crises associated with infant mortality and lower life expectancy. The most severely polluted areas were listed as Upper Silesia (Poland), North Bohemia and North Moravia in the present Czech Republic, the Sofia region of Bulgaria, Jesenica (present Slovenia), and Resita and Copsa Mica (Romania).

The evidence to the Commission that much needed to be done was echoed within the CEEC by public opinion. As early as January 1990, in one of the first surveys carried out in the former Czechoslovakia, 83 per cent of people regarded environmental improvement as a primary task for government (Moldan 1996). And in that same country, democratisation and the creation of a market economy were linked in the 1990 Rainbow Programme to a basic right – the right to a healthy environment. The political mood within CEEC was thus coinciding with that in EU member states, and also with the articulation of European Commission ideas on a market-based approach to environmental improvement.

It is not the intention to describe here the detailed environmental experience of CEEC as they underwent transformation. However, Gorzelak (1995) has pointed to evidence of declining pollution levels since the late 1980s. In Slovakia, for example, particulate matter emissions decreased by 43 per cent between 1988 and 1992. While the argument that falling pollution was related to falling industrial production is true to some extent, the decline in emission levels was more rapid than that of GDP. According to Gorzelak, the most striking feature of the early period (1988–92) was the increase in the share of expenditure aimed at air protection. A valuable overview and several case studies are provided by Carter and Turnock (1996) and, while confirming the European Commission's views that there was still much to do, they did measure significant progress in some areas.[2] Furthermore, experiments in water-quality improvement in Hungary's Lake Balaton indicated that higher standards could be achieved at relatively low cost.

On the other hand, Carter and Turnock note continuing problems over liability for cleaning up contaminated sites and operations, which were seen as a possible obstacle to inward investment by over 1,000 firms surveyed by the World Bank. The need for environmental investments, including technology, is set against the problem of conflicting priorities, and Carter and Turnock found that there was a temptation to place development above environmental protection. It is appropriate at this point, therefore, to analyse the importance of outside help in improving environmental conditions.

Tackling the problems: the role of external assistance

As the true scale of the environmental degradation in CEEC emerged, it soon became apparent that the ability to slow down, let alone halt or reverse, the decline would be limited by resources constraints. Considerable investments would be needed, not only in the hardware of environmental protection – clean technologies, monitoring equipment, and so on – but also in training and education. Russell (1991a, 1991b) saw three challenges ahead: to clean up the errors of the past, to halt the current rate of deterioration and, crucially, to ensure that future economic development was carried out in an environmentally sustainable way.[3] For maximum effectiveness to be achieved there was clearly a need to link national and local actions with the international level (Alcamo 1992). Financial resources from the latter were to be vital in implementing national environmental policies. Fortunately, the urgency and magnitude of the assistance needed were recognised. Bilateral aid has been considerable and a wealth of country case-study material exists elsewhere (Lofstedt and Sjostedt 1996). Consequently, discussion here focuses primarily upon assistance from EU sources and from the World Bank.

As Chapter 2 has indicated, the EU's Phare programme was quickly to become a major mechanism to support the objectives of the EAs being signed with CEEC. From its initial operations in Poland and Hungary, Phare had expanded to eleven countries by 1993. While the environment was identified as one of the major areas for support, it should be pointed out that, of a budget of ecu 3,285 million in the first three years, only 9 per cent was allocated to environment and nuclear safety (see Table 2.3). Initially, Phare supported 'urgent actions', for example the supply of equipment to monitor air and water pollution. Grants were also given for studies – soon leading to the criticism that these were at the expense of action on environmental protection (Carter and Turnock 1996). In addition, assistance was given to aligning legislation and to improving standards. Responding to criticisms, Phare attempted to adopt a more strategic approach, by developing policies and programmes for key areas, such as waste treatment.

From the very beginning of the programme, nuclear safety was perhaps *the* priority area.[4] Here, Phare's activities included safety studies, improving management and control procedures, and setting up a rapid alert system. An early example of such support was the Kozloduy nuclear plant in Bulgaria, where ecu 20 million were allocated to overcome safety problems. Regulatory and safety authorities were supported, and advice given on decommissioning nuclear plants within the framework of national energy policies. While supporting this type of assistance, critics have pointed out that Phare has been rather slow to act in the 'Sulphur Triangle', and also could have done much more to support NGOs (Carter and Turnock 1996).

More recently, the European Commission (1997a) offered its opinions on the operation of Phare in the candidate countries, and pointed out some of the shortcomings of the recipients during implementation. While these comments were related to the programme as a whole, the environment is generally highlighted as a major component. Four countries attracted particular criticism: the Czech Republic experienced complications in targeting funds on priority areas; Hungary had an overwide spread of programmes, limited absorption and management capacity and cumbersome administrative procedures; Romania had a lack of commitment to policy reform in some areas; while Poland had experienced initial difficulties but had shown improvement by the fifth year. Only Slovenia received unreserved praise for making effective use of Phare funds. But one should note that much of the effectiveness of this type of programme lies in collaboration with other donors; and that this region has been a major recipient of aid from other agencies, notably the World Bank and the EBRD.

Since the start of the decade the World Bank has been collaborating with the European Commission and the OECD in implementing environmental improvements. These bodies worked together in 1993 to produce the Environmental Action Programme for Central and Eastern Europe. The World Bank has assisted eleven countries in the region with formulating national environmental strategies and has helped to reform policies, strengthen institutions and encourage public participation. In addition the Bank has facilitated the development of appropriate economic incentives and regulations. The financing of environmental projects led to over $1.3 billion being committed by 1996 for a dozen projects. Beyond this, it has supported the environmental components or objectives of more than twenty-five major investments. As an implementing agency of the Global Environment Facility (GEF), the Bank has also financed projects in biodiversity protection, climate change protection and the phasing out of ozone-depleting substances.

The significant impact of World Bank assistance can be shown by the example of Poland's 'Strategy for Environmental Management', which was implemented on the basis of an $18 million credit. The implementation period of the programme was from 1990 to 1996 and its purposes were to specify the most important ecological problems and to decentralise the system of environmental management. With additional support from bilateral foreign assistance, Phare grants and internally generated resources, it was possible to establish the information, legal and institutional foundations so crucial for a candidate country in the pre-accession period. About 64 per cent of the allocation went to management and training and the purchase of office and computer equipment; the rest to water, air and nature protection.

The programme was implemented via four components. The first component was directed at creating an effective system of environmental management. This resulted in the installation of a new 'Environment' computerised system for the Ministry of Environmental Protection, Natural Resources and Forestry. The need to find collective solutions to acute environmental problems was demonstrated by an assessment of the impact of pollution on human health, in which the Ministry of Health and Social Care participated. Since environmental policy increasingly emphasises monitoring and enforcement, the second component, 'inspections of effectiveness and obeying of environmental protection requirements in industry', consisted of ecological inspections of thirty-eight plants in three Polish provinces (Katowice, Krakow and Legnica) notorious for a range of polluting industries. There was a significant element of training for local specialists in all aspects of inspection.

One of the most acute environmental problems, poor air quality, was tackled in the third component of the programme. In the provinces of Katowice and Krakow some $3 million was spent on a pilot project to establish networks for automatic monitoring of air quality, smog-warning systems and factory inspections. In the same part of the country $8.4 million was spent on the final component, the introduction of an integrated approach to water management in the Upper Vistula catchment area. The Regional Boards of Water Economy purchased specialist equipment for their ecological laboratories and ten screening stations for the monitoring of water quality. Once again, there was an emphasis on training as well as on purchase of hardware.

A further international organisation playing an environmental role in CEEC is the EU-sponsored EBRD, which was established 'to foster the transition towards open market-oriented economies and to promote private and entrepreneurial initiative in the Central and Eastern European countries' (EBRD 1996:1). In the present context it should be noted that the EBRD was the first international financial institution to have been given a proactive environmental mandate. Thus, Article 2.1vii of the Agreement establishing the Bank charged it to 'promote in the full range of its activities environmentally sound and sustainable development' (EBRD 1996:1). To give meaning to this general principle, the Bank produces a sector and country strategy which describes the environmental implications of its operations. It also requires proposals to submit a range of initial environmental information, including mitigation measures, liability, environmental assessment and audit reports. The Bank carries out environmental appraisals and emphasises to countries the importance of public consultation and the provision of information.

Two recent initiatives illustrate the widening scope of the EBRD's support for environmental improvement. First, in August 1995 a new sector team was created for 'Municipal and Environmental Infrastructure'. Municipal authorities have emerged as an important client group, and most projects have dealt with water supply, sewerage and wastewater treatment, sanitation, solid-waste management and district heating. Several key issues continue to create difficulties for environmental improvement, including a lack of recent investment, unclear legal and regulatory frameworks, and political influence over key financial decisions, such as user charges. Nevertheless, the EBRD has managed to support large, stand-alone projects such as the Tallinn wastewater project in Estonia, has aided groups of small municipalities in the same country, and has helped develop a specialised credit facility in Slovenia. In Maribor, Slovenia, the Bank supported private-sector investment whereby it was granted a concession to finance, build and operate a wastewater treatment plant. These so-called Build–Operate–Transfer packages might eventually be a model for injection of private cash into municipal environmental schemes.

More recently, in December 1997, the EBRD announced an agreement with the French company, CDC-Participations, and Belgian and Swiss interests, to create an investment fund with an initial capital of ecu 22 million (5 million from the EBRD), rising to ecu 50 million by the end of 1998. This emphasises an important response to environmental problems in the region – through exploiting the potential for provision of environmental protection equipment and services. The fund is investing between ecu 1 and 6 million in small and medium companies, and there is clearly a link between this investment and the requirement for candidate countries to meet EU environmental standards. The type of companies being supported include service providers such as operators of power plants or recyclers, as well as manufacturers of insulation, bio-fertilisers and filters. The full schedule (EBRD 1997) indicates the potential importance of this sector to any restructured economy. The main geographical focus is on the Czech Republic, Slovakia, Hungary, Poland and Romania, but it is possible that other countries will benefit. In keeping with the nature of venture capital support, the fund is taking a (minority) shareholding, and is expecting the companies to expand by attracting additional capital within three to five years or obtaining a listing on a stock exchange. Although the fund has a projected life-span of ten years, it is the intention to move out of companies to new clients and, in parallel with UK government prompting to British companies, the EBRD sees potential here to introduce local companies to Western partners.

A third example of assistance is perhaps the most imaginative. Debt-For-Environment Swaps (DFES) were first introduced between the USA and Bolivia in 1987, and they have been used by a number of indebted countries to reduce their external debt obligations in exchange for a commitment to mobilise domestic resources for environmental protection. Advantages certainly exist for the creditor, in that international and global environmental objectives can be met and public image can be enhanced. For the debtor, DFES can bring substantial injections of funds to small environmental management budgets, while institutions are strengthened because financing management capacity is required to negotiate and administer successful swaps (Georgieva 1995). Poland was the first country in the region to sign such an accord, replacing some external debt to the USA, France and Switzerland with an Eco-Fund. By 1995 this fund covered an official debt of over $450 million. A second agreement, between Bulgaria and Switzerland, was signed in October 1995. Here the agreement was to swap SF 20 million (20 per cent of Bulgaria's debt to Switzerland) against a commitment to set up an equivalent fund in local currency. Bulgaria committed itself to making eight successive semi-annual instalments into an Eco-Fund Trust, and projects funded from this trust must be additional to the normal Bulgarian state budget for environmental protection.

The reaction to externally funded environmental projects has not always been favourable. The underlying tension between sustainability in its 'economic development' as opposed to ecological meaning, suggested above, is exemplified by World Bank support to the forestry sector. In 1994 an $80 million loan was negotiated with the Slovakian Ministry of Agriculture (VLK Forest Protection Movement 1994). The major objectives of the loan were, first, development of environmentally and economically sound management, and, second, to ease the transition of the forestry and wood industry sub-sectors into, respectively, multiowner management and market conditions. Two Slovakian NGOs – the VLK (Wolf) Forest Protection Movement from Presov and the Green Perspective Foundation – evaluated the six components of the $200 million scheme, and identified the loan as yet another example of accelerating exploitation of natural resources to achieve short-term income. They pointed to the irony of terms such as 'ecological management of forests' in circumstances where old dirt roads would be paved, or over 15,000 hectares of new forest created to fuel biomass power plants. Given the common criticism of the wasteful use of energy throughout the region, the NGOs argued that the most environmentally sound way to 'produce' energy was to invest in energy-saving measures.

The World Bank was again at the centre of controversy when it agreed a loan with Poland to help its struggling forestry industry in 1993. Apart from any question of the final costs of the loan, including interest payments, critics saw the plans to increase logging as flying in the face of environmental protection (Adhemar and Petersen 1994). Bialowieza, in the east of Poland, is a forest ecosystem found nowhere else on the European continent. As Europe's last remaining lowland primeval forest, it is listed as a World Heritage Site and a UNESCO Biosphere Core Area, and part of it is designated as a national park. In 1992 the area received $4.5 million under the pilot phase of the World Bank's GEF. The scale of this loan, when compared with the aid to the forestry industry ($146 million), led to the view that GEF support was nothing more than a 'green smokescreen' to conceal the Bank's true priority. Whatever validity there may be in this critique, it became clear that the emphasis in environmental aid tended to be on 'scientific investment'. Other themes in assistance, such as establishing EU-compatible laws or institutional capacity building, result in an overemphasis on the 'top down'. NGOs are continually pressing for ' bottom-up' approaches which deal with the needs of the area in question and link environmental and social priorities. It is this sort of view from the grassroots environmental movement that needs to be heeded more in programme design.

Despite the many problems that have arisen, external assistance has been vital in both tackling major problems and in preparing the countries of the region for possible EU membership. That there is still much to be done is a theme explored through an analysis of the environmental issues emerging from *Agenda 2000*.

Agenda 2000: for a more environmentally sustainable Europe?

The three main strands of the European Commission's report – developing the Union and its policies, the impacts of enlargement on the Union as a whole and the financial framework beyond 2000 – are discussed elsewhere. Here attention will focus upon environmental issues, both in the context of the development of overall EU policy and the issues, problems and recommendations relating to this aspect of the applications of the ten countries of CEE.

Two earlier decisions by the European Council shaped the Commission's evaluation. The Copenhagen meeting of June 1993 set out the three criteria for establishing an Opinion on the application of the Associated countries. For the environment, the third of these was of particular importance: the applicants' ability to take on the obligations of membership (the *acquis*). Subsequently, the 1995 Madrid Summit requested the Commission to take forward its analysis of the impact of enlargement on the EU. The Commission's overall finding, in the summary accompanying *Agenda 2000*, was that 'substantial investments will be needed in areas such as environmental protection', as well as many other areas, and, highlighting a particular area of concern, that 'in countries which obtain energy from nuclear power stations, the Commission expects applicants to cooperate fully to bring their levels to internationally accepted safety standards in order to protect the life and health of all citizens' (Commission 1997a:11). The feeling was clearly that the environment posed a challenge not just to the applicants, but also to the EU itself.

Amid the scenes of celebration at the end of March 1998, when formal negotiations began, there was still a message from *Agenda 2000* which applied not just to the environment: the actual timetable for accession depended on progress made in the individual countries in adopting, implementing and enforcing the *acquis*. In this respect, an early, and important, proposal to emerge from *Agenda 2000* was for a 'reinforced pre-accession' strategy. As part of this, the Commission set out to bring together the different forms of support (including a reoriented Phare) into a single framework: the Accession Partnership (see Chapter 2 and Appendix II).

For a stronger and wider Europe: progressing the EU's environment policy

The importance of the environment should be understood not just in terms of the challenges of enlargement, but also as a central element requiring attention in Union policy development and reform. The environment displays many of the current problems of operation as well as potential for change.

In Volume 1, Part 1 of *Agenda 2000* (the Policies of the Union) the

development of internal policies was made a first priority. Four directions were discussed, with the environment contributing to the fourth –
improving living conditions. Initial comments were linked to the importance of being able to respond to the environmental challenge in an
enlarged Union, and went on to call for better implementation and
enforcement of the environmental *acquis* as well as further integration
of environmental considerations into all relevant Community policies.
Implementation problems occur time and again in the evolution of EU
environmental policy, for example with the adoption of 'horizontal'
measures such as Environmental Impact Assessment of projects and the
disputes over a draft Directive on Strategic Environmental Assessment.
Thus experience has proven that CEEC will become involved in an
already contested policy area. The environment was also discussed in a
later section, dealing with economic and social cohesion. The
Commission advocates structural support to *all* applicants, including
those joining in further expansions, with emphasis on bringing infra-
structures up to Community standards, particularly in the (transport
and) environment fields.

Judged by financial, political and social criteria, perhaps the most
important dimension to developing environmental policy within the existing Union and CEEC is the reform of the CAP. Deepening the reforms
initiated in 1992 would deal simultaneously with a number of burgeoning
problems. First, the CAP currently accounts for a little over 50 per cent of
the entire EU budget. The economic and social impacts, therefore, of
applying existing CAP measures to CEEC are potentially damaging to the
Union's financial and political credibility. The 1992 reforms stressed the
environmental dimension of agriculture as the largest land user. Likewise,
some twenty years of effort to devise a coherent rural development policy
began to recognise the interrelationship of three policy fields: agricultural,
structural *and environment*.

The importance of the natural environment and the need to evaluate
the environmental effects of human activity had steered policy into the
direction of so-called 'agri-environmental' measures. While these
measures had gained public approval and were well received by farmers,
the Commission was aware of the inadequate scale of support. With agriculture and forestry as the main land users in the existing and enlarged
EU, there were good arguments for investigating the economic and other
benefits of redirecting CAP money into public payments for the protection
of natural resources, environmentally sustainable farming practices, and
contributing to the economic and social stability of rural regions: a truly
holistic approach to the environment was necessary in the future. The
Commission set out a number of elements in a strengthened agri-environmental policy. Existing instruments could be applied to overlapping
spatial areas: of high nature value, less favoured areas (LFAs) and

Objective One areas, for example.[5] In addition, targeted measures, for example alpine cattle-keeping and wetland management, would have potential in areas such as south-east and north-east Poland.

The challenge of enlargement

Volume 1 continued with an analysis of the major challenges. The crucial issue, here, was the capacity to take on the obligations of membership, which included the whole range of policies and measures that constitute the environmental *acquis* of the Union. While the White Paper (Commission 1995) set out environmental measures in relation to the functioning of the Single Market, this was only part of the story. The Commission recognised that 'for most of the countries significant and far reaching adaptations will be needed in the field(s) of environment' (Commission 1995:39). A pessimistic assessment was offered at an early stage: 'None of the candidate countries can be expected to comply fully with the acquis in the near future, given their present environmental problems and the need for massive investments' (Commission 1995:43). The seriousness of this issue was highlighted by commentary upon the potentially disruptive consequences should a gap between existing and new members be allowed to persist; that is, different environmental standards would distort the functioning of the Single Market. Thus the problem of compliance had to be viewed not only in the context of legislative and administrative efforts but also investment. The Commission confirmed the long-held view of analysts (Alcamo 1992; Lofstedt and Sjostedt 1996) that national budgets alone could not bear the likely costs. But, ominously, it was emphasised that the Union could not bridge the gap. Without specifying likely sources, CEEC were encouraged to seek out important domestic and foreign financial resources, in particular from the private sector.

Partial help has come via the reorientation of Phare within the SPAR. Assistance has been focused on two key priority areas: institution building and finance of investment projects (30 per cent and 70 per cent of the budget, respectively). Bearing in mind the past criticisms of Phare (see Chapter 2), efforts have been made to improve effectiveness: through concentration on projects to implement the *acquis* (prioritised by the Accession Partnership); increasing the average size of projects; and continuing to decentralise the management in favour of recipient countries. While the message from the Union was that the principle of full adoption of environmental *acquis* was not to be compromised, it was clear that for this policy field some transitional arrangements would have to be negotiated from March 1998 onwards. From the Commission came the request for realistic long-term strategies for gradual effective alignment. Implementation of these strategies had to commence before accession; thus priority areas were highlighted (water and air pollution in particular), and key objectives had to be fulfilled by the date of accession and the timetable for full compliance agreed. The forthcoming Accession Treaties would incorporate such obligations, and it was also stressed that all environmental investments, not just those through Phare, will have to comply with the *acquis*.

The effects on the Union's policies of enlargement to the applicant CEEC

Although described as an 'Impact Study' (Commission 1997b), it was difficult to discern in the Commission's work any accepted methodologies, calculations or formal evaluations to support the views expressed. The emphasis was on highlighting possible problems and strains for the environment – which were predicted to be considerable. Nevertheless, the Commission's purpose in its reporting was to ensure that the integration of new members would evolve smoothly and as quickly as possible, both before and after their succession, without creating major tensions or undermining the Union's achievements.

Several sections of the Impact Study deal with the environment. Given later comments on the current phase of EU policy, where the objective is to deal with mitigation of the effects of diffuse, hard-to-control sources, it was disappointing to note the very short commentary on environmental issues in the sections dealing with agriculture and transport. In the former, the earlier comments on the possible reform of the CAP were linked to analysis derived from a 1995 study on agriculture in CEEC which suggested that a switch from price support to direct-income support could lead to spending on environmental initiatives. With regard to transport, the principal emphasis was upon major investment in all transport modes, with the environment warranting a mention only in relation to the quality of transport fleets(!), presumably associated with levels of vehicle emission.

Fortunately, Sections 6 (horizontal policies) and 7 (sectoral policies) offered a fuller discussion. Thus in Section 6.2 ('Environment') the Commission went over very familiar ground in acknowledging the legacies of the pre-transformation period. The need to clear up past liabilities, for example hazardous waste, was stressed, as was the threat to human health. There was a mention, but no examples given, of some problems that had intensified during the rapid transformation (the pollution consequences of rapidly growing road transport might be one). Air and water pollution, particularly in the urban-industrial regions, were major elements in making the situation far worse than currently in the EU, hence the special priority in the pre-accession strategies. Conversely, progress was noted as a result of improvements in production technologies, as was the beneficial effect of plant closures as market conditions bit. However, an analysis of the employment and social effects of such write-offs was not included.

As CEEC use more traditional, 'end-of-pipe' methods to tackle problems, the 'moving target' of environmental management was stressed. Not only would candidates have to adapt to EU legislation, but more research, policy coordination and management would have to be devoted to new problems: 'the diffuse, hard-to-control sectors'. Apart from those already discussed above, there would, in future, have to be environmental assessments of tourism, energy and the structural funds: any future benefits from such funds would require considerable investment in environmental appraisal skills.

The report attempted to be upbeat. Without any calculations being presented, it stated that the acceding countries would find 'significantly higher marginal environmental benefits of investments'. Moreover, it was asserted, these investments would also address transboundary problems, which would bring cost savings to existing member states, while EU-based firms in the environmental and related sectors would see important new markets develop for their products and services. Given the possibly large contributions to sustainability (that is, sustainable economic growth), some attempt at calculation would have been worthwhile in order to justify future public spending on environmental protection, despite attempts to switch the burden to the private sector.

Some warnings in the report were as much political as economic. Environmental efforts devoted to CEEC were viewed as 'inward-looking', and it was suggested that this might make it more difficult to support sustainable development activity.[6] A further warning related to the dangers inherent in allowing the environmental gap to continue for a long time after accession – this would pose strains on cohesion and distort internal competition: low environmental standards could not be used for competitive advantage, the Commission maintained.

After so much emphasis on the asymmetric relationship between 'club' and 'candidate', the Commission's study noted, rather belatedly, that many candidate countries had different, but efficient, approaches in this field; and that some had developed expertise in areas such as nature conservation and preserving biodiversity. This might suggest that CEEC membership could lead to new ideas being put on the EU policy agenda.

In Section 7.2 the main policy objectives for energy were set out. These were mainly derived from the 1995 Commission White Paper and included protection of the environment, improving energy efficiency, implementing high environmental standards in energy production, and nuclear energy.[7] For the latter there were crucial issues surrounding health, safety, transport and waste management. Of these, nuclear safety became the major issue. Nuclear safety was seen as a problem that required a solution even independent of enlargement: upgrading might be possible via improving the plant or constructing replacements. The 'nuclear safety culture' was seen to be set at a lower standard than in the West. But, perhaps with one eye on the interests of the EU's existing nuclear industry, the Commission stated in Section 7.2 that 'public opinion is likely to be increasingly sensitive to nuclear safety as a consequence of some nuclear power problems in acceding countries *and this could affect major Community policy development in the field*' (Commission 1997b:45, emphasis added).

The overall conclusions of the Impact Study discussed the direct budgetary and financial implications for internal policies, including the environment. These argued for a concentration of available funds in a reduced number of programmes to prove their added value. Once again, the investment requirements were stressed and future policy changes in energy and environment were hinted at in order to better meet the needs of the new members. A more general problem was also flagged in the conclusion: with acceding members having a lower level of economic development, this could impede the development of Community policies. For the environment, as for other areas, a basic conclusion was that the impact of enlargement on the Union and its policies, and especially the scale of possible problems, would depend to a very large extent on the preparations during the pre-accession period. Here the Commission stressed the efforts required by the candidates themselves. So, for the 105 million people of the CEEC 10, the general picture that emerged from *Agenda 2000* in relation to the environment was that there were massive tasks ahead – to clean up the past; deal with the present; adapt to the EU's requirements; learn very quickly; sustain the effort; and, of course, generate the necessary funds to pay for it all!

Commission Opinions on the environment: the ten country reports

What was to be of more immediate concern to the candidates were the Opinions presented in the country reports. While the environment was only one element, it was emerging as an important aspect of the overall evaluation of the readiness of each country to take on the obligations of membership.

The organisation of Opinions on the environmental situation of each country followed a common format. In the Introduction there was a section on the pre-accession strategy which occasionally contained brief comments on environmental projects supported via Phare. The main body of evidence, however, was presented in Chapter 3, which covered the ability to assume the obligations of membership. Within this chapter environment was dealt with in a sub-section entitled 'Quality of Life and Environment' (3.6). An earlier section within Sectoral Policies dealt with energy. From the earlier remarks on implementation, one should note the importance of Chapter 4, which offered an Opinion on the administrative capacity, including departmental responsibilities and, crucially for enforcement of the *acquis*, the strength and effectiveness of any inspectorate activity. Each section was prefaced with the relevant EU policy objectives. Thus for the environment this meant that both the environment and the energy sections contained relevant statements.

Table 6.1 The capacity of CEEC to take on the environmental *acquis*

Environment Key conclusion	Descriptor	Countries
1 Effort	Very important[a]	B, H, R, Sla, Sle
	Very substantial[a]	C, E, La, Li, P
2 Investment	Massive	All
3 Administrative capacity to enforce legislation	Strengthen	All
4 Compliance with *acquis*:	Full: long term	C, E, La, Li, P, Sle
	Full: long to very long term	H, Sla
	Full: very long term	B, R
	Partial: medium term	C, E
5 Necessity for compliance	Increased public expenditure	B, H, La, Li, P, R, Sle

Energy Key conclusion	Descriptor	Countries
1 Nuclear safety	Modernise to international safety standards	B, C, H, Li, Sla
	Close where agreed/necessary	B, Li, Sla
2 Nuclear waste	Find a solution	H, R, Sla, Sle
3 Compliance with *acquis*	(Full) medium[b]	E, P
	Work to prepare *acquis*	La

Notes: B = Bulgaria; C = Czech Republic; E = Estonia; H = Hungary; La = Latvia; Li = Lithuania; P = Poland; R = Romania; Sla = Slovakia; Sle = Slovenia.
[a] Significance of descriptor not known.
[b] With provisos.
Source: Extracted from EC DOCs 97/11-20, Brussels.

A common format also led to a common stock of descriptive and evaluative terminology. Table 6.1 draws together the major conclusions covering environment and energy (particularly nuclear). For the environment the first three conclusions were common to all countries – very important/substantial effort, massive investment and the strengthening of administrative capacity were necessities. The timescale to comply with the *acquis* consisted of four categories, with Hungary and Slovakia and Bulgaria and Romania having longer time horizons attached to expected full compliance. The Czech Republic and Estonia were each placed in two categories, as both were expected to achieve partial compliance in the medium term. For seven of the ten states increased public expenditure was stressed, although it is uncertain whether the other three (the Czech Republic, Estonia and Slovakia) had reached required levels. Two major areas were identified in relation to nuclear power and the environment: operational issues which either necessitated upgrading of plant to internationally acceptable standards or decommissioning, and the need to find a solution to the problem of disposal of nuclear waste.

The current challenge: alignment and 'following the road map'

A key aspect of *Agenda 2000*'s evaluation was the degree to which candidates had already aligned their environmental laws to the entire body of EU legislation. There exist some 300 legal acts, including Directives, Regulations, Decisions and Recommendations. In addition, numerous other policy documents and communications inform environmental policy (Commission 1996, 1997c). Consequently, as has been suggested, the alignment task is daunting. Experience with implementation (non-, partial or ineffective) up to the mid-1990s resulted in the Commission publication *Implementing Community Environmental Law* (1996). This provided some key definitions, which informed the Commission when carrying out its analysis of the candidates' claims on ability to meet the environmental *acquis*. This process began with the provisions of the 1995 White Paper, and consisted of candidates supplying information on the alignment of national laws to those Directives and Regulations pertaining to products and the environment. This covered approximately half of EU environmental legislation. The subsequent Commission country Opinions were confirmed as correct by national governments, so that, at June 1997, the overall picture was very disappointing. This confirmed the need not only for the candidates to produce realistic strategies for gradual and effective alignment, but also to plan for full implementation.

A first step in this process was to identify lead responsibilities in each of the CEEC. Single contact points were established in relevant Ministries (see Table 6.2), as well as maintaining links through the Missions to the EU. For the latter, the practice had varied, but in most cases specialist counsellors dealt with a number of policy issues, for example regional policy and technology. In the smaller Missions the counsellors tended to operate as a 'postbox'.

In August 1997 DG XI produced a Working Paper (Commission 1997c) to help senior policy makers and officials in countries preparing for accession to the EU to deepen their understanding of the entire body of EU environmental legislation. The paper is described as a kind of 'road map' representing the ground that countries must cover if they are fully to adopt EU rules and standards. It explains the three key elements of

Table 6.2 Lead responsibilities in CEEC for the environmental pre-accession strategy on the approximation of environmental legislation (at 12 September 1997)

Country	Lead responsibility
Czech Republic	Director, International Relations Department, Ministry of Environment
Estonia	Permanent State Secretary, Ministry of Environment
Hungary	PMU and International Cooperation Department, Hungarian Ministry for Environment and Regional Policy
Poland	Vice-Director, Department of Environmental Protection, Natural Resources and Forestry
Slovenia	Heads of Departments for European Affairs, Environmental Legislation, Ministry of Environment and Physical Planning
Bulgaria	Head of Legal Division, Ministry of Environment
Latvia	Adviser of State Secretary, Ministry of Environmental Protection and Regional Development
Lithuania	Adviser on European Integration, European Integration Unit, Environmental Protection Ministry
Romania	Director for Strategies and Regulations for the Protection of the Environment, Ministry of Water, Forests and Protection of the Environment
Slovakia	Head of the Foreign Legal Relations Division, Environmental Legislation Department, Ministry for the Environment

Source: Commission (1997c).

approximation – transposition, implementation or practical application, and enforcement. The scope of approximation is spelt out so that all aspects of EU environmental legislation will be covered by the candidate: products, activities or production processes and environmental quality, as well as procedures and procedural rights. A step-by-step guide is offered to the approximation of EU Directives. Annexe 3 of the Working Paper is particularly important as it provides an example of a table of concordance with EU legislation which may be used to monitor progress on approximation of an individual Directive.

The nomination of Desk Officers in Section A.4 of DG XI to work with the nominated contact persons in the Ministries of candidate countries allowed for workshops to be set up and training to be given. Interviews by the author with Missions confirmed the usefulness of DG XI's initiative. It appeared, however, that this approach was not fully replicated in other Directorates. Despite this assistance, the notion of the 'road map' was showing another side – in that the terrain, problems and need for learning referred to in the Preface of the paper were proving to be arduous.

As at May 1998, the pre-accession strategy that had been mapped out since mid-1997 was proving difficult for both sides. One report found that the Commission was calling on candidates to go back and design much tighter national programmes, with clear 'milestones' for implementing the environmental *acquis* (Turner 1998). And, despite the emerging problems within the Union of incorporating environmental considerations into sectoral spending, the demand from the Commission was that any future loans to the region should be compatible with EU environmental legislation.

Conclusion

After a decade of clean-up, studies, strategies, training and investment, the environment still poses major challenges to the CEEC. While, from 1990 onwards, there was undoubtedly a strong desire to make development more sustainable and to strengthen environmental protection, 'the pace of change and the economic problems of the transition, have subsequently made it hard to give the environment as much priority as desired in some of the countries' (Osborn 1997:260). Moreover, the European Commission made it plain that the continuing problems identified in *Agenda 2000* would require massive investment; and that no candidate country would be fully able to comply with the environmental *acquis* in the near future. Doeke Eisma (European Parliament 1997) introduced the Environment Committee's Opinion by confirming that EU environmental legislation is one of the major stumbling blocks for the enlargement of the Union. The political difficulties of demanding full compliance with the *acquis* are such that it has been estimated that no new member state would be able to accede for about twenty years!

As European environmentalists were celebrating Earth Day in April 1998, the Czech Environment Ministry announced that the nation would have to find at least $15 billion to bring the environment up to EU standards. In terms of priorities for the near future, water-treatment facilities for small towns and villages would require $3 billion. Czech Greenpeace warned, however, that the figures were the minimum necessary to comply with EU standards, and that much larger sums would be needed to move towards the higher environmental quality of many existing EU members (Legge 1998).

A recent EU estimate (European Parliament 1997; Turner 1998) suggested that the CEEC 10 would need to spend around ecu 120 billion to reach the required standards. Even with Phare funding of ecu 1.5 billion a year and the proposed special environmental fund, resources will still be insufficient. While some of these costs would have to be incurred even without accession to the EU, time constraints are now being perceived with the start of negotiations. The question of apportioning future costs seemed straightforward in *Agenda 2000*, with the Commission stressing that most investment would come from CEEC themselves. As the EP pointed out, however, the key question is whether the private sector is prepared to make such a commitment.

The dilemmas for negotiators quickly become apparent. On the one hand, it might be possible to argue that the benefits of access to the internal market will make it worthwhile for business to bear the extra costs of complying with the full range of the environmental *acquis*. If these costs were too high, however, they would act as a break on economic growth, and surely diminish public support for environmental protection (European Parliament 1997). Thus, a key element discussed above becomes important in the Opinion of the EP that 'efforts must be made to induce the international monetary bodies to give priority to environmental investments in the CEEC, and there needs to be a sound degree of coordination between such bodies' (European Parliament 1997:6).

What must be appreciated from the EU side is that since 1989 there have been great advances in environmental policy making. Poland, for example, adopted a National Environmental Policy as early as 1991, and by the time of the publication of the Agenda 21 Progress Report (1997), could report innovations in financing environmental protection, including national, regional and municipal funds. Recent reports from Estonia (Ratas and Raukas 1997; Ministry of the Environment of Estonia 1997) stress the role of NGOs in the implementation of the sustainable development strategy. An audit of best practice across the existing member states of the Union might reveal that some of the candidates are well ahead in key areas such as biodiversity protection and eco-agriculture.

The passing of the EU presidency from the UK to Austria in July 1998 could have a potentially important effect on one aspect of environmental policy: nuclear safety. Austria has a long-running concern over safety standards in CEE, especially in Slovakia and the Czech Republic. Martin Bartenstein, Austria's Environment Minister, stated at the beginning of the presidency that 'fulfilling Western safety standards will play an important role in negotiations on entering the EU' (Jakl 1998).

Finally, it is important to make the accession criteria realistic. The EP argued that the Commission should draw up a list of the most important elements of EU environmental legislation which candidates must satisfy at the time of accession. This was not seen as a way of avoiding obligations, however, as a transition period of more than five years seems generally unacceptable as far as the environment is concerned. Apart from meeting full or partial demands of the *acquis*, the financing of environmental improvements in CEEC remains a loosely costed and unresolved item on the agenda of the EU. With the invitations to the Czech Republic, Estonia, Hungary, Poland and Slovenia to enter negotiations for accession, the wrong signals may be going out as far as the environment is concerned. There is likely to be a perception that economic and political issues are more pressing. Indeed, it seems probable that this will be the outcome over the next months, despite Commission rhetoric to the effect that none of the environmental *acquis* is negotiable. In consequence, the warning issued by the EP (1997:64) must be considered to have great significance: 'The great danger in all this is that the environment is not given the same priority as economic criteria and the functioning of the internal market. Not only is this detrimental to environmental policy in the CEEC, but it will also put a brake on the further development of EU environmental policy.'

Notes

The author would like to thank officials in the following offices for their help via interviews, identifying sources and suggesting contacts: DG XI of the European Commission; the Mission of the Republic of Estonia to the EU; the Mission of the Republic of Slovenia to the EU; the Mission of the Republic of Poland to the EU; and the Office of the Committee for European Integration, Warsaw.

1 This was a special session of the UN General Assembly held to review and appraise the implementation of Agenda 21.
2 Carter and Turnock analyse the rise of Green parties and environmental NGOs. Some were effective in the last years of communism, particularly in Hungary and Bulgaria.
3 Russell's initial assessment of the environmental situation in Eastern Europe related to six countries – the former Czechoslovakia and East Germany, and Bulgaria, Poland, Hungary and Romania. Seventeen indicators were used and each was scored on a 4-point scale, with 4 indicating 'catastrophe'. Of the 102 possible entries (17 times 6 countries), one was catastrophic – water pollution in Poland. Another 16 were 'major' and 32 'serious'. Across the region as a whole, the most serious problems were water and atmospheric pollution, followed by pollution threats to general health, erosion/soil breakdown, habitat and species destruction, and forestry damage. The most pressing problems at the start of the decade were a shortage of environmental technology, shortcomings of environmental law and inadequate environmental infrastructure, including ecologists and data recording. In the short term (up to 1995) the situation was predicted to get worse, but by 2010 improvements were expected.
4 In the case of the NIS of the former Soviet Union, EU assistance is provided by the Tacis programme. Nuclear safety has been such an important issue in this region that it received 17 per cent of all funds allocated. The legacy of Chernobyl means that assistance is given to improving the safety of nuclear power-generation. But beyond this, there is a serious nuclear hazard from military uses. Here British Nuclear Fuels, in partnership with three other Western companies, has been undertaking a design study for a safe interim storage

facility for spent nuclear submarine fuel. And, beyond Tacis, the World Association of Nuclear Operators has been organising exchange programmes so that, for example, assistance has been given to all stations in the Moscow region.

5 The Commission announced legislative proposals in March 1998 to give effect to the *Agenda 2000* provisions. Current eligibility criteria for support for LFAs will be modified to improve the integration of environmental goals into rural development policy. The LFAs scheme will be gradually transformed into an instrument to maintain and promote low-input farming systems. Other agri-environmental measures will be aimed more specifically at the environment.

6 Here it might have been fair to have acknowledged the contributions of CEEC to such efforts already, for example Poland's work on the United Nations Environment Programme.

7 The critical importance of nuclear power for some states can be illustrated by the case of Hungary, where the Russian-designed PAKS nuclear station supplies 40 per cent of the country's electricity. Some ecu 200 million have been allocated to safety upgrade. Lithuania operated two large RBMK (Chernobyl-type) reactors at Ingalina, which produce 85 per cent of the country's electricity. The Commission expressed concern at the lack of full implementation of all urgent recommendations.

References

Adhemar, A. and Petersen, J. (1994), Hour of Destiny for Bialowieza Primeval Forest, *Green Brigades*, 2, 20–1.
Alcamo, J. (ed.) (1992), *Coping with Crisis in Eastern Europe's Environment*, Carnforth, Parthenon.
Bachtler, J. (ed.) (1992a), *Socio-economic Situation and Development in the Neighbouring Countries and Regions of the European Community in Central and Eastern Europe*, Brussels, Commission of the European Communities, DG XVI.
Bachtler, J. (1992b), Regional Problems and Policies in Central and Eastern Europe, *Regional Studies*, 26, 665–71.
Caddy, J. (1997), Harmonization and Asymmetry: Environmental Policy Coordination between the European Union and Central Europe, *Journal of European Public Policy*, 4, 18–36.
Carter, F. W. (1985), Pollution Problems in Post-war Czechoslovakia, *Transactions*, Institute of British Geographers, 10, 17–44.
Carter, F. W. and Turnock, D. (eds) (1996), *Environmental Problems in Eastern Europe*, London, Routledge.
Commission (1995), White Paper, *Preparation of the Associated Countries of Central and Eastern Europe for the Integration into the Internal Market of the Union*, COM(95)163, Final.
Commission (1996), *Preparation of the Associated CEECs for the Approximation of the EU's Environmental Legislation*, Working Document.
Commission (1997a), *Agenda 2000 – For a Stronger and Wider Union*, COM(97), Final.

Commission (1997b), *Agenda 2000 – the Challenge of Enlargement*, COM(97), Final.

Commission (1997c), *Enlarging the Environment*, DG XI.

EBRD (1996), *Environmental Policy*, London, European Bank for Reconstruction and Development.

EBRD (1997), ECU 22 Million Environmental Fund Set to Invest in Central and Eastern Europe, Press Release 104, 19 December.

European Parliament (1997), *Opinion on the Commission Communication 'Agenda 2000 – For a Stronger and Wider Union'*, Committee on the Environment, Public Health and Consumer Protection, DOC EN\RR\340\ 340348, 60–7.

Georgieva, K. (1995), Bulgarian–Swiss Debt-for-Environment Swap, *World Bank Environment Bulletin*, 7:4, 6.

Gorzelak, G. (1995), *The Regional Dimension of Transformation in Central Europe*, London, Jessica Kingsley.

Jakl, R. (1998), Nuke Power Foe Rules EU, *The Prague Post*, 8–14 July.

Legge, M. (1998), Nation Faces a Major Mop-up of Environmental Mess, *The Prague Post*, 22–28 April.

Liefferink, J. D., Lowe, P. and Mol, A. P. J. (eds) (1993), *European Integration and Environmental Policy*, Chichester, Belhaven.

Lofstedt, R. E. and Sjostedt, G. (eds) (1996), *Environmental Aid Programmes to Eastern Europe*, Aldershot, Avebury.

Ministry of the Environment of Estonia (1997), *Keskkond 1996 Estonian Environment*, Tallinn, Environment Information Centre.

Moldan, B. (1996), Environment in the Period of Transformation, in Z. Pavlik (ed.), *Human Development Report Czech Republic*, Prague, Charles University, 59–67.

Osborn, D. (1997), The Way Forward Beyond Agenda 21: Perspectives on the Future from Europe, in F. Dodds (ed.), *The Way Forward – Beyond Agenda 21*, London, Earthscan.

Ratas, R. and Raukas, A. (1997), *Main Outlines of Sustainable Development in Estonia*, Tallinn, Ministry of the Environment.

Rugg, D. S. (1985), *Eastern Europe*, London, Longman.

Russell, J. (1991a), *Energy and Environmental Conflicts in East–Central Europe*. London, Royal Institute of International Affairs.

Russell, J. (1991b), *Environmental Issues in Eastern Europe: Setting an Agenda*, London, Royal Institute of International Affairs.

Turner, M. (1998), Clearing the Fog for Eastern Europeans, *European Voice*, 28 May–3 June.

VLK Forest Protection Movement (1994), Campaign to Stop World Bank Loan to Forestry Sector in Slovakia, *Green Brigades*, 2, 22.

Security issues in the wider Europe: the role of EU–CEEC relations

Security issues have lain at the heart of EU–CEEC relations from the outset. In 1990, from the perspective of the Community:

> The peaceful revolution which swept Eastern Europe in 1989 is probably the most significant event in global terms of the past 45 years. It is happening on the very doorstep of the European Community. It represents a challenge and an opportunity to which the EC has given an immediate response. (Commission 1990a:5)

Central to that challenge was the need to provide support for transformation in CEEC, while simultaneously ensuring that the EU's internal processes of integration were safeguarded. Thus protection of the EU itself, as the stable core of Europe, was a prerequisite for building EU–CEEC relationships in a manner which would contribute positively to the security of Europe as a whole.

From the perspective of CEEC, the reorientation from East to West of external policies quickly became a priority for the governments installed after the 'velvet revolutions' of 1989. This represented a shift of perception and of policy so fundamental that it can be seen as a third transformation, alongside the processes of democratisation and market reform. Thus the 'triple transformation' which CEEC have been attempting 'represents a change so multifaceted and so profound that there are few precedents in history' (Smoke 1996:104).

For the peoples of CEE the experience of these transformations produced deep anxieties and broad, if unfocused, perceptions of insecurity. These related both to the destabilising effects and perceived uncertainty of internal transformation processes; and to the belief that, since loss of the old certainties of WTO membership and Soviet protection, CEEC had been affected by a 'security vacuum'. Here a central paradox lies in the fact that the general public across CEEC expresses strong feelings of insecurity, as do CEE security specialists and political elites. At the same time, however, all three groups have consistently emphasised that external threats are few (Dunay 1995; Kramer and Smoke 1996).

This chapter is primarily concerned with perceptions of security and insecurity in CEEC, and with the policy choices of CEE governments. While the principal focus is upon the security dimension of EU–CEEC relations, the changing role of NATO is also briefly discussed. Here the emphasis is upon the extent of complementarity between NATO and EU policies towards CEEC.

For two reasons, this focus demands consideration of debates within international relations about the meaning of security in the post-Cold War environment; and, in particular, arguments that the traditional under-standing of security – as freedom from external military threat – be extended to include alternative sources of risk. First, the EU itself is not a military power and access by the EU to military instruments is both indi-rect and uncertain. Second, and more importantly, perceptions of insecurity in CEEC are not primarily focused upon traditional security concerns. There is little sense of external military threat; indeed, it is clear that, 'For most people, the most pervasive and immediate insecurity is the profound and never-ending economic crisis of their country' (Boguszacova *et al.* 1996:35).

Post-Cold War conceptualisations of security

The ending of Cold War bipolarity brought fundamental changes to the structures and processes of international politics, and inevitably presented major challenges both to analysis and practice. The euphoria which greeted the revolutions of 1989, and associated expectations of a 'peace dividend', quickly evaporated following the outbreak of violent conflict in the Caucasus and the Balkans early in 1991. Evidently the end of the Cold War had not brought peace to Europe; rather, it had been a source of rapid and potentially destabilising change. In Eastern Europe this was associated with a range of new, and essentially unpre-dictable, security risks. The responses of security analysts to this radically changed environment ranged from nostalgia for the relative predictability of Cold War confrontation, to attempts to reformulate the concept of security itself.[1]

For traditional security analysts of the realist school, the premises of historical pessimism suggested that the ending of the Cold War would have disastrous consequences for Europe. From this perspective 'the Cold War was principally responsible for transforming a historically violent region into a very peaceful place' (Mearsheimer 1990:51). Consequently, the West 'has an interest in the continuation of the Cold War confronta-tion; developments that threaten to end it are dangerous' (Mearsheimer

1990:52). Despite the subsequent dissolution of the Soviet Union, such assumptions have underlain a lengthy debate among American security analysts about the enlargement of NATO – indeed, they continue to do so (MccGwire 1998; Ball 1998). From the US perspective, as Mandelbaum (1995:9) has noted, 'NATO expansion is about *Russia*'.[2] The continued dominance of traditional security analysis in this area undoubtedly demonstrates 'how little progress academic security studies has made in converting new security ideas into practical policies' (Ball 1998:44).

Those analysts who seek to extend the meaning of security are aiming, essentially, to develop a conceptualisation which will encompass the 'new' issues of the post-Cold War security agenda without abandoning the concerns of traditional analyses. In examining the security dimensions of EU–CEEC relations, the framework developed by Barry Buzan and his collaborators of the 'Copenhagen School' provides a useful starting point (Buzan 1991; Wæver *et al.* 1993; Buzan *et al.* 1998). For these authors, the 'defining core' of security studies is 'the survival of collective units and principles – the politics of existential threat' (Buzan *et al.* 1998:27).

Their approach invites consideration of security as a social process, in which issues which may not, in practice, constitute a genuine threat to survival are actively constructed in these terms in order to gain political priority or advantage. This, in turn, allows the adequacy of traditional, realist assumptions to be questioned, on two principal grounds – the centrality of the state as the referent object of security, and the almost exclusive emphasis upon military threats to survival.

First, the central focus in realist analysis upon the state as the referent object of security is challenged on the grounds that this privileging of 'national security' fails to capture the essence of the post-Cold War security agenda. This is significant, in the present context, due to the perceived need to protect the EU, or more specifically the integration process, in the interest of maintaining stability and security in Europe as a whole. Thus there have increasingly been attempts to identify the process of integration as a referent object of security. Should integration fail, the Commission warns us darkly: 'Europe, a mere geographical entity, will come under the influence of outside powers which will extort the price of its dependence and its need for protection' (Commission 1990b:5).

Since the end of the Cold War such warnings have frequently been re-iterated. This has included an explicit framing of integration *per se* as the guarantor of security and stability in Europe. Thus, for example, the late President Mitterrand, in his farewell speech to the EP (Mitterrand 1995:48), declared that 'Europe will be a people's Europe only if people feel secure in Europe, and because of Europe.' Clearly this framing of the EU as both security referent object and guarantor of security is central to our discussion of the EU's security roles.

Of particular significance to perceptions of insecurity in CEEC is the concept of societal security, which enables us to conceive of large-scale social units as referent objects of security (Wæver *et al.* 1993). Societies exist independently of, and potentially in opposition to, the state – as the velvet revolutions of 1989 clearly demonstrated. Societal security concerns 'the sustainability, within acceptable conditions for evolution, of traditional patterns of language, culture, association, and religious and national identity and custom' (Wæver *et al.* 1993:23). Thus, essentially, societal security involves the protection of collective identity. The relevance of this concept to discussion of security issues in post-Cold War Europe has been amply demonstrated; whether by the tragic conflicts in the Balkans or by the Czech–Slovak 'velvet divorce'.

In moving beyond state-centric approaches, an extended concept of security also challenges the state as the institution whose representatives are uniquely qualified to identify security threats, and hence to demand whatever extraordinary measures or sacrifices may be deemed necessary when survival is threatened. Difficulties arise here, in that official representatives of the state are clearly identifiable and more evidently possess the authority to frame security agendas; whereas a range of individuals or groups may make competing 'security' claims on behalf of societies. Buzan *et al.* (1998) address these issues through the concept of 'securitisation', which denotes the social processes through which issues come to be perceived and responded to as security threats. This concept is applied below in examining perceptions of security and insecurity in CEEC.

The second major area in which an extended concept of security challenges the assumptions of traditional analysis lies in the latter's overwhelming emphasis upon military threats to security. Here, in order to encompass a range of sources of threat which may be perceived as challenging the survival of collective entities, Buzan *et al.* (1998) have developed the notion of 'security sectors'. In addition to traditional military threats, which continue to have salience both for states and societies, four additional security sectors are identified – economic, environmental, societal and political. Each of the sectors is characterised by distinctive patterns of interaction between referent object and source of threat. In practice, of course, the sectors do not exist independently – environmental unsustainability and economic crisis may coexist; each is likely to impinge upon the political and societal sectors. These last are the security referent objects which principally concern us here.[3]

In the case of political security the referent object is primarily the state, although the concept can equally be applied to the EU. Here security threats involve challenges to 'relationships of authority, governing status and recognition' (Buzan *et al.* 1998:7); that is, to the legitimacy of the political system. In the case of societal security the referent objects are 'societies' or large-scale social units. Here security threats involve challenges to collective identity associated with fears of socio-cultural domination, dilution or marginalisation by the ideas, or physical presence, of non-members. Thus the processes of integration or migration, or the rights of ethnic groups, can be the subject of a securitising discourse. In the context of EU–CEEC relations, all these societal 'threats' have relevance.

While the concept of societal security is useful, it should be noted that it has attracted criticism. For example, Huysmans (1995) warns that including societal 'threats' within a security discourse will have negative consequences, including attempts to construct or protect the collective identity of a particular 'we group' through negative stereotyping of non-members of the group. Thus securitisation of migration, as Huysmans points out, casts the migrant as a threat to the survival of society; it also suggests the adoption of extraordinary measures to counteract this threat. While sympathising with the argument that 'desecuritisation' of such matters is to be encouraged, our concern is to explore the evolving meaning of security as reflected in contemporary usage and practice in CEEC.

Security issues and policy responses in CEEC

Following the revolutions of 1989, CEE governments were faced with the need to formulate external policies which would meet their security needs, both 'new' and traditional. This 'third transformation' may appear to have been relatively unimportant when compared with the momentous task of internal economic and political reform. However, the three transformations are intimately linked, and in the political and economic sectors external support for the transformation processes was sought from the outset. While the initial response from Western governments and institutions, through G24 and the EC, may have been inadequate, it was certainly prompt.

In the traditional security sector, however, the urgency of policy reorientation was less immediately apparent. In 1989 the WTO was in place and the Soviet Union remained a great power. Thus, for the foreseeable future, CEE policy choices in terms of military security appeared to be relatively constrained when compared with other sectors. While CEE governments began negotiations with the Soviet government for the removal of Soviet troops from their territories, and emphasised their support for enhancement of the pan-European Conference on Security and Cooperation in Europe (CSCE) process, there was neither space nor necessity for policy innovation. Indeed, in March 1990, CEE governments publicly expressed support for continuation of the WTO (NATO 1995:320).

The initial period after 1989 was thus characterised by uncertainty, given the potential tension between increasing economic orientation towards the West and continued military involvement with the East; and by moves to resolve this uncertainty through gradual disengagement from the Soviet Union. From mid-1991, however, the external policy environment changed both rapidly and fundamentally. The outbreak of war in Yugoslavia in May 1991, and the subsequent disintegration of the Yugoslav Federation, caused dismay throughout the region, although inevitably concern was greatest in Hungary, which has borders with Slovenia, Croatia and Serbia and a substantial expatriate population in the Serb province of Vojvodina. Of even greater significance, however, was the disintegration of the Soviet Union, which had 'seemed for such a long time to be so mighty, so threatening and so permanent'. This was experienced, throughout the region, as a shock 'so great that it took some time for the reality of it to sink in' (Kalicki 1996). The apparently inexorable processes of destabilisation and fragmentation in Eastern Europe subsequently continued with the separation of Slovakia from the Czech Republic at the end of 1992. The magnitude of change affecting the external environment of CEEC is exemplified by the position of Poland which, by January 1993, was entirely bordered by 'new' countries – the unified Germany, the Czech Republic, Slovakia, Ukraine, Belarus, Lithuania and Russia (Kaliningrad).

These major changes during 1991–92 necessitated a fundamental reorientation of all aspects of CEE external policy – both for practical and psychological reasons. Thus the formal disbandment of the WTO in early 1991, and the subsequent disintegration of the Soviet Union, were perceived, in circumstances where feelings of insecurity were already intense, to have created a potentially dangerous 'security vacuum'.

Below we consider CEE responses to these unsettling changes. Since the interaction of popular and elite attitudes and perceptions contributes significantly to the construction of security issues and agendas, public attitudes and perceptions are discussed as a prelude to examining CEE policy responses.

Public perceptions of security in CEEC

In the four CEEC included in the 1992–94 Security for Europe Project – the Czech Republic, Hungary, Poland and Slovakia – it was overwhelmingly apparent that the internal crises of their countries were perceived, by the public, as 'a *security* issue' (Boguszakova *et al.* 1996.[4] There was a clear perception that chronic economic instability was linked to a range of social disorders, in particular rising crime, prostitution and other forms of exploitation; together with more inchoate fears that uncontrollable demonstrations or riots would threaten the social fabric and jeopardise their countries' political future. In Hungary, Poland and Slovakia (but not the Czech Republic), distrust of the government was 'almost universal' (Boguszakova *et al.* 1996:35).[5]

These perceptions of internal crisis and political inadequacy indicate high levels of societal insecurity, associated with the existence of a multitude of 'threats against which no adequate countermeasures are available' (Buzan *et al.* 1998:4). Although the Security for Europe Project did not consider public responses by ethnicity or gender, it is axiomatic that perceptions of insecurity varied across these, and other, social dimensions. This is very evident in the case of the gender impacts of transformation; indeed, the falling birth rate in CEEC provides a particularly strong indication of societal insecurity (see Chapter 5).

In addition to the deep insecurities generated by the internal transformations, CEE publics also identified a range of external security threats. First among these were fears of danger from unsafe nuclear power stations, which were evident throughout the region, as were fears of some other form of environmental disaster (Boguszakova *et al.* 1996:37). There was also a strong perception that CEE governments were incapable of dealing with these environmental security threats, and that substantial assistance would be required from the West.

A second, widely expressed fear was of a threat to societal security arising from an influx of migrants from the former Soviet Union and/or the Balkan region.[6] There has, indeed, been increased permanent migration into CEEC, particularly the Czech Republic and Hungary but also Poland, from these sources and also from the West (Salt and Clarke 1996:517). This reflects relative economic success and includes a substantial proportion of returning 'nationals', particularly in the case of Hungary, which has a large expatriate population.[7] However, CEEC have also experienced considerable irregular and 'transit' migration, destined for EU countries, from a wide range of origins.[8] The size of this informal migrant population is difficult to establish but in Poland, in 1995, it was estimated at between 300,000 and 350,000 and in the Czech Republic between 100,000 and 140,000 (Salt and Clarke 1996:520). Moreover, as the EU has increasingly taken steps to prevent the entry of migrants, there is a sense that the CEE region 'has become a waiting room' (Salt and Clarke 1996:521).

Despite this, fears concerning the level and impact of migration have evidently not been realised; since the proportion of CEE publics expressing fear of migrants 'flooding our country' decreased from one-third (in 1992) to one-fifth by 1996 (Haerpfer and Wallace 1997:16).[9] The only exception here is Slovakia, where anxieties increased, despite the fact that Slovakia actually receives relatively few migrants. This may be attributable to the 'rising xenophobic rhetoric of Slovak political leaders' (Haerpfer and Wallace 1997:17).

The third issue identified as a security threat, throughout the region, was international crime, or 'mafias'. Again there was a perception that state agencies were not adequately trained or equipped to deal with this 'especially visible and worrisome' threat to political and societal security (Boguszakova *et al.* 1996:37).

These non-military sources of external threat to security – international crime, potential environmental disasters and the possibility of large-scale migration – were identified, in the focus-group discussions organised by the Security for Europe Project, 'more quickly, and with a stronger emotional sense of anxiety, than any military danger of any kind' (Boguszakova *et al.* 1996:37–8). Only in Hungary, where there were fears of being drawn into the conflict in ex-Yugoslavia, was concern expressed about issues relating to military security. Throughout CEE there were, nevertheless, widespread yet non-specific anxieties associated with more traditional security matters.

Anxiety about the future character and intentions of the Russian regime was foremost among the traditional security concerns identified by CEE publics. These concerns were more strongly felt in Poland than other CEEC, and were reflected in the opinion that Poland's eastern border should be strengthened. This view also related to the perception that Russian mafias were highly active in Polish cities; and to concerns that Russian troops stationed in Kaliningrad might be involved in incursions across the border 'if they become indisciplined or simply hungry'. It would, however, be 'nonsense to imagine any organised invasion' (Stefanowicz 1996:112). The future stability and intentions of Russia were, nevertheless, the only areas where public anxiety increased (by an average of 10 per cent) in the period 1994–96. This period coincides with the conflict in Chechnya, which inevitably caused concern in CEEC. It is interesting to note, however, that it was in those countries whose governments were most actively seeking NATO membership, and where such issues were the subject of public discussion, that anxiety about Russia was particularly evident (that is, the Czech Republic, Hungary and Poland). Indeed in Ukraine, Bulgaria and Romania anxiety about Russia fell during the same period (Haerpfer and Wallace 1997:3–8).

Concerns about relations with Germany were also expressed across CEEC. While these were articulated primarily in terms of potential economic dominance, attitudes in the Czech Republic and Poland were more complex. Czechs are said to feel 'a deep and highly nuanced ambivalence' about relations with Germany, although the overall impact of German influence is seen as threatening to Czech culture (Boguszakova and Gabal 1996:68–9). In Poland there were concerns about German territorial expansion, albeit in non-military ways, which were expressed through hostility towards purchase of Polish land by German individuals or companies (Starzynski 1996:56). Although anti-German sentiments had diminished in other CEEC by 1996, they remained high in Poland and the Czech Republic; indeed, they were expressed by almost half the population (Haerpfer and Wallace 1997:8).

The final issue identified by CEE publics as a security threat was the rise of nationalism. Here it is interesting to note that increasing nationalism was widely, and spontaneously, identified as a dangerous consequence of political manipulation. Indeed, there was a strong conviction that 'rising nationalism is being deliberately enflamed by politicians for political motives' (Boguszakova *et al.* 1996:40). This opinion was advanced in all four CEEC and also in Ukraine. It provides a clear reflection of the tensions between societal and political security in the unstable context of economic transformation; and in circumstances where democratic consolidation is uncertain and the legitimacy of the regime correspondingly weak. Here it is worth noting that today, of the four CEEC studied in 1994, it is only in Slovakia that extreme expressions of nationalism by politicians have subsequently increased. During this period, of course, it has become evident that Slovakia's membership of Western organisations is a distant prospect. We return to this matter below.

Concerns over the rise of nationalism were directly linked, by CEE publics, to the issues of territorial borders and national minorities. There was a strong sense that controversy over borders was a potential threat to security; and an equally strong consensus, bolstered by the Yugoslav experience, that no attempt should be made to change existing borders, despite the lack of accordance between territories and peoples. Here there was generally strong support for the notion of a 'borderless Europe' implied by future EU membership, which was seen as potentially resolving this problem. The exception here was Poland, where there was a desire to maintain the border with Germany (Boguszakova *et al.* 1996:51).

In all countries except the Czech Republic, where there is a relatively close coincidence between people and territory, there were concerns about relations with internal ethnic minorities and/or co-nationals resident abroad. In Poland internal minorities were not an issue, but there was widespread anxiety about the treatment of the large Polish population in Lithuania. There was a belief that the Polish government should 'exert pressure, perhaps strong pressure' on the Lithuanian government to improve the treatment of the Polish minority (Starzynski 1996:59).

It was in Hungary and Slovakia, however, that anxieties about minorities were strongest. And, here, there were also concerns about future relations between the two countries. In Slovakia, the Hungarian minority is concentrated in the south, close to the Hungarian border, and comprises around 11 per cent of the total population. Since the end of the Cold War, when overt political organisation and protest have been permitted, the Hungarian minority has been vociferous in its complaints about infringements of rights, and in demanding increased regional autonomy. The

Slovak public is deeply concerned about this issue. There are fears both of internal Slovak–Hungarian conflict and of some form of action by the Hungarian government in support of the demands of the Hungarian community in Slovakia. These latter fears diminished following the Hungarian general election of 1994, when the new government adopted a more conciliatory posture towards its neighbours (Taracova and Chmelikova 1996). However, fears of internal interethnic conflict remained high in Slovakia in 1996, whereas they had diminished elsewhere in the region (Haerpfer and Wallace 1997:15).[10] For the Hungarian public, the issue of Hungarian minorities abroad – in Serbia, Ukraine and Romania as well as in Slovakia – is 'a difficult, painful and complicated subject' (Hann 1996:83). Minorities abroad comprise one-third of all Hungarians, and concerns about their treatment are mixed with fears that overly strong advocacy on their behalf could be counterproductive.

In summary, it is evident that CEE publics feel deeply insecure; and that this reflects the cumulative impact of a range of perceived threats, both internal and external, against which reliable countermeasures are considered to be unavailable. However, traditional military threats are not the major source of insecurity; indeed, the principal external threat was perceived (in 1994) to be environmental. Overwhelmingly, the Security for Europe Project reveals the significance of societal security for CEE publics. With the partial exception of the Czech Republic, there was little confidence in the ability of societies successfully to complete the processes of economic and political transformation and to retain cohesion. This lack of confidence in the future was compounded by uncertainty about relations with potentially unstable neighbouring countries, which combined with fears of large-scale migration and interethnic tension within and between CEEC. These issues were perceived as security threats precisely because their potential cumulative impact was seen to challenge the collective identity, indeed the survival, of CEE societies.

Thus far, the construction of security issues has been examined from the perspective of CEE publics. The social process of securitisation, however, inevitably involves interaction between public perceptions and the pronouncements and policy choices of political elites. It is to this latter that we now turn.

CEE policy reorientation: the construction of Central Europe

The most evident and consistent response of CEE elites to the crises affecting their societies has been the reorientation of policy towards the West; in particular, the desire to join the EU. As will be evident from other chapters of this book, EU membership has been perceived by CEE elites as the most appropriate means, and frequently the only viable option, for addressing challenges in all non-traditional security sectors.[11] This includes the most problematic, and arguably the most significant, sector; that of societal security.

In its broadest sense, this is reflected in the notion, frequently proclaimed across CEEC, of the 'return to Europe'. This highly political idea has two major functions. First, it establishes, on behalf of the society, a claim to membership of a pan-European cultural community based on essentially Western principles; indeed, it emphasises that such membership has merely been interrupted during the Soviet era. This resonates with the depiction, originally proposed by Milan Kundera in 1984 and intended as a moral and political appeal to the West, of the CEE region (or, more specifically, 'Central Europe') as 'A Kidnapped West' (Neumann 1993:357). Consequently the notion of a 'return to Europe' implies an expectation that CEEC will be welcomed home. Second, in alluding to the common historical experience of Soviet domination, and claiming a shared, Western cultural identity, the idea of a 'return to Europe' proposes a common future as part of the peaceful and prosperous European core. Consequently it has an important collective identity function; it is intended to promote societal security in circumstances of rapid political and economic change and social destabilisation.

Kolankiewicz (1994:218) summarises these twin functions of the 'European idea', which

> acted successfully as a political-cultural as well as an economic template . . . an ideological shorthand standing for participatory democracy, the market economy, the rule of law, constitutional order and social citizenship . . . the east Europeans believe that as long as they adhere to this formula then entry to the EU is assured.

A third, related use of the 'return to Europe' notion has been in attempts actively to construct hierarchies of preference among CEEC. Thus, in advancing the claims for Western status of particular CEEC over those of their neighbours, the intention has been to obtain priority in terms of Western support and, in particular, to achieve early membership of the right Western clubs – primarily the EU, but also NATO.

A principal manifestation of this process of differentiation has been in the strenuous efforts, on the part of elites in Poland, Hungary and (initially) Czechoslovakia to (re)establish the notion of Central Europe; and to separate 'Central' from 'Eastern Europe'.[12] The construction and prioritisation of Central Europe (or, in some formulations, East Central Europe) have been supported by a number of Western commentators.[13] In addition to advancing claims on behalf of particular societies for preferential treatment by the EU, this construction also contributes to the processes of collective identity formation in CEEC by emphasising the Western vocation of a particular 'we' group (Czechs, Poles, Hungarians) in contrast with the 'Eastern' orientation of outsiders (Romanians,

Ukrainians, Russians). This process of constructing non-members of a society as 'alien others' is an important aspect of collective identity formation. As Neumann and Welsh (1991:331) have observed, identity 'is perceived as much in terms of what it is *not* as in terms of what it *is*'.

A useful device in considering the broader security implications of these processes of differentiation is the 'cosmos–chaos' model proposed by Tunander (1997). In contemporary Europe, Tunander maintains, Cold War 'friend–foe' structures are no longer dominant. Of greater significance, today, is a cosmos–chaos structure, at the centre of which is a relatively stable, peaceful and prosperous core, or cosmos. This model is hierarchical in terms of closeness of values rather than geographical proximity, thus signifying a departure from the territorially based structure of the past, when friends and foes were separated by a dividing wall. Moreover, the cosmos is not a territorial state, nor is it precisely defined in geographical terms; it comprises the EU and closely associated countries which share its values. Thus, through processes of assimilation and approximation, it is possible to move into the ambit of, or even become part of, the cosmos.

In this analysis Cold War divisions have been partially overcome through the development of networks of interaction and communication, which extend outwards from the central core. It is through strengthening and further extending these networks, and avoiding the creation of new 'walls', that European security can best be assured. There is a danger, however, that the competitive processes associated with the desire to identify with the cosmos will create a new, destabilising dynamic of inclusion and exclusion. In this model, the 'other' against which collective identity is measured and mobilised is no longer an external enemy; today the other is 'chaos' – backwardness, inefficiency, instability – which exists at the periphery, beyond the circles of authority and influence. Here a key issue is that, while the Balkans and the Caucasus epitomise 'chaos' in this model, the position of Russia and Ukraine is uncertain.

In the rhetoric of CEE politicians a 'cosmos–chaos' model has frequently been apparent – for example, Polish Foreign Minister, Krzystof Skubiszewski, proclaimed in 1992 that:

> as a consequence of the end of the Cold War, contemporary security relations on our continent have lost their simplicity and may be geographically described as concentric circles progressing from the stable nucleus of the countries of the European Communities, to the most unstable peripheries ... The association of the three countries [Czechoslovakia, Hungary and Poland] is relevant to their security but also to that of the West: the hard core of Europe will comprise a bigger territory.
>
> (Quoted in Neumann 1996:12–13)

For political elites seeking to move closer to the 'cosmos', the need to be dissociated from the 'chaos' of the periphery has been urgent. This has been pursued not only through policy orientation towards the West, and denunciation of 'non-European' or 'Asiatic' neighbours; but also, where necessary, through a process of 'amputation' (Tunander 1997:34). The policy of the Hungarian government from 1995 can be seen in this light, in that the new Prime Minister publicly declared himself to be 'Prime Minister of 10 million Hungarians', thus metaphorically 'amputating' the Hungarian minorities abroad in a direct repudiation of his predecessor's claim to represent, 'in his soul', 15 million Hungarians (Tunander 1997:34).

The Czech–Slovak split constitutes a more literal amputation, through which the Czechs freed themselves from Slovak traditionalism and inefficiency. 'Alone to Europe or together to the Balkans' was the apparent choice (Czech weekly *Respekt*, quoted in Tunander 1997:34). Thus, in a move that was politically and psychologically as well as geographically significant, the Czech Republic moved its centre of gravity westwards, distancing itself in every sense both from the Balkans and from the territory of the former Soviet Union (Had and Handl 1996:131). Slovakia, conversely, was increasingly distanced from Western Europe. Czech rhetoric now includes Slovakia among its alien others, and the notion of Slovaks as 'Asiatic' is 'routinely invoked to demarcate the border between the two' (Neumann 1996:14). From the perspective of Slovak academic commentators, 'the repeated efforts of some European countries [to establish their Western credentials] often take quite undignified forms' (Bombik and Samson 1996:148). The rhetoric of Slovak politicians, as noted above, has been less nuanced.

A similar process of constructing a culturally defined cosmos–chaos hierarchy has also been evident in the Balkans. Here Slovenian claims to a 'Central European' identity have been constructed, in part, with reference to the 'Balkan' character of neighbouring countries. In the Baltic region, also, the independence of Estonia, Latvia and Lithuania represents not only an expression of national identity but also a move westwards, towards the Nordic countries and the EU – and away from the inefficiency and potential instability of Russia. As in the case of other 'Central European' countries, Western commentators have contributed to these constructions. Thus the signing of EAs by these countries, we learn, indicated that 'Trouble-free Slovenia starts on road to EU membership' (*Guardian*, 16 March 1995); or 'symbolized the return of the Baltic States to the European family' (Council of the European Union 1995).

The construction of 'Central Europe' in the rhetoric and practices of CEE elites has formed a central element of the overall reorientation of CEEC towards the West. In security terms this reorientation potentially contributes to political security, through providing a future-oriented formula for legitimation of the new regimes; and to societal security, through its role in the construction of collective identity. Here the developing relationship with the EU has been of particular significance since, in addition to contributing to the broad needs of political and societal security, EU–CEEC relations play a major role in the economic and environmental sectors. In the military security sector, however, the role of the EU is at best problematic. Since the TEU came into force there has been, in principle, a potential for the EU to utilise the 'operational capability' of the WEU (Article 17 ex Article J.7). In practice, however, many impediments remain to the achievement of an EU military capability and, in this sector, the principal focus of CEE elites has been upon the development of relations with NATO.[14]

CEE policy reorientation: the military sector

In the immediate aftermath of the 1989 revolutions, CEE elites considered adopting a neutral or non-aligned security stance. However, this option was quickly abandoned as a consequence of the feelings of insecurity which increasingly affected CEE publics and elites. Early hopes that the CSCE (now OSCE) would develop into a pan-European collective security organisation were also abandoned, when the Paris Summit of November 1990 'provided the sobering insight that the organization would not and could not take on the role envisaged for it by Central Europeans' (Wohlfeld 1995:45). Consequently, since the collapse of the WTO in March 1991, CEE elites have regarded the westward reorientation of security and defence policies as an essential element of the 'return to Europe' (Had and Handl 1996; Matus 1996). The Czech position, here, is typical:

> Like other small Central European countries that are inherently unable to defend themselves against large countries in the region, the Czech Republic has no choice but to find its security in some larger structure. The Republic needs, in essence, a security guarantee from a powerful organization, alliance or entity that is genuinely able to provide it. (Had and Handl 1996:138)

The allusion here is clearly to NATO. Close cooperation with NATO is central to the new security and defence policies developed by all CEE governments. Nevertheless, in 1994 nine CEEC (all the EU candidates except Slovenia) became Associate Partners of the WEU. This reflects the general orientation towards the West, as well as hopes that the EU–WEU relationship might prosper in the future. A further factor here has been the perception that, in contrast with NATO, Russia will not be accorded special status in the WEU. Despite this, full membership of NATO remains the ultimate goal of most CEEC. In pursuit of this goal CEE elites have employed a number of tactics, with varying degrees of success.

In the early years there was a strong tendency to make 'dramatic pleas for western security guarantees ... based on exaggerations of the threats and risks to their security' (Wohlfeld 1995:36). Inevitably this has contributed to perceptions of insecurity among CEE publics, as noted above. In practice, also, this approach was counterproductive – not least because, in encouraging Western perceptions of instability in the East, it potentially undermined the broader effort to construct the countries of 'Central Europe' as those most appropriate for early membership of Western organisations.[15] CEE elites have since learned that the 'return to Europe' will not be accomplished through emotional appeals to a latent sense of moral responsibility in the West; rather, there is a requirement to demonstrate *eligibility* – through 'appropriate' behaviour and determined efforts to carry out difficult and painful internal reforms.

In the traditional security sector, appropriate behaviour for CEEC involves, in particular, the development of good neighbourly relations. Hence there has been a need to demonstrate the reduction of tension in intra-CEEC relations. To this end, numerous bilateral treaties have been concluded which concern, *inter alia*, the treatment of minorities and the inviolability of existing borders.[16] However, as the Hungarian Foreign Minister has observed, such treaties are 'only the institutional precondition to improving bilateral relations' (Kovács 1997:10).[17]

Fundamental internal policy reform, and restructuring of CEE militaries, are further tests of eligibility. Transformation here, as in other areas, is a highly complex process. As NATO's Special Adviser for Central and East European Affairs has recently acknowledged, military transformation continues to present a major challenge: 'The magnitude of the difficulties faced by armed forces in transition, and the problems of Central and Eastern European countries in establishing effective management of defence and security policies, is only just being recognized' (Donnelly 1997:15). The post-1989 CEE governments inherited a military whose organisational structure reflected its function as an instrument of the previous regime, while its deployment was predicated upon the assumption of a threat from the West. In consequence there was an urgent requirement both for depoliticisation of the military, and for development of national defence and security policies, appropriate to the post-Cold War environment, to guide the processes of military transformation. In practice, however, there was an element of incompatibility between these requirements, since the closed and secretive nature of CEE militaries under the former regimes ensured that neither the newly elected politicians nor civilians in defence ministries had expertise in military matters. Despite efforts to train civilian experts, this is a problem which persists (Wohlfeld 1995; Donnelly 1997).

For a variety of reasons the defence doctrines formulated by the new CEE governments have been problematic. Due to an inability, or reluctance, to identify any external military threat, the need to ensure the defence of *all* borders was adopted as a guiding principle of military restructuring. This is regarded by security analysts as an ineffective defence posture. Indeed, it is argued, 'No credible strategy and military planning are conceivable without an identification of potential threats and a ranking of them according to their importance' (Dunay 1995:5). Moreover, the principle of defending all borders, which involves relocation of forces from Western borders, has proved difficult, and costly, to implement. It was formally abandoned by the Bulgarian government as early as 1993 and has been 'tacitly' abandoned, or indefinitely delayed, elsewhere (Wohlfeld 1995:42).

Reform of the armed forces, in terms of depoliticisation and professionalisation, has also proved difficult. The 'de-Sovietization' of the officer corps was an early priority. In the former Czechoslovakia all professional soldiers were screened and more than five thousand high-ranking officers were released.[18] While this process was less far reaching in Hungary and Poland, it nevertheless resulted in the replacement of approximately 75 per cent of high-ranking officers (Wohlfeld 1995:40). Training of replacement officers proved expensive, however, and levels of retention after training have been poor.[19] Similar problems beset the aim of professionalisation. Conscripts make up approximately 50 per cent of CEE militaries, and their replacement by professional soldiers, even at reduced levels of personnel, cannot yet be fully implemented due to resource constraints. Moreover, poor pay and conditions and low levels of public respect for the military have caused recruitment problems (Donnelly 1997:17).[20]

The issue of professionalisation has important implications for the desire of CEE governments to contribute to multinational peacekeeping efforts, which is an aspect of the broader aim of demonstrating eligibility for NATO membership. Here the Security for Europe Project, while finding broad support for such participation, reported a strong feeling, on the part of all CEE publics, that 'it is definitely not legitimate ... to put conscript soldiers in danger by making them take up peacekeeping duties in foreign lands' (Boguszakova *et al.* 1996:43).

The persistent problems which beset efforts to transform CEE militaries have greatly complicated reform in the area with which Western officials and politicians have primarily been concerned, that is, democratic control of the military. Here the focus of NATO efforts has been upon the formal mechanisms required for political direction of the military. As Donnelly (1997) points out, however, this focus has been too narrow. In circumstances where politicians and civilian officials are ignorant of military matters; where civil–military relations are poor and where the armed forces are 'in a shambles', a more broadly based strategy is required.[21] Ultimately, however, this is a matter for CEE governments and societies to resolve. 'Western institutions cannot and will not step in and solve problems like this, whatever some Central and Eastern European countries may think' (Donnelly 1997:17).

While the problems affecting CEE militaries are evidently intractable, their significance must be assessed in the broader context of the triple transformation being attempted by CEEC. Given the urgency of economic and political transformation, and the strong feelings of insecurity which these processes have aroused among CEE publics, particularly when contrasted with their lack of anxiety about external military threats, it is unsurprising that military transformation has been relatively neglected. Moreover, it is evident that CEE governments do not seek NATO membership solely on military security grounds. Rather, it is viewed in the broader context of the desire to *belong* – to the West and to the major Western organisations. In the case of the Czech Republic, for example:

> There is a tendency in Czech policy and psychology to see Western structures, chiefly the EU and NATO, as organizations that the Czech Republic deserves to belong to, as a result of its smoothly working democracy and economy. Membership would not only be an emblem of success, but also would largely guarantee a successful completion of the remaining phases of a difficult transition. Membership would be the decisive symbol, not merely that one epoch has ended but that a new and favorable one has begun. (Had and Handl 1996:143)

Clearly, belonging to the West, becoming part of the cosmos, is seen as the only effective means of meeting the security needs of CEEC across all sectors. We examine, below, the responses of Western organisations to this challenge. Before comparing the security roles of the EU and NATO, the EU's contribution to European security is assessed.

Extending security: the role of the EU

In the period following the 1989 revolutions, CEE governments looked towards the EU both as a model for their own transformations and as a source of assistance and support. Indeed, the strongly positive perceptions of the EU, at this time, led the Commission to conclude that 'The European Community has what might be termed a mystical attraction and is seen as an ideal by the people of Central and Eastern Europe' (Commission 1990a:31). In security terms, the EU's particular attraction for CEEC was its development as 'a real community of security within which it is inconceivable that there would be the slightest threat of recourse to force as a means of settling disputes' (Commission 1997a:27).

In the interest of the security and stability of Europe as a whole, if for no other reason, the EU was obliged to respond to the urgent needs and demands emanating from the East. However, the first priority, as has been argued, was to safeguard the integration process itself. If the EU was to serve as a model, and an anchor, for its Eastern neighbours, it was essential that integration should not falter. In this sense the EU, as presence rather than actor, has fulfilled an important function for CEEC.[22] Nevertheless, the EU has responded actively to CEEC needs and expectations. It has developed progressively close bilateral relationships with CEEC, thereby supporting the processes of transformation and guiding progress towards adoption of the principles and policies of the *acquis communautaire*. Increasingly, the EU has adopted a supervisory, 'mentor' role towards 'candidate' countries, which has left CEE governments little room for manoeuvre. As one Czech diplomat commented, 'What can we do? If we want to become members of the Union, we have to accept what is decided' (Václav Kuklik, quoted in *The European*, 12–18 September 1996).

Clearly EU–CEEC relations have developed considerably since 1990. However, their contribution to the security of the wider Europe must be assessed in relation to three major challenges:

The need to extend eastward the stability and prosperity enjoyed within the EU.

The need to avoid reinforcing the exclusion–inclusion dynamic already evident among CEEC.

The need to extend communication and support networks beyond CEEC, in particular to Russia and Ukraine, to mitigate the potentially destabilising effects of an emergent 'cosmos–chaos' hierarchy.

A wide range of EU policies towards CEEC contribute to the extension of stability and prosperity. Since other chapters in this volume discuss in detail EU support for economic and political transformation, and also the EU's contribution to environmental security, these matters are not revisited here. It is worthy of note, however, that the external threat most readily identified by CEE publics, that of unstable nuclear power stations, has been a particular EU concern. Thus the major part (56 per cent in financial terms) of the EU's environmental policy towards its Eastern neighbours has involved financial and technical assistance with improving the safety of nuclear installations (Commission 1997b:149–50).[23]

In the areas of political and societal security, early perceptions that the EU was reluctant and ungenerous in its relations with CEEC caused disillusionment among CEE elites and publics alike; and between 1993 and 1997 *Central and Eastern Eurobarometer* recorded a gradual, but steady, decline in public support for EU membership. This suggested that orientation towards the EU was an unreliable source of legitimation for CEE governments. However, publication of *Agenda 2000*, and the formal opening of accession negotiations with five CEEC, has had a positive effect on support for EU membership across all ten CEE candidates except Romania (Commission 1998:2–3). In the five 'selected' CEEC there has also been a marked increase in public approval of government policies, and of optimism for the future (Commission 1998:30). This suggests that the prospect of full EU membership has impacted positively upon political and societal security.[24] Here it is significant that only 2 per cent of *Eurobarometer* respondents believe that EU membership poses a threat to collective identity (Commission 1998:34). This also indicates that concerns about excessive German influence within the EU have diminished since 1994.

Anxieties about minorities and about migration were also facets of societal insecurity among CEE publics in 1994. Treatment of minorities has been a matter of great concern for EU policy makers, and was a major consideration when the Commission's Opinions on eligibility for accession were formulated (see Chapter 5). While the EU continues to play a positive role in relation to treatment of minorities, particularly in relation to the treatment of the large Russian minority in Estonia, the situation with regard to migration is rather different. Here, the increasing stringency of EU policies has impacted upon CEEC, creating the 'waiting room' effect referred to above. Moreover, EU insistence that the five CEEC currently involved in accession negotiations must strengthen their external borders has been a source of considerable tension. New policies introduced early in 1998, in response to EU pressure, have been particularly damaging to relations between Poland and its three eastern neighbours – Russia, Ukraine and Belarus. The borders between the Czech Republic and Slovakia, and between Slovenia and Croatia, are similarly affected (*Guardian*, 9 February 1998).[25] This strengthening and *de facto* extension of the EU's external borders illustrate the dangers of 'securitising' migration. They denote the erection of barriers in circumstances where considerable effort has been invested in creating links.

In the past, care has been taken to avoid appearing to prioritise among CEEC. Even following identification of the chosen five in *Agenda 2000* there was an effort to maintain the appearance of parity of treatment between all ten membership candidates. In practice, however, the EU has contributed to the inclusion–exclusion dynamic. Through imposing stringent criteria for eligibility, and subsequently according broadly similar treatment to all applicants, the EU effectively established an apprenticeship scheme which made little provision for participants with 'special needs'. Consequently those countries which succeeded in demonstrating their 'Western' orientation at an early stage have been privileged. It is only since publication of *Agenda 2000* that the notion of 'catch-up' strategies has been introduced – to placate the excluded. These strategies are clearly undermined by insistence, as a condition of accession, on more effective policing of borders, including those with the 'pre-in' countries, Slovakia and Romania. These countries, together with Bulgaria, increasingly appear to be permanently excluded.

Until recently the EU avoided actively contributing to the inclusion–exclusion dynamic operating among CEEC. From the outset, however, EU policies contributed to the establishment of a sharp distinction between CEEC and NIS. This was formalised, *inter alia*, through the differing aims and impacts of the Phare and Tacis programmes.[26] Essentially, inclusion in the Phare programme denotes a position closer to cosmos. The EU's 'asymmetric approach' to CEEC–NIS has not gone unnoticed – in Russia, for example, it is deeply resented (Borko 1997:205).

The CEEC–NIS division was greatly reinforced by EU policy towards the Baltic states. In 1991, when according formal recognition to the three new states, the EU celebrated the resumption of 'their rightful place among the nations of Europe' (EPC Bulletin 1991). Subsequently, in a move which had important symbolic as well as practical implications, at the end of 1991 the EU transferred – and in a real sense *promoted* – the Baltic republics from the Tacis to the Phare programme. Effectively, the Baltic states became CEEC. Perhaps ironically, the subsequent decision to open accession negotiations only with Estonia has created a new inclusion–exclusion dynamic in a sub-region where the EU had previously been involved in the promotion of cooperative initiatives. Indeed, the European Commission is the only non-state member of the Council of Baltic Sea States.

The relationships with CEEC and NIS developed by the EU since 1991 have increasingly reflected a hierarchical structure. At the apex are the five CEEC which began accession negotiations in March 1998. Below them are the remaining five CEEC applicant countries deemed, as yet, unready to begin accession negotiations. A third group of NIS countries, including Russia and Ukraine (for whom the EU is devising 'Action Plans'), has been drawn into the orbit of the EU 'without any prospect of membership' (Sperling and Kirchner 1997:115). With these three groups, albeit with differing intensity, the EU continues to maintain networks of communication and to exert influence.

The EU relates quite differently to a fourth group of countries, which are effectively beyond its influence in the chaotic periphery. This group comprises Albania and the republics of the former Yugoslavia (except Slovenia), where the UN and subsequently NATO have been extensively involved, and the more unstable NIS, in particular Belarus and Tajikistan, where EU efforts have been less strenuous than elsewhere.[27] The essentially centralising tendencies of the cosmos–chaos structure suggest that the chaotic periphery is likely to be neglected or, where necessary, subdued. Thus it is in the context of potential interventions in the periphery rather than in territorial defence of the core – which is today a residual category – that issues of military security retain their salience. Here it should be noted that the 1997 Treaty of Amsterdam specifically aims, through facilitating action by coalitions of the willing, to strengthen the EU's capacity in relation to 'humanitarian and rescue tasks, peacekeeping tasks and tasks of combat forces in crisis management, including peacemaking' (TEU Article 17 ex Article J.7). While the Amsterdam provisions have yet to be put into practice, the Italian-led Multinational Protection Force deployed in Albania in the spring of 1997 provides a model for intervention in a low-level conflict situation by an EU-led coalition of the willing.

A key issue for European security is the situation of those countries which fall between cosmos and chaos and whose uncertain transformations suggest that they will not easily, or quickly, move close to cosmos. Russia and Ukraine fall within this category, as do the five 'non-select' CEEC. Anxiety that Russia, in particular, will move towards chaos is one of the principal justifications for NATO enlargement to CEEC. However, the cosmos–chaos model suggests that strengthening the EU's networks of communication, in order more effectively to support the transformation processes in Russia, would meet Europe's long-term security needs more effectively than extending NATO's defensive walls. Below we briefly compare EU and NATO policies towards CEEC.

EU and NATO security roles compared

All CEE applicants for EU membership have also expressed a desire to join NATO. In principle, this places responsibility upon policy makers, in both organisations, to ensure that there is complementarity between their policies; and that they avoid creating a mutually reinforcing, exclusionary dynamic. In practice, however, there has been no formal coordination of EU and NATO policies towards CEEC. This is not accidental; it reflects the US government's reluctance to involve non-NATO members of the EU, even indirectly, in discussions which impinge upon the future NATO. It also reflects fears that aspirant members might use one set of negotiations to gain leverage in the other.

In common with the EU, NATO responded positively to overtures from the East. There has been a similar, incremental development of structured links with CEEC–NIS – who came to be known in the NATO context as 'cooperation partners'. The initial relationship was political, involving CEEC–NIS, collectively, in the North Atlantic Cooperation Council. In response to pressure for a fuller relationship, and in order to defer making a decision on the difficult question of enlargement, NATO launched its

Partnership for Peace (PfP) initiative in 1994. PfP involves a series of bilateral arrangements, with twenty-five CEEC/NIS, which vary in scope and
intensity. They are based on practical military cooperation and are seen as
providing, *inter alia*, anticipatory socialisation for aspirant members. It is
in this context that NATO has provided support for military transformation in CEEC. However, an unanticipated benefit of PfP has been its role
in supporting NATO forces in Bosnia, where fifteen PfP are involved.
Thus, despite its creation, essentially, as a delaying tactic, PfP is considered to have succeeded 'beyond the Alliance's initial hopes' (Balanzino
1997:10). It did not, however, deflect CEE governments' demands for
NATO membership.

To a large extent, in the early phases of 'anticipatory socialisation',
there was complementarity between EU and NATO policies. However,
the subsequent parallel debates about EU and NATO enlargement have
taken somewhat different forms. To a considerable extent these reflect the
contrasting functions and character of the two organisations.

NATO is an intergovernmental military alliance created during the
Cold War with the specific purpose of deterring attack from the (then)
Soviet Union. While it has adapted incrementally to the post-Cold War
environment, debates about its future, including those on enlargement,
continue to be conducted according to the premises of traditional security
thinking. As already noted, discussion of enlargement has focused almost
exclusively upon Russia, with protagonists divided between those who
consider that Russia needs still to be deterred and others who, in effect,
believe that Russia should be appeased. Neither side has been greatly
interested in Russia's actual military capability – revealed by the 'humiliating disaster' of Chechnya (Baev 1997:184).

Ultimately the issue was resolved, not on the basis of careful analysis,
but in the context of US domestic politics. Thus the principle of enlargement was endorsed, unilaterally, by President Clinton during his 1994
re-election campaign. The subsequent decision, at the 1997 Madrid
Summit, to extend membership invitations only to the Czech Republic,
Hungary and Poland was again imposed by the US government – in the
face of strong appeals, from European NATO members, for a wider, more
balanced expansion.[28] Interestingly, there was no strong lobby for inclusion of the Baltic states, despite the fact that some commentators consider
them to have particular need of NATO defence guarantees. Instructive,
here, is the conclusion of security analysts Asmus and Norrick (1996:134)
that the solution to Baltic insecurity lies in enlargement of the *European
Union* to 'at least one Baltic country'. This clearly supports the contention
that the EU is destined to play the more significant role in extending security across the region.

The outcome of NATO's Madrid Summit raises difficult issues of inclusion and exclusion. Efforts to address these issues include the signing of a

'Founding Act on Mutual Relations, Cooperation and Security between NATO and the Russian Federation', which established a programme of regular meetings at various levels and is intended to address Russian sensitivities concerning NATO expansion.[29] In relation to excluded CEEC, assurances were made at the Madrid Summit that there would be further enlargements – 'We have committed ourselves to a robust "open door" policy' (Solana 1997:3); and that the existing PfP relationships would be substantially upgraded. Thus NATO launched its equivalent of EU 'enhanced pre-accession strategies for pre-ins'.

Clearly there are parallels between the EU and NATO enlargement processes. While in both cases there have been efforts to mitigate feelings of exclusion, the selection of candidates for accession has inevitably contributed to the construction of hierarchies of exclusion and inclusion. Indeed, the combined impact of EU and NATO enlargement places the Czech Republic, Hungary and Poland in a uniquely privileged position, which both reflects and reinforces construction of the notion of (non-Slavic) Central Europe. In the case of EU enlargement, however, this effect is ameliorated by the inclusion of Estonia and Slovenia among the first tranche of countries to open accession negotiations.

The decision to include these two countries denotes a significant difference between the two enlargement processes. EU enlargement is not 'about Russia', nor does it create the tensions associated with NATO enlargement; during the Cold War the role of the EU was to seduce rather than to deter the Eastern bloc. Moreover, the initial basis of EU external activity, upon trade, ensures that it is fundamentally oriented towards creating links; whereas NATO's principal task is the construction of defensive walls. Thus the inclusion of Estonia and Slovenia reflects concern to address the broader issues of European security and stability.[30] In widening the focus of enlargement to include countries relatively close to the chaotic periphery, it provides encouragement to the excluded and extends the links and networks of the cosmos towards uncertain and potentially unstable neighbouring countries.

In summary, there are parallels and areas of complementarity between EU and NATO relations with CEEC. Each provides support for transformation processes and anticipatory socialisation experiences, although the focus of NATO is inevitably much narrower. However, the processes and potential impacts of enlargement differ considerably. For the EU, enlargement is a deeply troubling prospect which demands fundamental reconsideration of internal policies and processes, and the risk of sacrificing the achievements of integration. For NATO, enlargement provides an opportunity to demonstrate continuing relevance in a security climate where its *raison d'être* is in question. While EU enlargement extends networks outwards, NATO enlargement includes new members within a defensive wall. For the governments and peoples of Hungary, Poland and the Czech Republic the prospect of acceding to both organisations would appear to address threats to security in all sectors. The broader, long-term security interest of Europe, however, will best be served by extension outwards of the prosperity and stability enjoyed within the EU.

Conclusion

Since the revolutions of 1989 the peoples of CEE have been troubled by deep feelings of insecurity. Overwhelmingly, the sources of insecurity have been non-traditional – they have emanated from the experience of rapid and fundamental change internally, exacerbated by perceptions of external threat to environmental or societal security. To accommodate the range of threats to survival identified by CEE publics, a reformulated concept of security has been utilised, which permits the inclusion of environmental, economic, political and societal threats within a security discourse.

In applying this conceptual framework to CEEC, the notion of societal security has particular salience. Throughout CEEC, collective identities have been challenged and destabilised, and are consequently vulnerable. Issues of societal security are a source of anxiety across CEE. They are associated, in particular, with the possibility of large-scale migration and/or tensions with ethnic minorities.

The response of policy elites to the crisis affecting CEE societies has been twofold. First, there has been a reorientation of policy, in all areas, towards the West. Epitomised by the notion of the 'return to Europe', the aspiration to join Western organisations has obliged CEE elites to demonstrate eligibility for incorporation into the cosmos, and hence to eschew the excessive nationalism of the chaotic periphery. Nevertheless, the perceived urgency of the need to become part of the stable, prosperous core has generated competition between CEEC – for support, resources and ultimately membership. In consequence the second element of the CEE elite response has been to seek privileged status, and preferential treatment, through claims of cultural proximity to the West – and at the expense of neighbours claimed to be 'non-Western'.

The EU has been the principal focus of these unhappy, competitive efforts. It has responded through developing a dense network of relationships with CEEC intended to assist in extending eastwards the stability and prosperity enjoyed within the EU. Although a division between CEEC–NIS was institutionalised at an early stage, efforts were made to avoid discriminating overtly between CEEC. However, in response to the insistent demands of CEE governments, the broad, outwardly oriented policies of the EU were replaced by a strategy for incorporating CEEC within the cosmos. In selecting five of ten CEE candidates to open accession negotiations, and subsequently insisting that the selected five strengthen their borders with their neighbours, the EU has reinforced the emergent, hierarchical cosmos–chaos structure in Eastern Europe. Inevitably, these developments impinge negatively upon societal security in excluded CEEC. Here the case of Slovakia is especially poignant.

The EU has nevertheless extended links widely across CEEC–NIS, and these have contributed to security in the environmental and economic sectors in particular. The traditional agenda of military security, however, remains an area where the EU's role is undeveloped. Here CEE governments have oriented their policies towards NATO. Despite a lack of formal policy coordination, the evolving relationship between NATO and CEEC has, in some respects, paralleled and complemented the EU–CEEC relationship. However, the implications of their respective enlargements are very different. In particular, there is a danger that the extension of NATO's defensive wall may undermine efforts by the EU to extend security across the wider Europe.

A further, and perhaps greater danger threatens the EU's ability to provide security and stability for the wider Europe, however. That is the challenge posed by the Eastern enlargement to the integration process itself. Ultimately a Union weakened by the internal strains of a difficult absorption process may be unable to sustain its efforts in support of non-member CEEC and NIS. Paradoxically, in meeting the security needs of the five least insecure CEEC, the ability of the EU to strengthen and extend networks of communication and support beyond its new borders may be diminished.

Notes

1 These debates are not in themselves new, although they are certainly a novel, post-Cold War concern for traditional security analysis. During the Cold War, peace researchers were centrally concerned with the meaning of peace and the fundamental conditions for its attainment. See, for example, Johan Galtung's (1969) seminal discussion.

2 Proponents of NATO enlargement, such as Brzezinski (1994:72), argue that there is a continuing need for containment of Russia, on the grounds that Russia's 'imperial impulse remains strong and even appears to be strengthening'. Opponents, however, are fearful that enlargement would 'provide a catalyst' that would reawaken Russia's territorial aspirations (Harris 1993:43).

3 In principle, of course, both the environment and the economy can also be referent objects of security – as is evident from admonitions that drastic action is required to save the planet or protect the liberal economic order.

4 In addition to these four CEEC, the Security for Europe Project also covered Russia and Ukraine. It made extensive use of focus-group activities in addi-

tion to opinion surveys. The research was conducted, and the reports produced, by researchers and experts from each of the countries concerned. The late Richard Smoke was codirector of the project, and its findings, together with updating material, form the basis of Smoke (1996).

5   Public confidence in the government greatly increased following the estab-lishment of the Czech Republic in 1993 and, in general, Czechs felt less insecure than other CEE publics in 1994.

6   In some countries, notably the Czech Republic, there were also concerns about an inflow of people from Western Europe who might buy up land and property, hence forcing up prices (Boguszakova and Gabal 1996:68).

7   In the case of Hungary there had also been a substantial influx of refugees in the period since 1988 – initially from Romania during the final phase of the Ceauşescu regime, but subsequently from Vojvodina in Yugoslavia. Between 1988 and 1992 approximately 100,000 refugees arrived in Hungary, placing a considerable burden on resources during the early stages of transformation.

8   In the Czech Republic in 1993, for example, 43,300 people from seventy-two countries were apprehended while attempting illegally to cross the border (Salt and Clarke 1996:520).

9   The conclusions of Haerpfer and Wallace are referred to in order to provide a broad comparison with the data emanating from the Security for Europe Project. Inevitably, differences in research design between the two studies make direct comparison problematic.

10 An exception here was Slovenia, where there had been an increase in percep-tions of threat from ethnic minorities since 1992. This is unsurprising, given the events in the former Yugoslavia during that period. Moreover, levels of threat perception (20 per cent) remained considerably lower than the 48 per cent recorded for Slovakia.

11 See, for example, a recent analysis by Slovenian economists, which evaluated a range of policy options but concluded that 'there seems to be not much choice for a small European country in transition like Slovenia . . . In theory there are other options but in practice they do not appear viable' (Stanovnik and Svetličič 1996:16).

12 While, in principle, the construction of 'Central Europe' may appear to be an attempt at region building, in practice cooperation, for example through the Visegrad–CEFTA formula, has not been a high priority for CEE elites. Rather, the Central European construction has been used, on behalf of each society, to advance its particular claim to cultural affinity with the West. The Baltic region is an exception here, since the Council of Baltic Sea States, with the support of the Nordic countries and the EU, had encouraged cooperation between Latvia, Lithuania and Estonia. It is ironic, therefore, that the EU subsequently chose to privilege Estonia, opening accession negotiations only with that country.

13 A number of Western academics have taken this line. See, for example, Adrian Hyde-Price's (1996:7) plea for the prioritisation of the countries of 'East Central Europe' (the Czech Republic, Hungary, Poland and Slovakia), which should be treated 'as a distinct group by virtue of their unique culture and history'; or the contention by Ash *et al.* (1991:19) that relations with the same group of countries should be the absolute priority of the EC.

14 For an excellent discussion of the development of the WEU, and of its relationship with the EU, see Deighton (1997).

15 Here it is of interest to note the observation, made in 1992, that:

> different threats are presented to different audiences, depending on the circumstances. One day the audience is confronted with a vision of domestic anarchy and foreign aggression. Another day the same politicians describe their country as exceptionally stable and surrounded by peaceful neighbours ... the latter vision is usually presented to Western bankers and investors; the former to security experts. (Jan Zielonka, quoted in Dunay 1995:8)

16 Part of this activity relates to the Pact on Stability (also known as the Balladur Plan), promoted by the EU as an aspect of its nascent CFSP. Following a series of regional conferences and preventive diplomacy initiatives between May 1994 and March 1995, supervision of the numerous bilateral agreements was entrusted to the OSCE.

17 Relations between Hungary and Slovakia have been particularly difficult – not only as a result of minorities issues, but also due to disputes over a dam scheme on the River Danube.

18 This included all generals, deputy ministers of defence, heads of military colleges, district commanders and political officers.

19 According to a recently retrained Czech commander of an 'elite airborne company', who had left the military to take up employment in the private sector, his company 'did not have enough parachutes, and there was not enough money to fix the photo-copier' (*The European*, 20–26 November 1997).

20 As is evident from other chapters, and in particular the discussion of democratic transition and consolidation in Chapter 4, these problems are not confined to the military sector.

21 Under its Phare and Tacis democracy programmes, the EU has supported a number of micro-projects which aim to improve civil–military relations. While these have a broad public awareness focus, their impacts are inevitably localised.

22 The notion of 'presence' is discussed by Allen and Smith (1990) and developed by Bretherton and Vogler (1999). In the context of EU external policy, presence is an important concept, in that it encompasses the frequently unintended external consequences of the integration process. Since the EU's presence tends to provoke responses from affected third parties, to which the EU is obliged to respond in return, presence is often the initial stimulus for action.

23 Of the ecu 912.4 million Phare/Tacis funding for environmental projects between 1991 and 1995, ecu 515 million were devoted to action on nuclear safety.

24 Here the case of Slovakia is of particular interest, since there has been a marked increase in support for EU membership, coupled with a strongly negative assessment of Slovak government policy. This indicates a divergence between political and societal security, based on awareness that the performance of the Slovak political system has been a major impediment to EU membership.

25 In the case of Poland, it is estimated that the new border controls and visa requirements introduced in January 1998 will have a damaging impact on the Polish economy. For example, the value of market trading, which largely depends upon itinerant Russian traders, was almost £4 billion in 1996.

26 The differentiation of EU policies towards CEEC–NIS, and in particular the aims of the Phare and Tacis programmes, are discussed in Chapter 2.

27 EU relations with a number of NIS are relatively weak. However, disapproval of the policy direction of Belarus and Tajikistan in particular has been reflected in interruption or reduction of funding support, respectively (Commission 1997c:6).

28 It was considered by the Clinton administration that only this limited enlargement would be acceptable to Congress. The French and Spanish governments strongly advanced the candidacy of Romania (and to a lesser extent Slovenia), both in the interest of balance and because military restructuring is considerably more advanced in Romania than in other CEEC.

29 A 'Charter on a Distinctive Partnership between NATO and Ukraine' was also signed. However, this contains only a general commitment to cooperation and consultation and lacks the formal arrangements provided for in the Founding Act with Russia.

30 While this is not the only argument in favour of their inclusion, it is a persuasive one. The decision was a source of controversy within the EU, and it is evident that it would have been possible to 'draw a line' after the Czech Republic, Poland and Hungary – not least because, when *Agenda 2000* was published in June 1997, Estonia and Slovenia had not yet ratified EAs.

References

Allen, D. and Smith, M. (1990), Western Europe's Presence in the Contemporary International Arena, *Review of International Studies*, 16:1, 19–37.

Ash, T. G., Mertes, M. and Moïsi, D. (1991), Let the East Europeans In!, *New York Review of Books*, 24 October.

Asmus, R. D. and Norick, R. C. (1996), NATO Enlargement and the Baltic States, *Survival*, 38:2, 121–42.

Baev, P. (1997), Russia's Departure from Empire: Self-Assertiveness and a New Retreat, in O. Tunander, P. Baev and V. I. Einagel (eds), *Geopolitics in Post-Wall Europe: Security, Territory and Identity*, London, Sage, 174–95.

Balanzino, S. (1997), Deepening Partnership: The Key to Long-Term Stability in Europe, *NATO Review*, July–August, 10–17.

Ball, C. L. (1998), Nattering NATO Negativism, *Review of International Studies*, 24:1, 43–68.

Boguszakova, M. and Gabal, I. (1996), The Czech Republic, in R. Smoke (ed.), *Perceptions of Security: Public Opinion and Expert Assessments in Europe's New Democracies*, Manchester, Manchester University Press, 64–71.

Boguszakova, M., Gabal, I., Hann, E., Starzynski, P. and Taracova, E. (1996), Public Attitudes in four Central European Countries, in R. Smoke (ed.), *Perceptions of Security: Public Opinion and Expert Assessments in Europe's New Democracies*, Manchester, Manchester University Press, 33–54.

Bombik, S. and Samson, I. (1996), Slovakia, in R. Smoke (ed.), *Perceptions of Security. Public Opinion and Expert Assessments in Europe's New Democracies*, Manchester, Manchester University Press, 146–63.

Borko, Y. (1997), Possible Scenarios for Geopolitical Shifts in Russian–European Relations, in O. Tunander, P. Baev and V. I. Einagel (eds), *Geopolitics in Post-Wall Europe: Security, Territory and Identity*, London, Sage, 196–216.

Bretherton, C. and Vogler, J. (1999), *The European Union as a Global Actor*, London, Routledge.

Brzezinski, Z. (1994), The Premature Partnership, *Foreign Affairs*, 73:2, 67–82.

Buzan, B. (1991), *People, States and Fear: An Agenda for International Security Studies in the Post-Cold War Era*, Boulder, Lynne Rienner.

Buzan, B., Wæver, O. and de Wilde, J. (1998), *Security: A New Framework for Analysis*, Boulder, Lynne Rienner.

Commission (1990a), *The European Community and its Eastern Neighbours*, Luxembourg, Office for Official Publications of the European Communities.

Commission (1990b), *Europe – A Fresh Start: The Schuman Declaration 1950–90*, Luxembourg, Office for Official Publications of the European Communities.

Commission (1997a), *Agenda 2000: Summary and Conclusions of the Opinion of the Commission Concerning the Applications for Membership of the European Union Presented by the Candidate Countries*, Strasbourg, DOC(97):8.

Commission (1997b), *Agenda 21 The First Five Years: European Community Progress on the Implementation of Agenda 21: 1992–97*, Brussels.

Commission (1997c), *The Tacis Programme Annual Report 1996*, Brussels, COM(97):400, Final.

Commission (1998), *Central and Eastern Eurobarometer*, 8, March.

Council of the European Union (1995), *Signing of the Europe Association Agreements with Estonia, Latvia and Lithuania*, PRES/95/173, 12 June.

Deighton, A. (ed.) (1997), *Western European Union 1954–1997: Defence, Security, Integration*, Oxford, European Interdependence Research Unit.

Donnelly, C. (1997), Defence Transformation in the New Democracies: A Framework for Tackling the Problem, *NATO Review*, January, 15–19.

Dunay, P. (1995), Debunking Certain Myths of Post-Cold War Military Security in Europe, in P. Dunay, G. Kardos and A. J. Williams (eds), *New Forms of Security: Views from Central, Eastern and Western Europe*, Aldershot, Dartmouth, 3–25.

EPC Bulletin (1991), *Statement by an Extraordinary EPC Ministerial Meeting Concerning the Baltic States*, 91:251, 27 August.

Galtung, J. (1969), Violence, Peace and Peace Research, *Journal of Peace Research*, 3, 167–89.

Had, M. and Handl, V. (1996), The Czech Republic, in R. Smoke (ed.), *Perceptions of Security. Public Opinion and Expert Assessments in Europe's New Democracies*, Manchester, Manchester University Press, 129–45.

Haerpfer, C. and Wallace, C. (1997), Perceptions of Security Threats in Central and Eastern Europe, *Studies in Public Policy*, 293, Centre for the Study of Public Policy, University of Strathclyde.

Hann, E. (1996), Hungary, in R. Smoke (ed.), *Perceptions of Security. Public Opinion and Expert Assessments in Europe's New Democracies*, Manchester, Manchester University Press, 79–86.

Harris, O. (1993), The Collapse of the West, *Foreign Affairs*, 72:4, 41–53.

Huysmans, J. (1995), Migrants as a Security Problem: Dangers of 'Securitizing' Societal Issues, in R. Miles and D. Thränhardt (eds), *Migration and European Integration: The Dynamics of Inclusion and Exclusion*, London, Pinter, 53–72.

Hyde-Price, A. (1996), *The International Politics of East Central Europe*, Manchester, Manchester University Press.

Kalicki, J. (1996), Background: The New and Old Europe, in R. Smoke (ed.), *Perceptions of Security. Public Opinion and Expert Assessments in Europe's New Democracies*, Manchester, Manchester University Press, 3–17.

Kolankiewicz, G. (1994), Consensus and Competition in the Eastern Enlargement of the European Union, *International Affairs*, 70:3, 477–95.

Kovács, L. (1997), Hungary's Contribution to European Security, *NATO Review*, September–October, 9–11.

Kramer, M. and Smoke, R. (1996), Concluding Observations, in R. Smoke (ed.), *Perceptions of Security. Public Opinion and Expert Assessments in Europe's New Democracies*, Manchester, Manchester University Press, 281–93.

Mandelbaum, M. (1995), Preserving the New Peace: The Case Against NATO Expansion, *Foreign Affairs*, 74:3, 8–24.

Matus, J. (1996), Hungary, in R. Smoke (ed.), *Perceptions of Security. Public Opinion and Expert Assessments in Europe's New Democracies*, Manchester, Manchester University Press, 164–86.

MccGwire, M. (1998), A Policy Error of Historic Importance, *Review of International Studies*, 24:1, 23–42.

Mearsheimer, J. J. (1990), Back to the Future: Instability in Europe after the Cold War, *International Security*, 15:1, 5–56.

Mitterrand, F. (1995), Programme of the French Presidency, *Debates of the European Parliament*, 4–456, Luxembourg, Office for Official Publications of the European Communities, 45–52.

Neumann, I. B. (1993), Russia as Central Europe's Constituting Other, *East European Politics and Societies*, 7:2, 349–69.

Neumann, I. B. (1996), European Identity, EU Expansion and the Integration/Exclusion Nexus, *Working Paper*, 551, Norwegian Institute of International Affairs.

Neumann, I. B. and Welsh, J. M. (1991), The Other in European Self-definition: An Addendum to the Literature on International Security, *Review of International Studies*, 17:4, 327–48.

North Atlantic Treaty Organisation (1995), *NATO Handbook*, Brussels, NATO Office of Information and Press.

Salt, J. and Clarke, J. A. (1996), European Migration Report, *New Community*, 22:3, 513–29.

Smoke, R. (1996), The Security Situation of the Central European Countries: Historical Background, in R. Smoke (ed.), *Perceptions of Security. Public Opinion and Expert Assessments in Europe's New Democracies*, Manchester, Manchester University Press, 89–106.

Solana, J. (1997), Letter from the Secretary General: Building a New NATO for a New Europe, *NATO Review*, July–August, 3.

Solana, J. (1998), On Course for a NATO of 19 Nations in 1999, *NATO Review*, 46:1, March, 3–5.

Sperling, J. and Kirchner, E. (1997), *Recasting the European Order: Security Architectures and Economic Cooperation*, Manchester, Manchester University Press.

Stanovnik, P. and Svetličič, M. (1996), *Slovenia and the European Union*, paper presented at the Experts' Meeting on the Economic Aspects of Slovenia's Integration into the European Union, Bled, 12–13 April.

Starzynski, P. (1996), Poland, in R. Smoke (ed.), *Perceptions of Security. Public Opinion and Expert Assessments in Europe's New Democracies*, Manchester, Manchester University Press, 55–63.

Stefanowicz, J. (1996), Poland, in R. Smoke (ed.), *Perceptions of Security. Public Opinion and Expert Assessments in Europe's New Democracies*, Manchester, Manchester University Press, 107–28.

Taracova, E. and Chmelikova, S. (1996), Slovakia, in R. Smoke (ed.), *Perceptions of Security. Public Opinion and Expert Assessments in Europe's New Democracies*, Manchester, Manchester University Press, 72–8.

Tunander, O. (1997), Post-Cold War Europe: Synthesis of a Bipolar Friend–Foe Structure and a Hierarchic Cosmos–Chaos Structure, in O. Tunander, P. Baev and V. I. Einagel (eds), *Geopolitics in Post-Wall Europe: Security, Territory and Identity*, London, Sage, 17–44.

Wæver, O., Buzan, B., Melstrup, M. and Lemaître, P. (1993), *Identity, Migration and the New Security Agenda in Europe*, London, Pinter.

Wohlfeld, M. (1995), The Former Non-Soviet Warsaw Treaty Organization Countries' Security Choices in the Post-Cold War Era, in P. Dunay, G. Kardos and A. J. Williams (eds), *New Forms of Security: Views from Central, Eastern and Western Europe*, Aldershot, Dartmouth, 36–54.

Part II

Country studies

The Czech Republic: the economic road to transformation

This chapter examines the components of the transformation process and the consequences for the Czech Republic's prospective entry to the EU using a threefold framework (Offe 1991). In the first two sections the processes of political, economic and social transformation are explained, with an emphasis on those aspects that attracted the attention of the European Commission (Commission 1997b). Once hailed as the economic miracle of Central Europe in the golden age of early 1990s transformation, the Czech Republic has, since 1997, entered a period of economic and political crisis. The third section locates the Czech Republic in its international setting and examines its foreign policy – the search for a 'return to Europe' – as exemplified by progress in Czech–EU relations.

The political transformation

The Czech and Slovak Federative Republic was dissolved at midnight on 31 December 1992, creating two independent republics. The causes of this 'velvet divorce' can be traced back to the historical differences in Czech and Slovak cultural development which came to shape their different approaches to economic and political reform after 1989 (Capek and Sazama 1993).

Czechoslovakia was created in 1918 out of the disintegrating Austro-Hungarian Empire, as a result of the Versailles peace agreement.[1] From the outset the ethnic problems of the former empire constituted the central problem for the new Czechoslovakia.[2] The creation of Czechoslovakia combined two substantially different economies – the more industrially developed Czech lands (Bohemia and Moravia) and the less developed agrarian Slovakia. The treatment of Slovakia as a colony of the Czech lands provided a 'potent catalyst for the rise of Slovak national consciousness and nationalism during the inter-war period' (Kaiser 1995:215). The gap in economic development intensified during the depression of the

1930s and Slovak dissatisfaction found an outlet in the Slovak Populist Party, which sought links to Nazi Germany and ultimately advocated Slovak independence.

During the interwar years, Czechoslovakia was not only the most prosperous of the CEEC, it was also the only democratic country in the region. In support of the claim for a rightful 'return to Europe', Czech commentators frequently refer to the egalitarian and democratic traditions put in place by Masaryk, the first Czechoslovak President, who created a stable constitutional state which held regular elections throughout the interwar period.

On 30 September 1938, the Czechoslovak leaders capitulated at Munich and surrendered extensive border territory to Germany. By March 1939 Czechoslovakia had been extinguished by Nazi forces; the Czech lands were declared a Protectorate and incorporated into the German military–industrial complex, while Slovakia became a puppet state.

In 1945, after the liberalisation by the Red Army, democracy was formally restored. The major influence of the Communist Party, supported from the outset by the Soviet Union, compromised the future of democracy through the prohibition of a majority of prewar political parties and the formation of the National Front from those parties which were permitted. Internal opposition and the founding of additional parties were prohibited. In the first postwar election in May 1946 the Communists were victorious, reflecting 'a European tide running towards Socialism, which flowed from the retrospective judgement that the depression of the 1930s had discredited liberal capitalism, from the experiences of war and from the need for state intervention to repair shattered economies' (East and Pontin 1997:72). The Communists did not obtain absolute majority and the threatened resignation of non-Communist ministers from the Communist-led coalition resulted in the seizure of power by Moscow in the *putsch* (the 'Prague coup') launched in February 1948.

Soviet totalitarian rule prevailed from 1948 to 1949 and the externally imposed command system created a marked shift in the economic fortunes of Czechoslovakia. The command system encouraged the over-expansion of heavy industry at the expense of light industry and services, insufficient pressure was exerted on enterprises to innovate, and the technological gap between Czechoslovakia and advanced industrial countries widened. As a concession to Slovak Communist unease over the centralisation of power in Prague, Alexander Dubček, the Slovak Communist leader, was appointed as First Secretary of the Czechoslovak Communist Party (KSC) in January 1968. Dubček's calls for liberal reform and a participatory democracy soon unleashed high levels of free expression as censorship was removed for the first time in a Communist state. The so-called

'Prague spring' of 1968 stimulated an enthusiastic debate on the prospect
of 'socialism with a human face' among the intelligentsia, including the
dissident playwright Václav Havel. The experiment was brought to an end
through the intervention of Warsaw Pact armed forces on 20 August,
resulting in the arrest of the leadership of the KSC. A period of 'normalisation' ensued after the replacement of Dubček by Husák as First
Secretary of the KSC when a hardline orthodox Communist regime was
installed, marking the end of the possibility of reform socialism 'from
above' in Czechoslovakia (Wilde 1993).

In November 1989, the 'velvet revolution' erupted simultaneously in
Prague and Bratislava and signalled the collapse of Communist rule in
Czechoslovakia. In Prague, a peaceful demonstration on 17 November
was brutally dispersed by the police. Two days later, leading dissidents
from Charter 77,[3] including Václav Havel, formed the Civic Forum in the
Czech lands together with a parallel organisation, Public Against
Violence, in Slovakia. The new non-Communist government was sworn in
on 10 December and within three weeks Havel was elected President. A
temporary 'Government of National Unity' was approved by the Federal
Assembly in December 1989 until the free elections of June 1990.

Controversies developed over the scope and pace of economic transformation. Two different scenarios of economic reform emerged: the
social democratic 'Komarek scenario',[4] which advocated a slower (gradualist) pace of marketisation, emphasising structural reconstruction and
modernisation; and the 'Klaus scenario', which favoured a more neoliberal (shock) treatment. This cleavage intensified during the 1990 election
campaign.

The free parliamentary elections held on 8–9 June 1990, in which more
than 96 per cent of the electorate participated, provided a firm foundation
for the emergence of a pluralist democracy. The outcome was a resounding defeat for the Communist Party (attracting only 13.6 per cent of the
vote) and a victory for the Civic Forum and Public Against Violence. Civic
Forum encompassed a wide variety of political positions and emphasised
the need to introduce a market economy and parliamentary democracy.
Post-electoral discord inside Civic Forum, however, resulted in a splinter-
ing into a series of parties, clearly differentiated into right and left wings
on the basis of preferences for the pace of economic reform. Similarly, in
Slovakia, Public Against Violence underwent the same process of disintegration. The strongest successor to Civic Forum was Klaus's Civic
Democratic Party (ODS), the champion of neoliberal economic policy; a
majority of Public Against Violence supporters followed the left- and
nationally-oriented Movement for a Democratic Slovakia (HZDS),
formed by the Slovak Prime Minister, Vladimir Meciar. HZDS adopted a
nationalist stance, favouring greater Slovak autonomy and an interventionist and gradualist policy of economic reform more suited to an

economy disproportionately suffering from unemployment and dependency on heavy industry and armaments (see Chapter 11). Klaus retained his post as Minister of Finance, but the departure of Komarek from the government provided the conditions for him to rigorously pursue his radical economic scenario. One of the key obstacles to achieving progress in economic policy arose from the mounting constitutional crisis centring on Slovak nationalism.

The June 1992 elections produced a clear-cut victory for Meciar's HZDS, matched by the success of Klaus's ODS. Nationalist sentiments were successfully mobilised by Meciar. Irreconcilable national, cultural and political identities played their part, as well as the economic inequality between the two republics. The federal constitution itself brought the conflict to a head, in that it gave a small majority of Slovak MPs an effective veto over reforms, thereby placing Klaus's economic strategy in jeopardy. Inevitably, the outcome, which many of the Czech and Slovak population did not want, was the 'velvet divorce'.

The emerging political crisis

The origins of the current economic and political crisis can be located in the results of the June 1992 general election which enabled the ODS to form a coalition with the Civic Democratic Alliance (ODA) and the Christian Democratic Union (KDU–CSL), with a working majority of 105 seats. This right-of-centre coalition was able to rule virtually unopposed from 1992 to 1996 due to the severely weakened and fragmented opposition parties on the political left. Economic reform dominated political debate, enabling Klaus to pursue his policies vigorously in the virtual absence from Parliament of representatives of the former Civic Forum dissidents (Innes 1993); the combination of Klaus's strong leadership style, coupled with his belief in the invisible hand of the market, allowed him to dismiss alternative ideas.

President Havel, in his 'role as moral guardian of public life' (Kettle 1995:36), launched his campaign for a civil society in his 1 January 1994 address, arguing that a civil society, working as a buffer zone between the citizens and the state, is vital for a functioning democracy. Klaus responded by accusing the advocates of civil society of trying to create new bureaucratic layers between the citizen and the state (Pehe 1998); for Klaus, maintenance of a centralised system is necessary for transformation to a market economy.

The failure to achieve a majority in the June 1996 parliamentary elections altered the balance of power within the government and allowed the Christian Democrats and the right-wing ODA to play a more significant role. However, the coalition experienced difficulty in reacting to rapidly growing trade and budget deficits and the slower growth of productivity relative to wage rises.[5] Klaus barely survived a vote of confidence in July, winning 101 votes to 99. A key threat to Klaus emerged from the detached attitude of the Christian Democrats who, under the leadership of Josef Lux, resolved to push for social market policies to resolve the country's economic problems.

Klaus and his cabinet, politically weakened for more than a year, were forced to resign on 30 November 1997 (the 'velvet defenestration') after its coalition partners, including the Christian Democrats, withdrew from the government over a financial scandal which enveloped the ODS.[6] On 16 December Havel named Josef Tosovsky, Governor of the Central Bank, head of a new caretaker government, still of the centre-right.

The 1998 elections gave the Social Democrats (CSSD), led by Milós Zeman, 74 seats in the 200-seat lower House of Parliament; unexpectedly, the ODS obtained 63 seats. The Communists came third with 24 seats, ahead of the centrist KDU–CSL with 20 seats and the right-of-centre Freedom Union – formed by the ODS rebels – with 19 seats. The election saw the collapse of the ultra-right Republicans, who had featured in government since 1989. In effect, the election reflected the end of economic confidence that had fuelled Czech elite claims to governing the most stable country in the post-Communist era (Pehe 1995, 1997). The following section pays particular attention to the successes and failures of this stress on an economic 'miracle' to achieve societal transformation.

The economic transformation

The experience of any economy undergoing transformation is a unique one. GDP fell more sharply in the Czech Republic than in Hungary or Poland. Productivity performance has been much weaker in the Czech Republic than in Hungary or Poland. Employment fell less sharply in the Czech Republic than in Hungary or Poland, while unemployment remains much lower,[7] and the proportion of output used for gross fixed investment is much higher. Table 8.1 gives the basic economic indicators for Czechoslovakia, and Table 8.2 gives indicators for the Czech Republic.[8]

Klaus, dismissive of a managed approach to transformation, identifies academic debate over gradualism and sequencing as an intellectual illusion (Jeffries 1993); macro-economic stabilisation with the control of inflationary expectations being more important than other objectives. Klaus identified the significance of market forces and foreign competition to force both consumers and producers to make rational economic decisions. Price and trade liberalisation, together with currency convertibility, were identified as the instruments through which this would occur (Blejer

Table 8.1   Economic indicators: Czechoslovakia, 1989–92

	1989	1990	1991	1992
Output[a]	1.0	−1.6	−14.7	−7.2
Inflation[b]	1.4	10.0	58.0	10.8
Unemployment[c]	0.0	1.0	6.8	5.1
Budget balance[d]	–	0.9	−1.0	−0.8
Current account balance[e]	0.3	−1.1	0.4	0.2

Notes:
[a] Average annual % change of real GDP.
[b] End-year % change in consumer prices.
[c] ILO definition.
[d] As % of GDP.
[e] In $ billion.
Source: OECD (various years).

Table 8.2   Economic indicators: Czech Republic, 1993–97

	1993	1994	1995	1996	1997
Output[a]	−0.9	2.6	6.4	3.9	1.0
Inflation[b]	21.0	10.0	9.0	8.8	8.5
Unemployment[c]	3.6	3.2	3.1	3.5	4.4
Budget balance[d]	0.0	−0.8	−2.2	−1.2	−2.2
Current account balance[e]	0.4	−0.2	−2.7	−7.6	−6.0

Notes:
[a] Average annual % change of real GDP.
[b] End-year % change in consumer prices.
[c] ILO definition.
[d] As % of GDP.
[e] 1993, in $ billion, as percentage of GDP.
Source: OECD (various years).

and Coricelli 1995). Restrictive fiscal and monetary policies were used to constrain domestic aggregate demand.

Four branches of economic reform have contributed to the achievements witnessed so far in the economic transformation of the Czech Republic. These are: price liberalisation; the liberalisation of foreign trade and internal convertibility of the currency; restrictive monetary and fiscal policies; and privatisation (Blejer and Coricelli 1995). In 1991 implementation of the reform package proceeded with the liberalisation of prices and foreign trade, internal convertibility of the Czech crown and small-scale privatisation and restitution (Ministry of Industry and Trade of the Czech Republic 1995). In 1992, large-scale privatisation began and prices and foreign trade were further liberalised. 1993 saw the division of the Czech and Slovak Federative Republic (CSFR) into the Czech Republic and Slovakia, together with changes to the structure of the taxation system, the separation of the Czech and Slovak currency, further progress on internal convertibility, and foreign trade liberalisation. In 1994 the second wave of large-scale privatisation commenced and the process of restitution continued, along with further reform of foreign trade and currency convertibility.

Price liberalisation

The liberalisation of prices began on 1 January 1991, leading to a dramatic leap in the rate of inflation of close to 40 per cent in the first three months of the year (Banerjee 1994). Prices (no longer set by the Ministry of Finance or local authorities) were determined by supply-and-demand forces for more than 94 per cent of goods and services. Some administered prices remained in non-competitive markets such as fuel and energy, residential rentals and postal services. By mid-1991 the monthly rate of inflation had returned to its more typical level of close to 1 per cent per month (Banerjee 1994; Blejer and Coricelli 1995). In 1993 the rate of inflation again increased with the introduction of value-added tax, and then quickly returned back to its former level.

Foreign trade liberalisation

During the 1980s Czechoslovakia's foreign trade was dominated by its Eastern neighbours, the Soviet Union being its largest trading partner in both receiving its exports and delivering its imports.[9] A number of factors precipitated the reorientation of Czechoslovakia's foreign trade. Reduced oil production in the Soviet Union, increasing world oil prices, the reluctance of the Soviet Union to purchase imports with hard currency and the increasing hard currency net indebtedness of the CMEA countries heralded major changes. Intra-CMEA trade fell by more than one-fifth in 1990 and by more than 50 per cent in volume in 1991 (Bakos 1993; Jeffries 1993; OECD 1992). With the narrowing of opportunities to trade with the Soviet Union, Hungary and Poland, Czechoslovakia's trade with Western Europe began to increase dramatically.[10]

Under communism, Czechoslovak foreign trade corporations owned by the state were the only organisations allowed to conduct trade with other countries. In 1990 the foreign trade corporations were permitted to extend the range of goods sold and bought abroad. The ownership of the foreign trade corporations was changed by the Foreign Trade Corporations Property Administration, an organisation set up specifically to facilitate this, and they became joint-stock companies. The legislation radically transforming such foreign trade activities, the Commercial Code (Act 513/1991), came into effect on 1 January 1992.[11]

The process of currency convertibility began on 1 January 1991, when firms were allowed to make financial commitments with non-residents, and extended in April 1992 to permit citizens conducting business to use foreign exchange. Following the monetary separation of the Czech Republic and Slovakia in 1993, the Czech crown was tied to two currencies, the German mark and US dollar, and allowed to fluctuate within a band of +/–0.5 per cent. In 1994 access to and the use of foreign currency were further liberalised: the quantity of Czech currency allowed to be taken out of and brought back into the country when travelling was increased; restrictions on the export of Czech securities were removed (Ministry of Industry and Trade of the Czech Republic 1995). Full convertibility of the Czech crown on the current account occurred on 1 October 1995 and capital account convertibility, planned for before 2000, was announced on 1 January 1996 (CzechInvest 1996a; Stolze 1997). Meeting the IMF charter and the OECD requirements for membership, restrictions on investing abroad have been removed, together with limits on borrowing. The Czech National Bank extended the fluctuation band to +/–7.5 per cent on 28 February 1996 to make it easier to cope with the large inflows of capital (OECD 1996; Boland 1996b).

Fiscal and monetary policy

The liberalisation of prices in Czechoslovakia did not result in the expectation of future rates of inflation of that level, and hence affect the decision making of individuals and enterprises. The use of the powerful tools of monetary and fiscal policy provides an answer to how Czechoslovakia avoided the scenario of out-of-control rates of inflation. The aim of macro-economic policy was the control of inflation and inflationary pressures (Dyba and Svejnar 1991). Control of the rate of growth of the money supply using interest rates and credit limits, together with restrictive fiscal policy measures such as the reduction of state subsidies to industry, the introduction of at first high and then falling rates of tax on profits and taxes on public-sector wage growth, were the instruments used to control inflationary pressures.[12] Macro-economic policy in Czechoslovakia has been both praised for its consistency (Winiecki 1994) and criticised for being too restrictive and resulting in a longer than necessary recession (Adam 1993).

Privatisation

Privatisation is by far the most significant policy implemented to transform the Czechoslovak economy; it stimulated the development of a private sector but, as we shall see, several negative consequences have been highlighted by the European Commission (Commission 1997b).

In January 1991, that the state sector was responsible for 96 per cent of GDP indicates the sheer magnitude of the government's aim to privatise the bulk of state-owned enterprises over a period of three years.

Privatisation in Czechoslovakia was to be the largest and most rapid privatisation project in the period. So comprehensive was its coverage of the new society's policy objectives that success in privatisation could be taken as a make-or-break indicator of societal transformation. The purpose of privatisation for the Czechoslovakian government was to uplift the economic efficiency of the economy and its constituent enterprises, reduce the pressure on state budgets to supply subsidies for loss-making enterprises and contribute to macro-economic stabilisation.[13] Emphasis was to be placed on the speed of the operation and, through the voucher scheme (see below), equality of opportunity to participate. The government was insistent not only in wishing to change the behaviour of enterprise managers and workers but also to encourage the mass of voucher holders to take responsibility for state enterprises (Simoneti 1993). Three main approaches were used: small-scale privatisation, large-scale privatisation and property restitution. The process can be regarded as successful if measured by the private-sector contribution to GDP alone. The private sector accounted for 74 per cent of GDP early in 1995 (EBRD 1996).

Small-scale privatisation, which represented an attempt to privatise property that could not be restored to former owners, started in 1991 and was formally closed on 31 December 1993.[14] In most cases the property was let on long-term lease to allow potential domestic entrepreneurs with limited purchasing power to participate in the process. Only a quarter of the properties were actually sold.[15]

Restitution is the process whereby previous owners (or their heirs) have been given back properties that were confiscated or nationalised following the Communist coup of 25 February 1948. The impetus behind the legislation (Act No. 403/1990 Coll.) rested on both political and moral considerations – to repair the alleged wrongs of the Communist past – and can thus be seen as part of a desire to return to democratic principles and the rule of law.[16] Real-estate transactions grew rapidly in response to the demand for office and retail floor space generated by both domestic entrepreneurs and foreign firms wishing to develop their operations in the Czech Republic. The Western-style temples of conspicuous consumption such as Marks & Spencer, Benetton, McDonald's, Pizza Hut and Esteé Lauder now jostle for position along the principal shopping streets of central Prague.

Large-scale privatisation was based on a flexible combination of the voucher method with other standard approaches, including direct sale to a specific (sometimes selected) buyer, public auction, public tender, transfer of ownership rights to a community or town and through transformation into joint-stock companies with subsequent share privatisation.

Citizens over the age of eighteen wishing to participate registered their interest by paying a symbolic fee of approximately $35 (1,000 Kč (crowns)), receiving in return a coupon booklet containing 1,000 points. A list of enterprises to be privatised was published, along with details of the sales, profits, number of employees, debts for the last three years, net assets and the percentage of shares offered in the coupon privatisation to be sold to foreign or domestic buyers or to remain in state ownership. Voucher holders could either use their points to bid for shares in up to ten enterprises of their choice or entrust their points to a private investment fund which would bid for shares on their behalf.

The voucher privatisation was organised into two waves. The first wave, launched in 1992, had five rounds and involved 998 enterprises with an estimated book value of Kč 300 billion, and was completed by mid-1993. The second wave, started in 1994, had six rounds involving 676 businesses with a book value of Kč 155 billion, and was completed at the beginning of 1995. The coupon method resulted in the privatisation of approximately 60 per cent of the total privatised property in the first wave (40 per cent of the property was privatised by means of standard methods). Interest among the voucher holders was high (some six million people participated) and their participation was more active than in the first wave; the investment privatisation funds only attracted slightly more than three-fifths of the voucher holders, compared with three-quarters in the first wave (Takla 1994).

One of the principal and negative features to emerge in the Czech privatisation process is the uncomfortably close relationship between the privatised enterprises, the investment funds,[17] the main banks and the state. The ten largest funds dominate the ownership of the newly privatised companies, six of which are subsidiaries of the major banks (Takla 1994). The Czech privatisation process has witnessed a concentration of capital dominated by banking power, labelled by some observers as the unofficial 'third wave' of privatisation (Vecernik 1996). The key role played by banking in the emergent private sector led to serious repercussions in the performance of the economy in 1997, its trajectory towards a functioning market and the Czech Republic's interactions with the EU (Commission 1997b). Although the first bankruptcy law was enacted in 1991, followed by amendments in 1993, there has been a reluctance to enforce it because of the social and political costs associated with mass bankruptcies (Robinson 1994).

Enterprise restructuring is motivated by the receipt of profits accruing to the owners from minimising the costs of production and maximising the revenue earned from sales, combined with the punishment of bankruptcy proceedings. Berle and Means (1932)[18] identified the weakening of this profit motive in corporations where the owners of a firm are not the managers. Their work, which spawned a vast research effort to consider the consequences of the separation (or divorce) of ownership and control,[19] is of heightened relevance to the Czech Republic, where an additional layer of separation can be identified, further weakening the profit motive. The additional layer of separation consists of two parts: the National Property Fund, with its continued significant ownership in many of the former state-owned enterprises; and the ownership stakes held by the investment funds.

The manner of privatisation and its speed has contributed directly to three pervasive issues in the economic environment, highlighted by the *Agenda 2000* Opinion (Commission 1997b). The Commission was critical of the web of cross-ownership of banks and investment funds and the banking sector in general, the opaque and poorly regulated capital market and the apparent ease with which illegal activities and asset-stripping could take place, the pace of restructuring and the level of governance within enterprises. These factors inhibit the allocation of resources by market forces and the incentives and capacity of enterprises to compete.

The approval process of projects for privatisation made by state-owned enterprises in 1992 more than doubled the number of industrial enterprises from 632 to 1,294 (Charap and Zemplinerova 1993). Additional factors which have changed industrial concentration in the Czech Republic have been the new private-sector enterprises stimulated by the liberalisation of prices and trade. Thus, following restitution, small-scale and large-scale privatisation, the concentration of industry diminished sharply as the large state-owned monoliths were broken up and sold or transferred to new owners. More recently, mergers have occurred among the leading enterprises, for example among the brewers, stimulated by foreign interest and part-ownership as well as new foreign trade opportunities (Anderson 1997b). Such activity is indicative of a reaction to market forces, either to strengthen an enterprise against the impact of its competitors, or to stifle a competitor.

Foreign investment

Foreign investment has played an important role in encouraging enterprises to undertake restructuring. With FDI of US$7.5 billion between 1990 and mid-1997, the Czech Republic has been successful in attracting foreign interest in spite of a lack of investment incentives such as tax breaks and cut-price land deals for foreign investors.[20] The largest annual FDI took place in 1995 and 1996, with US$2.5 billion and US$1.4 billion, respectively (CzechInvest 1996c; Done 1997). Some of the most alluring features of the Czech Republic for foreign producers are its geographical location, stability, and relatively low inflation and interest rates compared with Hungary, Poland and Slovakia, together with the liberal foreign exchange regime, infrastructure and relatively cheap, well-educated labour force (Done 1997).

European countries have been the dominant contributory sources of

FDI in the Czech Republic. Germany (29.6 per cent), Switzerland (13.5 per cent) and the Netherlands (13.5 per cent), together with the USA (14.5 per cent), were the four largest investors between 1990 and July 1996. The sectors of the Czech economy into which this investment has mainly been made are communication and transport (22.6 per cent), the automotive industry (17 per cent) and consumer goods and tobacco (14.1 per cent) (CzechInvest 1996b).[21] The large quantities of FDI demonstrate vividly the positive expectation of the potential for growth, sales and profits in the Czech Republic. The more recent investments in oil, telecommunications and electricity follow the deregulation and anticipate further liberalisation of prices in these sectors.

The inflow of FDI has stimulated restructuring beyond the enterprise into which the initial investment was made. For example, despite the substantial downward revision of Volkswagen's investment plans in the Czech Republic, the resulting impact on the components industry has been significant.[22] The focus of this restructuring was to raise both the quality and productivity of Volkswagen's suppliers and thereby reduce the costs of the required components. Although FDI is having a positive influence on developing a competitive productive base in the Czech Republic, it is not without its disadvantages. Competition inevitably results in some suppliers not meeting the required standards in terms of quality, productivity and cost.

In 1995 alone, Komercni Banka, the Czech Republic's largest commercial bank, estimated that of the US$10 billion which flowed into the country in that year, less than one-third took the form of FDI. More than one-third of it was long-term capital, the rest being portfolio investment and short-term capital (Done 1996c). Foreign capital, although going some way towards providing the investment finance and working-capital requirements needed to raise the productivity, quality and value-added nature of the Czech Republic's output, has not been sufficient to address the restructuring needs of all newly privatised enterprises.

The major problems facing the state-owned enterprises on privatisation were the high levels of interenterprise debt, the shortage of domestic capital to finance production and shrinking markets for the products being produced. The investment funds holding a majority of the coupons, together with the large stakes of enterprises held by the National Property Fund, made reorganisation difficult. An additional hurdle was the ownership and running of many of the investment funds by the banks, with any financing requirements needing approval from the part-owners of the enterprises themselves. In addition, the National Property Fund also owns large stakes in the banks. This web of cross-ownership constitutes a major obstacle to the restructuring of enterprises.

The investment privatisation funds, though at first cautious, were keen to cooperate with the managers of enterprises to improve company performance (Brom and Orenstein 1994). The removal of managerial corruption and incompetence and the use of bankruptcy and labour shedding were seen as necessary to establish a strong portfolio and enhance efficiency and profitability. Kenway and Klvacova (1996) argued that the National Property Fund's ownership of enterprises was essentially passive, despite appointing representatives on the boards of companies and participating in shareholder meetings.[23] The structure and ownership of the banking sector also inhibit restructuring.

The banking system

The Czech Republic has a two-tiered banking system: a central bank, the Czech National Bank, and more than fifty commercial banks, the majority of which are at least partly, if not wholly, foreign-owned. The functions of the Czech National Bank include the formulation of monetary policy, issuing bank notes and coins, controlling the circulation of currency, overseeing the payments and settlements system, supervising the other banks, and providing reports to Parliament and information to the public.

The commercial banking sector is dominated by four large banks, which collectively own 60 per cent of the banking sector's assets (Boland 1996b). These are Ceska Sporitelna, Komercni Banka, Ceskoslovenska Obchodni Banka and Investicni a Postovni Banka (IPB). Ceska Sporitelna, a savings bank, was reported to have, in mid-1995, an 80 per cent share of the retail savings market (Robinson 1995). Half of Ceska Sporitelna's balance sheet was given to interbank lending. The National Property Fund still retains a 49 per cent stake in this bank and in Komercni Banka, which is essentially a bank for the industrial sector. Ceskoslovenska Obchodni Banka provides trade finance for the top 100 Czech companies and is a net borrower from the interbank market for funds. The National Property Fund currently holds a 66 per cent stake, though a shortlist of bidders was drawn up in January 1999 for 51 per cent of its stake (Anderson and Wagstyl 1999).

The main problems facing the banking sector are problem loans.[24] These are not loans made prior to 1990, as most of the unrecoverable debt was taken up by the Consolidation Bank, but from poor lending decisions made since 1990. The collapse of some of the small banks impacts on the banking sector as a whole due to interbank lending. In addition, the lack of bankruptcy proceedings has led to the deferring of financial restructuring.[25] The failure of enterprises to restructure, together with good lending decisions cross-subsiding poor ones, have made it difficult for enterprises seeking loans to secure them on favourable terms (Borish et al. 1997). The decline in reported net profits in the first three-quarters of 1997 of 20 per cent for Ceska Sporitelna and over 60 per cent for both IPB and Komercni Banka added to this difficulty (Anderson 1997a).

Capital markets

A functioning capital market with easy access to capital funds for investment would enable enterprises to modernise their facilities and reward
shareholders with dividends. In the Czech Republic the capital market
does not function well.[26] The biggest problem is a lack of liquidity, in part
because the investment privatisation funds have retained their shares in
enterprises (Boland 1995a).[27]

There are four markets for trading in shares: the Prague Stock
Exchange, on which between 50 and 60 per cent of trading occurs
through either an automatic trading system or direct block trades; the
Securities Centre, which accounts for between 30 and 40 per cent of trade;
and the RM-System, accounting for about 10 per cent of trade (Done
1996b). The price of shares is different in the different markets, which has
made trading confusing but manipulation of the market relatively easy.
The capital market in the Czech Republic, under these circumstances, was
not one for either portfolio investors buying a variety of shares to spread
the risk, nor one in which enterprises could raise funds for restructuring
or investment by issuing new shares. It was a market for speculation.
Those participants with inside information or sufficient financial power
were able to make considerable gains. Poor corporate earnings from mid-
1996, the expected devaluation of the crown, economic slowdown and
summer floods, together with cuts in public spending and penalties
imposed on high wage growth after the currency crisis, have all
contributed to the difficulties faced by enterprises in general and the
capital market (Boland 1997).

The newly created Czech Securities Commission is an important step
towards creating a working system of supervision (Anderson and Done
1997). How successful it will be at improving market confidence,
however, will depend on how much power and influence it has and especially how much it uses that power. As confidence returns to the capital
market, enterprises will find the finance for restructuring in the equities
market, not just from bank borrowing, and the rewards from restructuring will be more evident. Further reforms to both the capital market and
the banking sector are anticipated.[28] These include a strengthening of the
stock exchange rules to ensure the full reporting of all trades and to ban
off-exchange dealing, a takeover panel to regulate the transfer of large
stakes in shares, and the full privatisation of Ceska Sporitelna,
Ceskoslovenska Obchodni Banka and Komercni Banka (Wagstyl and
Anderson 1998a).

The European Commission states that 'The Czech Republic can be
regarded as a functioning market economy' (Commission 1997b:81). This
is not the case. The currency crisis of May 1997, where the Czech crown
depreciated to the tune of 10 per cent in the wake of a flood of specula-

tive flows, the limited availability of key managerial expertise and tight labour market conditions (especially in Prague, with an almost zero rate of unemployment), together with the lack of restructuring and corporate governance described above, present a very different picture of the economic environment (Boland 1997). Privatisation, to a large degree, is over, though state control of a large proportion of industrial output is not, due to the large minority stakes still in the hands of the National Property Fund and its important stakes in the large banks. The response so far to both the currency crisis and key micro-economic restructuring, and the slow pace of putting financial market supervision in place, combine to make economic stability a goal yet to be achieved.

The social consequences of transformation

Economic transformation is being accompanied and sustained by changes in the social structure, especially the re-emergence of the middle classes. Thus Vecernik (1996) suggests that three post-1989 'partial revolutions' explain the emerging middle-class occupational structure. The 'capitalist revolution' has created a new set of opportunities for those with property and enterprise, especially the nomenklatura, who have converted their political power into economic power by transferring state property into their own hands or by transforming parts of state enterprises into private firms which they now own. The 'informational revolution' has opened the way for technological and organisational innovations, making it possible for highly qualified workers to seek advancement. The third revolution is the expansion of the service industry, signalling the emergence of a post-industrial society, creating new highly paid occupations in financial and business services. The removal of income regulation in the Czech business sector in July 1995 has also reduced the likelihood of the public sector (where more importance is attached to experience than educational quali-fications) catching up on earnings.

Deacon (1993) has outlined the pattern of losers and gainers in the process of post-Communist social change. The small group of short-term and possibly long-term beneficiaries include the newly emergent capitalist class, mainly recruited from the former nomenklatura. Clark and Soulsby's examination of the management structure of four large-scale mechanical engineering enterprises in Moravia shows 'that there is an overall continuity of the membership between the pre-1989 and post-communist elite structures, with greater persistence of the former *nomenklatura* and aspiring *nomenklatura* in the higher echelons' (Clark and Soulsby 1996:296). Winners also include those who have become successful in the shadow economy (including spivs and racketeers), those who have had their property restored, and beneficiaries of the voucher privatisation scheme. In contrast, the vast majority of society saw a diminution of their living standards in the early phases of transformation. The economic transformation has given rise to a 'new poverty' due to the rising cost of living created by price liberalisation, the inability of households to adapt to the new market conditions and open unemployment through restructuring. The 'new poor' are the once-secure urban proletariat, who now experience various degrees of impoverishment through actual or threatened unemployment and the reduction of state subsidies on rents, food and transport.

Perceptions of societal security

Charlotte Bretherton (Chapter 7), in keeping with the Security for Europe Project (Smoke 1996), offers a broad concept of security to encompass not only politico-military, but also economic, environmental and other insecurities perceived to be of significance by ordinary citizens as they live in the uncertainty of transformation. Lack of job security, democratic fragility and social disorders such as crime loom large in the catalogue of problems. Although generally internal insecurities were perceived to be much greater than external ones in all Visegrad countries, Czechs felt a growing sense of confidence that the worst of the transformation crisis was over after 1993 and that the economy was developing as well as could be expected. 'Raising the standards of living and, more generally, completing the transition to become "a normal European country" continued to be the public's main concern' (Boguszakova and Gabal 1996:64).

Despite the need for a social security net to cushion the adverse social impact of economic transformation, the policies adopted by the countries of East Central Europe varied. A comprehensive plan for social reform was prepared by the Federal Ministry of Labour and Social Affairs that broadly reflected the neoliberal orientation of the federal government and social democratic policies (Rhys 1995). This hybrid policy prevented social problems from creating a severe political backlash and enabled the early construction of welfare-state institutions. This compromise arose from an intense dispute between the neoliberal approach of the Finance Minister Vaclav Klaus and the Social Democrats; in order to gain voting support for his economic strategy, Klaus yielded to pressure for a social democratic brand of social policy. The short-term transitional measures implemented included compensation payments for cuts in consumer subsidies on food (these were gradually reduced from 1993, and only available to lower-income families, reflecting a policy shift of targeting of social benefits) and continued government subsidies on rent, heat, electricity and transport. In 1991, the Federal Parliament passed a law on the 'living minimum', which provided support for all citizens whose income fell below a minimum level and who were unable to supplement their income because of age or ill health. The Czech Republic was the only East Central European country to erect an effective social safety net, albeit to minimal standards in the early transitional period (Orenstein 1995).

In 1993 the government began to restructure the three pillars of the social welfare system (social insurance, state social benefits and social assistance), to a more effective and targeted social policy which would place greater responsibility on individuals and families and those in real need. The privatisation of health care has begun, along with the development of an insurance-based health service, which will result in the exclusion of entitlement for some; and several state-subsidised programmes, such as day-care facilities, have been reduced or eliminated.

Women in the post-Communist republic

The impact of transformation on Czech women reflects many of the conclusions reached in Chapter 5. The pursuit of equality between men and women, an important plank of the socialist political programme, was encouraged directly by the state through various Acts and policies which were associated with voting and representation, education, divorce, property and employment rights.[29] The proletarianisation of society additionally removed a whole stratum of occupations in business, commerce and self-employment which had been the traditional domain of male esteem.

The most important feature of socialist 'emancipation' was the raising of the level of female participation in the labour force. Thus in 1968, 46.1 per cent of the Czechoslovak workforce were women, rising to 48.4 per cent by 1989 – practically 94 per cent of all Czech and Slovak women (Siklová 1993). The high activity rate of women in the labour force was facilitated through the establishment of a heavily state-subsidised network of services, such as canteens, laundries and institutionalised nursery schools and child-care facilities, which gives the impression of the regime's full commitment to female emancipation and equality of opportunity. The costs may be measured through the reality of life for many overburdened women, reflected in their dual (or even triple) role as full-time paid workers supplementing the family income and their traditional role as bearers and rearers of children and domestic workers. Inevitably, the overburdening of women led to a high divorce rate and poor health. However, Havelková suggests that 'In the Czech case, the high employment of women ... was not resented as much as is sometimes claimed today in sweeping criticisms against the totalitarian system' (1993:64). Although discrimination was officially abolished, the formal equality of rights did not lead in reality to equality at work. Women now form the minority of entrepreneurs and the earnings differential between men and women has decreased slightly, with women now earning 74 per cent of male earnings in the Czech Republic, despite the formal adoption of EU directives on equal pay, fair treatment at work and maternity leave (Duncan 1996).

Abortion, legalised in Czechoslovakia in 1957, became the most commonly used method of fertility regulation. Estimates suggest that every third pregnancy (every second in the largest urban areas) is aborted (Heitlinger 1993). Abortion 'on demand' only became available in 1987. Since 1989, abortion has become the single most important women's issue on the otherwise apparently empty female political agenda. The debate has come to adopt a Western flavour, centring on the moral issue of the right of the mother to decide against the protection of the foetus.

Czech neoliberal policies since 1993 have resulted in a reduction in the previous network of childcare facilities, family allowances, and employment and unemployment-related benefits. Women became over-represented in less well-paid jobs such as teaching and health care and under-represented in leadership positions in the job hierarchy. Even in the field of health care, where 96 per cent of specialised jobs were female, only 11.9 per cent of women held leadership positions (Siklová 1993).

Czech women appear to be losers rather than beneficiaries in the transformation process in that they now have fewer job opportunities, they suffer higher rates of unemployment relative to men (non-registered job losses are high among women) and part-time work is on the ascendant as the standard mode of employment. One of the biggest changes is associated with decollectivisation of consumption and reductions in state benefits, which are impacting particularly on single mothers who are experiencing a renewed 'feminisation' of poverty.

Despite the post-1989 revival of civil society with conditions conducive to the formation of grassroots women's movements, enthusiasm for and membership of such groupings are conspicuous by their absence. With the exception of the abortion issue, women do not appear to be anxious to improve their situation, and this has led Wagnerová to lament that 'Most Czech women are totally uninterested in emancipation, the women's movement or even feminism' (1996:108). It could be argued that this attitude is a legacy of the socialist experience, in which the multiple burden denied women the time and energy to think and the totalitarian system rendered them impotent to mobilise. To this may be added 'the indifference of politics and the enmity of the market in relation to women' of the transformation period (Ferge 1997:175).

The external environment

Had and Handl (1996) suggest that Czech foreign and security policy is possessed by a cold and pragmatic realism which attaches importance to how international institutions can be used to achieve national policy goals. The singlemindedness of Czech foreign policy is apparent in the three strategic tasks embodied in the foreign policy guidelines. The first task is to create cooperative relations with each of the neighbouring states (Germany, Hungary, Poland, Austria and Slovakia), especially bilateral relations with Slovakia and Germany. The second task is to obtain membership of the main security, political and economic organisations of Europe: NATO, the WEU and, above all, the EU. The third task is to maintain good relations with the former Communist states, through trade and to assist in their stabilisation. Thus the most prominent institutional actors are the EU, NATO, the member states of the EU (especially Germany), and the members of the Visegrad Group (Poland, Hungary and Slovakia).

Before November 1989, the Czech Republic was an integral part of the economic, political and security structures of the former Soviet bloc, the most significant of which were Comecon and the Warsaw Pact until 1991. Following their demise (July 1991), the immediate objective was to secure Czechoslovakia's sovereignty and independence by extricating itself from the wreckage of the old order and establishing itself in the new European architecture, requiring a rapid withdrawal of Soviet troops (accomplished by July 1991). Immediately after 1989 efforts were made to identify a new Western-oriented economic and defence security identity by establishing links with all the significant interlocking multilateral organisations from which it might receive recognition and support for economic and social transformation. Already Czechoslovakia had been one of the founding states of the UN, and following the 'velvet divorce', the Czech Republic became a member in January 1993. In December 1995 the Czech Republic became the first post-Communist country to gain full membership of the OECD, which facilitates the exchange of economic information among policy makers. Acceptance by the OECD provided a useful additional credential for future EU entry, as did membership of the Council of Europe as Czechoslovakia (1991) and the Czech Republic (1993).

The Council of Europe requires evidence of acceptable democratic behaviour, the observance of human rights protocols and parliamentary democracy in joining countries; both the Council of Europe and CSCE have expressed concern about the Czech Republic's treatment of the Roma population. An invitation to join NATO (December 1997), extended also to Poland and Hungary, confirmed the Czechs' 'inclusive' status in the emergence of a post-Cold War European architecture (see Chapter 7).

Of the neighbouring Western European countries Germany is the most significant, but this is arguably true of all the Visegrad countries. Czech perceptions of Germany are complex and exhibit 'a deep and highly nuanced ambivalence' (Boguszakova and Gabal 1996:68), reflecting a

distinct generational difference between those who can recall the experience of Nazi oppression and fear the resurgence of German influence.
Younger Czechs do not appear to experience this fear but are cautious of
what the future may bring. Germany, a leading trading partner and investor
in the Czech economy, exerts a strong influence on the development of the
economy and governmental decision making. There are growing fears of
German economic hegemony and structural dependency.[30]

A high degree of dependency on German political patronage also arises
from the Czech Republic's relations with the EU. Jerábek and Zich argue
that 'countries such as the Czech Republic, kept on the waiting list to join
the EU, are open to political pressure from strong EU members such as
Germany' (1997:176). So far, within EU and NATO circles, Germany has
championed the cause of the Czech Republic becoming a full member.
However, the situation is complicated by the abiding national memory of
Nazi Germany's occupation of Czechoslovakia, which persists as a background factor, and the continuing animosity between the Czech state and
the expatriated Sudetan Germans. The Sudetan German issue poses diplomatic difficulties for both Czech–German relations and for Czech and
German national politics.[31]

Of the three other Visegrad countries, Slovakia is the most relevant for
the future of the Czech Republic. Following the division of
Czechoslovakia, relationships continue to be cordial and Czech foreign
policy guidelines recognise the desire to create stable relations, especially
in the light of differential progress towards EU membership between the
two countries (see below). After Germany, Slovakia is the Czech
Republic's most important trading partner, although the level of trade has
fallen.[32] Public attitude surveys reveal that Czechs generally feel that
Slovakia has far more problems and fewer economic and social resources
to deal with than the Czech Republic, and there is scepticism about the
ability of any Slovak government to form a competent administration in
the near future. As such, Slovakia is perceived as a source of potential
instability for the Czech Republic (Boguszakova and Gabal 1996).

Regional cooperation and competition

While waiting for signs of admission to the EU, the Central European
countries have formed a number of regional cooperation groupings, the
most important of which, for the Czech Republic and Slovakia, are the
CEI and the Visegrad Group. Czechoslovakia joined the CEI in May 1990
and the Czech Republic and Slovakia joined as separate members in
March 1993. At the fourth summit meeting of the CEI on 16–17 July
1993 in Budapest, the prime and foreign ministers of the member states
reaffirmed the importance of regional cooperation in the European integration effort. However, Klaus scathingly described the CEI as being

concerned solely with the building of roads and railways through neighbouring states (Reisch 1993). This statement was interpreted as a signal that the Czech Republic was attempting to shed its Central European image and forge ahead of the rest in a race for Europe.

Czech policy has been less than enthusiastic towards institutionalising the Visegrad Group; Klaus's personal view is that it is 'an artificial creation of the West' engineered by the EC to encourage intraregional cooperation and trade. Successful regional collaborative structures could always be seen as an alternative to EU or NATO structures or used as an argument to slow down admission. As a consequence of Czech policy there has been no joint meeting of state representatives of the Visegrad Group since 1992. Klaus has insisted that intraregional cooperation should focus on developing trading relations. The outcome has been active Czech support for the promotion of free trade among the Visegrad Group. The free-trade agreement removed a marked contradiction in trading conditions between the Visegrad countries brought about by their EC associate memberships in 1991, whereby the customs duties on certain EC products were much lower than the duties on the same products traded between the three countries. Valerie Bruce (1997) sees 1993 as a watershed in the development of the Visegrad Group in that it marks a shift away from cooperation between the members to one of overt competition, and it was then that member countries began to differentiate and acquire their own identities and self-confidence. Since 1993 there has been a strong incentive for these states to act separately and promote their competitive uniqueness towards Europe.

With regard to the Czech Republic, Illner argues that 'the specific geographic and geopolitical situation of the country and its economic, social and cultural heritage create relatively favourable preconditions for an orderly and successful transformation and political stability, provided that no external shocks occur' (1994:34). Perhaps the most important advantageous country-specific characteristic of the Czech Republic is its changed geopolitical situation as it became physically divorced from the Russian sphere of influence. It is the most western of the Visegrad countries, offering a regional dynamism able to accommodate economic transformation at a rapid pace and so attract higher levels of new investment. The leading role played by Prague will continue to grow apace, especially when the infrastructure linking the Czech lands with Western Europe is completed (the Prague–Nuremberg and Prague–Dresden motorway, the reconstruction of the main railway corridors and the enlargement of Prague airport). The planned network of transport corridors will create axes for economic development and will allow the integration of Prague into the system of European metropolises (see Gorzelak et al. 1994; Hall 1993).

Illner suggests other relevant country-specific factors deriving from the heritage of Czech history which have the potential to influence the course of the transformation of CEE. For example, with regard to Czech political history, during the interwar period, 'democratic models as well as standards of both political behaviour and institutions were established which have partly survived in the national memory and can be activated in the present process of transformation as points of reference and symbolic values. It is this which provides democracy with a good chance of realisation' (1994:32–3). Similarly, it is claimed that egalitarianism, which is considered to be a trait of Czech political culture, may exert an influence during the transformation process, through, for example, popular support for welfare-oriented policies. In similar vein, sobriety and scepticism, both features of the Czech mentality, 'have contributed to the rational economic and political behaviour of the Czech population and have made it relatively resistant to political extremism' (Illner 1994:33–4). For Czech political elites the Republic represents an important and carefully observed example of political and economic transformation of CEE and, as such, should play a vanguard role in CEEC 10 ambitions to 'return to Europe'. The extent to which that view is shared by the EU is explained below.

Czech transformation and the EU: the Commission's Opinion

The Czech Republic presented its application for membership to the EU on 17 January 1996, to be examined alongside applications from nine other CEEC. The Commission published its Opinion on 16 July 1997, applying the Copenhagen conditions (Commission 1997b). The Commission's verdict on the Czech Republic's application was in general positive and, as such, the EU has commenced accession negotiations within a reinforced accession process (March 1998). Here we examine some of the more problematic conclusions that may well form the basis of accession negotiations for the immediate future.

Political criteria

Though the Czech Republic satisfies the Commission on political criteria in that it has the characteristics of a democracy with stable political institutions that function smoothly, guaranteeing the rule of law, human rights and respect for and protection of minorities, there remain a series of problems in the application of the democratic process. With regard to the functioning of the Czech judiciary, the situation constitutes a major challenge for the country's integration into the EU. The courts are deemed to be overcrowded, and 'the average length of commercial law proceedings ... exceeds three years' (Commission 1997b:10). These problems are seen to stem from inadequate experience of the judges, who have to apply legislation which is often totally new and for which there is frequently no established legal precedent (see also Chapter 4). The three other important caveats relate to the lustration law, discrimination against the Roma population and access of the press to administrative documents.

Since the publication of the Opinion, the government has undertaken to cancel the lustration law by the year 2000, when a new civil service law will be in operation; a freedom of information law is in preparation, and a series of recommendations have been adopted by the Cabinet to improve the position of the Roma.

Economic criteria

Applying economic criteria, the Opinion regards the Czech Republic as having 'a functioning market economy, and it should be able to cope with competitive pressure and market forces within the Union in the medium term, and provided that change at the enterprise level is accelerated' (Commission 1997b:13).

However, the Opinion statement notes a deteriorating economic situation attributed to the lack of restructuring, a shortage of skilled labour and the fact that corporate governance is not always totally effective, partly as a result of the privatisation method used. The Commission was also not convinced that all market institutions are sufficiently strong and are completely operational. In particular, the financial and capital markets, both of which are essential features of a market economy, and public administration need to develop further. Regulation of the financial markets is considered inadequate and, in particular, the banking sector is not competitive and requires structural reform, the main problems being bad debts, the lack of competition and transparency, inadequate legislation and supervision, the interownership of banks and investment funds and under-capitalisation. Our own analysis confirms these criticisms, especially in the light of inconclusive election results (1998) that may further delay rapid reform measures, such as effective stock-market regulation, and measures to privatise the banks and sever the links between the banks, investment funds and privatised enterprises (Telicka 1998).

Capacity to take on the obligations of membership

While the Commission found in a medium-term assessment that Czech capacity to cope with membership obligations in most areas was achievable, there was particular concern for its capability in meeting the *acquis* in agriculture, environment and energy. In agriculture, efforts are needed to meet the implementation and enforcement of veterinary and phytosanitary requirements, and administrative structures to implement the CAP and further restructuring to improve its competitive capacity. Eight problems were identified in the field of energy: the adjustment of existing monopolies, import and export issues, access to networks, cross-subsidisation in pricing, below-EU targets for oil stocks, continued state intervention in solid fuels and uranium, energy efficiency and fuel quality standards. The environment and consumer protection were the two issues considered in terms of life quality. The Commission was very critical of environmental protection, while acknowledging the progress made so far. There is inadequate implementation and enforcement of the legislation, and major investment is required for the water, air and waste sectors. Effective compliance with EU standards would only be achievable in the long term and with massive political commitment.

There remained some concern over the ability of the various agencies in the field of border policing. Difficulty may arise if the Czech Republic's border is also the boundary of the EU, as it will be if Slovak accession is not forthcoming, and additional assistance (both financial and technical) will be required to enforce border controls. Tightening of the Czech/Slovak borders may well create new tensions between old partners, only avoidable if 'the Slovaks accede at the same time or as soon as possible' (Commission 1997b).

We have already mentioned the Commission's particular concern with regard to bank restructuring. To meet the *acquis* in the medium term, the operation of the central bank needs to be changed to prohibit its use to finance deficits. Privatisation and further competition in banking need to continue, together with supervision in financial markets.

The final element of the *acquis* relates to the administrative capacity of the Czech Republic. In this field the Commission made a number of recommendations, including the substantial modernisation of public administration, the requirement for an adequate legal basis for the civil service, the need to retain able public administrators (since many had left to work in the private sector), and vigilance against corruption. 'Significant and sustained effort' would be needed to administer the *acquis* in the medium term, a recommendation not dissimilar from others made to most of the CEEC 10.

Attitudes in the Czech Republic towards EU membership

'Although the majority of people want to be part of the EU, what you see is a very provincial country which finds it hard to cope with foreigners on its territory' (Pehe 1998). The evidence from a variety of public opinion polls suggests that there is a stable consensus on the desirability of EU membership. Joining the EU is the most prominent foreign policy goal and, for the majority, is seen as the best way forward for securing the well-being of Czech society. The consensus was already apparent in November 1993, when a national opinion poll showed that 85 per cent of the adult population supported EC membership (Illner 1994). A positive attitude existed among all groups of the population with the exception of the extreme left; stronger support was apparent among the better-educated, the better-off and the right wing.

The same features are also found in the 1995 National Survey (Nedomová and Kostelecký 1997). On the entrance of the Czech Republic into the EU, 50 per cent of respondents were in favour, 18 per cent were against and the remaining 32 per cent did not know. Attitudes towards the EU are influenced by the political orientation of the respondents; those on the left of the political spectrum generally expressed stronger reservations towards the EU than the rest of the population. Older and less educated people are also much more opposed to the idea of joining the EU. Nedomová and Kostelecký (1997) consider that different images of the EU are held by the population at large compared with the political elite. The majority of right-wing politicians perceive the EU as a symbol of successful capitalism, despite their accusation that the EU is 'an anti-liberal strong-hold of social engineering and bureaucracy, functioning under the influence of different kinds of socialists' (Nedomová and Kostelecký 1997:91). The majority of the left-oriented political elite tend to view the EU as a well-managed organisation upholding high social standards for employees, whereas a substantial part of the left-oriented respondents view the EU as serving the interests of multinational capital – a view which may be remaindered from years of Communist propaganda.

Public attitudes towards accession to the EU may still be intuitive, and based on the idea that membership is not only the ultimate reward of success and international recognition but a guarantee of the successful completion of the transformation, with little awareness of the precise costs and benefits of membership. The risks seen by the Czechs relate to the dangers posed to the business community of allowing completely free access to the Czech market and traditional anxieties about German domination.

A specifically Czech concern is ambivalence towards the prospect of a 'borderless Europe', the unwanted inflow of migration from the East and South as well as the West; Czechs are concerned that affluent Western Europeans will buy up land and bid up the price of apartments and houses, especially in Prague (Boguszakova and Gabal 1996). However, Central Europeans, with their keen sense of history and memories of repeated 'betrayal' by the West (at Munich in 1938, Yalta in 1945 and the Prague Spring of 1968), feel that refusal of admission to the EU would constitute yet another betrayal.

The latest survey of public opinion towards the EU published in March 1998 in the *Central and Eastern Eurobarometer* (Commission 1998) shows that opinions have remained stable and positive in the Czech Republic. It also reveals that the Czechs' general opinion of the EU is well below the average, and they show an above-average concern about the cost of EU membership for some groups of the population. This is linked to a growing pessimism about the efficacy of the market economy and a general concern about the future of the country.

Conclusion

Since the euphoria of the 'velvet revolution', followed by the traumas of the 'velvet divorce', the Czech Republic has made valiant efforts to prepare itself for its return to Europe, its foremost foreign policy objective. It has yielded to exacting adaptation pressures to ensure the compatibility of its economic, political and legislative structures and processes with the supranational norms and standards of the EU. In some respects it has shown greater tenacity and spirit of purpose than that of the validating organisation to which it aspires to belong. Enlargement poses a challenge to both sides and requires two-way adaptation. As Illner so rightly observes, 'the cooperation and integration of the Czech Republic into Western European structures cannot be based on a passive adaptive model according to which the new potential member should merely catch up with the EU and its standards' (1994:30).

Seeking membership of the EU has not been problem-free in the economic sphere. The liberal trade regime required by the EA left the Czech Republic open to an influx of imports competing with domestic output and subject to speculative flows culminating in the currency crisis of 1997.[33] The political and economic events apparent in the Czech Republic since mid-1997 have cast considerable doubts on the particular strategy of economic reform unleashed by Klaus, which plunged the country into a period of growing uncertainty of direction and destination. There is no greater testimony to this than the results of the latest *Central and Eastern Eurobarometer* (*CEEB*, March 1998) of public opinion towards the market economy. Of all the EU candidate countries, only the Czech Republic shows a clearly negative trend from 1990 (*CEEB7*) to 1997 (*CEEB8*). The year 1997 saw 'a sharp rise in critical voices (*CEEB7*: 41 per cent, *CEEB8*: 50 per cent) and a concomitant drop of positive ones (*CEEB7*: 42 per cent; *CEEB8*: 28 per cent) (Commission 1997a, 1998). The Czechoslovakian and Czech experiences provide a clear object lesson to other transforming countries on how the application of rigorous market-led policies is no guarantee for either domestic economic stability or, as previously assumed, a trouble-free ride to EU membership.

Notes

1 Thomas Masaryk, a Slovak philosopher, convinced the Allies that it made sense to unite the Czechs and Slovaks in a single nation because of close ethnic, cultural and linguistic similarities. His view was not universally accepted (see Bombik and Samson 1997).

2 In 1918 the population of Czechoslovakia comprised roughly 50 per cent Czechs, 15 per cent Slovaks, 25 per cent ethnic Germans and 6 per cent Hungarians (Bombik and Samson 1997).

3 Charter 77 was a statement of human rights and their abuse in Czechoslovakia during 'normalisation'. It attracted international attention and, together with Havel's talents as a playwright, made him a leading figure during political transition.

4 Komarek was the first deputy Prime Minister in charge of economic affairs in December 1989. He resigned from the Communist Party on 8 January 1990 and in April 1991 joined the Social Democratic Party (Jeffries 1993:378).

5 Following the adoption of austerity measures in April 1997, public disenchantment with the state of the economy and the government led to a fall of 10 percentage points for the Civic Democrats, compared with a 9 per cent lead established by the opposition Social Democrats.

6 The scandal included reports that investors had channelled money into the party's secret Swiss bank accounts in return for favourable treatment in privatisation deals.

7 The rate of unemployment in the Czech Republic reflects the tight labour market conditions and a failure of former state-owned enterprises to shed surplus labour. It is evidence of the priority given to privatisation rather than the restructuring of industry (Charap and Zemplinerova 1993).

8 Care needs to be taken when using any economic data; this is especially true of statistics from countries in transition. Their reliability makes any analysis of the data a precarious task. Only the main trends can be used with any degree of confidence (Zecchini 1997).

9 In 1980, 35.6 per cent of Czech exports and 43.7 per cent of imports were accounted for by trade with the Soviet Union. This trade increased to 43.7 per cent and 46 per cent in 1985 and 43.1 per cent and 40.3 per cent, respectively, in 1988 (OECD 1990:50).

10 In 1990 CSFR exports to the OECD area increased by 17.7 per cent, and imports by 33 per cent from the previous year. In 1991 exports and imports increased by 35.7 and 29 per cent and in 1992 by 39.6 and 71.4 per cent, respectively. Easier access to OECD markets enabled this reorientation of trade, granted in part by the EA's trade provisions (Bakos 1993; OECD 1993:122).

11 The number of foreign trade organisations increased from 'several dozen' in 1990 to more than 26,000 exporters and 46,000 importers by the end of 1993 (Ministry of Industry and Trade of the Czech Republic 1995:11).

12 Positive real interest rates and a zero growth of the money supply; budget surplus of at least 1–1.5 per cent in 1990 and 2–2.5 per cent in 1991, together with cuts in subsidies, were the targets set by macro-economic policy. Monetary control has been successful; the failure to meet budget targets can

in part be explained by the receipt of only 75 per cent of anticipated tax revenues (Dyba and Svejnar 1991; Gros and Steinherr 1995; Adam 1993).

13 A successful privatisation programme would also result in political gains as a demonstration of Czechoslovakia's determination to establish a fully fledged market economy.

14 Small-scale privatisation resulted in the disposal by public auction of 22,212 small state-owned businesses, principally retail and service outlets, hotels, restaurants and small workshops, with a total book value in the region of Kč 23.6 billion. Of the 22,212 businesses, 15,225 units were disposed of in 1991, 6,312 in 1992 and 855 in 1993.

15 The first round of auctions was reserved for domestic investors. Foreigners were given the right to participate in subsequent rounds. Accusations of manipulation by organised gangs or collusion agreements at auctions have been made (Mejstrik and Sojka 1994). Restitution and small-scale privatisation helped to develop a real-estate market in the Czech Republic and led to the emergence of a differential price or rent surface (Sýkora 1993).

16 Controversy surrounded the 1948 cut-off date for restitution. In 1994 restitution was amended to extend the process to Jewish families whose properties were taken by the Nazis in the Second World War. Thirty thousand industrial and administrative buildings, forests and agricultural plots, and seventy thousand commercial and residential units have been returned to their original owners or their heirs. It is estimated that the total value of assets returned in the period 1990–93 was between 70 and 120 billion crowns (Ministry of Industry and Trade of the Czech Republic 1995).

17 A minimum of Kč 1 million of registered capital and just two rules regulated the formation of funds: each fund had to spread its investment over the shares of at least ten joint-stock companies, and there was a 20 per cent ceiling on each fund's interest in any single company.

18 A good introduction to their work and its impact can be found in P. J. Devine, N. Lee, R. M. Jones and W. J. Tyson (1993), *An Introduction to Industrial Economics*, London, Routledge.

19 See for example, W. J. Baumol (1959), *Business Behaviour, Value and Growth*, London, Macmillan; R. Marris (1964), *The Economic Theory of 'Managerial Capitalism'*, London, Macmillan; O. Williamson (1963), Managerial discretion and business behaviour, *American Economic Review*, 53, 1032–57; H. A. Simon (1959), A behavioural model of rational choice, *Quarterly Journal of Economics*, 49, 253–83; R. M. Cyert and J. G. March (1963), *A Behavioural Theory of the Firm*, London, Prentice Hall.

20 After much debate over the efficacy of incentives to investors, the Czech Republic has now reversed its position (Anderson 1998a).

21 The largest investments to date have included Asea Brown Boveri, a Swiss-Swedish engineering group, in 1990; the German car producer Volkswagen in 1991; Nestlé and BSN (the Swiss and French food groups) in 1992; Philip Morris (an American tobacco and foods group) in 1993; KPN and Swiss Telecom (a Dutch–Swiss telecommunications consortium) in 1995; IOC (an oil consortium including Shell, Agip, Conoco and Total), also in 1995; and the largest British investment, in electricity, made by National Power in 1997 (Boland 1994; Anderson 1997b).

22 'The takeover by Europe's biggest carmaker of Skoda has triggered a big effort to restructure and modernise the Czech automotive components industry and has already led to the formation of more than 40 joint ventures between western components producers and Czech suppliers and the setting up of 15 greenfield site component plants' (Done 1996a).

23 A shift was discerned from the earlier case of greater involvement in governance and control of the enterprises by the investment funds. The power to change the top layers of managers, however, was limited by a reported shortage of good managers, limited information being released by managers and legislation preventing an investment company from having more than a 20 per cent stake in an enterprise. The cross-ownership of the banks provides an incentive for investment companies to cooperate to strengthen their position with respect to the companies in which they have shares, thus circumventing the 20 per cent rule.

24 The proportion of bad assets, those on which neither interest nor principal has been paid for thirty days or more, is 20 per cent, 23.5 per cent and 32.7 per cent for IPB, Ceska Sporitelna and Komercni Banka, respectively (Anderson 1997a).

25 The rescue of one small bank by the state has compounded the problem of unwise lending. It is reported that there is a strong belief that state intervention will be available to prevent the collapse of banks, despite the government repeatedly stating that this is not the case (Boland 1996a). Capital adequacy levels of the three large banks are 8.23 per cent for IPB, 9.9 per cent for Ceska Sporitelna and 10.23 per cent for Komercni Banka, just above the required 8 per cent level (Anderson 1997a).

26 Much of the trading that took place did so off-market. The lack of regulation allowed parties to withdraw from or dishonour a deal. The lack of reliable information about trades and the enterprises themselves contributed to the 'murky' trading environment (Wagstyl and Anderson 1998b; Boland and Robinson 1996).

27 At March 1996, only five stocks were sufficiently liquid to enable continuous trading, these being Komercni Banka, Ceska Sporitelna, CEZ, SPT Telecom and KB Investicni Fond (Done 1996b).

28 Piecemeal reforms to improve the performance of the capital market included quarterly financial reporting for the top thirty-five stocks and half-yearly reports being required for the rest (Done 1996b). In April 1996 measures to protect minority shareholders were enacted (Boland 1996a). Despite such measures, the Prague exchange was outperformed by Budapest and Warsaw in 1996 and 1997.

29 Wagnerová (1996) argues that 'collectivisation not only attacked capitalist power but also fundamentally limited the power of men', since the removal of their property deprived them of an important attribute of their social dominance.

30 This is illustrated by the way in which Volkswagen's corporate strength wielded asymmetrical bargaining power over the Czech state concerning the joint Volkswagen–Skoda venture between 1990 and 1993, and the subsequent increase in the dependence of Czech automobile parts producers on Skoda–Volkswagen.

31 The majority of Czechs are hostile to the opening of any dialogue with
    Germany on the Sudetan German issue. The dispute has served to impede
    otherwise generally harmonious relationships between the two countries, but
    the legacy has raised complications at the level of EU integration, in the form
    of a petition from the Sudetan German deportees to the EP requesting that the
    Czech and Slovakian applications for membership should not be accepted
    until their claims have been satisfied (Leff 1997).
32 In 1993 Slovakia accounted for 17 per cent of Czech imports and 21 per cent
    of Czech exports, falling to less than 10 per cent and 15 per cent, respectively,
    in 1996 (Commission 1997b).
33 A more recent example that coincided with the opening of accession negotia-
    tions (March 1998) related to Czech imposition of a 24,000 tonne annual
    import quota on EU apples, claiming protection of domestic producers. EU
    ministers responded by agreeing to suspend preferential import tariffs on
    Czech pork, poultry and fruit juice – 'a lovers' tiff before getting engaged'
    (Joseph Tosovsky).

References

Adam, J. (1993), Transformation to a market economy in the former
    Czechoslovakia, *Europe–Asia Studies*, 45:4, 627–45.
Anderson, R. (1997a), Banking: spotlight on sell-offs, *Financial Times*, 1
    December.
Anderson, R. (1997b), Brewing: merger fever hits, *Financial Times*, 1 December.
Anderson, R. (1998a), New incentives for investors, *Financial Times*, 30 April.
Anderson, R. (1998b), Limbo likely to continue, *Financial Times*, 14 May.
Anderson, R. and Done, K. (1997), A year of growing uncertainty: dangers may
    still lie ahead for the coalition government after the economic difficulties of
    1997, *Financial Times*, 1 December.
Anderson, R. and Wagstyl, S. (1999), Czech Republic: short-list for state sale
    expected, *Financial Times*, 11 January.
Bakos, G. C. (1993), After COMECON: a free trade area in Central Europe?,
    Europe–Asia Studies, 45:6, 1025–44.
Banerjee, B. (1994), Czech transformation enters new phase, *IMF Survey*, 24
    January, 17–21.
Berle, A. and Means, G. (1932), *The Modern Corporation and Private Property*,
    London, Macmillan.
Blejer, M. I. and Coricelli, F. (1995), *The Making of Economic Reform in Eastern
    Europe: Conversations with Leading Reformers in Poland, Hungary and the
    Czech Republic*, Aldershot, Edward Elgar.
Boguszakova, M. and Gabal, I. (1996), The Czech Republic, in Smoke, R. (ed.),
    Perceptions of Security, Manchester, Manchester University Press, 64–71.
Boland, V. (1994), Setbacks lead to reassessment, *Financial Times*, 19 December.
Boland, V. (1995a), Greater transparency on the way – while trading is slow,
    stock market mechanisms are under scrutiny, *Financial Times*, 2 June.
Boland, V. (1996a), Big need to tackle problem loans, *Financial Times*, 26 April.
Boland, V. (1996b), The problems run deep, *Financial Times*, 26 April.

Boland, V. (1997), Stock market: looking beyond recent turmoil, *Financial Times*, 1 December.

Boland, V. and Robinson, A. (1996), There are too many markets, *Financial Times*, 6 December.

Bombik, S. and Samson, I. (1997), Slovakia, in R. Smoke (ed.), *Perceptions of Security*, Manchester, Manchester University Press, 146–63.

Borish, M. S., Ding, W. and Noel, M. (1997), The evolution of the state-owned banking sector during transition in Central Europe, *Europe–Asia Studies*, 49:7, 1187–208.

Brom, K. and Orenstein, M. (1994), The privatised sector in the Czech Republic: government and bank control in a transitional economy, *Europe–Asia Studies*, 46:6, 893–928.

Bruce, V. (1997), The Visegrad Group: regional cooperation and European integration in post-communist Europe, in P. J. Katzenstein (ed.), *Mitteleuropa – Between Europe and Germany*, Providence and Oxford, Berghahn Books.

Capek, A. and Sazama, G. W. (1993), Czech and Slovak economic relations, *Europe–Asia Studies*, 45:2, 211–35.

Charap, J. and Zemplinerova, A. (1993), *Restructuring in the Czech Economy*, EBRD working paper, 2, March.

Clark, E. and Soulsby, A. (1996), The re-formation of the managerial elite in the Czech Republic, *Europe–Asia Studies*, 48:2, March.

Commission (1997a), *Central and Eastern Eurobarometer*, 7, Brussels, April.

Commission (1997b), *Agenda 2000 – Commission Opinion on the Czech Republic's Application for Membership of the European Union*, 15 July.

Commission (1998), *Central and Eastern Eurobarometer*, 8, Brussels, March.

CzechInvest (1996a), *Currency, Banking, Insurance Market*, FactSheet 7, July.

CzechInvest (1996b), *Czech Republic Investment Climate*, FactSheet 1, September.

CzechInvest (1996c), *Foreign Direct Investment in the Czech Republic*, FactSheet 2, September.

Deacon, B. (1993), Social change, social problems and social policy, in S. White, J. Batt and P. G. Lewis (eds), *Developments in East European Politics*, London, Macmillan, 225–39.

Done, K. (1996a), Asian investors take the plunge, *Financial Times*, 26 April.

Done, K. (1996b), Concern over corporate disclosure, *Financial Times*, 26 April.

Done, K. (1996c), Enviable reputation for stability and progress, *Financial Times*, 26 April.

Done, K. (1997), Foreign investment: need to build on early success, *Financial Times*, 1 December.

Duncan, S. (1996), Obstacles to a successful equal opportunities policy in the European Union, *European Journal of Women's Studies*, 3, 399–422.

Dyba, K. and Svejnar, J. (1991), Czechoslovakia: recent economic developments and prospects, *American Economic Review Papers and Proceedings*, May, 81:2, 185–90.

East, R. and Pontin, J. (1997), *Revolution and Change in Central and Eastern Europe*, London, Pinter.

EBRD (1996), *Transition Report*, London, European Bank for Reconstruction and Development.

Ferge, Z. (1997), Women and social transformation in Central-Eastern Europe, *Czech Sociological Review*, 5:2, 159–78.

Gorzelak, G., Jalowiecki, B. and Kuklinski, A. (eds) (1994), *Eastern and Central Europe 2000. Final Report*, Brussels, European Commission.

Gros, D. and Steinherr, A. (1995), *Winds of Change: Economic Transition in Central and Eastern Europe*, Harlow, Longman.

Had, M. and Handl, V. (1996), The Czech Republic, in R. Smoke (ed.), *Perceptions of Security*, Manchester, Manchester University Press, 129–45.

Hall, P. (1993), Forces shaping urban Europe, *Urban Studies*, 30:6, 883–98.

Havelková, H. (1993), A few pre-feminist thoughts, in N. Funk and M. Mueller (eds), *Gender Politics and Post-Communism*, London, Routledge, 62–73.

Heitlinger, A. (1993), The impact of the transition from communism on the status of women in the Czech and Slovak Republics, in N. Funk and M. Mueller (eds), *Gender Politics and Post-Communism*, London, Routledge, 95–108.

Illner, M. (1994), The international context of Czech transformation, *Czech Sociological Review*, 2:1, 21–34.

Innes, A. (1993), Political developments in the new Czech Republic, *Policy Studies*, 14:4, 22–30.

Jeffries, I. (1993), *Socialist Economies and the Transition to the Market: A Guide*, London, Routledge.

Jerábek, H. and Zich, F. (1997), The Czech Republic: internalisation and dependency, in P. J. Katzenstein (ed.), *Mitteleuropa – Between Europe and Germany*, Providence and Oxford, Berghahn Books.

Kaiser, R. J. (1995), Czechoslovakia: the disintegration of a binational state, in G. Smith (ed.), *Federalism: The Multiethnic Challenge*, Harlow, Longman.

Kenway, P. and Klvacova, E. (1996), The web of cross-ownership among Czech financial intermediaries: an assessment, *Europe–Asia Studies*, 48:5, 797–809.

Kettle, S. (1995), Of money and morality, *Transition*, 15 March, 36–9.

Leff, C. S. (1997), *The Czech and Slovak Republics, Nation versus State*, Oxford, Westview.

Mejstrik, M. and Sojka, M. (1994), Privatisation and regulatory change: the case of Czechoslovakia, in M. Moran and T. Prosser (eds), *Privatisation and Regulatory Change in Europe*, Buckingham and Philadelphia, Open University Press.

Ministry of Industry and Trade of the Czech Republic (1995), *Czech Republic Country Profile*, Prague.

Nedomová, A. and Kostelecký, K. (1997), The Czech national identity, *Czech Sociological Review*, 5:1, 79–92.

OECD (1990), The economies of Central and Eastern Europe, *Economic Outlook*, 48, December, 47–52.

OECD (1992), Economic developments outside the OECD, *Economic Outlook*, 51, June, 41–5.

OECD (1993), Developments in selected non-OECD countries, *Economic Outlook*, 53, June, 119–26.

OECD (1996), Czech Republic, *Economic Outlook*, 60, December, 84–6.

Offe, C. (1991), Capitalism by democratic design? Democracy theory facing the triple transition in East Central Europe, *Social Research*, 58, 866–92.

Orenstein, M. (1995), Transitional social policy in the Czech Republic and Poland, *Czech Sociological Review*, 3:2, 179–96.

Pehe, J. (1995), A leader in political stability and economic growth, *Transition*, 1:1, 30 January, 29–33.

Pehe, J. (1997), Czechs fall from their ivory tower, *Transition*, August, 22–7.

Pehe, J. (1998), The disappointments of democracy, *Transition*, 5:5, May, 38–42.

Reisch, A. A. (1993), The Central European initiative: to be or not to be?, *RFE/RL Research Report*, 2:34, 30–7.

Rhys, V. (1995), Social security developments: a return to reality, *Czech Sociological Review*, 3:2, 197–208.

Robinson, A. (1994), Towards a state of grace – a pro-business government has achieved political stability while maintaining economic growth, *Financial Times*, 19 December.

Robinson, A. (1995), Source of liquidity – profile: Sporitelna, the top Czech savings bank, *Financial Times*, 2 June.

Siklová, J. (1993), Are women in Central and Eastern Europe conservative?, in N. Funk and M. Mueller (eds), *Gender Politics and Post-Communism*, London, Routledge.

Simoneti, M. (1993), A comparative review of privatisation strategies in four former Socialist countries, *Europe–Asia Studies*, 45:1, 79–102.

Smoke, R. (ed.) (1996), *Perceptions of Security*, Manchester, Manchester University Press.

Stolze, F. (1997), The Central and East European currency phenomenon reconsidered, *Europe–Asia Studies*, 49:1, 23–41.

Sykora, L. (1993), City in transition: the role of rent gaps in Prague's revitalisation, *Tijdschrift voor Economic en Sociale Geografie*, 84:4, 281–93.

Takla, L. (1994), The relationship between privatisation and the reform of the banking sector: the case of the Czech Republic and Slovakia, in S. Estrin (ed.), *Privatisation in Central and Eastern Europe*, Harlow, Longman.

Telicka, P. (1998), For Czechs, EU application no longer a breeze, Central Europe Online, http://www.central europe.

Vecernik, J. (1996), *Markets and People, The Czech Reform Experience in a Comparative Perspective*, Aldershot, Avebury.

Wagnerová, A. (1996), Emancipation and ownership, *Czech Sociological Review*, 4:1, 101–8.

Wagstyl, S. and Anderson, R. (1998a), Czech securities watchdog starts to bare its teeth, *Financial Times*, 12 May.

Wagstyl, S. and Anderson, R. (1998b), Counting the cost of the golden years, *Financial Times*, 14 May.

Wilde, L. (1993), *Modern European Socialism*, Aldershot, Dartmouth.

Winiecki, J. (1994), East-Central Europe: a regional survey – the Czech Republic, Hungary, Poland and Slovakia in 1993, *Europe–Asia Studies*, 46:5, 709–34.

Zecchini, S. (1997), *Lessons from the Economic Transition: Central and Eastern Europe in the 1990s*, Dordrecht, Kluwer Academic.

The Slovak Republic: on the edge of Europe

This chapter examines the perilous condition of Slovak democracy since 1990 and the impact that political actions of successive governments have had on EU relations. According to Miháliková (1996), the main problems that characterise Slovak politics since independence concern: democratic transformation and disputes over representation; the relationships between state institutions (the President, the Prime Minister and the Constitutional Court); managing ethnic minority problems; the establishment of a market economy; the determination of foreign policy orientation and external security arrangements; and the creation of a civil society. The nature of the debate and its outcomes in several of these areas will be examined in this chapter.

Leadership, elections and party politics (1990–98)

Since the velvet revolution, Slovak politics has been dominated by Vladimir Meciar, who has held office for most of the period since 1990.[1] Stripped of power twice, each time he managed to return and exercise an increasingly authoritarian political style of leadership. As the self-defined champion of Slovak interests, his instinctive leadership style is a mixture of nationalism and populism. Despite numerous scandals attached to his political career, he has managed to retain a flair for political manoeuvring and control of the levers of power (Kettle 1996). He rebukes those who criticise both him and his policies, labelling them as damaging to Slovakia's interests. Meciar has benefited from being surrounded by both docile coalition partners and an ineffective opposition, the leaders of which tend to be urban intellectuals who cannot match his charisma and attraction in a largely rural country. He is viewed with suspicion by Western leaders, from whom he has attracted strong criticism for his disrespect for democratic procedures, and he is rarely invited to meet key Western leaders at an official level, which has contributed to Slovakia's

increasing isolation. The other leading actor in Slovak politics is Michal
Kovac, President from 1993 to 1998 and Meciar's most significant and
persistent critic.

Prior to independence and as a result of the June 1990 elections, the
Slovak republican government consisted of members of Public Against
Violence (VPN) in coalition with the Christian Democratic Movement
(KDH), headed by Ján Carnogursky, and the much smaller Democrat
Party. The VPN disintegrated over the question of nationalism and the
state of the federation. Prime Minister Meciar distanced himself from
VPN members and split the group to form a Movement for a Democratic
Slovakia (HZDS), which became the republic's most popular party.
Meciar's government fell in April 1991, when he was removed from his
post by the Slovak National Council's presidium on grounds of political
misbehaviour. He was replaced as Prime Minister by Ján Carnogursky,
supported by the rump of the VPN. Whilst Czech politics became more
secular and focused on economic issues, nationalist issues were on the
ascendant in Slovakia, successfully mobilised by Meciar's HZDS, which
convincingly won the June 1992 elections.[2] Meciar was now the first
Prime Minister of a *de facto* independent Slovakia, many citizens of
which, according to opinion polls, were not fully convinced that they
wanted an independent state (East and Pontin 1997).

Following the formal dissolution of Czechoslovakia (December 1992),
discord within the HZDS emerged over Meciar's abrasive and confronta-
tional leadership style and over the selection of the first President.[3] By
March 1993, Meciar's government had lost its majority, following the
defection of several disenchanted HZDS deputies to the opposition and
the withdrawal of its junior coalition partner, the Slovak National Party
(SNS).[4] The HZDS continued to rule as a minority government until
October, when it reached a new coalition agreement with the SNS. By
February 1994, Meciar's feud with President Kovac was public property
and Meciar experienced additional conflicts with Foreign Minister Josef
Moravcik. Moravcik, who claimed that Meciar had utilised the privatisation process for the financial benefit of the HZDS, defected and formed a
new party, the Democratic Union of Slovakia (DUS). The intervention of
President Kovac, who accused Meciar of populism, incompetence and
anti-democratic behaviour, contributed to Meciar losing a no-confidence
vote in the National Council and his loss of office for a second time on 11
March 1994. Moravcik became Prime Minister in a temporary grand
coalition government, comprising a broad left–right coalition of three
parties with Carnogursky's KDH on the right, the reformed Post-
Communist Party of the Democratic Left (SDL) on the left and defectors
from HZDS and SNS in the centre. The economic policy goal of this six-
month administration centred on stimulating marketisation and
privatisation through a second wave of voucher privatisation, meeting

with approval from the IMF and the extension of credits in July 1994 (Leff 1997).

President Kovac hoped that Meciar would not be returned to power; however, in subsequent elections, the HZDS exceeded expectations and obtained almost 35 per cent of the vote, enabling Meciar to form his third government. The HZDS was supported by a coalition of the nationalist SNS and the left–nationalist Workers' Association of Slovakia (ZRS, a recently formed breakaway party of the SDL), the coalition being collectively dubbed the 'red-brown' coalition by the centre-right opposition. The appointment of a ZRS deputy as privatisation minister provided a signal of the intended direction of economic policy – the government quickly halted Moravcik's mass privatisation programme. The new coalition, with 83 seats in Parliament, enabled Meciar to consolidate his position as Prime Minister, enabling him, as a first act of vengeance, to stage the 'Night of the Long Knives' of 3–4 November, which involved seizing control of key areas of political power through the sacking of the Chief Prosecutor and the Director of Slovak Television, and installing his own deputies to key parliamentary committees.

These and other actions taken by the Meciar government led to increasing disquiet on behalf of the international community as it became evident that the government's controversial domestic policies and general political behaviour were distant from acceptable democratic practice, so diminishing the chances of straightforward entry into Western multilateral organisations. Despite repeated external criticism, the ruling coalition continued to adopt policies that have divided Slovak society. Between 1994 and 1995, the emphasis was on controlling parliamentary and state organs and the electronic media. In 1996, the coalition continued to exert control on local administrations, foundations, universities and cultural institutions (Fisher 1997).

One of the most significant and controversial political conflicts in the period after the 1994 elections was the struggle between Meciar and President Kovac, which had been incipient since Kovac's call in December 1993 for Meciar's resignation. Once back in office, Meciar embarked on a persistent campaign to remove the President from office. In May 1995 the President experienced several votes of no confidence, and was portrayed as a betrayer of Slovakia's interests because of his criticism of government policies in domestic and international settings. In April 1995 Kovac reluctantly agreed to hand over control of the Secret Service to the government; Kovac denied Meciar's claim that the Secret Service had been used to spy on him. Also, in June 1995, further presidential powers were lost through the transfer by the National Council of the function of head of the armed forces. In 1996 the government passed a vote of no confidence in the President, but Meciar failed to persuade Parliament to do likewise. Meciar accused the President of using his office to lend support to the opposition which had been excluded from any effective involvement in supervising government activity, including representation in the leadership of parliamentary committees. Until late 1997, for example, no opposition member was appointed to panels overseeing the Secret Service.[5] The President also publicly commented on the extent of government control over the media; that the anti-government press suffers from harassment; and that the independence of the public prosecutors has been compromised. Meciar has kept tight control on the state media and much of the private media by applying economic pressures on opposition newspapers, some of which have been purchased by Meciar supporters. Other developments to cause concern included the enactment in 1996, under pressure from the extreme right of the ruling coalition, to restrict freedom of speech, the autonomy of universities and the right to speak minority languages, and the impedence of the work of NGOs (Done 1996b; see also Chapter 4).

The pariah state?

Meciar's persistent campaign to remove President Kovac has created the potential for a major constitutional crisis, and has been a contributory factor to the issuing of diplomatic notes from both the EU and the USA to the Slovak government since 1995, 'expressing concern about possible actions against the president of the republic which could negatively affect the development of democracy in the Slovak Republic'. Despite recommendations made by the EU in a number of démarches and declarations, the struggle continues and, as we shall see, there has been no noticeable improvement. In the theatrical excitement of Slovakian politics the key danger is that 'both Meciar and the opposition see their opponents not merely as political rivals but as threats to Slovakia itself. The opposition fears that the pattern of his actions represents a latent authoritarian agenda. Meciar himself regards this opposition as wholly illegitimate' (Leff 1997: 156).

Slovak politics is marked by a high degree of polarisation, one of the key issues being not whether the goal of European integration is desirable, but the culpability of each side in the political struggle for damaging Slovakia's chances (Henderson 1997). Mihálikova (1996) argues that there are two sharply contrasting views in elite and public discourse for explaining Slovakia's external image. One view, which is promoted by the present ruling coalition, may be referred to as a 'syndrome of persecution', whereby criticisms of Slovakia and warnings issued by international organisations such as the Council of Europe about 'anti-democratic' behaviour reflect an international anti-Slovak conspiracy. These criticisms involve a wide variety of interests, including foreign capital, which seeks revenge for its exclusion from the privatisation process; the Hungarian state, along with the ethnic Hungarian elite and the opposition, are accused of complicity in their attempts to annex Slovak territory. It is also contended that because most of the current opposition were against independence they have no right to participate in the building of the new state, reap its benefits and pontificate on domestic and foreign policy. Along with ethnic Hungarians, they constitute the political and social opposition in Slovakia's increasingly divided society. For the ruling coalition the solution to this problem lies in the creation of a more favourable external image marketed by the media, information agencies and diplomatic efforts, and through legislation limiting freedom of expression for those critical of the present regime.

The second view comes from those groups who openly debate the negative aspects of Slovakia's domestic and foreign politics and see the source of outside criticisms and warnings as arising from the ruling coalition's fundamentally undemocratic mode of political behaviour; clearly, the rules and norms of democracy have been sacrificed in order to retain political power. This view is strongly opposed by the ruling elite, who see themselves as the custodians of the independent and democratic Slovakian state and firmly believe that their interpretation (or redefinition) of democratic principles is justified in upholding the interests of Slovakian sovereignty. Supporters of this view see the solution requiring the adoption of respect for democratic principles and the rule of law and greater clarity in Slovakia's domestic and foreign policy intentions. Soon after independence it became obvious that the divisions causing conflict within Czechoslovakia were being transferred to the independent Slovakia. 'Today, this country is so deeply divided that it is reminiscent of the tensions between Czechs and Slovaks during the time of the federation' (Simecka 1997:16).

A recent manifestation of a lack of respect for democratic procedures in Slovakia is the government's disregard for the Constitutional Court's decision regarding the May 1997 referendum on future membership of NATO and direct elections of the President by popular vote rather than by parliamentary vote. On Meciar's instruction, the Interior Minister, in defiance of the court's ruling, ordered the printing of ballot papers without the question on the direct election of the President; the referendum was thereby thwarted. The Constitutional Court in February 1998 ruled that the Minister had violated citizens' constitutional rights. When Meciar took over presidential power in March, following the government's failure to choose a successor to President Kovac, Meciar cancelled the prosecution of those responsible for the referendum. For the opposition, the referendum was an opportunity to mobilise an apathetic society and demonstrate that the struggle for political power could proceed democratically. The referendum itself, along with a positive vote for membership of NATO, and the direct election of President Kovac for another term of office, to consolidate his position, could have been instrumental in changing the European image of Slovakia. By spoiling the referendum, Meciar guaranteed that Slovakia would not attain NATO membership in the near future; a majority positive response in favour of NATO would probably have meant the defeat of his coalition (Simecka 1997). The referendum crisis led to intense international criticism and contributed to the current block on accession to the EU and NATO.[6]

In response to both domestic and international concern a recent development in Slovak politics has been the consolidation of the major opposition parties into a single centre-right coalition, the Slovak Democratic Coalition (which came together in August 1997 after the referendum campaign), in an attempt finally to oust Meciar from office. Gould and Szomolanyi (1977) consider that both the government and opposition constitute 'a fragile coalition of diverse and potentially conflicting interests'. The HZDS (with an agenda based on nationalism and scepticism towards economic reform) forms the populist core of the administration. It is in a coalition with Jan Luptak's labourist breakaway faction from the SDL, known as the ZRS, and the SNS, an extreme right-wing nationalist party. In May 1994 the SNS refused party membership to ethnic minorities. Together, they have little shared interest beyond nationalism and the defence of Slovak sovereignty. The opposition coalition includes the KDH, now more nationalist and left wing, along with the liberal DUS and the Hungarian parties. The SDL, the socialist party of Peter Weiss, which is internally divided, has so far not cooperated with any other opposition party, but offers a potential link across the political divide. Gould and Szomolanyi (1997) argue that the fragmentation within each camp may enable some defection to the other side or the creation of a new centre ground; currently, the whole political elite configuration is predisposed neither to democracy nor to authoritarianism. There is potential for 'the opposition to create a middle ground, that, if prepared carefully, could provide a bridge across the chasm running through Slovakia's polarised society' (Gould and Szomolanyi 1997:74).[7]

Economic transformation

In its short period as a united, liberal and democratic country, Czechoslovakia achieved, relatively successfully, macro-economic stabilisation through the use of tight fiscal and monetary policies. Most prices were liberalised and the trade regime was opened up. Privatisation encouraged the strong growth of private-sector economic activity, resulting in reduced budgetary subsidies to state enterprises. In Czechoslovakia the emphasis of privatisation was on the transfer of ownership; issues of governance and control were of secondary importance. Prior to the separation of the republics, Slovakia had disproportionately suffered from the impact of economic transition.[8] In 1991 the rate of unemployment was more than twice as high in Slovakia as in the Czech lands (OECD 1991). As Czechoslovakia reoriented its trade towards Western markets, Slovakia's exports faced limited access for its major outputs of food products and steel. In addition to the problems facing the Czech Republic in transforming its economy – unprofitable enterprises, expensive and restricted access to bank credit, a growing budget deficit due to sharp falls in the tax base, tax avoidance and high levels of social spending – Slovakia also had to cope with the difficulty of converting its defence production into marketable output. Whilst the Czech Republic successfully attracted a substantial volume of FDI, Slovakia attracted only modest levels of foreign capital.

The return to economic growth in Slovakia was slower than in the Czech Republic. The reduction in employment of levels in excess of 20 per cent were more frequent in Slovak districts, in particular those with a high dependence on agricultural employment and recently established industry. Such dramatic falls in employment were not reported for the Czech Republic (Myant 1995). Winiecki (1994) argues that the fall in output in Slovakia was inevitable, because of the general legacy of central planning which left in its wake characteristics such as oversized stocks of inputs and over-investment, features common to all post-Communist states in Eastern Europe.

An additional factor contributed to the fall in output, namely the reduction in military expenditure. After the Second World War, Slovakia was of strategic importance to the USSR, with military production concentrated in six districts of north-western Slovakia. Following the velvet revolution and Havel's proclamation that profiting from arms sales was amoral, a federal policy of arms conversion began in earnest. Between 1988 and 1992 the production of armaments fell by 89 per cent as a result of the reduction in defence budgets after the end of the Cold War, the collapse of the Soviet Union and political and economic transformation, in addition to federal restrictions on the export of arms (Brzica *et al.* 1997). A substantial and important consequence of the contraction of arms production was the large increase in unemployment. Defence-related unemployment was of the order of 12–18 per cent in Slovakia compared with 3–8 per cent in the Czech Republic (Smith 1994).[9] The modernisation of Slovakia's arms industry has had an advantageous effect. With Slovakia's weapons becoming more compatible with the weapons held by NATO, the likelihood of future membership has possibly been enhanced.

The differing impact of economic transformation was certainly instrumental in the separation and dissolution of the Federation. An important contributory factor was the different directions the federal government believed to be appropriate for future economic reform, especially concerning the second wave of privatisation. As we saw in Chapter 8, in

Czechoslovakia and then the Czech Republic, a deliberate decision was taken to privatise first and allow restructuring to occur afterwards. Such a policy stemmed from a neoliberal acceptance of letting the market choose the winners – enterprises that would flourish – and the losers – enterprises without a hope of becoming competitive. Disillusionment with the consequences of this approach in Slovakia led to a rejection of the second wave of coupon privatisation. Dissatisfaction with coupon privatisation arose from two factors: first, the slowness with which effective ownership structures emerged; and second, a strong belief in the ability of industrial, social and regional policies to progress restructuring. Miháliková (1996) reveals the following views of Slovaks on economic transformation: 50 per cent believed that state ownership should prevail over private ownership; 74.1 per cent believed that the economy could not progress without serious state intervention and 85.6 per cent considered that the state should organise cooperation among banks, entrepreneurs, employees and trade unions. Thus the dominant view held by Slovaks is that the government should take an active role in industry (Isa 1996). Such a view gives credence to Winiecki's observation that Slovak industry on its own lacks the ability to adapt to changing patterns of demand (Winiecki 1994).[10]

In spite of these difficulties, Slovakia has achieved considerable success in economic transformation, as Table 9.1 shows. Slovakia has maintained high rates of economic growth, relatively low rates of inflation, and high but falling rates of unemployment, though the balance of payments does remain a problem. The current account deficit responded to the reintroduction of an import surcharge, and in 1998 was closer to 7 per cent of GDP. At this level it is a concern if it constrains the import of investment goods needed for economic growth. Domestic interest rates have risen sharply, thus increasing the costs of restructuring, and the 1998 election heightened uncertainty about the prospects for future reform.

The politicisation of economic transformation

Despite the successes, economic policy and, in particular, privatisation in Slovakia became increasingly politicised under Meciar's direction. The Fund for National Property (FNP) became directly supervised by the Privatisation Minister, Meciar taking over the privatisation ministry himself in June 1993; members of the presidium of the FNP were to be appointed by the government. Having been accused of abusing the privatisation process, Meciar was removed from his position as Prime Minister in March 1994. On his return to power in December 1994 an amendment to the law on large-scale privatisation allowed the FNP to sell property without Cabinet approval and without revealing the selling price to the public (Fisher 1995a).

Table 9.1 Economic indicators: Slovakia, 1993–97

	1993	1994	1995	1996	1997
Output[a]	–4.1	4.9	6.8	6.9	6.5
Inflation[b]	23.2	11.7	7.2	5.4	6.4
Unemployment[c]	14.4	14.8	13.1	12.5	11.5
Budget balance[d]	–7.5	–0.4	0.1	–1.3	–3.3
Current account balance[e]	–0.6	0.7	0.6	–1.9	–1.4

Notes:
[a] Average annual % change of real GDP.
[b] End-year % change in consumer prices.
[c] ILO definition.
[d] As % of GDP.
[e] In $ billion.
Source: OECD, various years.

Privatisation proceeded with direct sales in which most enterprises were sold to the management and workers of the enterprises concerned at preferential prices. The payment initially of 10 per cent of the value of the assets enabled sales to take place. Additionally, funds to restructure could be used to offset part of the price paid for the enterprises. In the last six months of 1995, over $1 billion of assets were sold in what has been called 'family circle privatisation'. With the aim of creating a native entre-preneurial and managerial class, Meciar's rapidly established privatisation programme involved the sale of assets to individuals loyal to him (Boland 1995). Criticism of this privatisation comes not just from public disap-pointment that the popular second wave of coupons was cancelled,[11] but from the secrecy in the timing of the sales and the lack of transparency in the prices paid for the enterprises. This lack of transparency fuelled fears that the new owners of the enterprises were not necessarily the most able. The OECD expressed concern over the lack of accountability involved and the 'risk of politicisation of enterprise management' (OECD 1996:134). The European Commission was also critical of the lack of fair-ness and transparency as well as the exclusion of foreigners from most of Slovakia's privatisations (Commission 1997b).

The political squabbles over privatisation with allegations of profiteer-ing, theft of state property and political interference (Boland 1994) have resulted in foreign investors being concerned about the future course of reform (Done 1995, 1996a) and has also led to the downgrading of Slovakia by the three leading credit-rating agencies (Done 1998b).[12] Despite having attracted lower levels of FDI than the Czech Republic, Slovakia has had some success in modernising and rehabilitating former state-owned enterprises. A good example is the oil-refining company Slovnaft. After blocking advances to form joint ventures with foreign companies, Slovnaft launched a major investment programme financed through selling shares, foreign bank loans and reinvesting profits. As a result, productivity has almost doubled (Harris 1998).

Slovakia suffers from similar problems in the sphere of banking and capital markets as those witnessed in the Czech Republic. The state banks control in excess of 70 per cent of the sector's resources, though private banks are increasing their competitiveness in the fields of new asset growth, new lending, deposit mobilisation and new capital (Borish *et al.* 1997).[13] Whilst improvements in the state-owned banking system have been made in response to increased competition, there remains a need for substantial restructuring. Restructuring is required to address bad loan portfolios,[14] lending practices, the evaluation of credit risk, fund management and the adaptation to new supervisory arrangements in relation to international accounting standards and requirements of disclosure (Borish *et al.* 1997). Tight regulation by the National Bank of Slovakia[15] has contributed to these improvements through the imposition of tough capital adequacy rules, a 10 per cent limit on shareholding in non-financial companies and a ban on lending to companies which have more than a 10 per cent stake in the bank (Anderson 1997a). However, two factors combine to make domestic banks a difficult place to find the finance necessary for enterprise restructuring; these are the very high interest rates (in the region of 16 per cent) and the Revitalisation Act (passed in May 1997). The Revitalisation Act not only encourages the non-payment of debts, but prevents banks from foreclosing on loans and allows enterprises to receive state help in order to meet their obligations.[16]

The continued independence of Slovakia's Central Bank came under threat from government plans to change the legislation governing its operation in October 1997. The proposed amendments would have allowed the government to appoint half of the members of the board of the Central Bank, increase the financing of the budget deficit, transfer approval of the National Bank's budget from the bank's board to Parliament, and remove the casting vote of the Governor of the Central Bank (Anderson 1997a). These plans were withdrawn, thus alleviating concerns over the impact on the Slovak crown, inflation and international views of Slovakia (Done 1998a).

One further problem is the chronic lack of liquidity in Slovakia's capital markets. Only a few companies are actively traded on the stock market (Brzica *et al.* 1997; Boland 1994) and 90 per cent of trading takes place outside the official systems.[17] The European Commission's Opinion takes the view that capital markets in Slovakia are fragmented and illiquid, placing much of the responsibility for this on the cancellation of the second wave of voucher privatisation and the restrictions placed on investment privatisation funds (Commission 1997b).

Slovakia's external environment

The Slovak Republic is facing international reproach, having been excluded from the first wave of countries to apply for membership of NATO and the EU; its application for membership of the OECD has also been delayed, following doubts over the transparency of the Slovak financial system and the health of its democracy. Of the four Visegrad countries seeking full membership of the EU, it is the only one to have failed to satisfy the political criteria for admission. Despite having made considerable strides to marketise its economy and the evident wish of the majority of its population to be integrated with (Western) Europe, its government seems to be destroying any chance of doing so by failing to address repeated international criticisms and warnings about its disregard for democratic norms. The velvet divorce created a changed geopolitical situation for Slovakia, rendering it more distant from the markets and investment potential of the West and closer to the politically unstable East. A large ethnic Hungarian minority and unresolved Slovak/ Hungarian animosities maintain the prospect of future conflict. With these problems, a vital challenge for Slovakia is to shed its poor external image of being the most politically unstable Visegrad country (Obrman 1992).

An ambivalent foreign policy

In 1993 the inexperienced sovereign and independent Slovakia was faced with the task of defining its own foreign policy interests. However, Slovakia inherited the international treaties and agreements of the former CSFR, which strongly influenced the orientation of policy; in particular, a Western orientation had been established through the EA entered into by the CSFR with the EC, which, after renegotiation, applied to the Czech and Slovak Republics after January 1993. Slovakia's official security and foreign policy goals were twofold – integration into Western political, economic and security structures and the development of good relations with its neighbours.

Eastward orientation – Slovakia and Russia

Despite the official Slovak stances, a sceptical view of and a high level of uncertainty regarding Slovakia's foreign policy has developed in Western political circles. It was felt that Slovakia did not display full identification with the West and that it was attempting to establish a balance between Eastern and Western interests. One source of Western confusion concerning Slovakia's lack of foreign policy identity came from the views expressed by individual representatives of Meciar's coalition partners, such as Klement Kolmick, the former Deputy Chairman of the Workers' Union of Slovakia, and Josef Slota, the anti-Hungarian and anti-Semitic leader of the Slovak National Party. Both of these political leaders made radical anti-NATO and EU statements in pre-election discussions in 1994 (Rehak and Kirillov 1995).

Bombik and Samson (1996) describe three domestic perspectives on Slovakia's importance to the rest of the world, which arise from its sensitive geographical position after the collapse of the bipolar world and which have influenced Slovakian foreign policy and security analysis. First, the notion of Slovakia as a bridge between East and West, based on the belief that Central Europe, and Slovakia in particular, has a unique and major geopolitical advantage which is marketable to both East and West. Second, there are those who see Slovakia acting as a neutral or nuclear-free zone. The third security concept is that of Slovakia as a buffer zone between the West and the two nuclear powers to the East, Russia and Ukraine. In a scenario for future conflict, Slovakia's position would form a 'first line of defence' for the West. Collectively, these concepts seem somewhat naïve in attaching such a degree of importance to Slovakia's geopolitical position; however, the 'bridge' concept, in particular, occupied a prominent position in Meciar's thinking about Slovakia's foreign policy direction.

Meciar governments since 1990 have attempted to develop a close economic relationship between Slovakia and Russia, of which we may observe two phases. The first, between 1990 and 1991, reflected the need to minimise the negative impact on Slovakia's economy consequent on the breakdown of the CMEA; the second, between 1992 and 1993, was based on the strategic notion that Slovakia (which Meciar perceived as having a 'special status' with Russia) should become a vital economic bridge between the West and the East; Meciar considered that closer relations between Russia and Slovakia would elevate the importance of Slovakia in the eyes of the West.

Duleba (1996a, 1996b) argues that Meciar's strategic vision relied on three plans, which all met with Russian approval. First, Slovakia, which inherited the system of natural gas and oil pipelines leading from the Soviet Union, should remain Russia's principal partner for transporting oil and natural gas to the West. Second, a joint Slovak–Russian company, Slovrusgas, based in Bratislava, would coordinate Russian natural gas exports. Third, a joint Slovak–Russian bank should be established in Bratislava. This strategy overestimated the significance of Slovak–Russian cooperation and has not produced any significant results. Slovakia will cease to be Russia's primary partner in the export of natural gas on completion of the planned high-capacity Jumal–Europe gas pipeline, traversing Poland; Slovrusgas has not materialised; and the Clearing Bank Association created in 1993 makes the idea of a further bank redundant.

Duleba suggests that the real reason for Meciar's 'special-status' policy towards Russia and inconsistent, vague policies towards NATO and the EU lies in economic explanations. The improvement in Slovakia's macro-economic indicators from 1994 to 1996 arises from the enhanced performance of some 20–30 per cent of Slovakia's largest flagship industrial firms such as Slovnaft and Slovensky Plynarensky, which have benefited from access to oil and gas at prices considerably below world market prices. However, in 1996 Russia made efforts to bring its gas prices up to world levels. It would appear that Slovakia's early 'special-status' economic relationship with Russia may have assisted the revival of the Slovak economy, but the changing economic conditions would suggest the need for a revised Western policy orientation.

Slovakia's relationship with Russia would appear to be problematic. On the one hand, a priority in this relationship concerns trade, on account of Slovakia's almost complete dependence on Russia for energy sources; Russia supplied 80 per cent of Slovakia's oil requirements and all of its gas needs from 1993 to 1995. Slovakia has not taken any steps to reduce its dependency on this source; indeed, under the 1995 agreement on the construction of the Mockovce nuclear plant, Slovakia accepted Russia's condition that only Russian uranium would be used in Slovakian plants, thereby making Slovakia completely dependent on Russian energy sources. According to Magda Vascaryova of the Slovak Policy Association, there is therefore the risk that 'Russia could probably use Slovakia's dependence on its energy supplies to retain its influence' (Butora 1995:24). Slovakia wishes to restore the balance by persuading Russia to use its export credits to purchase Slovak products. On the other hand, the experience of forty years of communism and the fear of too close a connection with a potentially authoritarian regime with serious economic problems of its own implies that a degree of caution is required in Slovakia having close economic relations with Russia.

Westward orientation – Slovakia and the EU

Since 1993, Slovakia's official foreign policy priority has been to secure full membership of the EU and NATO. Czechoslovakia acquired associate-member status on 16 December 1991, and following the bifurcation of Czechoslovakia, an EA was signed with Slovakia in October 1993 which entered into force in February 1995. The Meciar government submitted a formal application for full membership on 27 June 1995. The memorandum accompanying the Slovak application declared that 'the strategic objective of the Slovak Republic is to become a fully-fledged member in the EU within the time horizon around the year 2000' (Commission 1997a). Slovakia's apparent eagerness to be integrated was evident in that it was the first of the Visegrad countries to submit a completed Commission questionnaire on 19 July 1996.

Despite public pronouncements by Meciar of Slovakia's commitment to respect for democracy,[18] and the improvement in macro-economic indicators, within months of the formation of Meciar's government in 1994 criticisms of its disrespect for human rights and controversial policies were launched by the international community (Fisher 1996a, 1996b). Concern was expressed over the Meciar government's lack of tolerance of other political views and the constitutional implications of the feud between President and Prime Minister. In November 1996 the EP noted the erosion of freedom of expression in the media, and in March 1996 a US State Department report on Human Rights (US State Department 1997) catalogued instances of police abuse of authority and intimidation of the political opposition. Various explanations (Fisher 1996c; Henderson 1997) have been put forward to account for the growing difficult relationship between the EU and the Slovakian ruling coalition. Some of this related to Slovakia's new independent statehood and a lack of diplomatic expertise within the Civil Service. At a more fundamental level the government also blames Slovakia's deteriorating external image on 'lies' told to the outside world by the opposition and the President, with the objective of bringing their policies into disrepute and thus distortions of the truth finding their way into international and diplomatic discourse. There seems to be a marked government tendency to underestimate the importance of démarches, which have been presented as merely 'friendly warnings' to the public. The government clearly refuses to accept responsibility for its policies, preferring to blame the diplomatic corps, some of whom, at ambassadorial level, have been sacked but not replaced. In October 1996 Slovakia had no ambassador in London, Rome or the UN (Boland 1996), and few foreign heads of government willing to represent its case.

Since 1995, when the terms of the EA with the EU took effect, the Meciar administration has taken little heed of external criticism and has passed further legislation which appears to defy EU norms and expectations. Illustrative of this is the amendment to the penal code on the protection of the Republic, which is designed to criminalise attempts to slander Slovakia overseas (approved in March 1995), and the minority language law (approved in November 1995). The latter Act is worthy of more detailed examination here because it reveals the force of ethnicity and nationalism in the determination of Slovakian policy.

Nationalism and the ethnic Hungarian minority

National independence for Slovakia in 1993 did not resolve the conflicts over the question of nationhood and national identity. In post-1993 Slovakia, as the Czech–Slovak tensions subsided, resurgent Slovak

nationalism centred on Magyar–Slovak relations. Almost 13 per cent of
Slovakia's population of 5.3 million belong to ethnic minorities, most of
which are Hungarian (10.6 per cent), the Roma (1.4 per cent), Czech (1.0
per cent), Ruthenian (0.3 per cent), Ukrainian (0.3 per cent), German (0.1
per cent) and Polish (0.1 per cent). The ethnic Hungarians are concentrated in close-knit communities between the southern border of Slovakia
and the Danube, where they comprise in excess of 90 per cent of the population. So far, the Czechs and the Slovaks have engaged in symbolic
political conflict rather than open physical conflict, although 'the fear
persists in some Western quarters that a suppression of the Hungarian
minority in Slovakia might trigger in central Europe a crisis of
Yugoslavian proportions. In an attempt to alleviate NATO concerns, both
countries signed in October 1993 a five-year bilateral military cooperation agreement' (Brzica *et al.* 1997:226).

The sources of tension in the Slovak–Hungarian relationship lie in
mutual historical resentments. For the Slovaks, their long period of political servitude prior to 1918 under Austro-Hungarian rule lingers in the
historical memory, which has created the distrust now exploited to good
effect by Slovak nationalists. For the Hungarians, there is the humiliating
legacy of the Trianon Treaty of 1920, which shifted the border, leaving
them outside the protection of the Hungarian homeland. The potential for
conflict is exacerbated by the fact that the rights of the Hungarian minority are strongly championed by the Hungarian state. The ethnic
Hungarians were strongly opposed to Slovakian independence in that it
would leave them exposed to a tide of rising Slovak nationalism; their
demands for minority rights and territorial autonomy in the face of
nationalism have produced 'the next serious ethno-territorial conflict
facing Eastern Europe' (Kaiser 1995:232).

The ethnic Hungarian minority has active political representation
through three political parties – Coexistence, the Hungarian Christian
Democratic Movement (and the Hungarian Civic Party, but since 1994
they have become increasingly isolated, unable to muster much support
from the opposition, and their perceived radical demand for minority
rights has provided ammunition for nationalist politicians. Little legislation advocated by this minority has been approved. However, with support
from Hungary they have attracted the attention of the international
community to their cause. The potential for interstate conflict exists, as
evidenced by Hungary's threat to veto Slovakia's Council of Europe
membership (along with strong pressure from EU members); in the event,
Hungary abstained, but only in return for Slovakian representatives'
promises to reform minority rights. The Council attached to Slovakia's
admission strong recommendations that Slovakia should enact legislation
allowing previously forbidden bilingual signs in towns and villages (an
early symbolic nationalism), and should repeal the Czechoslovakian law of

1950 preventing the registration of names in birth registers in their natural language.

Since the electoral victory of Slovak nationalist interests in 1994, Meciar has attempted to strengthen the national identity and has used language as the key instrument in the Slovakisation of society.[19] In November 1995, the controversial State Language Law was approved in the face of strong opposition from Hungary and the international community. It restricts the use of other languages in various aspects of daily life and requires the use of Slovak in official encounters; however, ethnic Hungarians have made much of the fact that this is in contradiction of Article 34 of the Slovak Constitution, which grants minorities the right to use their own language in official contacts. Other controversial provisions include the banning of bilingual documentation in schools, which some Slovaks regarded as a form of historical justice (Fisher 1995b).

A vivid and alarming manifestation of the power of Meciar's brand of Slovak nationalism to engender fear occurred when the language bill came before Parliament. The HZDS proposed, in a televised parliamentary session, that each deputy should state his position aloud after his name was called. Afraid of being branded 'anti-Slovak', most opposition deputies voted in favour. President Kovac, also wishing not to appear anti-Slovak, also signed the bill, but threatened to involve the Constitutional Court if the ruling coalition did not honour its promise to forward a bill on minority languages in the near future (Fisher 1995b).

The conflict between the majority Slovaks and the minority Hungarians highlights a conceptual gap that exists over the definition of democracy. The Hungarians take a 'collective rights' perspective, arguing that in a democratic multinational state the state should provide support for the preservation of the minority culture and identity on the same basis as the majority; they desire the right to the use of their language guaranteed by the state through the provision of Hungarian-language schools. The Slovak government upheld the notion of majority rule on their own native territory as their perspective on democracy, arguing that each citizen has constitutionally 'individual rights' (Leff 1997; see also Chapter 4).

In March 1995, Meciar signed a bilateral treaty with Hungary on good-neighbourliness and friendly relations. The significance of this lies not so much within its content as in its international political significance. Both Hungary and Slovakia were anxious to sign the treaty in order to demonstrate their democratic credentials to the West, a requirement for membership of NATO and the EU. The treaty addresses two issues: Hungarian guarantees of the inviolability of the Slovakian border and the protection of Hungarian minority rights in Slovakia. Long-standing Slovakian fears of Hungarian annexation of its territory appear to be resolved by the treaty, although some representatives of the Hungarian minority desire territorial autonomy for their districts. Slovakia argues that these areas are not homogeneous but of mixed composition. The issue of territorial autonomy continues to simmer.[20]

Slovakia and EU membership

'Slovakia does not fulfil in a satisfying manner the political conditions set out by the European Council in Copenhagen, because of the instability of Slovakia's institutions, their lack of rootedness in political life and the shortcomings in the functioning of its democracy' (Commission 1997b:98–9).

In its conclusions and in its country Opinion, the Commission dwells on Slovakia's contemporary political circumstances. Their analysis is heavily critical. Slovakia is the only CEEC seeking membership of the EU to fail the political criteria, and in support of its judgement the Commission covers much of the ground examined above. Thus it criticises: the lack of respect of Constitutional Court decisions; the disregard shown to the rights of the opposition; the problems between the government and the former President; concern over the use made by the government of both the police and secret service; a lack of independence in the judicial system; and an ineffective pursuit of the removal of corruption. The treatment and situation of minorities in Slovakia require attention, and the Commission also notes that recommendations made by the EU in the form of démarches and declarations have been ignored.

In sharp contrast to the political criteria, the Commission is very positive about Slovakia's ability to meet the economic criteria. Most of the reforms to establish a market economy have been implemented, though concern is expressed over the impact of the Price Law in 1996 and the Revitalisation Act intervening with market forces. Further progress is needed in the regulation of bankruptcy, capital markets and enterprise restructuring. Similarly, as the analysis in Chapter 2 (Table 2.4) illustrates, Slovakian capacity to take on the obligations of membership looks not unduly problematic, when compared with some other applicants. 'Continued and sustained efforts' need to be made in a number of areas,[21] and no evaluation of judicial capacity could be made without clear evidence of improvement in the field of human rights. Interestingly, no problems are envisaged in meeting the *acquis* in the fields of common foreign and security policy in the medium term.

Further progress is required in transport, especially in relation to road freight and the railway sector, with integration into the European transport network seen as essential. Financial controls are needed for the application of Community rules on regional policy and cohesion. Safety standards in Slovakia's nuclear power plants need to be modernised and a long-term solution found for nuclear waste. The environment is singled out as being the only element in which the obligations will be met in the long to very long term.

Explicit in its conclusion is that once sufficient progress has been made in satisfying the Copenhagen criteria, negotiations for accession would be opened. Implicit is the assumption that a Meciar-led government, or any such similar future government, stands firmly across a route to accession and as such forms a political barrier to the eastern boundary of the EU.

The Slovak response

Just five months prior to the publication of *Agenda 2000*, after the Third Association Council meeting of the EU and Slovak Republic (Commission 1997a), an upbeat assessment of progress was made, particularly with regard to the progress Slovakia had made on democratisation.[22] The subsequent Opinion of the Commission (July 1997) has been heavily criticised by the Slovak government, and in August 1997 the Ministry of Foreign Affairs produced a thirty-one-page rebuttal describing examples of the Opinion statement that are based, in its view, on 'imprecise, mistaken, incomplete and distorted information' (Ministry of Foreign Affairs of the Slovak Republic 1997:2). The rebuttal begins by making plain the Slovak view that the recommendations made by the European Commission do not 'fully correspond to the wording of the conclusions of the Copenhagen summit', and goes on to state that the Commission's Opinion on Slovakia 'resembles the justification of a political decision' (Ministry of Foreign Affairs of the Slovak Republic 1997:2).

Whilst the authors would not seek to uphold all the views expressed in Slovakia's critique of the Opinion, we would agree that aspects of this rebuttal are in part supportable. The Opinion takes a very different stance from the position after the Third Association Council meeting; it provides no positive remarks whatsoever in its evaluation of Slovakia's political environment (for instance, the emergence of NGOs), except to state that fair and free elections take place. However, the lengthy Slovak response is interesting when read in conjunction with the Commission's Opinion. Some of the criticisms are little short of pedantry;[23] other criticisms by the Commission induce no substantive response. An example of this is the criticism of the privatisation process in Slovakia, which was described as not transparent and inequitable. The minimal response by the Slovak government was that the results of the process were the best and the lack of foreign investors was deliberate.[24] A similar 'assertive rebuttal' is made regarding the Commission's comments on FDI.[25]

The Opinion was chiefly critical of the lack of respect shown by the Slovak government to the role and responsibilities of other political institutions, a criticism which strikes at the centre of the Slovak democratic process. The Commission gives two examples of where this has happened: the first is totally ignored in the Slovak response (the tension between the government and the President); to the second (concerning the threats of sanctions to civil servants not signing a petition seeking to dismiss the President), the response given is that 'the employees signed the petition of their own initiative and no sanctions were imposed on anyone who did not sign the petition' (Ministry of Foreign Affairs of the Slovak Republic 1997:5). The Slovak response seems inadequate, not only because this particular criticism is not addressed, but also because the accusation is rebutted by simple denial; there also appears to be a misunderstanding (wilful or not) of the boundaries between political loyalty and administrative neutrality – a necessary and defining feature of a (European) democratic process.

A final example of the Slovak response to the Opinion concerns the position of the Roma in Slovakia. The Opinion states that the Roma continue to suffer considerable discrimination in daily life, are the target of violence from skinheads and receive inadequate protection from the police. The response rejects this view and argues that the Roma have the same rights as all Slovak citizens, that the Roma deserve this treatment because they participate in more criminal activity, that racially motivated crimes are not statistically significant, and that none of the attacks inflicted on the Roma are of any great magnitude and are investigated fully. The Slovak rebuttal of the Opinion simply and proudly proclaims that the Slovak Republic fully respects ethnic minorities.[26]

The European Commission's Opinion on discrimination is supported by, amongst other international critiques, the US Human Rights Report (US State Department 1997), which provides evidence of the severity of racial attacks on the Roma by skinheads. It cites evidence of a failure of the police to investigate incidents of abuse and take statements of witnesses to attacks, and the use of countercharges to pressurise the Roma to drop their complaints of police brutality. It provides examples of several serious incidents consisting of two deaths, serious woundings, four assaults and other injuries to the Roma from skinhead attacks. The weight of evidence supports the view taken by the European Commission (see also Chapter 4).

The EU and the Slovak citizen

Despite the pessimistic Commission assessment of the ability of the Meciar government to function within a democratic framework, Slovak citizens continue to show interest in their country's association with the EU. In surveys undertaken after the *Agenda 2000* recommendations, the *Central and Eastern Eurobarometer* (November 1997) demonstrates a marked improvement of public opinion in Slovakia towards the EU. It shows a very critical attitude of Slovaks to domestic politics in Slovakia, especially with regard to the functioning of the political system and the future direction of the country, though a less negative attitude to human rights is evident.

Of those surveyed, 48 per cent said that the future of Slovakia lay with the EU (an increase of 10 per cent from the previous survey), 46 per cent held a positive image of the EU (an increase of 12 per cent), whilst 62 per cent said that they would vote for entry into the EU were a referendum to be held, a substantial increase of 16 per cent (Commission 1998). On being asked about the groups which might benefit or lose as ties with the EU become closer, all groups were said to be net beneficiaries.[27] In a very real sense the EU is perceived as a barrier against the cynical manipulation of power so far experienced in the new democracy.

Whilst attitudes were very positive about the EU, attitudes towards Slovakian institutions were quite negative, particularly manifest by the response to questions about the market economy, democracy and the direction of the economy. Thus, 35 per cent said the creation of a market economy was right for Slovakia; 45 per cent said it was wrong. Twenty-five per cent of respondents were satisfied with the way democracy is developing in Slovakia; 75 per cent were not satisfied. Twenty-seven per cent were satisfied with the way democracy works in Slovakia; 70 per cent were not. On being asked if they felt Slovakia was going in the right or wrong direction, 26 per cent said the right direction, and 64 per cent said the wrong direction.

Despite international criticism, citizens' views on human rights in their country have changed positively. In the surveys conducted in 1995 and 1996, the net response was negative (–9 per cent and –21 per cent, respectively). By 1997 the response was equally divided between those stating that there is more respect for human rights and those stating that there is less respect. Slovaks were asked by the *Central and Eastern Eurobarometer* about their country's readiness to join the EU, and asked if the Opinion was accurate. Fourteen per cent said it was very accurate, 50 per cent said it was quite accurate, 28 per cent said it was not very accurate and just 2 per cent said it was not at all accurate (Commission 1998:Annexe 58).

Other surveys conducted support the negative opinions described above about the lack of confidence in the way the country is governed. The low confidence of the Slovak population in political institutions is evident in that the office of the President is the only institution in which more than 50 per cent of the population have confidence (Miháliková 1996).[28]

Conclusion

On gaining independence, the foremost challenge for the Slovak government was to prove that its already tarnished international reputation was unfounded (Obrman 1992). The fear that it might become relegated to a 'second-tier post-communist country' has taken root through the EU's decision to exclude it from 'first-wave' applicant status. After 1994, the West's increased loss of confidence in the Meciar government's authoritarian style and disregard for constitutional norms has led to increasing isolation of the state. Of the Visegrad countries, Slovakia is unique in that since 1990 it has struggled with problems of national identity and institution building – a struggle reflected in a political cleavage that centres on issues of nationhood (Henderson and Robinson 1997). On an optimistic note, evidence of economic transformation seems reasonably positive and the institutional framework, though somewhat battered, is in many respects 'quite robust' (Henderson and Robinson 1997:375). The best hope for the country is the popular removal of Meciar at the 1998 elections and the installation of a government more committed to the already existing rules of the democratic game. Only this will sustain Slovakia's 'Western European' orientation. Inevitably, therefore, the EU must continue to assist Slovakia in the process of transformation, for without such support a scenario of increasing isolation, attended by continuing volatile politics and social polarisation, would seem unavoidable. The consequences for the security of Europe, East and West, in such a scenario, are not pleasant.

Notes

1 Elections took place in 1990, 1992 and 1994.
2 HZDS won 37.3 per cent of the vote and 74 seats in the 150-member Slovak National Council.
3 Meciar's and his fellow HZDS members' preferred candidate for the presidency, Roman Kovac, was rejected by Parliament and Michal Kovac, with whom Meciar had a problematic relationship, was selected as a compromise candidate.
4 Meciar persuaded Kovac to dismiss his key rival, Foreign Minister Milan Kuazko, in March 1993 and SNS Chairman Ludovit Cernak resigned in sympathy as Economy Minister and withdrew his party from the 'informal' coalition (Nic *et al.* 1993). Kuazko and Cernak considered that Meciar wanted to exercise personal control over their ministries.
5 The alleged improper and overt political use of the Secret Service and police is well illustrated by the alleged involvement of the Secret Police in the kidnap of the President's son (31 August 1995). Despite the existence of an apparently incriminating tape of a telephone conversation between the Head of the Secret Service, Ivan Lexa, and the Interior Minister, which was leaked to the media, Meciar claims that it has not been proved that Kovac Jr was abducted,

nor that the Secret Service and police acted improperly.

6 In a similar vein, the US State Department has referred to the case of Frantisek Gaulieder as 'a serious step backwards in Slovakia's democratic development'. The case is also cited in the Commission's Opinion (Commission 1997b). Gaulieder, a dissident member of Meciar's HZDS, was expelled from Parliament by means of a disputed letter of resignation; he has been refused reinstatement, despite a ruling from the Constitutional Court in July 1997 that his constitutional rights were violated (Anderson and Done 1997).

7 In the run-up to the September 1998 election, the opinion-poll rating of the HZDS fell from its 35 per cent support at the last election to about 26 per cent. The opposition coalition is ready to offer the three ethnic Hungarian parties seats in the government, but the ruling coalition is using anti-Hungarian sentiments as a weapon against them. In order to maximise his power base, Meciar has been considering modifications to the electoral system by seeking to change the current party-list system of voting to either a German-style combination of first-past-the post and proportional representation or a British-style first-past-the post, his preferred alternative (Anderson 1997b).

8 In 1918, the Czech lands were industrially developed whilst Slovakia was less developed and agrarian. Under central planning the wide disparity in economic conditions in their economies was reduced substantially in terms of income, labour productivity and industrial output between 1948 and 1989. The structure of the Slovak economy was heavily reoriented to industrial production and away from its dependence on agriculture (see Capek and Sazama 1993). Under central planning, investment in the heavy engineering sector and the steel and chemicals industries took place with the aim of fast growth and rapid industrialisation (Smith 1995).

9 Smith also argues that unemployment in areas dependent on armaments production was still below average, unemployment being highest until 1993 in agricultural and single-industry areas. Unemployment in the armament-dependent areas was hidden by reductions in the length of the working week, the workforce being absorbed into private enterprises or smaller units of the former enterprises.

10 Winiecki states that in order to accelerate growth in Slovakia, 'The state enterprise sector's structure of supply is maladapted to the newly emerging pattern of demand (because of the oversized heavy industry) and its behavioural aptitude to search for new demand is lower' (Winiecki 1994:722).

11 Over three million Slovaks had signed up when it was cancelled in summer 1995 (Boland 1996), which constitutes 90 per cent of eligible citizens (Fisher 1995a).

12 Moody's downgraded Slovakia at the end of March 1998 from investment grade Baa 3 to speculative grade Ba 1. Standard & Poor reversed the outlook for Slovakia from stable to negative in April 1998. IBCA, another leading credit-rating agency, gave Slovakia its lowest investment grade in August 1996, citing the long-running conflict between Meciar and Kovac as a factor, and warned in late 1997 that weakening the central bank's independence could trigger a downgrade (Done 1998a).

13 Slovakia's banking sector is dominated by five institutions: Vseobecna

Uverova Banka; Investicna Banka Rozvojova (IRB); Slovenska Spoirtelna Bratislava; Konsolidacna Banka; and Slovenska Zaruchna. At the end of 1995 there were thirty-one banks in Slovakia; thirteen had minority state ownership, eight indirect state majority share and three were wholly state-owned.

14 At the end of 1996 32 per cent of bank loans were classified as sub-standard or worse and 18 per cent of loans had insufficient provisions held against them (Anderson 1997a).

15 The National Bank of Slovakia was established as Slovakia's central bank (by Act No. 566/1992) and has the following functions: to issue notes; be a banker to the government, other banks and financial institutions; to administer monetary reserves; to design and implement monetary and exchange policy; to control the money supply; to coordinate the payments and settlement of accounts between banks; and to supervise the performance of banking activities (Slovak Information Agency 1997).

16 The widespread implementation of the Act is likely to result in a weakening of the (hard) budget constraint, and thus drive funds away from enterprises seeking to finance investment projects and modernisation programmes (Anderson 1997a; OECD 1998). Concern over the health of the banking sector also resulted from IRB being taken under direct central bank supervision in mid-December 1997 because of a lack of liquidity and its quantity of non-performing loans (Done 1997a).

17 Slovakia has three exchanges on which shares can be traded: the Bratislava Stock Exchange, the Bratislava Option Stock Exchange and the RM-S computerised system (Brzica *et al.* 1997).

18 For example, the signing in 1995 of the Slovak–Hungary State Treaty. As a condition of membership the EU and NATO require the resolution of conflicts outstanding between neighbouring countries.

19 The first indicator of tension over minority rights appeared in October 1990, when Slovakia's First Language Law was approved. This allowed for the use of a minority language in public and official dealings in communities with an ethnic minority of at least 20 per cent.

20 At the interstate level, the question over whether the Gabcikovo–Nagymaros project should be demolished or completed has caused a diplomatic rift between Hungary and Slovakia and came before the International Court of Justice in The Hague in May 1994 (Lanyi and Jencik 1997). The project was originally conceived by both countries as a way of jointly exploiting the Danube to prevent flooding, improve navigation and provide hydroelectric power. For Slovakia, 'the dam was a positive symbol of nationalism' (Anderson 1997b). In 1992, Slovakia built a lateral dam along the joint Danube border, limiting the reservoir to Slovak territory. In retaliation, Hungary unilaterally diverted the river, causing extensive environmental damage by reducing the flow of water into the bed of the Danube. There seems little prospect of a resolution of this issue until after the 1998 elections.

21 Of most concern are the following areas in which substantial efforts are needed to meet the *acquis* in the medium term: standards and certification; industrial and intellectual property; competition; public procurement; insurance; telecommunications; customs; the environment and labour law; health and safety at work; and an autonomous labour inspectorate.

22 For example: 'The European Union welcomes recent developments in the field of democratisation in Slovakia. The EU is encouraged by recent parliamentary discussions and decisions, in particular concerning the amendments to the penal law and changes in the composition of some important parliamentary committees' (Commission 1997a:3).

23 The first comment made in the economic criteria section by the Ministry of Foreign Affairs argues over the wording used to describe the division of the CSFR, stating that the use of the words 'split from' for Slovakia and 'division into' for the Czech Republic, views the same process as more negative for Slovakia than that for the Czech Republic.

24 '[T]he criticism of the lack of openness to foreign investors in Slovak privatisation lies in the understandable preference for Slovak business people ... The macroeconomic results achieved in Slovakia ... serve to confirm that the right method of privatisation was chosen' (Commission 1997a:6).

25 The full text states: 'Although Slovakia does not have enough foreign investment, the Slovak Republic has achieved the best macroeconomic results of the Associated Countries, and it is assumed that if the amount of foreign investment increased, such results would be even better' (Commission 1997a:17).

26 'The assessment of the situation as regards the respecting and position of ethnic minorities in Slovakia is in marked contrast with reality ... Slovakia applies the highest European standards for their protection and development' (Ministry of Foreign Affairs of the Slovak Republic 1997:13–14).

27 The groups which might benefit the most were private business (49 per cent), the educational system (47 per cent) and the armed forces (45 per cent). Those which might benefit the least were manual workers (13 per cent), low income groups (8 per cent) and farmers (7 per cent) (Commission, 1998).

28 Reasons given for lack of confidence in the Cabinet, Parliament, coalition and opposition deputies were: the inability of the new elite to respect the interests of common people; the very strong sense of impoverishment; the fear of economic failure from social insecurity; and the pessimistic evaluation of the effects of economic transformation (Mihálliková 1996).

References

Anderson, R. (1997a), Banking: hamstrung by tight policy, *Financial Times*, 28 October.

Anderson, R. (1997c), Politics: toughest challenge for Meciar, *Financial Times*, 28 October.

Anderson, R. and Done, K. (1997), Facing isolation in the heart of Europe: time is running out for Slovakia to put its house in order and start addressing the concerns of the international community, *Financial Times*, 28 October.

Boland, V. (1994), Never mind the politics – a second round of privatisation is about to start, *Financial Times*, 16 December.

Boland, V. (1995), Shares for all no longer the favourite policy – sell-off procedures are being revised to ensure tighter control of key national assets, *Financial Times*, 20 December.

Boland, V. (1996), Sell-offs give rise to suspicions, *Financial Times*, 23 October.

Bombik, S. and Samson, I. (1996), Slovakia, in R. Smoke (ed.), *Perceptions of Security*, Manchester, Manchester University Press, 146–63.

Borish, M. S., Ding, W. and Noel, M. (1997), The evolution of the state-owned banking sector during transition in Central Europe, *Europe–Asia Studies*, 49:7, 1187–208.

Brzica, D., Polackova, Z. and Samoson, I. (1997), The Slovak Republic: bridge between East and West?, in P. J. Katzenstein (ed.), *Mitteleuropa – Between Europe and Germany*, Providence and Oxford, Berghahn Books, 192–239.

Butora, D. (1995), Magda Vasaryova: the role of Slovak foreign policy, *Transition*, 28 April, 23–5.

Capek, A. and Sazama, G. W. (1993), Czech and Slovak economic relations, *Europe–Asia Studies*, 45:2, 211–35.

Commission (1997a), EU/Slovak Republic: third meeting of the Association Council, press release, 25 February, Brussels.

Commission (1997b), *Agenda 2000 – Commission Opinion on Slovakia's Application for Membership of the European Union*, 15 July.

Commission (1998), *Central and Eastern Eurobarometer*, 8, Brussels, March.

Done, K. (1995), Healthy capital flow – speed of growth has confounded the sceptics, but foreign investors remain wary, *Financial Times*, 20 December.

Done, K. (1996a), Money supply triggers anxiety, *Financial Times*, 23 October.

Done, K. (1996b), The news is making news, *Financial Times*, 23 October.

Done, K. (1997), Crisis in Slovakia as big bank needs rescue, *Financial Times*, 19 December.

Done, K. (1998a), Benchmark eurobond for Slovakia, *Financial Times*, 2 April.

Done, K. (1998b), Multi-tranche bond issue for Slovakia, *Financial Times*, 12 May.

Duleba, A. (1996a), Pursuing an eastern agenda, *Transition*, 20 September, 52–5.

Duleba, A. (1996b), *The Blind Pragmatism of Slovak Eastern Policy: The Actual Agenda of Slovak–Russian Bilateral Relations*, Occasional Paper 01, Research Centre of the Slovak Foreign Policy Association, Bratislava.

East, R. and Pontin, J. (1997), *Revolution and Change in Central and Eastern Europe*, London, Pinter.

Fisher, S. (1995a), Privatisation stumbles forward, *Transition*, 26 May, 44–9.

Fisher, S. (1995b), Ethnic Hungarians back themselves into a corner, *Transition*, 29 December, 58–63.

Fisher, S. (1996a), Meciar retains control of the political scene, *Transition*, 9 August, 32–6.

Fisher, S. (1996b), Domestic policies cause conflict with the West, *Transition*, 20 September, 56–61.

Fisher, S. (1996c), Making Slovakia more Slovak, *Transition*, 29 November, 14–17.

Fisher, S. (1997), Slovakia heads toward international isolation, *Transition*, 7 February, 11–13.

Gould, J. and Szomolanyi, S. (1997), Bridging the chasm in Slovakia, *Transition*, 4:6, November, 70–6.

Harris, F. (1998), Can cronyism work?, *Business Central Europe*, April, 11–13.

Henderson, K. (1997), *Slovakia Attitudes to EU Accession in a Polarised Society*, paper presented at East–Central Europe: prospects for accession to the European Union, workshop, University of Leicester, 21/22 February.

Henderson, K. and Robinson, N. (1997), *Post Communist Politics – An Introduction*, London, Prentice Hall.

Isa, J. (1996), New stage of economic transtition in post-socialist countries, *Slovak Sociological Review*, 1, Spring, 12–22.

Kaiser, R. J. (1995), Czechoslovakia: the disintegration of a binomial state, in G. Smith (ed.), *Federation: The Multiethnic Challenge*, Harlow, Longman.

Kettle, S. (1996), Slovakia's One-man band, *Transition*, 23 August, 12–15, 64.

Lanyi, A. and Jencik, G. (1997), What to do with Gabcikovo?, *Transition*, June, 92–5.

Leff, C. S. (1997), *The Czech and Slovak Republics, Nation versus State*, Oxford, Westview.

Mihálikova, S. (1996), The painful birth of Slovak democratic political culture, *Slovak Sociological Review*, 1, Spring, 51–68.

Ministry of Foreign Affairs of the Slovak Republic (1997), *Slovak View on the Commission's Opinion on Slovakia's Application for Membership of the European Union*, 28 August.

Myant, M. (1995), Transforming the Czech and Slovak economies: evidence at the district level, *Regional Studies*, 29:8, 753–60.

Nic, M., Obrman, J. and Fisher, S. (1993), New Slovak government: more stability?, *RFE/RL Research Report*, 2:47, 26 November, 24–30.

Obrman, J. (1992), Uncertain prospects for independent Slovakia, *RFE/RL Research Report*, 1:49, December, 43–8.

OECD (1991), Economic developments outside the OECD, *Economic Outlook*, 50, 53–7.

OECD (1996), Developments in selected non-OECD countries, *Economic Outlook*, 59, 133–6.

OECD (1998), Developments in selected non-member countries, *Economic Outlook*, 63, 149–53.

Rehak, L. and Krillov, V. (1995), Slovakia as a new factor in European politics, *International Relations*, 12:5, 47–64.

Simecka, M. (1997), Slovakia's lonely independence, *Transition*, 3 August, 14–21.

Slovak Information Agency (1997), *The European Union Questionnaire for the Slovak Republic: Summary*, Bratislava, Slovak Information Agency.

Smith, A. (1994), Uneven development and the restructuring of the armaments industry in Slovakia, *Transactions of the Institute of British Geographers*, NS 19:4, 404–21.

Smith, A. (1995), Regulation theory, strategies of enterprise integration and the political economy of regional economic restructuring in Central and Eastern Europe: the case of Slovakia, *Regional Studies*, 29:8, 761–72.

US State Department (1997), *1996 Human Rights Report: The Slovak Republic*, Bureau of Democracy, Human Rights, and Labor.

Winiecki, J. (1994), East–Central Europe: a regional survey – the Czech Republic, Hungary, Poland and Slovakia in 1993, *Europe–Asia Studies*, 46:5, 709–34.

Hungarian economic transformation: gradual progress towards accession?

Since 1989 there has never been much debate in Hungary about joining the EU, and the political consensus among the major economic elites, political parties and among the public for membership has been a mostly positive one. The focus of interest and debate was rather the speed of the accession, as both the public and many politicians anticipated rapid progress to membership. This expectation partly derives from the state socialist period. Hungary was the most liberalised state socialist country (apart from the former Yugoslavia) and introduced many of the elements of a market economy as well as some political freedoms prior to 1990 (Holmes 1997).[1] This early liberalisation tended to produce a public and elite complacency which belied the fact that market forces and economic institutions existed only in an embryonic form. Indeed, it could be argued that they existed in name only, while expectations, values and behaviour remained largely unchanged. Perhaps as a result of this, the expectations and emerging requirements of the EU have not been fully· appreciated, especially by the public.

In this chapter we will discuss the factors that have assisted Hungarian economic and political transformation and have led to the relatively favourable Opinion reached by the Commission on the possibility of Hungarian accession to the EU (Commission 1997). In order to explore these factors we first examine the legacies of Hungarian state socialism and its disintegration, and then analyse the most important elements of the transition in Hungary in the 1990s. Finally we discuss the most problematic issues of the accession process.

The evolution and disintegration of the state socialist regime in Hungary

Two crucial factors that shaped the development of state socialism in Hungary, when compared with other state socialist countries, were the lessons absorbed by the political leadership from the uprising of 1956, and the consequences of the several economic reforms, especially the New Economic Mechanism (NEM) of 1968. The latter was to give Hungary the 'enduring reputation as the most innovative and economically liberal of the Soviet bloc states' (East and Pontin 1997:52).

Hungary adopted central planning in the late 1940s. Macroeconomic plans were formulated at the political centre; these plans allocated production inputs directly to enterprises, which in turn were linked together in a chain of directives that specified production, investment, employment, wage levels and customer–supplier relations. On the basis of central planning, Hungary achieved rapid output growth and primary industrialisation.

The political slogan of the Hungarian Socialist Workers' Party (HSWP) after 1956, 'Who is not against us is with us', was reflected in both economic and social policy. From 1956, the most important political priority was to ensure a stable and visible increase of living standards on a year-to-year basis (thus ensuring popular support from, or at least neutrality of, Hungarian citizens) and so avoid the need to return to openly repressive measures – although covert repression was used against opposition until the mid-1980s. This policy provided the basis for a system nicknamed 'gulyas-communism' or 'refrigerator-socialism', in which people were encouraged to have their own houses and second houses, furnish them, and travel to Western countries once every three years; in which long queues were unknown (except for cars and public housing), and a large proportion of household income (40 per cent by the early 1980s) derived from transfers.

However, in the mid-1960s, in Hungary as in other Eastern European countries, production reserves of the economic transformation and bureaucratic central planning started to dry up and the rate of economic growth began to decline. At the level of decision making the problem manifested itself in difficulties in switching from the extensive use of productive resources (additional investment and additional labour) to using those resources more intensively; that is, achieving higher productivity, greater intensity of production, and better motivation of economic agents. To deal with the situation it seemed that the solution was reform of the mechanism of economic regulation. This emerged in 1968 as the NEM.

The NEM aimed at reforming certain basic features of the traditional central planning model without undermining the basic tenets of socialism. The most important change was the elimination of directives from the centre, in particular the allocation of inputs and outputs. Enterprises were given autonomy to make micro-economic decisions subject to uniform regulations. The NEM also attempted to promote a more direct relationship between the domestic and external sectors by introducing a unified exchange rate, closer links between domestic and foreign prices, and greater freedom in foreign trade. The common aim of all these reforms was to implement the priorities of central planning authorities through market-based incentives (Berend 1990).

However, the informal hierarchical relationship between enterprises and their supervisory bodies (ministries and local governments) continued to be crucial after the introduction of the NEM, since the methods of appointment, evaluation and remuneration of managers were unchanged and the allocation of a significant proportion of investment resources was centralised. Enterprise autonomy thus became one of the focal points of the battle over 'market socialism' – between advocates of further liberalisation and those preferring informal centralisation and only formal autonomy. From the mid-1970s the latter group was in retreat.

The State Enterprise Act of 1977 attempted to loosen the ties between enterprises and ministries. It opened the way to establish supervisory boards, responsible for overall strategic guidance; thus managers enjoyed greater autonomy in operational matters. In 1980 a single Ministry of Industry was formed from three industrial branch ministries, while their price-setting and marketing responsibilities were transferred to the National Materials and Price Office. In the first few years, the new Ministry was very much involved with the implementation of its own structure; consequently enterprises acquired further autonomy from the Ministry of Industry.

Although regulation problems and the interests of the major actors pointed towards further reforms, the major driving force of the reforms of the 1980s was the changed economic situation of Hungary. In 1975, advisers to policy makers and the bureaucracy proposed to the political leadership that the negative effects of the 1973–75 recession could be financed via external borrowing. By 1979 Hungary was at the brink of insolvency. This was a combined effect of the unfavourable external climate and the decision to base economic development on foreign loans at a time when the country was not ready for the efficient use of large amounts of additional resources.[2]

In 1982, in an attempt to ease external debt, Hungary joined the World Bank and the IMF, a move which corresponded with the interests of the growing financial bureaucracy. From this date, monetary and fiscal policy, and the bureaucracy associated with it, have acquired an overwhelming importance in the macro-economic management of the Hungarian economy. The bureaucracy gained a *de facto* veto on any economic policy issue and focused on a full transformation of the state socialist economic system. In order that such transformation be achieved, two important preconditions had to be met: preventing the political leadership's intervention and gaining the support of the large companies. These steps did not require any particular conspiracy: they came axiomatically from the logic of the reforms, the disintegration of the state planning system, and the direct and personal aims of an emerging new elite – in addition to pressure from the IMF.

The economic policy applied between 1980 and 1984 culminated in the 1984 Reform Package, which contained the following innovations: the development of a two-tier banking system; the introduction of a value added tax and personal income tax system; abolition of the controlling rights of the ministries over companies (aimed at removing the Ministry of Industry from formulation of economic policy); and extension of the legal scope of the private sector. In order to achieve political acceptance of the reform package, economists promised economic growth – again, based on external borrowing – to the political leadership (Vigvári 1991). But the aims of the economic growth policy and the Reform Package contradicted each other. The policy rapidly led to indebtedness, and hence to the reintroduction of monetary restrictions. Consequently, managers of large companies, who were interested in growth, finally turned away from the state socialist system when the Company Act of 1985 and (especially) the Company Act 1988 and the Transformation of State Owned Enterprises Act (1989) were approved. The Company Act (1985) removed supervisory control of company management from ministries and intro-duced Company Councils. Half the members of the Councils were delegated by the management of the company, while the other half were elected by the employees of the company. The Company Council exer-cised employment rights over senior managers of the company, and determined managerial salaries and bonuses, as well as hiring and firing senior staff. Since half the Council's membership was delegated by the management, the management of the company exercised not only managerial, but also *de facto* ownership rights. The 1988 and 1989 Acts opened the way to the transformation of state-owned enterprises into joint-stock or limited companies and the establishment of Boards of Directors and Supervisory Committees – consequently opening the door to external investment. The Acts were also widely abused since they created the opportunity for early and unregulated 'spontaneous privatisation'.[3]

As well as company directors and factions within the state bureaucracy, the new stratum of private entrepreneurs was another crucial contributory factor to the disintegration of the remains of central planning. In 1982, the establishment of small private companies (up to thirty-nine owners and thirty-nine employees), either on a rental or private property basis, was permitted. The employment limit was gradually increased and finally abolished in 1989. According to the Central Statistical Office, about 10 per cent of the workforce was involved in these private enterprises, either as their main or second employment.

Parallel with these changes, the macro-economic system was also transformed as new institutions were created which could not be controlled within the already disintegrating central planning system. In 1987 the two-tier banking system was established, that is, the central banking and commercial banking functions were institutionally separated; 35 per cent of prices were completely freed. As well as the introduction of personal income tax and value added tax, a universal right to foreign trade was in place by 1989.

Such a liberalisation in the economic sphere and power shift within the elite necessarily resulted in a liberalisation of the political system. In 1987, the government was reshuffled and in an extraordinary party conference in May 1988 the political leadership was replaced, with János Kádár removed to the role of General Secretary of the HSWP.[4] By this time economic decision making clearly shifted to the Prime Minister, as the Central Committee was denied crucial information to make such decisions. In 1988, in parallel with the economic liberalisation, progress towards legalisation of the multiparty system, freedom of association and rehabilitation of people persecuted for political reasons were well advanced (Kulcsár 1994).[5] By September a populist movement, the Hungarian Democratic Forum (MDF), had established a formal conservative opposition. In November a Liberal Alliance was also created (SZDSZ), and in January 1989 a multiparty system was legally established.

During 1989, negotiations were started between these opposition parties and the HSWP on the further transformation of the political system. Later the trade unions and the left-wing, non-HSWP movements joined the negotiations as the 'third side'. During these negotiations the political and economic institutional systems of liberal democracy (including banning party organisations in the workplace and abolishing the privileged situation of the HSWP) and steps to legally establish free elections were the main issues. Although some of the parties refused to sign the final agreements as a means to establish their separate, more radical identities, 'steps to legally establish free elections' were the main issues. With these 'round-table' negotiations Hungary arrived at the point of political transition. Finally, in October 1989 at, as it transpired, the final Congress of the HSWP, reformers whose agenda remained the dismantling of the state socialist system gained control and established the Hungarian Socialist Party (HSP). In December the Hungarian Parliament voted for its own dissolution and in March/April the first multiparty elections returned a centre-right coalition that was to be led by Józef Antall, leader of the MDF.

The Hungarian political system in the 1990s

The Hungarian Constitution, though heavily amended, is built around the basic law of 1949, and the political system is based on the formal separation of legislative, executive and judicial powers.[6] The stage is headed by a President, indirectly elected by Parliament, and having relatively weak powers.[7] Legislative power is limited by a strong Constitutional Court and referendums. The Constitutional Court has the right to annul existing laws under parliamentary consideration if these contradict the Constitution and, since 1990, the Constitutional Court has made a number of significant landmark rulings.[8] The important role of the Constitutional Court (see below) derives from the fact that it is accessible to the government, MPs, groups of citizens and individuals alike. Parliament must hold a referendum if 100,000 electors demand it (except for certain issues, such as budgetary questions).

The Executive has little discretion to interpret laws, as the Hungarian legal system does not recognise secondary or regulatory legislation; nevertheless, the Executive has from time to time attempted to expand its delegated power. The main power of the Executive derives from the Prime Minister, to whom ministers are collectively responsible. They are also answerable to but not removable by Parliament.[9] The Prime Minister also enjoys the protection of a German-style 'constructive' vote of no confidence. Szoboszlai (1996:126) argues that the Hungarian Prime Minister has acquired similar powers to those in a *Kanzlerdemokratie*. Ministers (equivalent to Secretaries of State in the UK) do not necessarily have to hold parliamentary seats and are assisted by a political state secretary responsible for relationships with Parliament, who acts as deputy in the absence of the minister. The administrative state secretary is responsible for civil service issues. Although this role is non-political, politicians have also been appointed to this position as well as the position of under-state secretaries.

There are a large number of quasi-autonomous state institutions (with the right to appointment mainly resting with the Prime Minister), such as the Competition Office and the Court of Auditors. Although these institutions enjoy wide-ranging powers and rights, the Executive has often ignored their recommendations, for example the several critiques of the Court of Auditors on privatisation policies. An important Hungarian institution is the National Interest Reconciliation Council, in principle a tripartite, consultative organisation which discusses a wide range of issues from economic legislation to the annual state budget. Paradoxically, this organisation played an important role in policy creation, even though intermediary organisations (trade unions and employers' associations) are relatively weak in Hungary (Ladó 1994). Such is the political structure within which economic transformation has taken place, and to which we now turn.

The political economy of transformation: shock therapy verus gradualism (1990–93)

The background for the transfer of power from the HSP to the coalition that won the 1990 election, consisting of the Hungarian Democratic Forum (HDF), the Smallholders' Party and the Christian Democratic Party, was the drift of the Hungarian economy first into stagnation, then into recession. In 1990, instead of the projected growth of 1 per cent, GDP fell by 3.5 per cent, and in 1991 by 12 per cent, while unemployment increased from virtually zero to above 10 per cent. Although the government expected economic growth to begin in 1992 and exports to recover strongly, the recession continued, though at a slower pace. GDP fell by 5 per cent in 1993, but the economy started to grow in the second half of that year. However, due to the low accumulation potential of the domestic economy and the preceding recession period, the economy could not produce sufficient resources and so imports (especially of capital goods) increased significantly, while exports fell, partly because of the problems in agriculture and partly because of the deteriorating terms of trade. These factors resulted in a record deficit in current account ($3.5 billion). In 1994 the government failed to work out a comprehensive economic policy and implemented only those measures which were necessary to maintain the solvency of the country, while the new government needed time to create its own macro-economic policy.

First shocks

During the summer of 1990 the new Antall-led government started to develop its macro-economic policy. The most important conditioning factor of macro-economic policy at that time was the large decrease of international reserves (falling to the value of two months of imports). In this situation, the new government needed further support from the international organisations (the tough budget measures implemented by the last Communist government was a result of a one-year stand-by agreement with the IMF). In this early period, throughout the region, the only economic programme supported by the IMF in return for credits was shock therapy (see Chapter 3 and Gowen 1995). In short, this meant that the government had to try to achieve its structural aims (reduction in state ownership and budgetary transfers, reinforcing financial disciplines and capital imports) while attempting, simultaneously, to stabilise the economy.

This first phase of the shock therapy enjoyed the support of the main opposition party, the Alliance of Free Democrats (AFD). An agreement was reached in an informal pact between the HDF and the AFD, which aimed at easing the modification of certain laws requiring a qualified parliamentary majority (66 per cent plus one vote). Politically there were three major parts to this pact. First, there was strong pressure from the West to establish a grand coalition or to agree an informal coalition. Second, the government's economic programme was only marginally different from the economic ideology of the AFD. Third, the policy involved replacement of the top management of large, state-owned enterprises, which could have opened the way to major change in the economic elite (Sárközi 1991).

The pact was terminated when the government, under pressure from one of the junior coalition partners, attempted to introduce a law on the limited restitution of properties confiscated during the state socialist period. This failed when the Constitutional Court declared unconstitutional the government's proposal to provide restitution in kind only and in respect of one type of property – land. After also failing to replace the top management of state-owned companies, the government commenced centralised control of privatisation.[10] In practice this meant that the optional transformation of state-owned enterprises into joint-stock or limited companies was made compulsory. Since these company forms require external boards that exercise the ownership rights, the government could not only replace the management of state-owned companies through votes of the Board, but could also appoint its clientele to the boards of companies. These boards were also used to exercise a very close control on the day-to-day management of the companies (Whitley and Czaban 1998), and thus to reallocate resources and cross-subsidise activities (Voszka 1995).

The Antall government therefore settled on what was seen as an 'active privatisation programme', that is, the selection of a number of large companies for sale to foreign investors. Managers of the companies were excluded from the process. The success of 'active privatisation' was crucial to shock-therapy policy, since it was projected that the main elements of the shock therapy – deregulation and full liberalisation – would result in a large current account deficit and fall in production; capital inflow from the success of the active privatisation programme would, it was hoped, address these problems.

The shock therapy had failed by late 1990, partly because the coalition partners of the major government party (the HDF) and some of its own major factions politically opposed it; partly because of the diminishing support for the government (defeat in the local elections and the taxi-driver blockade of October);[11] and partly because of the deteriorating external conditions of the transition. These factors resulted in intragovernmental conflicts, in which the Economic Policy Secretariat of the Prime Minister's office emerged in opposition to the shock therapy!

The question of privatisation

The second period of the macro-economic transformation (1991–93) was much less radical, accepting that the implementation of a similar deregulation and liberalisation programme would involve a much longer time scale. During this period, almost all price controls, wage controls, foreign trade control and direct subsidies were abolished and Parliament passed Acts defining and regulating the Central Bank, Commercial Banks, Accounting and Bankruptcy, among others. Despite these steps, however, the original programme of liberalisation and deregulation was seriously impaired by the continued failures of privatisation policy. 'Active' privatisation programmes had proved that centralised (directed) processes were too slow; and that effective privatisation required committed participation by the managerial elites.

During 1991 a number of factors combined to bring about changes in economic policy. These included the deep recession affecting all CEEC, the relatively easy access to international capital markets and a surplus in the current account which, together with the lack of domestic capital and the financial consequences of the monetary restrictions, resulted in the considerable devaluation of the existing state assets and largely uncontrolled privatisation through liquidation procedures. These developments forced the economic elites within the government to retreat from *laissez-faire* perspectives and establish an Economic Policy Work Group headed by the Privatisation Minister at the end of 1991.

The Economic Policy Work Group submitted its report to the government in early 1992 (Gazdasagi Munkacsoport 1992). Besides proposing widespread state intervention (export guarantee, credit consolidation, state involvement in research and development, state holding, and so forth) and criticising the economic policy of 1990–91, the report stated that the war against the management of state-owned companies was destructive and had to end – not only for economic reasons, but also because the management of these companies was one of the potential sources of a future Hungarian bourgeoisie. In this was the admission that only a unified elite was able to manage the transition and legitimise it, for if factionalism arose, the transformation itself might become endangered (Czaban 1998).

The last element of this phase was the creation, in August 1992, of a state asset-holding company (SAMCO), which meant inevitably that large-scale economic units would remain in the hands of government for the foreseeable future. The privatisation laws of summer 1992 thus legalised the then existing situation: the exclusive control of the government over privatisation and state asset management.

The macro-economic management problems described above, a relatively favourable external balance of the country and increasing political unpopularity prompted the government to extend the change in economic policy still further and, with substantial state support, help companies to stabilise their position. In the second half of 1992, the government implemented the proposals of the Economic Policy Work Group, and between 1992 and 1994 spent HUF 300 billion (about 10 per cent of GDP) on the recapitalisation of banks and debt forgiveness.

By 1993 the slow pace of privatisation and the low level of foreign interest in Hungarian companies, as well as the now more positive electorate, encouraged the government to change its philosophy of privatisation completely: thus use of subsidised loans, employee and management buy-outs, and 'quasi'-free distribution of state assets became characteristic of a new philosophy. This move, therefore, achieved a series of political compromises among several elite groups and offered assets to those who were the potential source of the Hungarian bourgeoisie: that is, the management of state-owned companies and technocrats moved from central bureaucracy to business; the entrepreneurs of the 1980s and, to a lesser extent, the descendants of the traditional upper middle class. In the meantime, compensation schemes and employee buy-outs secured the neutral position of relatively broad social groups during the transition.

Inevitably there was to be a price for these more populist methods. A government policy for economic growth resulted, quite rapidly, in economic disequilibrium. Since economic growth was based on machinery imports as well as large state contributions this, coupled with recession in the most important export markets, was to lead to a deteriorating current account from the beginning of 1993. External debt started to grow rapidly, not only because of the current account deficit but also because state intervention and support for economic growth resulted in a budget deficit so large that it far exceeded domestic savings. From the second half of 1993, economic growth already affected household incomes, and so imports of consumer goods also increased rapidly. By the end of 1994, this disequilibrium became unmanageable and in March 1995 the HSP/AFD government, now led by Gyula Horn, decided to implement an austerity programme.

Consolidation of the transition: downsizing of public finances and enterprise transformation

In the election of May 1994, the centre-right coalition parties suffered a very serious defeat, while the HSP won more than half the seats.[12] The causes of this defeat were visible in 1992 (Lengyel 1992), and include the lack of trust between the companies and the government, administrative incompetence, political arrogance (especially over the independence of the media; see Chapter 4), sleaze and a hostile relationship between the government and sections of a still significant intelligentsia. All of these factors combined to generate a 'nostalgia' for the relative comfort of previous socialist administrations. Furthermore, as a Eurobarometer opinion survey suggested (Commission 1994), the people of Hungary had become frustrated by official denunciations of everything from the state socialist period (interview with Magyar Hirlap, May 1998).

Although the HSP won 209 of the 394 seats, in the interests of stability, to extend the political and social base and because of the closeness of the state socialist period, HSP entered into negotiations with the second largest parliamentary party, the AFD. As a contrast to the coalition of the previous government, these two parties prepared and published a very detailed coalition agreement. The distribution of posts, however, did not fully reflect the distribution of seats; moreover, the AFD obtained a *de facto* veto on cabinet decisions. Although the coalition had a 72 per cent majority, it announced that it would only change laws requiring a qualified majority if at least one of the opposition parties gave support.

While the new government enjoyed considerable popularity, there was a clear division between the government's aims and the expectations of its largest social base. Thus those groups comprising the social base of the HSP anticipated an easier life, with a larger welfare state, more jobs and higher employment security; while the government aimed at fine-tuning the political and economic system, introducing further institutional reform, completing privatisation and making all necessary preparations for joining the EU (Koaliciós 1994). The situation changed dramatically during the second half of 1994 and the first quarter of 1995. International markets, cautious about the huge current account deficit of the previous two years and the large budget deficit, threatened an accelerating external indebtedness; the Mexican financial crisis also contributed to this instability. Additionally, the IMF, which had never publicly criticised the previous coalition government, issued warnings about Hungary's macroeconomic situation after just a few months of the new government. In addition, the problem was heightened by government policy towards the privatisation process. Because of the merging of various agencies involved in the privatisation process, the sale of state assets slowed significantly in the second half of 1994. Furthermore, the Prime Minister personally intervened in a very public sale of a hotel chain, claiming that the offer price was too low.

All these events resulted in rapidly deteriorating expectations of investors in Hungary, at a point when the country needed their trust more than at any time before. We have already mentioned the austerity package introduced in March 1995, in part to deal with this growing problem of diminished domestic and international confidence. This package contained elements that would reallocate income from wage earners to entrepreneurs in order to reduce domestic demand, reduce budgetary expenditure (welfare state), promote exports (crawling-peg exchange rate policy) and defend domestic production (customs duty policy). It also demonstrated (as emphasised in Chapter 3) that shock therapy and the gradualist approach are not dichotomies, but alternatives – and the transitional countries, depending on the circumstances, must of necessity switch them.

The austerity package had a double effect on the economy; it disturbed the slow economic growth that had commenced in 1994 and extended the stagnation by about eighteen months. However, it also rapidly restored the trust of foreign investors. As the Constitutional Court's ruling on some elements of the package required additional policy measures, while delaying implementation of the original ones, the government decided to balance the books through a substantially accelerated privatisation. In the second half of 1995, the Hungarian government extended the privatisation of state assets to the utilities: gas, electricity and water supply and the energy sector. These characteristically capital-intensive industries and natural monopolies promised, and delivered, considerable privatisation revenue to the budget. In spite of the pressure from unions and employers' associations, pressure groups and backbench MPs, the coalition government used this revenue entirely for the reduction of state debt. This measure prolonged the period of slow economic growth, but it relieved the government from the economic policy constraint of external debt. By the end of 1997 the share of the private sector in the net debt of Hungary increased to 45 per cent (National Bank of Hungary 1998).

Out of this third privatisation campaign (which continued in 1996) and some additional large privatisation deals (for example, the floatation of some chemical industry companies on the stock exchange and the sale of all the large and medium-sized state-owned banks) came an ownership structure characteristically different from other former state socialist countries. Of the 200 largest companies in Hungary, 80 per cent are partly or wholly foreign-owned (Figyelo 1997) and the share of these companies in Hungarian exports exceeds 70 per cent (EBRD 1997). This very high concentration of foreign ownership in the large company sector is found, within the EU, only in Ireland. By the middle of the 1990s investment by multinationals (both green-field and brown-field) and the output of their subsidiaries reached a level at which they had also achieved a major impact on the small and medium-sized sector. The multinational corporations started to source components from Hungarian producers through their first-tier suppliers, who, to ensure the quality and the reliability of the supply, acquired a stake in the Hungarian suppliers (Czaban and Henderson 1998).

At the beginning of 1998 it seemed that the socialist–liberal coalition would easily win the election. However, the Alliance of Young Democrats (FIDESZ) had, by that time, repositioned itself as a centre-right liberal–conservative party and launched a successful election campaign which emphasised law and order and the need for economic growth. At the same time, the HSP, in what transpired to be a political error, placed the Land Act (which allowed the acquisition of land by foreigners) before Parliament just a few months before the election (interview with Magyar Hirlap, 21 May 1998). This allowed the nationalist card to be used against the government.

In the first round of the elections, although the HSP gained the most votes nationally, the defeat of the coalition became a possibility, as the combined votes of the opposition promised large gains in the second round and because the junior partner of the coalition (the AFD) showed poor results. In the second round this possibility became a reality and FIDESZ was able to form a coalition government with the HDF and the Smallholders' Party. Accession to the EU is one of the fragile elements of this new coalition government as FIDESZ is committed to joining the EU (*Financial Times*, 27 July 1998), while the junior partner, the Smallholders' Party, has often expressed strong reservations about membership. This means, ironically, that as the possibility of accession has increased since the *Agenda 2000* conclusions, Hungarian political conditions in support of the EU have become problematic.

Accession issues

As suggested earlier, ever since political transition there has been a concord among the largest Hungarian political parties that joining the EU is of crucial national interest. However, the relationship between the EU and Hungary has not always been harmonious.

Politicians of the first democratically elected government believed in early accession: sometimes they put it as early as 1993 or 1995.[13] It became clear, however, that although Hungary could expect support from the EU both financially (for example, loans for refilling the international reserves in 1990) and in terms of technical assistance (Phare), accession would be a lengthy process influenced by a number of factors, including the internal affairs of the EU and political developments of the region. Despite this recognition, Hungary submitted its application for membership in 1993.

The collisions between the EU and Hungary have typically related to the sensitive industries: textiles, agriculture and steel. After the collapse of the CMEA, the Hungarian textile and garment industry became a very important source of export revenue since it could capitalise on the low level of wages. Agricultural producers also sought to switch from the CMEA markets to OECD markets, while the steel industry was important as a large employer in the north-east region. The disputes included an anti-dumping procedure against the steel industry in 1992, while controversies over the articles of the EA related to outward processing in trade in the garment industry, the ban on unprocessed bovine products in 1993 and the unilateral modification of some of the customs duties by the Hungarian government in 1993. However, these issues were less important in Hungary than in other accession countries – partly because the recession of the first half of the 1990s greatly reduced the duplications in the Hungarian economy, and partly because foreign investment from EU countries played such a large role in the privatisation of state assets in Hungary.

Although per capita GDP in Hungary is still very low compared with the EU average, the influence of FDI gives strength to the Hungarian government in negotiations with the EU. However, Hungary's responses to the country questionnaires circulated by the Commission in 1996 showed many weaknesses in macro-economic management and in the operation of macro-economic institutions. These relate to the transparency of the procedures and some compatibility problems in competition policies (state aid) and customs practices. Nevertheless, as Chapter 2 illustrates, Hungary is seen to be in a relatively strong position regarding application of the Copenhagen criteria. Consequently the major concerns regarding accession progress would seem to be associated with political factors.

Of the political issues, the most important is the relationship with neighbouring countries. This historical problem derives from the loss of large Hungarian territories after the First World War and with the existence of substantial Hungarian minorities, mainly in Romania and Slovakia.[14] This issue was used for political purposes in the early 1990s, but the socialist–liberal coalition, partly in response to pressure from the EU, managed to conclude agreements with the neigbouring countries. Although there are nationalist sentiments in the junior parties of the present coalition government, these were more publicly evident prior to their entry into government.[15] Thus, from the perspective of Hungary, this issue does not seem to pose a major threat to the further development of cross-border relations with these countries.

On face value the minority problem in Hungary does not seem to cause difficulties for accession, since strong institutions are present to safeguard minority rights. In recent years there has been an improvement in the minority rights of the large gypsy population in Hungary, and minority self (local)-governments have been elected. Nevertheless, anti-gypsy sentiments remain strong in a very large proportion of the Hungarian population. Since the institutions which provide democratic rights to the gypsy minority are in place, this is essentially not a political, but an economic issue. A very large proportion of the gypsy minority are unskilled, migrant workers, who are particularly vulnerable to the impact of economic recession. Consequently the rate of unemployment in this segment of Hungarian society is very high.

The minorities issue appears in another form, however. Implementing the border-crossing policies of the EU would almost certainly mean debarring a large proportion of the Hungarian minority in the neighbouring countries from entering Hungary. This is a sensitive political issue, which may give rise to nationalist feelings in some layers of Hungarian society. Very recently the Hungarian government expressed willingness to reinforce its borders in exchange for financial assistance from the EU (*Financial Times*, 27 July 1998).

An issue that has recently become an important concern in relation to accession procedures is the growth of organised crime. The number of criminal acts has rapidly increased since 1990 and this increase is associated with Hungary's transformation. Thus there is ambiguity concerning traditional values, while the new 'rules of the game' remain unclear – in relation to the reallocation of assets (privatisation), income (taxation) and liberalisation (smuggling and the grey economy). By the mid-1990s it had become clear that many of these criminal acts are related to economic crime (domestic and foreign), and there remains a danger of its penetration into the state administration. Nevertheless, there is a political will to combat this problem (it was a strong point in the election campaign of the current government), and it is anticipated that with additional resources, technical assistance and the further consolidation of the market economy and political democracy, the situation will improve in the future.

Conclusion

Hungary, with the considerable advantage of early liberalisation during the 1980s, has made great progress in consolidating political democracy and the market economy. In effect, Kádárite socialism 'left polity with some features of civil society and a population that, however cynical and jaded, was used to certain freedoms and ready for more' (Brown 1994:81).

Its institutional system is largely based on the postwar German institutions with historical and cultural legacies of Hungary and some Anglo-Saxon influence. Although this makes the Hungarian institutional system different from that of most EU countries, this divergence is not unusual in the context of the EU (Lane 1992). By the mid-1990s, the operation of these institutions had become routine and, although their competencies are weak at some points and attempts to assert political influence on the operation of these institutions have been frequent, the evidence of improvements is strong and is recognised by the Commission. There is no significant political movement or public sentiment in Hungary that would question the values of political democracy or the need for transparent procedures and trust in the legal system. The safeguard measures in the legal and institutional system introduced in the early period of the transition, and in particular the role of the Constitutional Court, proved to be efficient in separating the legislative, executive and judicial powers. The country has undergone three general elections, with changes in the government, and the transition from the incumbent to the new government has been smooth in all cases.

The Hungarian economy has been one of the slowest growing in CEE. However, this slow economic growth (that also resulted in low per capita GDP) resulted from prudent budgetary policies and was seen as the price of the macro-economic stabilisation of the early 1990s, which provided a solution to the indebtedness of the state. With regard to privatisation, Hungary avoided the various quasi-privatisation measures and, relying heavily on foreign investment, it achieved a privatised economy not only in manufacturing and agriculture, but also in the service sector, including utilities and some of the welfare services. Foreign investment, after a long waiting period, has been the crucial factor in the transformation – not only in terms of macro-economic management, but also in restructuring of the company sphere. As a result, Hungary has many state-of-the-art companies and has become integrated into the production chains of multi-national firms. In the sphere of macro-economic management it has been crucial that, by the mid-1990s, the autonomy of civil servants was established, with 'technocrat' ministers accepted as part of the Executive (for example, the current Minister of Finance, Zsigmond Jaray).

The political consensus in Hungary to 1998 has ensured that, even if gradually, Hungarian governments have implemented measures required by the EU in the context of accession – and in this they have enjoyed the support of opposition parties. In this respect, however, inclusion of the anti-EU Smallholders' Party in the governing coalition in May 1998 can be seen as a 'fairly negative sign' in relation to attitudes towards the EU and, indeed, attraction of foreign investment (Central Europe Online 1998). Ultimately, as in all CEEC, continued progress towards accession depends on the maintenance of political consensus and public acquiescence to the government's overall aims; together with a willingness to accept the pain of applying uncomfortable EU conditionalities. In the case of Hungary, the relatively early start to transformation, and the incremental progress of reform since 1989, suggest an absence of major impediments to accession.

Notes

1 It remains debatable whether it was Hungary or Poland that was first to lead CEEC towards post-communism. Holmes (1997:68) argues that by April or May 1990, 'Hungary had unambiguously reached post-communism. It had done so with a minimum of fuss; the whole process had been very civilised.'

2 By the mid-1980s Hungary was the most heavily internationally indebted country in the world, with a currency debt of approximately 62 per cent of its GDP in 1986.

3 Spontaneous privatisation normally meant that the senior management established a venture, with stock and private ownership, involving one of the units of the enterprise. Not only was the state's share undervalued in these ventures, but soon the senior management used its position to transfer business from the state-owned enterprise to the privately-owned venture. At a later stage the state was bought out, resulting in a 'pure' private company. The principal issue in 'spontaneous privatisation', therefore, is not a moral one; rather, it is the huge waste in assets involved in the process.

4 Kádár was General Secretary of the HSWP from 1956 to 1988.

5 An example of the new political freedoms during this period was a mass demonstration of some 30,000 people in Budapest in September 1989. They were protesting against the environmental impact and economic cost of the Gabcikovo–Nagymanos hydroelectric dam. This protest led to the suspension of work on the scheme a few months later.

6 The Hungarian constitutional changes predate the establishment of a free parliamentary system, thus 'parliamentarianism was more a result of, rather than a framework for the transition of state socialism to pluralism' (Szoboszlai 1996:118).

7 However, as the media war of 1991–94 showed, these weak powers can be used effectively: the President refused to endorse the appointment of the new president of Hungarian Radio and Television and the Constitutional Court ruled that no time limit could be imposed upon the President's consideration of the candidate proposed by the Prime Minister.

8 The Court has, for instance, played a significant role in debates over media freedoms during both the Antall and Horn governments. In 1995 it also declared unconstitutional several elements of the government's economic programmes which infringed rights assured under existing social security legislation.

9 Thus, for example, Parliament rejected the answers of the Privatisation Minister to questions of MPs on seven occasions between 1992 and 1994, with no political consequences.

10 For a review and analysis of the changing institutional system of privatisation, see Henderson *et al.* (1995).

11 As a protest against a huge increase in petrol prices that had previously been denied by the government, taxi and lorry drivers blocked the bridges and main junctions in Budapest. The protest then spread across the country, bringing it to a standstill. The action enjoyed popular support and the government was finally forced to negotiate with the employers and unions in the Interest Reconciliation Council. The entire negotiation was broadcast on Hungarian television and the public became convinced that the new politicians were both arrogant and incompetent (Lengyel 1992).

12 In the elections of May 1994, four months after the death of Antall, the HDF was beaten into third place with less than half of its 1990 vote of 25 per cent. The HSP, in contrast, increased its vote threefold, to 33 per cent.

13 This information is based on extensive interviews with Hungarian politicians

and Commission officials, conducted by the author between 1993 and 1996.
14 These issues are, of course, discussed in Chapter 9, on Slovakia, and also in the treatment of perceptions of security in Chapter 7.
15 For example, a former opposition leader, now a junior member of the governing coalition, described the 1994 treaty normalising relations with Ukraine as an act of treason for accepting the existing borders between the two countries.

References

Berend, I. (1990), *The Hungarian Economic Reforms 1953–1988*, Cambridge, Cambridge University Press.
Brown, J. F. (1994), *Hopes and Shadows – Eastern Europe after Communism*, Harlow, Longman.
Central Europe Online (1998), Hungary urges EU to judge aspirants on own merit, *Archive*, 8 April, http://www.centraleurope.com/ceonews/98040902.html.
Commission (1994), *Central and Eastern Eurobarometer*, Brussels, March.
Commission (1997), *Opinion on Hungary's Application for Membership of the European Union*, DOC/97/13, 15 July.
Czaban, L. (1998), Ideologies, economic policies and social change: the cyclical nature of Hungary's transformation, in J. Henderson (ed.), *Industrial Transformation in Eastern Europe in the Light of the East Asian Experience*, London, Macmillan.
Czaban, L. and Henderson, J. (1998), Globalisation, institutional legacies and industrial transformation in Eastern Europe, *Economy and Society*, 27:4, 585–614.
East, R. and Pontin, J. (1997), *Revolution and Change in Central and Eastern Europe*, London, Pinter.
EBRD (1997), *Transition Report*, London, European Bank for Reconstruction and Development.
Figyelo (1997), A ketszaz legnagyobb magyar gazdasagi tarsasag [Top-200], *Figyelo*.
Gazdasagi Munkacsoport (1992), *A Gazdasagi Munkacsoport jelentese* (Report of the Economic Policy Work Group), report to the Hungarian government.
Gowen, P. (1995), Neoliberal theory and practice for Eastern Europe, *New Left Review*, 213, 3–60.
Henderson, J., Whitley, R., Czaban, L. and Lengyel, G. (1995), Contention and confusion in industrial transformation: dilemmas of state economic management, in E. Dittrich, G. Schmidt and R. Whitley (eds), *Industrial Transformation in Europe*, London, Sage, 79–108.
Holmes, I. (1997), *Post Communism – an Introduction*, Cambridge, Polity Press.
Koaliciós (1994), *Megallapodas a Magyar Szocialista Part es a Szabad Demokratak Szovetsege kozott* [Coalition Agreement Between the Hungarian Socialist Party and the Alliance of Free Democrats], Budapest.
Kulcsár, K. (1994), *Ket vilag kozott. Rendszervaltas Magyarorszagon 1988–1990* [*Between Two Worlds. The Change of the System in Hungary 1988–1990*], Budapest, Akademiai Kiado.

Ladó, M. (1994), *Workers' and Employers' Interests – As they are Represented in the Changing Industrial Relations in Hungary*, Working Paper No. 3, Krakow, University Council for Economic and Management Education Transfer.

Lane, C. (1992), Business systems and institutional systems, in R. Whitley (ed.), *European Business Systems*, London, Macmillan.

Lengyel, L. (1992), *Utfelen [Off the Road]*, Budapest, Szazadveg.

National Bank of Hungary (1998), *Annual Report*, Budapest.

Sárközi, T. (1991), Vita a tarsasagi torvenyrol [Debate about the Company Act], *Figyelo*, 14 March.

Szoboszlai, G. (1996), Parliamentarianism in the making: crisis and political transformation in Hungary, in A. Liphart and C. H. Waisman (eds), *Institutional Design in New Democracies – Eastern Europe and Latin America*, Boulder, CO, Westview, 117–36.

Vigvári, A. (1991), Reform es rendszervaltas [Reform and the change of the system], *Eszmelet*, 9:10, 11–33.

Voszka, E. (1995), *Agyaglabakon allo orias. Az AV Rt letrehozasa es mukodese [A Giant on Clay Feet. The Creation and Operation of the State Holding]*, Budapest, Penzugykutato Rt.

Whitley, R. and Czaban, L. (1998), Institutional transformation and enterprise changing an emergent capitalist economy: the case of Hungary, *Organization Studies*, 19:2, 259–80.

Poland: the return to Europe

With a population of over 38.6 million and an area of over 312,000 square kilometres, Poland is by far the largest of the countries of CEE seeking membership of the EU. Its location, between Germany and the patchwork of states that emerged from the former Soviet Union, gives it a particular geopolitical sensitivity, thus 'Poland brings into sharper focus than perhaps any other the dilemmas of enlargement for both applicant and EU' (Preston 1997:3).

This chapter, first, places Poland's progress towards EU membership in the contexts of a turbulent history, a severely limited democratic experience, and a long struggle to re-emerge politically and economically as a democratic society. The discussion then stresses the importance of trade and aid in stimulating Poland's economic transformation. Poland rapidly locked into the EU trading system and was the recipient of about $36 billion in assistance between 1990 and 1994 (US General Accounting Office 1995). The focus then moves to the central theme of Poland's 'return to Europe'. The history of association agreements and progress towards membership is analysed, with particular emphasis upon the significance of the period 1995–98, from the alignment to the Single Market, to the *Agenda 2000* Opinion and the actions stemming from it. The arrangements operating from 1998 are outlined and some controversies, and questions for negotiation, suggested.

Since 1989 the strategic importance to Poland of EU membership has been confirmed on many occasions, so it is first of all important to understand Poland's vision and motivation for this.

Poland: vision and motives

Proud of its role in European history and Christianity, Poland views membership of the EU as fulfilling its historical destiny. But, given the structure of Polish society as 'a partly traditional and partly industrialised society' (Weclawowicz 1996), one should not assume that this is a universal view. Moreover, at a time when the realities of alignment and restructuring are beginning to be fully appreciated in Poland, it is important to recognise the obstacles to accession. Nevertheless, Rolf Timans, the EU representative in Poland, has said, 'I would not like to speak of obstacles, I would rather speak of challenges' (Oljasz 1997:5).

Despite the uncertainties and difficulties which will inevitably attend accession, one can immediately appreciate the significance of applying to join the Union from the views recently expressed by the Minister of Foreign Affairs, Bronislaw Geremek: 'for Poles, it is an indisputable fact that a permanent and successful anchoring of Poland in the sphere of Western civilization is a task of fundamental importance'. His position on the EU is unequivocal: 'the European Union has become the most important political and economic structure of the modern world. It guarantees, and is a model for, the respect of democratic principles. It has also become the center toward which most international entities gravitate.' He sums up the domestic symbolism of this process by stating that, 'to most Poles, membership in the EU will be proof of Poland's new place in Europe and the world as a democratic and modern state' (Geremek 1997:3).

Jonas (1997), Weclawowicz (1996) and many others have set out a wide range of motives for Poland's integration into the EU. These reflect a mixture of pragmatism and idealism. First, one must appreciate the Polish desire for political security from a potential Eastern threat. Poland's President wrote of 'inscribing Poland into the mosaic of Euro-Atlantic structures' (Kwasniewski 1997:2), while the head of Poland's European Integration Committee posed the question: 'What is Poland's *raison d'être* at the end of the 20th century? In my opinion it is state security and the well-being of its citizens . . . I am convinced the best two ways to realise these objectives is to join NATO and the European Union' (Czarnecki 1997:4).

Jonas points out that, for Polish politicians and intellectuals, EU membership brings the prospect of embracing a system of European values based on religious tradition, Greek philosophy and the French Revolution. Cultural, ethical and moral principles are therefore crucial within this European value system. But, most significantly, he sees the adoption of these values 'even against some local forces and opinions. In this way, membership of the EU will provide a specific external insurance policy against potential internal threats' (Jonas 1997:3). The short duration of previous Polish democracy lives on in the memories of older Poles; and the hope is that, today, democracy will prove more solid and acquire deeper roots. In contemporary political discourse, notions of a civic society mean that Poles hope for a much closer connection between citizens' desires and the actions of the state, as well as a more active, and devolved, style of governance.

In economic terms, Poland hopes for, and is certainly now enjoying, an inflow of foreign investment which will do much to reduce backwardness. New technology will provide a basis for the modernisation process and linkage to the global economy. The evidence of long-term economic growth, and the benefits for living standards, have impressed many Polish commentators; and the ability to provide a higher quality of social welfare is seen as vital. For a society that has long enjoyed high levels of education, career prospects look brighter. And for a previously frustrated group of potential entrepreneurs, the new rules offer great opportunities. Finally, Poland sees the evidence that Western European countries such as Austria and Finland, successful in the past by 'going it alone', have made a recent judgement that better prospects lie in joining the EU. Ultimately, however, Poland's turbulent history might mean that the main reason for joining is a fear of being left outside 'fortress Europe'; and, here, this 'better out than in' pragmatism may make some within the EU suspicious of Poland's motivation (Cloonan 1996).

Poland in historical context

Poland's historical links with Western Europe can be traced back for over 1,000 years. From the fifteenth century onwards close cultural and political links developed, ranging from the enthusiastic adoption of architectural, artistic and musical styles, through to sharing important ideas in Catholic theology, the Reformation, the Enlightenment and Humanism. Successive waves of German settlers enriched Poland via merchant capital, technology and legal frameworks (Aniol et al. 1997). Poland entered into military alliances and gave leadership at critical moments in European history, the most celebrated being at the Battle of Vienna (1683), when the Turks were repulsed from Western Europe.

The Republic of Poland, established in 1918, enjoyed only a brief period of Western-style parliamentary democracy, as in 1926 a military coup was staged. A semblance of parliamentary life returned from 1935 to 1939, but the opposition was emasculated. The martyrdom of Poland from 1939 to 1945 witnessed the greatest proportional loss of life of any participant in the Second World War (some 25 per cent). Moreover, the consequences of peace for democratic life were, once more, to be negative. The imposition of the Soviet model of economic and political development was strengthened by the 1947 election, and then settled by the forcible merger of the Socialists with the Communists into the PUWP in 1948. For the next thirty years Poland experienced a number of violent protests at the loss of political and economic freedom. The 'Polish October' of 1956, when riots took place in Poznán, led to some reform and a leadership change. The principal opponent of the Communist state, the Catholic Church, gained some concessions. However, as was to become the pattern in Communist Poland, the impact of reform soon faded. It took another violent demonstration, centred on Gdansk at the end of 1971, to produce further concessions and another change of leadership.

One year before these events, there was a very significant development in Poland's bilateral relations with members of the EU. The German Federal Chancellor, Willy Brandt, visited Poland as part of his policy of *Ostpolitik*. This visit was important to Poland's progress towards its return to Europe, for at least three reasons: West Germany recognised the postwar borders of Poland;[1] full diplomatic relations were established; and access was given to Western financial markets. By their very nature, these changes lessened Polish dependence upon the Soviet Union since images of NATO, and especially West Germany, as a security threat were less sustainable. While negative stereotyping of Germans would continue, Poles began to appreciate the possibilities arising from West Germany's economic strength and growing political influence both within the EU and globally.

In the short term there were benefits to the Polish economy, for example in the ability to use credits to import foodstuffs and consumer goods, and the potential for increased inward investment, but the gains were soon swept away by the OPEC oil price increases and the international economic problems that followed. In 1975–76 Poland responded to the crisis by imposing massive price rises, but, learning from past public unrest, the authorities undertook strong preventive measures. This time, however, there was a major difference because in 1976 the Workers' Defence Committee (KOR) had been set up. KOR has been described as 'a politically potent labor movement', which was 'supported by dissident intellectuals and a powerful Catholic Church' (Aniol *et al.* 1997:39). In 1980 a further round of increases in the price of foodstuffs led to the now famous strikes centred on the Gdansk shipyards.[2] The creation of the independent, self-governing trade union, Solidarity, hastened the end of another Communist leadership, but the political 'gridlock' of 1980–81, and the threat of outside intervention, led to a declaration of martial law in December 1981. But this was to be relatively short-lived, not least because Poland had an important international voice in the shape of Pope John Paul II. He had paid a triumphal visit to Poland before the events of 1980, and his return in 1983 played some part in persuading the Communist military rulers that concessions were unavoidable.

For the next five years the economic crisis continued unabated, with foreign debt rising to $39 billion. Wages and productivity fell and industrial unrest continued. In June 1986 Poland took the (to some unpalatable) step of applying for membership of the IMF. In order to improve its image, both abroad and at home, the Jaruzelski government submitted its 1987 programme of (yet more) price rises and promised democratisation through a referendum. Rejection of the proposals signalled the impending end of the Communist Party's monopoly of power (Weclawowicz 1996). From February 1989 round-table talks began between the government and the opposition, led by Solidarity. The latter's demand for legalisation was confirmed in April 1989 and freedom of the press allowed. General elections were then organised. Even at this late stage, the Communists tried to retain their dominant position by reserving two-thirds of the 460 seats in the Lower Chamber of the Sejm (Parliament). Solidarity not only won all 161 seats that could be freely contested, but in the Upper Chamber, the Senate, it won 99 of the 100 seats.

In August 1989 Tadeusz Mazowiecki led the first non-Communist government in CEE. This set the stage not only for rapid domestic economic reform, but also for local democracy (Regulska 1993) and, significantly, for external links to European and international institutions to be strengthened.

The commencement of radical economic reform and political change

On the political front, the start of the decade saw the PUWP voting to disband and re-form as the Social Democratic Party and Poland's application to join the Council of Europe. However, 1 January heralded the start of a major, and still ongoing, economic reform programme. It is the subsequent speed (or its lack) which has had repercussions, not only on Poland's own domestic economy and politics, but on the evolving relationship with the EU. A tough austerity programme had been approved by the IMF, in 1989, to tackle hyperinflation of 550 per cent. Poland did, however, attract generous levels of aid from the West.

Mazowiecki's economic reforms had four major objectives: to manage the transition from a centrally planned to a market economy; to initiate measures to fight inflation and the budget deficit; to draft privatisation, competition and tax-reform programmes; and to modernise the banking system. What was particularly radical was the use of so-called 'shock therapy' tools. State subsidies were to be abolished, except in the case of a limited number of products such as fertilisers, pharmaceuticals and fuels. One has to consider, however, the gap between these intentions and the real progress, particularly bearing in mind some of the European Commission's views in *Agenda 2000* (Commission 1997a). It was also the intention to abolish remaining price controls and impose a wage freeze. The dismantling of monopolies was proposed, as was the privatisation of the economy through reorganisation of the cooperative system and foreign investment. Development of capital markets, including the creation of a Stock Exchange, rationalisation of credit policies and establishing the convertibility of the zloty, were the other essential features of the reforms.

Two particular elements that have proved to be vital to the transformation, not only in Poland but in other CEEC, are FDI and the creation of joint ventures. In 1986, three years before the fall of communism, a 49 per cent maximum stake had been set and a foreign investment agency, responsible to the Prime Minister, supervised proposals fairly closely. By 1991 a new law had been promulgated which removed the minimum capital contribution from overseas and eliminated restrictions on profit repatriation; and by 1997, according to the Polish Agency for Foreign Investment, Poland ranked first in CEE in FDI – with $6.6 billion invested. Moreover, by the end of December 1997, foreign companies had invested over $20.6 billion. This success, however, was to take some years to achieve – for the start of the economic reform process took place in the context of raging inflation. At the beginning of 1990 the inflation rate was 684 per cent. There was a fall in living standards during 1990 of some 20 per cent and foreign debt had accumulated to $48 billion. But progress was made, so that by the end of 1991 inflation had fallen to 60 per cent.

The Act on the Privatisation of State-Owned Enterprises and the Office of the Minister of Privatisation Act were passed by the Sejm in July 1990 and the regulations on privatisation were produced in November 1990. These allowed for the creation of a ministry to administer ownership changes, with the power to coordinate and regulate the privatisation process. The mechanisms to sell shares in existing state-owned enterprises, or increase share capital by issuing new shares, were set out. Finally, rules on preferential entitlements to shares for employees in private enterprises and foreign-owned share capital were made.

With regard to domestic politics, the impact of the austerity programme and accusations of delays in implementing economic and political reforms led to a split in Solidarity during 1990. The result was that Mazowiecki ran for President against Lech Walesa. The victory of the latter, and the poor showing of the former behind an unknown, right-wing, returned émigré, led to Mazowiecki resigning as Prime Minister in December 1990. The new Prime Minister, Jan Bielecki, was an economist and the new government included the IMF-backed Leszek Balcerowicz.

In January 1991 the first privatisation share sales took place. Further loans were forthcoming during 1991 to support the economic reforms, but unemployment was rising and living standards declining. The difficulties of the government were overtaken by the first post-Communist, fully free elections. After much negotiation, a new coalition emerged. The government pledged to adopt a more gradual approach to market-based reform and, once again, domestic political priorities were re-emphasised by the pledge to concentrate on helping ailing state industries. Two more administrations followed in quick succession, and at the election of October 1993, the ex-Communist Democratic Left Alliance (SLD) and the Polish Peasant Party polled strongly. Subsequently, in 1995, the ex-Communist SLD leader, Aleksander Kwasniewski, narrowly defeated Lech Walesa in the presidential election. The re-emergence of the Left and the continuing problems of building coalitions remain crucial factors in Poland's domestic politics, but membership of the EU continued to be the strategic objective of Polish foreign policy. President Kwasniewski, who had been a junior minister in the last Communist government, confirmed Poland's commitment to EU membership at the College of Europe in Natolin, near Warsaw, on 6 November 1996:

> Participation in the natural integrative processes of our continent is part of our understanding of Polish sovereignty. For us, the prospect of European integration is a historic challenge. We are thinking not only of the benefits we will gain from accession to the European Union. We are also aware of the obligations incumbent upon us from our role in the unification of the continent. (Quoted in Commission 1997b:6)

An important contribution to the analysis of some dimensions of Poland's economic and political transformation has been made by Aniol *et al.* (1997). They see the emergence of two camps in Polish politics. While Poland subscribes publicly to the 'return to Europe' through its primarily urban 'cosmopolitans', the opposing camp views European integration as a threat. The geography of the second round of the 1995 presidential elections saw the latter group supporting Lech Walesa. Traditional, rural, Catholic south and east Poland contrasted with the north and the west, the main areas of Kwasniewski's support. The 'isolationists' see that transformation has led to a loss of influence for the Catholic Church. As for the Church itself, the Primate of Poland, Cardinal Glemp, has viewed EU membership as not just an economic but also a moral issue. One reading of this position might be that, just as Poland resisted communism and foreign domination before 1989, so it needs now to face the secular commercialism of the EU. As we saw in Chapter 5, an important manifestation of this view has been prolonged and bitter controversy over women's rights and, in particular, the issue of abortion.

It is to Poland's evolving relationship with the EU that we now turn.

The establishment of Polish/EU relations: frameworks for trade, cooperation and assistance

The first mutilateral contacts between Poland and the EC had been in summer 1988 when a joint declaration was signed between the EC and the

CMEA. This was followed by the first TCA between non-Communist Poland and the EC, signed in November 1989. The stimulation of trade was an early and vital step on the road to integration. Poland was given greater access to the Single Market through mechanisms such as the granting of MFN status, inclusion in the Generalised System of Preferences (GSP), and lifting of quantitative restrictions. The GSP meant that, *in theory*, Poland could export industrial goods to the Community free of customs duties and without imposition of ceilings or quotas. However, the exclusion of ECSC products as well as other so-called 'sensitive' goods was to prove a source of continuing irritation. Poland benefited from GSP from 1 January 1990, initially for a five-year period.

It was at this time that the Commission proposed the incorporation of new elements into future agreements with Poland and other CEEC which would, it was hoped, facilitate their participation in aspects of the integration process; and hence also support the processes of economic and social transformation. These new elements moved beyond economic and financial cooperation to embrace cultural cooperation, political dialogue and free movement (of goods, capital and people). At a special summit of the European Council held in Dublin in April 1990 it was agreed that a free-trade area between Poland and the EU should be established. The date of 12 December 1990 was to prove significant in EU/Polish relations, as on this day the Council approved a series of Directives which enabled the Commission to negotiate Association Agreements with Poland, Hungary and Czechoslovakia. On 16 December 1991, Poland and the EU signed an agreement, by then known as an EA, through which Poland embarked on changes to prepare itself for the Single Market, and with the possibility of future accession.

The most significant elements of the EA included the phasing-in over a ten-year period of a free-trade area on goods (with the Community removing its tariffs and quotas at a faster rate than Poland); the gradual liberalisation of the services sector; financial and technical assistance of various kinds; approximation of existing and future legislation with that of the Community; adoption of Community state aid and competition rules; and the establishment of political dialogue (Cloonan 1996; Preston 1997). A non-trade issue which has the potential to cause problems in the current negotiations stemmed from Title 4, concerning the movement of workers, and the agreement provided for non-discrimination against Polish nationals working in the EU. The trade provisions came into force on 1 March 1992 under an Interim Agreement, while the main Agreement commenced on 1 February 1994.

The terms of the trade agreement specified steel, textiles and chemicals as 'sensitive' products subject to restrictions, and agriculture – a sector of great significance for Poland – was outside the scope of the Agreement. Trade restrictions were soon to develop into a source of bitterness in

Poland, for in the areas where its products were most competitive there were numerous quotas, voluntary export restraints and anti-dumping measures in operation. The Commission (1997b) noted a number of implementation difficulties in the trade field, notably with the Polish import surcharge, certification, restructuring of the steel industry and measures in the motor vehicle and oil sectors. Nevertheless, between 1989 and 1995 EU exports to Poland increased by more than 300 per cent, totalling ecu 15 billion in 1995, while EU imports from Poland increased by more than 200 per cent and amounted to ecu 12.2 billion. The Commission argued that the trading deficit represented Poland's re-equipment needs. The degree of trade connectivity was demonstrated by the fact that, in 1995, 70 per cent of Polish exports went to the EU and 65 per cent of its imports came from the EU.

As political dialogue progressed, the Community became conscious of the need to stimulate Poland's transformation, not just through trade, but also through various forms of assistance. Indeed Cloonan (1996), among others, draws parallels between Western Europe's postwar recovery through Marshall Plan aid and the recovery of the CEEC from the 1990s onwards.[3] The coordination of aid to CEE at the Paris Summit of July 1989, and the role of the G24, is discussed in Chapter 1. Here we review the particular and early contribution of the Phare programme to Poland's immediate transition needs and subsequent economic transformation.

Poland and the Phare programme

The Phare programme was established by an EU Council Regulation at the end of 1989 to provide immediate grant assistance to Poland and Hungary to support the process of economic transformation. Initially aid was provided in four main areas: agriculture, improving access to the Single Market for Polish goods, cooperating in projects to improve environmental quality, especially in industrial regions like Upper Silesia, and encouraging investment in Poland.

In 1990 food aid was a high priority, with half the funds made available devoted to supplies of animal feed, pesticides and credits for the farming sector. However, there was a failure to take up some of the credit lines owing to the decline in Polish farm incomes (Bobinski 1993), and in succeeding years the allocation of funds to this sector was low, estimated at about 7 per cent of spending. In contrast, the area of training proved more successful. A 1990 Commission proposal provided for the creation of a European Training Foundation; Phare identified the educational sector as a priority area for reform; and the Trans-European Mobility Scheme for University Studies was adopted by the Council in May 1990. The major goal of this scheme was to contribute to the medium- and longer-term development of higher education and training systems through joint activities and increased staff and student mobility. In Poland the priorities identified included management and business administration, applied sciences and technologies, modern European languages, agriculture and agribusiness, and environmental cooperation.

Phare also made financial assistance available to support privatisation, financial reforms and industrial restructuring. Experts were funded to work in the government-owned Industrial Restructuring Agency and to advise the Ministry for Industry. Such help was invaluable in dealing, for example, with Pilkington, which set up a joint glass-making venture in Sandomierz, south-east Poland, and Volkswagen, which bought into a light truck manufacturing operation in Poznán.

As with many other forms of external financial aid, difficulties emerged with the Phare programme. First, Poland's absorption capacity, or the ability to spend the allocations on time, soon became a problem. In 1991 and 1992 only 60 per cent of the funds allocated was spent, although by 1995–96 the situation was much improved. Second, the annual sums involved, typically ecu 225 million from 1993–95, were small in relation to the needs identified. Third, and crucially, the processes involved in attempting to reconcile the Commission's priorities with those in Poland tended to be time-consuming and difficult.[4]

By 1993 the Phare programme had started to shift focus, partly because of external criticisms of the high proportion of funding going to highly paid Western consultants, and partly because of Polish desires to see increased emphasis upon direct investment projects in high unemployment areas. To meet this need, the Phare–Struder (Small and Medium-Sized Enterprises Grant Scheme) programme was set up in Poland in May 1993. It provides support in selected regions for local economic restructuring, through assistance to organisations and through encouraging the creation, development and nurturing of SMEs. One of the first steps to implement the programme was the creation of the Polish Agency for Regional Development, whose mission is to foster self-sustaining regional economic growth in Poland. Apart from components such as training and advisory services and small infrastructure projects, the programme contains three regional financial measures: the Grant Scheme, the Guarantee Scheme and Regional Investment Funds (Konopielko and Bell 1998). Formal eligibility criteria were established, but the most important requirement has been the test of technical, economic and financial feasibility. Thus the emerging Polish banking system, in this case either the Polish Development Bank or the Bank for Socio-economic Initiatives, appraises the projects. While Konopielko and Bell note that the programme is still in operation, and thus the total impact has yet to be determined, they conclude that the scheme has positively affected the behaviour of the regional banks.

While this example shows one aspect of Phare's evolution, it should be pointed out that multilateral and bilateral aid for Poland has spawned many similar schemes towards SMEs. A second example illustrates the widening forms of external financial support for Poland's economic transformation.

The EBRD

In order to support Poland's efforts to create a favourable environment for foreign investment, the G24 countries agreed to reinforce their promotion and protection of investments, and to support joint enterprises and other forms of industrial cooperation. The EBRD, inaugurated in London on 15 April 1991 on the initiative of the EU, became an important player in progressing Poland's transformation. Its functions were: to promote, in consultation with the IMF and the World Bank, productive investments in Poland and the other CEEC; to reduce the financial risks associated with such investments; to facilitate the transition to a market-based economy; and to accelerate the necessary market adjustment.

The Board approved the Bank's Strategy for Poland in August 1996. In advancing the economic transformation, the Strategy focused on three objectives:

> to improve the participation of the domestic financial system in enterprise financing, including wholesale financing of financial institutions, further privatisation and consolidation of the banking and insurance sectors, diversification of capital markets and participation alongside Polish institutions in specific transactions;

> to mobilise investment capital needed for growth, especially investment capital in commercial infrastructure, by raising and mobilising finance and developing financial products and financing structures consistent with more complex types of transactions now appearing in Poland, for example municipal bonds, public–private partnerships;

> to take a leading role in encouraging and financing structural reform in key sectors, by focusing on restructuring in steel, chemicals, oil and gas, shipbuilding and agri-business, by expanding interactions with the former state-owned trading organisations and by supporting the Mass Privatisation Programme and equity and venture capital funds.

By the end of December 1997 the EBRD had approved seventy investment projects (excluding projects which had been cancelled), involving direct Bank investment of ecu 1,186 billion. Table 11.1 summarises the major project categories, total cost and EBRD contributions.

One of the key dimensions of the modernisation process is modern communications, and especially telecommunications. Expenditure indicated in Table 11.1 includes the largest investment loan for the CEE telecommunications industry. This was made in June 1996 to Netia

Table 11.1 EBRD: Board-approved operations in Poland at 31 December 1997
(million ecu)

	Total project cost	EBRD financed
Joint ventures	2,642	397
Polish corporates	645	168
Banks and other financial institutions	183	88
Equity funds	615	133
Mass privatisation	174	105
Transport	569	95
Telecoms	509	88
Power	90	30
Property	439	79
Total	5,868	1,186

Source: EBRD office, Warsaw.

Telekom SA: the Bank provided $75 million of its own funds, a consortium of Polish banks another $85 million and the Nordic Investment Bank $20 million. In a project costing $350 million in total, Netia's eight operating subsidiaries will install 350,000 telephone lines. An interesting, and frustrating, part of this investment, which caused delay, were the inadequacies of Polish law to recognise holding companies.

The overall conclusion is that the contribution of international assistance to Poland's transformation has been vital (Fitz 1997).[5] However, with new lending in the range of $400–500 million a year, Poland will have to raise its absorptive capacity if the potential of these investments is to be realised (Knotter 1997). The donors have clearly identified the problem of further adjustments required in the Polish economy and, while delays might not be disastrous, they would certainly make accession to the EU much more difficult. The progress that has been made in adjusting to EU requirements is now discussed.

Polish adjustment measures: the period up to the publication of *Agenda 2000*

Following signature of the 1991 EA, Poland acted swiftly to establish new structures to take forward the preparations for an anticipated early accession. The Office of the Government Plenipotentiary for European Integration and Foreign Assistance was established in 1991 (Preston 1997). The Polish Council of Ministers gave it three tasks: to initiate specialised studies of the impact of EU membership on the Polish economy and legal system; to prepare public servants for accession; and to disseminate information both within central government and to all interested parties. At the parliamentary level, the Sejm passed a resolution in July 1992 recognising the fundamental importance of the EA to the future of the country and to the transformation of the Polish economy. In January 1993 the government announced a Programme of Measures for Adapting the Polish Economy and Legal System to the Requirements of the Europe Agreement (Committee for European Integration 1998). Annual progress reports on the adjustment process were published. The Office of European Integration commissioned a detailed review of Polish legislation, and the thirty-four reports were published in 1994. At this point Poland faced the choice of either directly transposing all EU law and removing all pre-existing Polish legislation, or gradually aligning Polish legislation as the reform programme progressed; the latter course was preferred (Preston 1997). In March 1994 the Council of Ministers decided to require that all new draft legislation conform to EU norms.

A limitation of Poland's (and other CEEC) EA was that it did not guarantee full membership of the EU, and thus did not discuss the necessary preparations for such status. As discussed in Chapter 2, the Copenhagen Summit of June 1993 proved significant, as it set out the political and economic requirements as well as the responsibilities of membership which would lead Poland eventually to the negotiating table. The encouragement given by the Copenhagen decision, the progress being made to harmonise Polish legislation and the working-through of economic reforms led to Poland making an official membership application on 8 April 1994. By late 1995 the process of internal alignment had been advanced to the point that both pre-existing legislation and new draft statutes being prepared by the Sejm were being subjected to a screening process for EU compatibility.

The Commission's White Paper on the Internal Market (1995) was of special significance to Poland's adjustment processes, as it included important recommendations regarding the priorities and sequence to be followed in adapting Polish laws to the regulations of individual sectors of the Single Market. The importance attached to the task of adopting the key *acquis* (the stage one measures indicated by the White Paper) is shown by a number of developments: the Government Plenipotentiary was charged, by the Council of Ministers, with producing a supplementary work schedule for all Ministries during 1995–96; each Ministry was also required to establish an EU Integration Unit; twenty-nine working groups were set up to work on the pre-accession strategy; and the Polish government published, during 1996, a series of legal studies setting out the path to approximation.

This period was made even more frenetic by the December 1995 decision of the European Council to request the Commission to prepare Opinions on Poland and the other applicants. In consequence the Commission produced a lengthy questionnaire seeking information deemed necessary to the formulation of its Opinion, which arrived at the Office of European Integration in April 1996 – to be completed by the end of July 1996. The Office coordinated the responses of the Ministries to the relevant DGs of the Commission and, as Preston (1997) suggests, the exercise both provided a test of the structures put into place to manage the integration process and showed sectoral Ministries what would be expected of them in the future.

One of the lessons drawn from the experiences to 1996 was that more effective coordination was required at the political level, in particular to resolve disagreements between ministers. A response to this problem came in August 1996, when the Committee for European Integration was established. This Committee was accorded new statutory powers to coordinate and steer policy and to make decisions on accession issues; and, as an indication of its importance, it was chaired by the Prime Minister (Dziennik Ustaw 1996). Following a resolution of the Sejm in March 1996 the government, through the new Committee, produced a National Strategy for Integration (Committee for European Integration 1997a). Its purpose was to summarise the measures taken to date, to formulate priorities for adjustment processes, and to set out the challenges associated with accession.

The report was structured around seven main areas: general political objectives, adaptation of the economy, adaptation of legislation, external affairs, justice and home affairs, training and human resources, and information activities.[6] It confirmed that EU membership continued to be a strategic objective of the Polish government, and that proper preparation of the Polish economy in the pre-accession period was crucial. It argued, furthermore, that the rate of economic reform should be accelerated. Phare was seen as one of the main instruments for financing the adjustment process.

The key elements of economic policy were reviewed in Part II and included reform of the national insurance system, privatisation of the largest state-owned enterprises, and completion of the process of restructuring and privatising the financial sector. Macro-economic policy, given the right combination of monetary and fiscal policy and the exchange rate, would, it was hoped, lead to a permanent lowering of the rate of inflation. In a discussion of the costs of economic transformation, the Committee argued that these would have to be borne whether or not Poland joined the EU. It was considered that, in the long term, the economic benefits of accession would greatly outweigh the costs of adjustment.

The Strategy was also concerned with preparatory work for the accession negotiations expected to open in 1998. It called for an acceleration of the work of experts on the balance of costs and benefits of membership – so that Poland's position on transition periods, exemptions and, especially, transfers could be established. Also set in motion were analyses of other accession treaties previously negotiated and evaluations of member state performance in the initial membership period. The tactics of influencing external opinion relevant to the accession process were set out: channels of political influence included diplomacy, the media and opinion makers. A form of SWOT analysis seems to have been employed, which led to particular attention being paid to countries and interest groups that might be hostile to Poland's membership.

The National Strategy for Integration was considered by the Sejm on 21 May 1997, and a set of implementation measures was drawn up, setting out the work for individual government institutions. March 1997 saw the setting-up of an Inter-ministerial Team for the Preparation of Documentation for Poland's Negotiations Regarding Membership in the European Union. The team comprised twenty-eight sector and five horizontal teams. Ongoing work stemming from the 1995 European Commission White Paper on the Internal Market resulted in a schedule of measures to adapt the Polish legal system being approved by the Council of Ministers on 15 July 1997.

Agenda 2000: the Commission Opinion

On the day after the Council of Ministers approved the measures to align Polish law, the Commission presented its Opinion on Poland's application for membership of the EU to the EP (Commission 1997b). In the light of its analysis, the Commission recommended the initiation of accession negotiations with Poland. Nevertheless, the need was stressed for continued internal adaptation in order fully to meet the conditions of membership; in consequence the Commission emphasised the importance of strengthened pre-accession strategies for all candidate countries.

The Polish Opinion highlighted a range of concerns, mostly regarding the capacity to take on the obligations of membership. Under political criteria, efforts to improve the operation of the judicial system and to intensify the fight against corruption were mentioned, as were certain limitations on press freedoms and the need to complete procedures on property compensation. Under economic criteria, there was seen to be a case for reforming the pension and social security systems, the banking sector was in need of further reform, and financial services were undeveloped. Two of the greatest challenges, not just in economic but also in social and regional terms, were agriculture and the larger state-owned enterprises.[7]

The third section of the Opinion dealt with capacity to take on the obligations of membership. A number of problems were identified here, including – on the highly significant issue of agriculture – the need to establish a coherent rural policy and to strengthen the administration that would apply the CAP. Also highlighted was the need for further work on public procurement, data protection, competition and the liberalisation of capital movements, while legislative adaptation in the field of technical rules and standards was considered to be proceeding only slowly. Some sectors – telecommunications, fisheries and consumer protection – were highlighted as requiring substantial efforts. Despite the significant progress discussed in Chapter 6, the Commission stressed the major problems facing the environment, including water and air pollution and waste management. In the case of transport policy, the need to invest in the European network was stressed, while in the energy sector questions were raised over coal industry intervention, energy pricing and import barriers for oil products. In employment and social affairs there was a need to adapt legislation on health and safety at work to conform with EU standards.

Some critical comments had certainly been anticipated by the Polish government, so that criticisms concerning regional policy coincided with the final report of Poland's Task Force for Structural Policies – which led, in turn, to a more coherent, ministerially led approach before the end of the year. Moreover, progress in economic policy was affirmed by the fact that the Commission saw no reasons why Poland should not be able to participate in the third stage of EMU. Finally, the significant problems in justice and home affairs, especially drugs, border management and transnational crime, were seen as challenges that Poland would respond to effectively.

Poland's formal response to the Opinion was prepared through the Office of the Committee for European Integration, being adopted by the Ministerial Committee on 26 September and approved by the Council of Ministers on 14 October 1997. The response adopted a very positive tone and used the Commission's comments to identify priorities for all the institutions of the Polish administration (Committee for European Integration 1997b), and to embark on the Programme of Preparation for membership of the EU.

Preparing for membership

In December 1997 the European Council adopted a SPAR as proposed in *Agenda 2000*. The strategy's objective was to provide Poland and other associate members with practical and financial assistance to implement reforms which are a prerequisite for full EU membership. Two horizontal requirements received the most attention: strengthening of administrative structures and the creation of mechanisms for their efficient operation, and implementation of Community standards regarding the operation of businesses.[8]

It was decided to create a new instrument, the Partnership for Accession, as well as ensuring the fuller utilisation of procedures under the EA and providing for greater participation in Community programmes and *acquis* mechanisms. The Commission's document, 'Partnership for Accession', was approved by the European Council in March 1998 in a Decision which set out the principles, priorities, intermediate objectives and conditions contained in the Accession Partnership. The Partnership document presented to the Polish government listed short-term (1998) and medium-term (to 2002) priorities for action and financial support from the EU, and it included an annexe summarising all the recommendations of the 1997 Opinion.

In order to be able to respond immediately to the EU's Partnership for Accession, Poland's Office of the Committee for European Integration began work in December 1997 on a draft 'Programme of Preparation for Membership in the European Union' to implement the EU's priorities. The draft list was approved by the Committee for European Integration at the end of January 1998, and the draft Part 1 was approved by the Council of Ministers at the end of March 1998. The priorities were listed under the six headings of Economic Policy, Internal Market, Employment and Social Affairs, Home and Justice Affairs, Sectoral Policies and Other Fields. Detailed annexes in Part 2 set out the prioritisation of tasks within each of the twenty-five areas. Table 11.2 sets out the priorities related to Sectoral Policies.

Taken together, the Programme of Preparation for Membership and the Partnership document confirmed that 'Poland will, in the course of the coming years, have to embark on a series of complex adjustment measures (whose list is by no means limited to those which the EU plans to support with financial aid) so as to achieve maximum readiness for the acceptance of the rights and duties associated with full membership in the European Union' (Committee for European Integration 1998:15). The Partnership introduced a uniform framework for financing adjustment priority implementation: Phare is to be the basic instrument and a financial memorandum has now taken the place of the various programme documents. In addition to the Phare funds, Poland is to finance the adjustment priorities from its own resources and from credits delivered by international financial institutions; the grant resources from Phare may thus be viewed as a catalyst for credits from these institutions. In this way funds for a number of large investment projects will be forthcoming, but in vital areas such as transport infrastructure, especially the motorway programme, private-sector funding will be crucial.

Table 11.2   Agreed draft list of adjustment priorities for Poland's sectoral policies

Steel	Drafting a programme for restructuring and a schedule for its implementation
Energy	Starting to implement programme of restructuring, including continuation of privatisation and modernisation of refineries, and petroleum stockpiling
Cars	Defining the criteria for production and industrial assembly
Enterprises	Creation of favourable conditions for development and improvement of competitiveness, especially SMEs
Environment	Preparation of the programmes and creation of the conditions for fulfilment of the requirements set by the frame directives on environmental protection, and starting the implementation of EC standards in that area
Environment	Adjustment of the Polish Ecological Policy to the 5th Community Action Programme on the Environment
Environment	Staff improvement (institution building) and financial support for environmental protection institutions
Agriculture	Creation of coherent rural policy aimed at encouraging positive changes in the agriculture sector
Agriculture	Adoption and implementation of phytosanitary and veterinary provision; establishment of proper services and infrastructure on the future external borders of the EU
Agriculture	Modernisation of the food-processing industry (including dairy and meat) and upgrade of quality-control systems
Telecommunications	Privatisation and law adjustment
Transport	Modernisation of transEuropean infrastructure
Transport	Harmonisation of laws and adjustment of standards aimed at efficient passenger and commodity traffic
Transport	Strengthening of institutions, administration and training for carriers on the rules of the common transport policy
Taxation	Continued harmonisation of laws in area of direct taxation
Taxation	Strengthening of fiscal authorities, including the procedures to counteract tax offences
Financial	Continued adjustment of laws and infrastructure
Financial	Establishment of State Agency for Financial Information and prevention of money laundering
Statistics	Continued adjustment to EC requirements
Audiovisual	Adjustment of laws by amendment and implementation of the Act on Radio and TV Broadcasting

Source: Programme of Preparation for Membership in the European Union (Warsaw, Office of the Committee for European Integration, 1998).

Recent developments and conclusions

Accession talks commenced on 31 March 1998. For a variety of reasons – including some controversial EU pronouncements and actions in 1997, the need for Poland to set out an initial negotiating position, the re-

opening of issues dating back to 1945, and the increasingly negative attitudes of some sections of Polish society – the stage appears to be set for
some interesting times ahead!

The question of transition periods for parts of the Polish economy,
notably heavy industry and agriculture, as well as more time to clean up
the Polish environment, have all figured in early pronouncements from
Jan Kulakowski, Poland's chief negotiator. From the EU side, Poland
faces the prospect of a delay, perhaps as long as ten years, on the free
movement of labour. What has also swiftly emerged as a controversial
political question concerns the Second World War and its aftermath.
Thus, while Germany has recognised Polish sovereignty over territory that
was part of the prewar Reich, it considers private land claims open
(Bowdler 1998b). For its part, Germany fears legal claims from its citizens
if it absolves Poland of any liability, while for Poland there is a need to
consider the likely EU negotiating position concerning the right of non-
discrimination in purchases of land and property.

Positive views in Poland towards the EU were certainly damaged at the
end of 1997 by a ban on Polish dairy products. In October an EU inspection of four dairy plants found two not up to standard, resulting in the
overall ban. The Polish government argued that the ban was political and
that competitors, notably the French, could hardly be seen as dispassion-
ate analysts of Poland's agricultural standards (Grodsky 1997a). Shortly
after this incident, Poland faced the pronouncement that its Special
Economic Zones set up to attract FDI breached the competition rules of
the EU and Poland's obligations under the EA. It was argued from the EU
side that Poland was supporting not just investment costs but also production costs, and that the total package exceeded the allowable ceiling
(Grodsky 1997b).

While opinion polls have generally shown Poland to be one of the most
enthusiastic supporters of the EU (Commission 1998), certain caveats
attach to this view. Bowdler (1998a) cites one recent poll where 55 per
cent of the population believed that Poland would feature in the EU only
as a second-class member. Thus the 1997 National Strategy for
Integration saw the need for a concerted information campaign, particularly as negative images emerge during negotiations. Indeed negative
opinions towards the EU have already moved towards expressions of
hostility by some sections of Polish society. Notably, in February 1998,
some two thousand farmers marched through Warsaw, declaring that
Poland's accession to the EU would take place 'over their dead bodies'
(Bowdler 1998a). One of the most dramatic demonstrations of opposition
to the EU occurred in March 1998, when employees of the Ursus Tractor
Factory in Warsaw staged a rally against the company's collapse and
likely insolvency. To emphasise where they thought the blame lay, the
EU's blue and gold flag was burned.

In terms of the Accession Partnership arrangements, a particularly difficult moment came when the Committee for European Integration was told in May 1998 by Ryszard Czarnecki, the coordinating Minister, that Poland had failed to obtain 34 million of the total of ecu 212 million allocable Phare funds. None of the other nine associated states were similarly affected, and the immediate domestic political casualty was the deputy minister responsible for preparing Phare projects (Oljasz 1998e). Among the fourteen projects rejected by the Commission were initiatives covering some of Poland's most urgent needs: environmental protection (four projects), agriculture (three) and one in telecommunications. The explanation from the Commission was that some projects were not in line with the priorities of the Accession Partnership or with the Polish government's plan for legal alignment, while others were inadequately specified. As political recriminations continue to fly, there is certainly a lesson to be learned over the effectiveness of coordination mechanisms.

Analysing Poland's future from an international perspective, the World Bank's representative in Poland has argued that, for Poland to be prepared for EU membership, there are a number of key tasks still to be pursued with vigour (Knotter 1997). In terms of macro-economic policy, Poland needs to maintain high rates of economic growth (ideally 7 per cent or more) while inflation, interest rates and budget deficits need to be reduced, public debt needs controlling, and a market-determined competitive exchange rate is required. Moreover, the role of the state and state-owned enterprises requires urgent attention. Knotter pointed, in particular, to the excessive share of GDP produced by state-owned enterprises (some 40 per cent in 1995). He used the rule-of-thumb calculation that every 10 per cent share of the public sector in GDP tends to lower average growth by 1 per cent per annum. Here, the prime candidates for restructuring are the energy and metallurgy sectors, but for coal and steel there are crucial social and regional issues to be considered. Finally, stressing the high costs of social policy provision, he argued that the social security and pension systems are not sustainable in the medium to long term.

Austria assumed the presidency of the EU from July 1998 at a relatively early stage in the process of screening Poland's legislation. It has therefore been important for Polish negotiators to discern any signals for the near future. The Austrian Ambassador to Poland has confirmed his country's favourable stance on enlargement, subject to careful preparations (Zygulski 1998). He has emphasised the importance of Poland maintaining its economic performance so that incomes continue to rise (currently only one-third of the EU average). The fear otherwise, and one certainly not unique to the Austrians, is of mass outmigration of Polish labour and the resulting tensions in domestic labour markets. With an eye to possible future adverse public opinion, the Austrian Ambassador suggested the need to educate the public in the existing member states to convince them that EU enlargement is in their interest. One possible positive development may be the acceptance of Austria's suggestion that some non-controversial negotiations take place in parallel to continued screening. It remains to be seen if this symbol of good will is agreed by the member states.

Ultimately one hopes that Poland's future relationship with the EU will involve the fulfilling of historical destiny; however, it may be a love affair that turns sour. From the Polish perspective, 'the main issue for today's EU, apart from the introduction of the Euro, must be guaranteeing the Central European states' participation in the continent's integration' (Kwasniewski 1997:2).

Notes

The author wishes to convey special thanks to the following organisations for interviews, and identifying contacts and sources: the Mission of the Republic of Poland to the EU, Brussels; the Integration Policy Department, Office of the Committee for European Integration, Warsaw; the Department of Environmental Policy, Ministry of Environmental Protection, Natural Resources and Forestry, Warsaw; *The Warsaw Voice* and *The Warsaw Business Journal*.

1 The issue of land and property rights of expelled Germans was more difficult; it remains contentious today.
2 The longer-term impact of the Twenty-One Points covering economic and social reform, issued by Solidarity leader Lech Walesa, was felt in the burgeoning opposition groups of CEE.
3 In the aftermath of the Second World War, with the onset of Cold War tensions, Soviet pressure had denied Poland and other CEEC access to assistance via the Marshall Plan.
4 These matters are discussed in some detail in Chapter 2.
5 In addition to the examples reviewed above, one can cite the approval of $4.1 billion from the World Bank for projects covering most major sectors of the Polish economy: energy, transport and municipal infrastructure, support of the market economy, the financial sector, social security, health and education. The EU-based EIB has also provided loans to CEEC, including Poland, primarily for the provision or upgrading of basic infrastructure. The Wroclaw–Gliwice motorway provides an example of an EIB-financed project in Poland.
6 An education and information campaign was to be initiated to increase awareness of and knowledge about the EU.
7 'Reversals in trade policy' were also commented upon. While the Commission felt that too many trade-related problems had arisen, most had been resolved.
8 A long list was given of specialists to be trained, ranging from environmental protection to veterinary inspection. Trading principles, working conditions and production control processes were examples cited in relation to the operation of businesses.

References

Aniol, W., Byrnes, T. A. and Iankova, E. A. (1997), Poland: returning to Europe, in P. Katzenstein (ed.), *Mitteleuropa: Between Europe and Germany*, Providence and Oxford, Berghahn Books.

Bobinski, C. (1993), Preparing for eventual membership of EC, *Financial Times*, Survey: Poland, 17 June, 11.

Bowdler, N. (1998a), Poland's EU negotiations; the gloves are off, *Business Central Europe*, April.

Bowdler, N. (1998b), Kohl extends hand of friendship to Warsaw to heal wounds of war but Germans stir up old fears by laying claim to land in Poland, *Guardian*, 12 June.

Cloonan, M. (1996), *Poles Apart? The Widening and Deepening Debate in the European Union*, University of York, Department of Politics.

Commission (1995), White Paper, *Preparation of the Associated Countries of Central and Eastern Europe for Integration into the Internal Market of the Union*, COM(95)163, Final, 3 May.

Commission (1997a), *Agenda 2000 – For a Stronger and Wider Union*, COM(97), Final.

Commission (1997b), *Agenda 2000 – Commission Opinion on Poland's Application for Membership of the European Union*, DOC 97/16.

Commission (1998), *Central and Eastern Eurobarometer*, DG X, Information, Communication, Culture and Audiovisual, Brussels.

Committee for European Integration (1997a), *National Strategy for Integration*, Warsaw.

Committee for European Integration (1997b), *Position of the Government of the Republic of Poland Regarding the Commission's Opinion on Poland's Application for Membership of the European Union*, Warsaw.

Committee for European Integration (1998), *Programme of Preparation for Membership in the European Union*, Part 1 (draft), 27 March, Warsaw.

Czarnecki, R. (1997), Good for Poland, good for the EU, *The Warsaw Voice*, Special Supplement: Knockin' on the Union's door, 50:477, 4.

Dziennik Ustaw (1996), *Establishment of the Committee for European Integration*, Warsaw, Official Journal NO. L 494, 8 August.

Fitz, R. (ed.) (1997), *The First Polish Economic Guide*, Warsaw, Common Europe Publications.

Geremek, B. (1997), Strengthening our continent's shared identity, *The Warsaw Voice*, Special Supplement: Knockin' on the Union's door, 3.

Grodsky, B. (1997a), Milk bar, *Warsaw Business Journal*, 8–14 December, 1, 14.

Grodsky, B. (1997b), Investors alarmed by conflict with EU over special economic zones, *Warsaw Business Journal*, 15 December, 3.

Jonas, A. (1997), Euro-hope, *The Warsaw Voice*, Special Supplement: Knockin' on the Union's door, 2–3.

Knotter, P. (1997), Thoughts on the medium-term economic prospects of the Polish economy and the World Bank assistance strategy, speech to the American Chamber of Commerce, in R. Fitz (ed.), *The First Polish Economic Guide*, Warsaw, Common Europe Publications.

Konopielko, L. and Bell, J. (1998), Reinventing aid for SMEs in Eastern Europe:

lessons from the implementation of the STRUDER programme, *Regional Studies*, 32, 290–4.

Kwasniewski, A. (1997), Adding to the European mosaic, *The Warsaw Voice*, Special Supplement: Knockin' on the Union's door, 2.

Oljasz, T. (1997), Stability and variety with size, *The Warsaw Voice*, Special Supplement: Knockin' on the Union's door, 5.

Oljasz, T. (1998e), PHARE fallout, *The Warsaw Voice*, 7 June, 5.

Preston, C. (1997), *Poland and EU Membership: Current Issues and Future Prospects*, UACES Conference, Enlarging the European Union – The Way Forward, Birmingham, July 1997.

Regulska, J. (1993), Democratic elections and political restructuring in Poland, 1989–91, in J. O'Loughlin and H. van der Wusten (eds), *The New Political Geography of Eastern Europe*, London, Belhaven.

US General Accounting Office (1995), *Poland: Economic Restructuring and Donor Assistance*, Report to Congressional Committees.

Weclawowicz, G. (1996), *Contemporary Poland: Space and Society*, London, UCL Press.

Zygulski, W. (1998), Bringing Poland closer to the EU, *The Warsaw Voice*, 12 July, 8.

Appendix I
Chronology

Linda Middleton

The Cold War and Europe (1945–88)

1945

February   At the Yalta Conference, the 'Declaration on Liberated Europe' (11 February) promises free elections and democracy for every European country; however, the Allies also agree to allow the USSR to maintain positions in Eastern Europe.

July–August At the Potsdam Conference, the Polish Provisional Government is recognised by the Allies and discussions take place regarding the future of Germany.

November   In Yugoslavia, Josip Broz Tito's National Front wins an election which is boycotted by opposition parties, and a Yugoslav Republic is declared.

1946

March   Churchill's 'Iron Curtain' speech (5 March) in Fulton, Missouri, warns of Soviet expansionism in Eastern Europe and signals the end of the US's and Britain's wartime alliance with the USSR.

May   The Communist Party in Czechoslovakia wins 38 per cent of the vote in elections.

August   The USSR signs trade agreements with Eastern European states.

1947

January   The Communist Party wins elections in Poland.

March   Truman proclaims his 'Truman Doctrine' (12 March), which aims to contain the spread of communism wherever possible.

June   The European Recovery Programme or 'Marshall Plan' is announced (5 June) in order to combat European economic crisis.

July   Poland and Czechoslovakia accept the Marshall Plan, but then reject it two days later because of Soviet pressure.

               A Committee of European Economic Cooperation is set up in Western Europe.

July–August In order to compensate for the loss of American aid, the USSR establishes a number of bilateral trade treaties with Eastern European countries under the Molotov Plan.

August   In Hungary, the Communist-dominated leftist bloc wins 46 per cent of the vote in elections. Communists now dominate the government and National Assembly.

September   Establishment of the Communist Information Bureau (Cominform) to reinforce the USSR's ideological dominance of the Eastern bloc.

October   Signature of the GATT (23 October).

1948

March   The Treaty of Brussels is signed by Belgium, France, Luxembourg, the Netherlands and the UK (17 March). The treaty calls for 'collective self-defence' and for further 'economic, social and cultural collaboration'.

April   The OEEC is established (16 April). This coordinates the distribution of Marshall Aid.

May	The Communist-dominated National Front wins elections in Czechoslovakia.
June	Beginning of the Berlin blockade.
	Formal expulsion of Yugoslavia from the Cominform.
December	In Poland the Socialist and Communist Parties merge to form the PUWP, which embraces a programme of state-led collectivisation and industrialisation.

1949

January	The CMEA, or Comecon, is created by the USSR as an Eastern European response to the Marshall Plan.
April	The North Atlantic Treaty is signed in Washington (4 April), marking a formal commitment by the US and Canada to participate in a system of collective military security for Western Europe. NATO is subsequently set up to give institutional expression to the commitments of the Washington Treaty.
May	End of the Berlin blockade.
	Establishment of the Council of Europe (5 May) to promote Western European political, economic and social ideals.
September	The FRG is established.
October	The GDR is established.
	Adenauer declares that the FRG is to be considered the sole representative of the German people (‘*Alleinvertretungsanspruch*’). This policy is supported by the Western allies in September 1950 and results in the Hallstein Doctrine, by which the FRG’s predominant foreign policy aim is to undermine the GDR’s international status.

1950

May	The Schuman Declaration (9 May) calls for the pooling of coal and steel production between France and Germany.
June	Outbreak of the Korean War.
October	Launch of the Pleven Plan for a European Defence Community (EDC).

1951

April	The ECSC Treaty is signed in Paris (18 April).

1952

March	The USSR begins a major campaign to prevent the FRG from joining the EDC.
July	Entry into force of the ECSC Treaty (27 July).

1953

March	Death of Stalin.
May–June	Riots occur in Sofia, Prague and East Berlin.

1954

August	The French National Assembly fails to ratify the EDC Treaty.

October	The Paris Agreements (23 October) amend the Brussels Treaty and provide for the FRG and Italy to join the Treaty's existing members in a new organisation to be known as the WEU.

1955

May	The FRG becomes a member of NATO. A week later, the WTO is created.
	A Joint Memorandum by the Benelux countries (18 May) calls for a customs union among the members of the ECSC, and further integration in the fields of transport, and nuclear and conventional energy.
June	The Benelux plans for the creation of a Common Market are accepted at a meeting of ECSC Foreign Ministers in Messina.

1956

February	Khrushchev's 'secret speech' attacks the personality cult of Stalinism. At the Twentieth Party Congress in the Soviet Union, Khrushchev argues that differing national avenues towards socialism exist; this marks the beginning of a process of de-Stalinisation, which results in the decline of direct Soviet control over Eastern Europe.
	It is reported that over 1.5 million Germans have fled to the FRG.
April	Dissolution of the Cominform.
July	Liberalisation attempts in Poland stimulate similar movements throughout the Soviet bloc, and especially in Hungary.
October	In Hungary, Imre Nagy becomes Prime Minister and the first Soviet invasion takes place. Nagy announces democratic reforms, and on 31 October he also announces Hungary's withdrawal from the WTO.
November	Second Soviet invasion of Hungary. Nagy is replaced by János Kádár.

1957

January	Kádár espouses a hardline conservative policy and a return to the 'dictatorship of the proletariat'.
	The USSR's Institute of World Economics and International Relations publishes a document entitled 'Seventeen Theses on the Common Market', in which the formation of the EEC is condemned.
March	Signature of the EEC and European Atomic Energy Community (EAEC or Euratom) Treaties in Rome on 25 March.
October	First application of the Hallstein Doctrine by the FRG: when Yugoslavia enters into diplomatic relations with East Berlin, Bonn rescinds its diplomatic ties with Belgrade.

1958

January	Entry into force of the Rome Treaties (1 January).
June	The execution of Nagy in Hungary brings to an end the first period

| | of Eastern European revisionism. |
| *November* | Khrushchev precipitates a second Berlin crisis by proposing that control of Berlin should be transferred to the GDR. |

1959
July The EEC's Economic and Social Committee argues that the coordination of foreign trade policies among member states is particularly important with regard to East–West commerce, as artificial Eastern European prices could disrupt free trade within the EEC.

1960
May Entry into force (3 May) of the Stockholm Convention establishing the EFTA.
July The EEC's Council of Ministers adopts a resolution calling on member states to include an 'EEC clause' in bilateral trade agreements with non-members. This would provide for the alteration or annulment of such bilateral agreements once an EEC Common Commercial Policy came into force. However, member states fail to include any such binding clause in agreements with CMEA countries.
December The OEEC is replaced by the OECD.

1961
August The Berlin Wall is erected.

1962
January Establishment of the EEC's CAP.
August On 26 August, the USSR's Academy of Sciences publishes the 'Thirty-Two Theses', officially entitled 'Concerning Imperialist "Integration" in Western Europe ("The Common Market")'.
September The EEC Council initiates an Action Programme containing concrete measures for adopting a Common Commercial Policy.
October Cuban missile crisis.

1963
January De Gaulle's veto (14 January) of Britain's application to join the EEC enables the USSR to claim a significant success in its *Westpolitik*, since it had campaigned vigorously against British entry into the Common Market.
De Gaulle and Adenauer sign a Franco-German Treaty, forming the basis of the Paris–Bonn axis which is to play an important part in both Western European integration and EC policy towards Eastern Europe.

1964
October Khrushchev is replaced as CPSU General Secretary by Leonid Brezhnev.

1965

April   Signature in Brussels of the 'Merger Treaty' (8 April) between the ECSC, EEC and EAEC to form the EC.

1967

January   Romania becomes the first Eastern European state to establish relations with the FRG. The FRG's attempt to improve Eastern European relations results in a renewal of friendship and cooperation treaties signed in the late 1940s between the Soviet Union and its Eastern bloc allies, except for Romania. (The existing Soviet–Romanian Treaty nevertheless remains in force.)

July   Entry into force of the EC Merger Treaty (1 July).

August   A trade agreement is concluded between the FRG and Czechoslovakia.

1968

January   The NEM is introduced in Hungary.
Alexander Dubček becomes head of the Czechoslovak Communist Party, heralding the beginning of the Prague Spring.

August   Warsaw Pact invasion of Czechoslovakia.

September The wider consequences of the Czechoslovak invasion are emphasised by the USSR's assertion of the doctrine of limited sovereignty of Socialist states. This becomes known as the Brezhnev Doctrine.

1969

January   The USSR calls a meeting of the CMEA Executive Committee in order to promote Communist economic integration. Soviet leaders attempt to introduce supranational elements into the CMEA, but these plans fail because of the opposition of other Eastern European leaders to an organisational framework which is liable to increase the USSR's influence.

June   At a world conference of Communist parties in Moscow, Romania dissents over the Brezhnev Doctrine.

December The EC Council decides that a unified trade policy is particularly important in relation to Eastern Europe, and adopts a regulation stating that no bilateral trade agreement between an EC member state and an Eastern European country should be in force by the end of 1974. However, some member states have already signed agreements extending beyond this transitional period. In practice, the Common Commercial Policy is not applied to the state trading countries until the end of 1975.

1970

March   The FRG and GDR discuss the normalisation of relations.

May   The FRG recognises the GDR, and agreement is reached on access to Berlin; concurrently, four-power talks on Berlin resume for the first time since 1959.

Poland introduces economic incentive measures to increase productivity.

August   The Soviet–German Treaty of Non-Aggression between the FRG and the USSR, recognising postwar borders, is signed in Moscow (12 August).

November   First meeting of EC Foreign Ministers under European Political Cooperation.

December   Signature of the Warsaw Treaty between the FRG and Poland. As in the Moscow Treaty, the FRG explicitly recognises the Oder–Neisse line.

1971

July   The CMEA agrees a 'Comprehensive Programme' for greater economic integration, but the intergovernmental principles of the 1960 CMEA Charter are maintained.

September Signature of a Four-Power Agreement regarding the status of Berlin.

1972

March   The USSR indicates that it is willing to recognise the Common Market provided that the EC recognises the CMEA as the trade representative of Eastern Europe. The EC rejects this offer on the grounds that the two organisations do not have comparable legal status. However, negotiations between the EC and the CMEA continue intermittently up to the end of the 1970s.

1973

January   The UK, Ireland and Denmark join the EC (1 January), despite Soviet opposition to enlargement.

July   The CSCE opens in Helsinki as a forum for East–West dialogue and negotiation.

1974

May   The EC puts forward a series of proposals to individual CMEA countries for negotiating new trade agreements to replace the expiring bilateral agreements between its member states and Eastern Europe. However, this initiative fails.

June   The provisions of the CMEA Charter are amended in order that 'international agreements may be concluded with the member countries of the council, third countries, and international organizations'.

1975

June   The Twenty-nineth CMEA session reaches agreement on measures to increase economic integration.

August   The CSCE Final Act is signed in Helsinki (1 August).

1977

January   The introduction of the Common Fisheries Policy strengthens the EC's bargaining power in East–West economic relations.

October   A CSCE Follow-up Meeting begins in Belgrade.

1978
March   The Belgrade CSCE meeting closes without reaching agreement on any new proposals.

1979
March   Introduction of the EMS within the EC.
December   The Soviet invasion of Afghanistan leads to a deterioration in East–West relations. A week after the invasion, the West German firm Ruhrgas announces the inauguration of a long-term project with the Soviet gas trading agency Soyuzgazexport. This is the start of the Urengoi pipeline dispute, which causes serious tensions between the US and the EC during the early 1980s.

1980
April   Yugoslavia signs a new preferential trade and cooperation agreement with the EC.
May   Death of the Yugoslav leader Tito.
July   An increase in Polish meat prices leads to protests and demands for pay rises. Widespread strikes across Poland follow.
September   Formation of Solidarity as an independent trade union.
November   A CSCE Follow-up Meeting begins in Madrid.

1981
January   Greece becomes a member of the EC (1 January).
March   Following continuing unrest in Poland and the threat of Soviet intervention, the EC issues a warning to the USSR and offers economic aid to Poland.
December   Western banks agree to reschedule Polish debts of $2.4 billion. Solidarity issues a new series of demands, including free national elections, access to the media and joint union–party control of the economy. The PUWP General Secretary, Wojciech Jaruzelski, responds by declaring martial law and announcing the formation of the Military Council for National Salvation.

1982
June   The Thirty-sixth CMEA session discusses the economic implications of the Polish crisis.
October   New union laws in Poland aim to dismantle Solidarity.
November   Brezhnev dies and is succeeded by Yuri Andropov.

1983
June   The USSR brings the EC before the European Court, accusing it of unjustified anti-dumping measures; thus the Soviets implicitly acknowledge the EC's competence over foreign trade issues.
July   Martial law is lifted in Poland, and a limited amnesty is declared for political and other offenders.
September   End of Madrid CSCE meeting.

1984
February   Andropov dies and is succeeded by Konstantin Chernenko.
June   The CMEA announces that it is to improve commercial ties with capitalist countries.
October   The Rome Declaration (27 October) by the WEU Council of Ministers marks the reactivation of WEU as a means of creating a Western European security identity and encouraging cooperation between member states in the field of defence policy.

1985
March   Chernenko dies and is succeeded by Mikhail Gorbachev.
June   Publication of the Cockfield White Paper on completion of the EC's internal market.

1986
January   Spain and Portugal become members of the EC (1 January).
February   Gorbachev proposes a 'radical reform' of Soviet economics and politics.
             Signature of the SEA by the twelve EC member states (17 February in Luxembourg and 28 February in The Hague).
June   Poland's entry into the IMF and World Bank is approved.

1987
June   Kohl proposes a joint Franco-German Brigade as a first step towards a European fighting force.
July   The SEA enters into force (1 July).
October   Extensive political and economic reforms are introduced in Poland. The CMEA Prime Ministers' meeting in Moscow agrees on a long-term reform of the intrabloc trading system.

1988
May   In Hungary, Kádár is removed after thirty-two years in power.
June   The EC and the CMEA issue a Joint Declaration (25 June) on the establishment of official relations between the two organisations.
July   CMEA members, with the exception of Romania, announce plans to create a unified market.
September   A trade and economic cooperation agreement between the EC and Hungary (26 September) provides for the phased abolition of quantitative EC restrictions on imports from Hungary.
October   Chancellor Kohl visits Moscow accompanied by over sixty West German industrial leaders.
December   At the European Council meeting in Rhodes (2–3 December), the Community indicates its willingness to advance economic ties with reformist CMEA members.

The development of relations between the EC/EU and CEEC (1989–98)

1989

February   Round-table talks begin in Poland between government and opposition leaders.

March   In a speech to the Italian Communist Party Congress, Aleksandr Yakovlev, the Secretary of the CPSU Central Committee, sets out the USSR's new policy towards the EC by arguing that Russia (*sic*) should be included in the process of European integration.

Hungary becomes the first Eastern European country to accede to the UN Convention on Refugees.

April   At the Luxembourg Summit, EC Foreign Ministers decide to coordinate their policies towards Eastern Europe within the EC framework.

EC Foreign Ministers also suspend negotiations on a more wide-ranging trade and cooperation agreement with Romania (replacing that of 1980) because of the country's abuses of human rights.

Solidarity and the Polish government reach an agreement regarding elections; 35 per cent of seats in the Sejm, or lower house of Parliament, and all 100 seats in the newly established Senate, or upper house, are to be contested.

May   The EC suspends negotiations with Bulgaria because of the latter's abuses of the rights of the Turkish minority.

Hungary begins the removal of the Iron Curtain on its border with Austria (2 May).

June   Elections are held in Poland (4 and 18 June). The PUWP is heavily defeated, with Solidarity and independent candidates winning (after the second round) 99 out of 100 seats in the Senate and all 161 of the contested seats in the Sejm.

Shortly after the Polish elections, negotiations begin in Hungary between government and opposition forces.

The EC Commission Vice-President, Frans Andriessen, states during a meeting in Moscow that the Community is determined to mobilise the policy instruments at its disposal in order to promote the objectives of political reform and economic liberalisation in Eastern Europe. He also argues that the SEA, which contains provisions covering both political cooperation and economic integration, has enabled the EC to promote East–West cooperation in a coherent and dynamic way.

July   In a speech to the Council of Europe, Gorbachev talks of a new, united Europe stretching from the Atlantic to the Urals.

The G7 meeting in Paris decides to set up the G24 Western aid programme to Poland and Hungary in order to support the reforms taking place in these countries, and it is agreed that the European Commission should coordinate this assistance. The Commission subsequently sets up its own Phare programme, which aims to deal mainly with the financing and provision of technical assistance for economic restructuring in Poland and Hungary.

EC Agriculture Ministers approve a 110 million ecu emergency food programme for Poland (24 July).

Jaruzelski resigns his post as PUWP First Secretary to become President of Poland.

August   The PUWP abandons attempts to form a government and gives the task to Solidarity, but it retains the 'sensitive' positions of Interior and Defence Ministers in the new government headed by Prime Minister Tadeusz Mazowiecki.

September   The post-Communist coalition government led by Tadeusz Mazowiecki assumes power in Poland.

The EC Commission puts forward a new 300 million ecu aid package for Poland and Hungary (one-third for Hungary and two-thirds for Poland).

A cooperation agreement is signed between the EC and Poland (19 September).

Over 13,000 East Germans cross the Hungarian border into Austria, and another 17,000 leave the Soviet bloc via the West German embassies in Warsaw and Prague.

The Hungarian government and opposition parties agree that a multiparty system will be introduced in 1990.

October   In East Germany, large-scale public demonstrations for democracy are accompanied by the continuing emigration of young and professional people. These developments result in the removal of Erich Honeker as party leader and head of state. He is replaced by the youngest member of the Politburo, Egon Krenz.

At a specially convened HSWP Congress, the old party is dissolved and replaced by a new HSP modelled on Western democratic Socialist parties.

On the thirty-third anniversary of the 1956 uprising a new, democratic Hungarian Republic is proclaimed.

A meeting of Warsaw Pact Foreign Ministers in Warsaw (26–7 October) confirms the abandonment of the Brezhnev Doctrine.

November   In East Germany, the government resigns (7 November), followed within a day by the whole Politburo. The opening of the Berlin Wall takes place (9 November) as the GDR abandons travel restrictions for its citizens and opens its borders.

The EC decides to scrap all quantitative restrictions on Hungarian and Polish industrial exports from 1 January 1990, rather than phasing them out over five years as originally planned.

The British government puts forward the first proposal for EC association agreements with those CEEC displaying a firm commitment to economic and political reform.

An informal meeting of EC heads of state is called (18–19 November) at the Elysée Palace to discuss a collective EC policy towards Eastern Europe. It is agreed that the EC will assist economic reform in CEEC in return for democratic reform, respect for human rights and the organisation of free elections. This is the first time the EC has attached specific conditions to the provision of aid to CEEC.

In Czechoslovakia, anti-Communist demonstrations take place in Prague and elsewhere. Civic Forum is founded on 19 November as a broad anti-Communist social movement, and on 25 November a major demonstration involving 750,000 people takes place. The authorities initally resist this popular pressure for reform, but the protests soon result in the downfall of the government and party leadership and the abandonment of the Communist Party's leading role.

December   In the GDR the new Politburo resigns (3 December), two days after the Parliament has ended the Communist Party's monopoly of power and its leading role in the constitution.

At a meeting in Kiev (6 December), the French and Soviet Presidents express worries about a possible German reunification. However, following a negative response to this meeting by Western European states, Mitterand returns to the strategy of the Paris–Bonn axis within the EC.

The Strasbourg European Council (8–9 December) states that the EC is 'the corner-stone of a new European architecture and ... a mooring for a future European equilibrium'. Support is expressed for German reunification. Agreement is reached on the establishment of the EBRD, with an initial capital of 10 billion ecu to be subscribed by the G24 countries to promote private enterprise and infrastructure development in Eastern Europe. The European Council also endorses the concept of an appropriate form of association agreement with reforming CEEC.

In Czechoslovakia, the first majority non-Communist government since 1948 comes to power (10 December). Václav Havel becomes President, and Alexander Dubček becomes President of the Federal Assembly. However, as fundamental reforms have not yet been inaugurated the EC signs only a limited trade agreement (19 December) with the Czechoslovak government.

A ten-year trade and cooperation agreement is signed between the EC and the USSR (18 December).

A short-lived but bloody civil war in Romania ends with the capture, trial and execution of deposed leader Nicolae Ceaușescu and his wife.

1990
January   The CMEA's trade and payments system is criticised during the organisation's Forty-fifth session in Sofia (9–10 January), and it is agreed that the organisation must be restructured in accordance with market principles.

Mass emigration of East Germans to the West continues; by the end of the month over 4,000 per day are leaving. Reunification is seen increasingly as a solution to this problem.

The Solidarity government's 'shock therapy' economic reforms take effect from 1 January and result immediately in price rises for many basic foods. Meanwhile, the PUWP splits into two social democratic groups.

Phare commences operations in Poland and Hungary.

February The USSR accepts the prospect of German reunification.

A merger of the East and West German currencies is announced, but with no clear timescale.

In response to the request of the December 1989 Strasbourg European Council, the Commission produces suggestions regarding an appropriate form of association between the EC and CEEC.

March Lithuania declares independence from the USSR (11 March).

General elections take place in East Germany (18 March). However, given the prospect of reunification, the elections concern little more than the power bases which can be built up in the East by West German political parties. The result is a victory for the Christian Democratic Union (CDU), which has existed throughout the GDR's history but is now under the influence of its much more powerful West German counterpart. CDU leader Lothar de Maizière becomes Prime Minister.

The Czechoslovak government decides to revoke multilateral agreements on exchange rates with CMEA countries (22 March).

The Estonian Supreme Soviet decides to begin the restoration of the country's independence (30 March).

April An Extraordinary Meeting of the European Council takes place in Dublin to consider the EC's response to the transformation in Eastern Europe. It is decided that EAs will be drawn up with those countries which have made clear progress towards democracy and the establishment of a free market, i.e. Hungary, Poland and Czechoslovakia. No reference is made to future membership of the Community for Central European states. However, a Commission report argues that the integration of the GDR into the EC as part of a reunified Germany constitutes a special case, and that Article 237 of the Treaty of Rome (relating to the accession of new member states) does not apply in this instance.

The first trilateral meeting between Hungary, Poland and Czechoslovakia to coordinate Central European *Westpolitik* takes place in Bratislava (9 April).

In Hungary, Democratic Forum wins 165 of the 386 parliamentary seats in the final round of the March–April elections and begins negotiations which result in the formation of a centre-right government in coalition with the Independent Smallholders' Party (44 seats) and the Christian Democrats (21 seats).

Lothar de Maizière forms East Germany's first non-Communist government.

May The Articles of Agreement of the EBRD are signed in Paris (29 May).

June A new trade agreement is signed with Romania (8 June) following the collapse of the Ceauşescu regime.

Free elections take place in Czechoslovakia (8 and 9 June). A 96 per cent turnout produces a clear majority for Civic Form and its

Slovakian counterpart, VPN, in both houses of the Federal Assembly. Marian Čalfa becomes Prime Minister and head of a wholly non-Communist government consisting of a coalition of Civic Forum and VPN representatives in association with the Christian Democratic Movement of Slovakia.

Negotiations begin on the creation of an EEA as an alternative arrangement between the EC and EFTA which falls between the existing free trade framework and full EC membership for EFTA countries.

July	German economic and monetary union takes place (1 July). Latvia declares independence from the USSR (28 July).
August	Beginning of Gulf crisis. The Commission produces further details on the aims and proposed content of the EA. This forms the framework for subsequent negotiations.
September	In Poland, the Citizen's Parliamentary Caucus (from Solidarity's list) forms a government which includes former Communists. Phare is extended to include Bulgaria, Czechoslovakia, Yugoslavia and East Germany (aid to East Germany ceases after reunification, and aid to Yugoslavia is suspended in 1991).
October	Formal reunification between the GDR and the FRG takes place (3 October).
December	The EC Commission begins negotiations with Czechoslovakia, Hungary and Poland on the content of EA. In Poland, Lech Walesa is elected President.

1991

January	Partial price deregulation takes place in Czechoslovakia (1 January) as the neoliberal Finance Minister Václav Klaus introduces 'shock therapy'. The political crisis between the Baltic states and the USSR culminates in violent crackdowns by the Soviet authorities in Latvia and Lithuania.
February	Hungary, Poland and Czechoslovakia issue the Visegrad Declaration (15 February), in which they announce the setting up of an East–Central European free trade area and intergovernmental cooperation.
March	Dissolution of the WTO.
April	EC Foreign Ministers decide (15 April) that EC membership can be mentioned in the preamble to EAs with Central European states as 'an ultimate, though not an automatic' aim. The EBRD becomes operational.
June	Dissolution of the CMEA. Slovenia declares independence from Yugoslavia (26 June).
August	An attempted coup in the USSR (19 August) fails, and is followed later in the year by the collapse of the Soviet Union.
September	The Soviet Union recognises the independence of the three Baltic states (6 September).

October	A Follow-up Meeting of the Visegrad Three is held in Cracow (6 October).
	A general election is held in Poland, with over 100 parties standing, but voter turnout is only 43 per cent. Among the twenty-nine parties which enter the new Parliament, there are no left-wing or blue-collar representatives.
December	At the Maastricht European Council (9–10 December), agreement is reached on the Maastricht Treaty. The European Council asks the Commission to examine the implications of other European states acceding to the EU under the terms of the new Treaty.
	EAs are signed between the EC and Poland, Hungary and Czechoslovakia (16 December).
	Phare is extended to Albania and the Baltic states.
	In Poland, Jan Olszewski becomes Prime Minister.
	The Minsk Agreement establishes the CIS, which is joined by all former republics of the USSR except the Baltic states.

1992

January	A centre-right government is formed in Poland after months of disagreement.
	Slovenia is recognised by the EC (15 January). Phare is subsequently extended to Slovenia in summer 1992.
February	Signature of Maastricht Treaty (7 February).
April	The EBRD begins operations in the former Soviet republics.
May	The EEA Treaty between the EC and EFTA is signed (2 May).
	The EC signs ten-year TCAs with Albania and the three Baltic states (11 May).
	In Poland, Olszewski is voted out of office.
June	The Danish electorate rejects the Maastricht Treaty in a referendum (2 June) by 50.7 per cent to 49.3 per cent – the first time an agreement between EC member states has not been ratified at national level.
	A referendum in Ireland (18 June) results in a 'yes' vote for the Treaty by 69 per cent to 31 per cent.
	In Poland, Waldemar Pawlak, leader of the Peasant Party, is endorsed by Parliament as Prime Minister (5 June). However, Pawlak is unable to form a government which can command parliamentary support.
	Elections in Czechoslovakia are followed by the rise of a Slovak independence movement.
	The Lisbon European Council (26–7 June) receives the Commission's report on the implications of further enlargement.
July	In Poland, Hanna Suchocka forms a seven-party coalition government.
	In Czechoslovakia, a grand coalition of the major political forces is formed (2 July) to arrange the division of the country into two states.
September	The French endorse the Maastricht Treaty in a referendum (20 September) with only 51 per cent of voters in favour.

November	The first EC cooperation agreement with a former Yugoslav state is signed with Slovenia (5 November).
	The EC Council decides to prolong the operation of Phare (which is due to expire at the end of 1992) until at least 1997.
December	The European Council meeting in Edinburgh (11–12 December) welcomes the Commission's report on closer association with CEEC, which focuses on improvements in political dialogue and market access.
	Signature of the CEFTA Treaty in Cracow (21 December).

1993

January	The SEM enters into force, and the EC becomes known as the EU.
	Establishment of the Czech Republic and of Slovakia (1 January).
February	The EU and Romania sign an EA (1 February).
	Václav Havel is inaugurated as President of the Czech Republic (2 February) for a five-year term.
	Phare initiates a 5 million ecu sponsorship of 'democracy projects' in CEEC (this initiative was launched by the EP in 1992).
March	Slovak President Michal Kovac is inaugurated (2 March) for a five-year term.
	The EU signs an EA with Bulgaria (8 March).
May	A further Danish referendum (18 May) produces a vote in favour of the Maastricht Treaty by 56.8 per cent to 43.2 per cent.
	In Poland, a vote of no confidence in Suchocka's government is passed (28 May) by one vote. The President calls new elections for 19 September, this time with an electoral threshold of 5 per cent (or 8 per cent for coalitions).
June	The Copenhagen European Council (21–2 June) offers the prospect of full EU membership to those countries which already have EAs with the Union, subject to the applicants meeting the *acquis communautaire*. The EU proposes increased political contacts, the accelerated abolition of trade barriers and the adaptation and improvement of the Phare programme.
	Jacques Attali is forced to resign as head of the EBRD following widespread political and press criticism regarding misuse of the bank's funds.
September	Following the Polish general election (19 September), Waldemar Pawlak, leader of the Peasant Party, becomes Prime Minister. The new left-wing coalition government is dominated by ex-Communists of the Democratic Left Alliance.
October	The EU signs EAs with the Czech and Slovak Republics (4 October).
November	The Maastricht Treaty enters into force (1 November).
December	The European Council meeting in Brussels (10–11 December) supports the idea of the Stability Pact or 'Balladur Plan' for CEEC, the aims being to avert conflicts, consolidate borders and deal with the problems of national minorities.

1994

February   Final declaration of the CEFTA countries (4 February) on trade liberalisation within five years.

March   Hungary applies to join the EU (31 March).

April   Poland applies to join the EU (5 April).

May   General elections take place in Hungary (8 and 29 May). These result in the defeat of the conservative government coalition, and a resounding victory for the Hungarian Socialist Party. Together with its junior coalition partner, the SZDSZ, the government has the two-thirds majority required to change the constitution.

June   The Corfu European Council (24–5 June) asks the Commission to prepare a report on the progress to date of cooperation with CEEC. This report subsequently forms the basis of a broad pre-accession strategy involving the phased adoption of the EU's internal market legislation, the development of transport networks through Phare, and cooperation in the spheres of justice and home affairs, foreign and security policy, and education, culture and training.

               President Yeltsin meets with EU leaders at the Corfu European Council and signs a PCA between the EU and the Russian Federation (24 June).

September–   Parliamentary elections take place in Slovakia (30 September–
October   1 October). Vladimir Meciar and his party, the HZDS, win the most seats.

December   The Essen European Council (9–10 December) adopts the broad pre-accession strategy. It also asks the Commission to produce further reports concerning the impact of enlargement on the EU, as well as a White Paper on CEEC and the internal market. It is further agreed that the issue of EU institutional reform must be tackled by the 1996 IGC before accession negotiations with CEEC can begin.

               In Slovakia, the HZDS forms a government with two coalition partners, the ZRS, an extremist Communist party, and the extreme right-wing SNS.

1995

January   Austria, Sweden and Finland become EU members (1 January).

March   Signature of the CEEC Stability Pact in Paris (21 March).

June   EAs are signed between the EU and the three Baltic states (12 June).

               Romania applies for EU membership (22 June), followed by Slovakia (27 June).

               The Cannes European Council (26–7 June) adopts the White Paper detailing the medium-term framework for the preparation of associated CEEC for integration into the EU's Single Market.

October   Latvia applies to join the EU (13 October).

November   A former Communist minister, Aleksander Kwasniewski of the Democratic Left Alliance, wins the Polish presidential election, beating Lech Walesa, despite strong opposition from the Catholic Church.

Estonia applies for EU membership (24 November).

December   Lithuania applies for EU membership (8 December), followed by Bulgaria (14 December).

The European Council meeting in Madrid (15–16 December) gives an assurance that all applications for EU membership will be considered on the basis of common criteria. It also asks the Commission to produce Opinions on the CEEC applications for EU membership as soon as possible after the conclusion of the forthcoming IGC. The Council hopes that negotiations with the CEEC will be able to commence at the same time as those with Cyprus and Malta.

1996

January   The first enlargement of the CEFTA takes place with the accession of Slovenia (1 January).

The Czech Republic applies to join the EU (17 January).

March   Opening of the EU's IGC in Turin (29 March).

May   Elections are held in the Czech Republic (31 May). The results are inconclusive, with the ruling coalition of the ODS, the ODA and the KDU–CSL losing six seats and its majority in Parliament. The CSSD increases its number of parliamentary seats to sixty-one, becoming the second strongest party behind the ODS.

Under a deal brokered by the Czech President Václav Havel, the Social Democrats agree to support a minority government formed by the coalition, and in return they are given important parliamentary posts.

June   Signature of an EA between the EU and Slovenia. On the same occasion, Slovenia applies for EU membership (10 June).

The European Council meeting in Florence (21–2 June) reaffirms the decisions of the Madrid Council regarding enlargement.

November   In the Czech Republic, elections on 15–16 and 22–3 November to the upper house or Senate give the three-party government coalition fifty-two seats in the eighty-one-member chamber. Despite a turnout of only about 30 per cent in each round of voting, this helps to stabilise the political situation after the general election result earlier in the year.

December   The European Council meeting in Dublin (13–14 December) again confirms the timetable for enlargement set at the Madrid meeting.

1997

May   A referendum takes place in Poland (25 May) on a new constitution which enshrines the values of free markets and democracy. It has taken eight years for successive post-Communist governments and the Church to reach agreement on this constitution, and it fails to receive an enthusiastic endorsement from the public; only 42 per cent of voters take part in the poll and, of these, a narrow major-

	ity of 53 per cent back the constitution.
June	At the European Council meeting in Amsterdam (16–17 June), agreement is reached on the Treaty of Amsterdam. It is stated that accession negotiations should commence with individual applicants 'according to the stage which is reached in satisfying the basic conditions of membership and in preparing for accession'.
July	Romania becomes a member of the CEFTA (1 July).

The Commission publishes its communication '*Agenda 2000*', together with Opinions on each of the applications for EU membership (16 July). This publication is the Commission's response to the Madrid European Council's requests in December 1995, and contains the Commission's view of the broad perspectives of EU development beyond the year 2000, the impact of enlargement on the Union, and the future financial framework of an enlarged EU. Of the CEEC applicants for EU membership, the Commission recommends that accession negotiations should be opened with Poland, Hungary, the Czech Republic, Slovenia and Estonia. It also proposes that reinforced Accession Partnerships should be set up with all ten CEEC.

September   General elections in Poland (21 September) result in the defeat of the ruling ex-Communists by Solidarity Election Action (AWS), a Solidarity-led group of almost forty rightist parties. The AWS wins 201 of 460 seats in Parliament's lower chamber, with the Democratic Left Alliance winning 164 seats and the liberal Freedom Union (UW) headed by Leszek Balcerowicz coming third.

October   Signature of the Treaty of Amsterdam (2 October) by EU member states.

In Poland, Jerzy Buzek, an academic and free market reformer, is appointed as Prime Minister to head a centre-right coalition of the AWS and UW.

November   An Extraordinary European Council on Employment is held in Luxembourg (20–1 November).

In the Czech Republic, the coalition government of Prime Minister Václav Klaus collapses (30 November) as a result of a financing scandal within Klaus's ODS.

December   The Luxembourg European Council (12–13 December) confirms that accession negotiations are to begin with CEEC in line with the Commission's recommendations. It decides to increase substantially pre-accession aid to CEEC, and endorses the Accession Partnerships as the key feature of the enhanced pre-accession strategy. It is also decided to set up a European Conference which will bring together present and aspiring EU member states in a broadening and deepening of cooperation.

Czech President Václav Havel appoints Josef Tosovsky, the Governor of the central bank, as head of a caretaker government.

1998

March   Slovak President Michal Kovac steps down at the end of his term of office (2 March), leaving no successor and provoking a constitutional crisis. Prime Minister Vladimir Meciar subsequently assumes some presidential powers, thus strengthening his own position.

The inaugural meeting of the European Conference takes place in London (12 March).

The Commission approves the Accession Partnerships for the ten CEEC (25 March).

The launch takes place of the CEEC accession process (30 March), with entry talks beginning on 31 March for five 'fast-track' applicants.

April   The Polish and Hungarian Presidents announce (15 April) that their countries are to form an alliance to further their common goals on European integration.

May   The centre-right FIDESZ Hungarian Civic Party unexpectedly defeats the governing Socialists in the second round of voting in parliamentary elections (24 May).

The EU Commission cuts aid for 1998 to Poland under the Phare programme by 34 million ecu (25 May).

June   Viktor Orban, the leader of FIDESZ, is named Hungarian Prime Minister (18 June) and given the task of forming a new coalition government.

General elections take place in the Czech Republic (19–20 June). The opposition CSSD gain 74 of the 200 seats in the lower house of Parliament, but former Prime Minister Václav Klaus' ODS wins 63 seats, thereby making it difficult for either party to produce a viable government coalition.

Sources

Avery, G. and Cameron, F. (1998), *The Enlargement of the European Union*, Sheffield, Sheffield Academic Press.

Bideleux, R. and Taylor, R. (1996), *European Integration and Disintegration: East and West*, London, Routledge.

Cloonan, M. (1996), 'Poles Apart? The Widening and Deepening Debate in the European Union: The Case of Poland', *Case Studies for Politics*, 18.

Commission (1992), *Europe and the Challenge of Enlargement*, Luxembourg, Office for Official Publications of the European Communities.

Commission (1993), *Europe in a Changing World: The External Relations of the European Community*, Luxembourg, Office for Official Publications of the European Communities.

Commission (1995), *What is Phare?*, Brussels, European Commission Phare Information Office.

Commission (1996), *Background Report: EU Relations With Poland*, B/10/96, London, July.

Dawisha, K. (2nd edn, 1990), *Eastern Europe, Gorbachev and Reform: The Great Challenge*, Cambridge, Cambridge University Press.

Lewis, P. G. (1994), *Central Europe Since 1945*, London, Longman.

Nugent, N. (ed.) (1993), *The European Community 1992: Annual Review of Activities*, Oxford, UACES/Blackwell.

Nugent, N. (ed.) (1994–7), *The European Union: Annual Review of Activities*, Oxford, UACES/Blackwell (1993–6 editions).

Preston, C. (1997), *Enlargement and Integration in the European Union*, London, Routledge.

Sedelmeier, U. and Wallace, H. (1996), 'Policies Towards Central and Eastern Europe', in H. Wallace and W. Wallace (eds), *Policy-Making in the European Union*, Oxford, Oxford University Press, 353–85.

Van Ham, P. (1993), *The EC, Eastern Europe and European Unity: Discord, Collaboration and Integration since 1947*, London, Pinter.

Vaughan, R. (1979), *Twentieth-Century Europe: Paths to Unity*, London, Croom Helm.

Internet sources

Central Europe Online http://www.centraleurope.com/
The Council of Europe http://www.coe.fr/
The EU http://europa.eu.int/
Institute of Baltic Studies http://www.ibs.ee/
The OSCE http://www.osceprag.cz/
The WEU http://www.weu.int/

Appendix II

Summary of *Agenda 2000* documentation and enlargement strategy

Structure of *Agenda 2000*

Volume I   For a stronger and wider Union

Part 1 The policies of the Union
Internal policies; economic/social cohesion; CAP; external policies.
Part 2 The challenge of enlargement
Accession criteria; principal problems (Impact Study); enlargement strategy; Cyprus; Turkey; European Conference; final recommendations.

Volume 2   The challenge: reinforcing the objectives of SPAR; methods/priorities

Institution building; enterprise and the *acquis*; objective setting; financial supports; Phare; agricultural/structural assistance.
Effects of the Union's policies of enlargement on applicant states (Impact Study) summary/ policies; conclusion.

Opinions on country applications (Bulgaria; Czech Republic; Estonia; Hungary; Latvia; Lithuania; Poland; Romania; Slovakia; Slovenia)

Introduction and context of Opinion; EU/country relations; membership criteria; the economy and membership; justice and home affairs; summary/conclusion.
Each Opinion similar in structure and approximate length.

Agenda 2000: the policies of the Union - the first priority?

Institutions

New IGC to confirm a prior political agreement on Commission size and QMV weighting, and to deal with other institutional matters, as soon as possible after 2000.

Growth and enlargement

Promotion of economic convergence and participation in single currency to achieve growth/employment; removal of market restrictions to SEM; strict application of *acquis*; competition rules enforced; SMEs promoted; environmentally sustainable production/consumption; TENs development and supporting funding.

Knowledge policies

Impetus to research technical development education and training and the information society.

Labour market and social reform

Coordination of national employment policies to establish best practice; labour mobility; effective social protection pensions and health schemes; long-term perspective to be taken. Policies towards a cohesive and inclusive society; improvements in public and environmental health; right to free movement operationalised. Comprehensive Union policy for migration/asylum; crime control.

Cohesion

Reform/redistribution of structural funding: simplification of objectives; greater concentration; reinforcement/reassessment of criteria; cohesion fund reviewed; pre-accession aid made available; enhancing cost effectiveness.

CAP reform

Deepen/extend 1992 reforms. Further shifts from price support to direct payments. Move towards a rural development policy. Development of an agri-environment policy.

Europe and the world

To extend the community of security to new member states and partnership countries including Russia; stabilisation complementary to NATO; gradual definition of a common defence policy; reinforcement of Mediterranean, Atlantic/Asia Pacific relations; deepening of CFSP, commercial policy, aid role of the WEU; search for complementarity between internal and external policies; increased EU eternal visibility.

Commission efficiency

Establishment of a citizens' European public service based on competence, independence and permanence. Commission to remain a dynamic force. Sound Efficient Management and Modernisation of Administration and Personnel initiatives. Key procedural streamlining through decentralisation, rationalisation and simplification.

The strategy for enlargement: composite analysis

Conclusions based on Copenhagen criteria, 1993 (see Chapter 2).

General principles

(1) Pre-accession period utilised to the full to ensure adequate membership preparations achieved.
(2) Substantial financial investment in certain sectors including environment; transport; energy; industrial and agricultural restructuring.
(3) Adaptation of standards in social sphere, primarily health, employment, health and safety at work – at suitable pace and with financial support.

Sectoral adaptation

(1) Agricultural production
Weaknesses in primary farming and agri-food industry necessitate transition (of varying lengths) to allow price adjustments and to mitigate excessive competition. No need for direct income support: applicants would receive aid for development of structures to prepare for inclusion in the new 'common agricultural market'.

(2) Cohesion policy
Applicants to receive pre-accession assistance, e.g. Phare programme comparable with existing poorer EU states. Co-financing in line with absorption capacity level; co-financing up to 85 per cent for projects in environment and TENs.

(3) Market development
Reinforced progress towards White Paper elements through specific procedures. Possible difficulties in agricultural trade and free movement in medium term foreseen.

Environmental standards

Severe problems tackled by: realistic national long-term strategies for gradual effective alignment in pre-accession period, in particular water/air pollution; key areas/objectives to be achieved by accession dates; further obligations as part of accession treaty: search for domestic/foreign and private investment (Union to contribute only partially).

Transport

High priority to investment in infrastructure through TENs-related corridors; specific measures for renewal in railway sector in line with common transport policy.

Nuclear safety

Improvement in nuclear safety to international standards by: technical assistance programmes; upgrading of ex-Soviet plant to international standards over 7–10 years; agreed timetable for closure of non-upgradable plant. Coordination of financial assistance programme (EBRD/Phare/EURATOM/World Bank).

Freedom, justice, security

Emphasis on upgrading external frontier controls and respect for international standards in asylum, visas, immigration. All applicant countries to confront organised crime, terrorism, drugs and human trafficking.

Border disputes

Use of processes under Stability Pact to be sustained to reserve remaining disputes. Use of International Court of Justice to achieve settlements if necessary.

Applying Community rules

Applicant countries to apply provisions of EAs above MFN or bilateral trade arrangements.

Accession negotiations

Basis:	the *acquis*
Aim:	(a) a balance of rights and expectations
	(b) no second class membership/opt-outs
Timetable:	dependent on applicant's progress to *acquis*, to be accelerated where applicable in parallel with accession negotiations.

Principles

(1) New members to take on rights/ obligations of membership on basis of *acquis* on accession.
(2) Expected to apply, implement and enforce *acquis*. SEM should be applied immediately.
(3) May agree transition measures – not derogations – in duly justified cases within a limited period of time. May apply particularly to agriculture and free movement.
(4) Progress towards *acquis* adoption to be monitored/reviewed on the basis of Commission reports.

SPAR

- To apply to all candidate countries.
- Directed at specific needs of countries to avoid long transition periods.

Objectives

(1) To provide a single support framework – the Accession Partnership.
(2) To allow joint activity between EU and applicant within a clear programme.
(3) To establish a calendar for achievement.
(4) To familiarise applicants with Union policies/procedures.

Basis of SPAR

(1) EAs.
(2) White Paper.

(3) Phare.
(4) Presidency-organised multilateral dialogue.

Financial support (from 2000)

- Phare (ecu 1.5 billion)
- agricultural development aid (ecu 500 million)
- structural aid (ecu 1 billion).

Accession partnerships

Assistance within a single framework implemented by a national programme:

- to involve country commitments to achieve *acquis* standards in democracy; macro-economic stabilisation and nuclear safety; plus a precise timetable for *acquis* adoption
- mobilisation of resources including Phare (30 per cent to institution building, 70 per cent to investment), with co-financing operations with the EIB, EBRD, World Bank (to be included in framework agreement)
- priorities given to deficiencies identified in Opinions
- annual monitoring of progress; strict accession conditionality for future financing.

Commission will:

- report to European Council annually
- judge extent of progress in *acquis* implementation
- make recommendation for launch of accession negotiations.

Applicant countries:

- may be given opportunity to participate in Community programmes
- Phare funding may be used to co-finance participation
- no rights of decision taking will be conferred from this participation
- encouraged to contact specialist Community agencies, e.g. Medicine Evaluation; Environment Agency, etc.

Community financial framework, 2000–06

Based on assumption of a first wave of accession towards the middle of the period.

Framework to cater for:

- impact of changes on member states of certain policies
- impact of first enlargement and transitional arrangements
- pre-accession aid.

Financed by

- sound light budgetary management
- own resources ceiling – 1.27 per cent Gross National Product
- substantial budget margin below ceiling
- economic growth rate of 2.5 per cent (4 per cent applicant states) to 2006.

Potential additional resources from growth forecast at ecu 20 billion (1997 prices).

Expenditure classification

CAP; Structural Action; other internal policies; external action; administrative expenditure; reserves.

Proposed reference framework

- 17 per cent increase in expenditure (2000–06)
- own resource ceiling 1.27 per cent.

This leaves significant margin should member states' growth rate fall below anticipated 2.4 per cent.

Index

foreign investment 79, 81–4
   (efficiency seeking 83–4;
     strategic asset seeking 84)
   privatisation 78–82
   shock therapy 74–8
   shortage economy 72
   women and 134–6, 142–3, 145–6
   see also communism, collapse of

Tacis programme 121–3
Towards a Closer Association 34
trade agreements 9–10

United Kingdom see Great Britain

Visegrad Declaration 13
   Czech Republic and 237

women, ch.5 passim
   abortion and 137–8
   comparative position of 140
   economic transformation and
     136–9, 150–2
   employment and 138–9
   equal opportunity 132–3, 140–5,
     149–50
   EU and 144–5, 148–50
   experience, variety of 133–4
   grassroots participation 147–8
   political participation and 145–9
   state socialism and 134–6, 142–3,
     145–6, 148
World Bank 165–6, 167–8